I0895773

KAWASAKI
THE GREEN MACHINE

ISLE OF MAN TT 1966–1986

MATTHEW RICHARDSON

PEN & SWORD
TRANSPORT
AN IMPRINT OF PEN & SWORD BOOKS LTD.
YORKSHIRE – PHILADELPHIA

First published in Great Britain in 2025 by
Pen and Sword Transport
An imprint of
Pen & Sword Books Ltd.
Yorkshire – Philadelphia

ISBN 978 1 03610 754 3

A CIP catalogue record for this book is available from the British Library.

Typeset in 12/16 pt Palatino
Typeset by SJmagic DESIGN SERVICES, India.
Printed and bound in the UK by CPI Group (UK) Ltd.

The Publisher's authorised representative in the EU for product safety is Authorised Rep Compliance Ltd., Ground Floor, 71 Lower Baggot Street, Dublin D02 P593, Ireland. www.arccompliance.com

For a complete list of Pen & Sword titles please contact

PEN & SWORD BOOKS LIMITED
George House, Units 12 & 13, Beevor Street, Off Pontefract Road,
Barnsley, S71 1HN, UK
E-mail: enquiries@pen-and-sword.co.uk
Website: www.pen-and-sword.co.uk

or

PEN AND SWORD BOOKS
1950 Lawrence Rd, Havertown, PA 19083, USA
E-mail: uspen-and-sword@casematepublishers.com
Website: www.penandswordbooks.com

MIX
Paper | Supporting responsible forestry
FSC® C013604
FSC www.fsc.org

CONTENTS

FOREWORD

This new book on Kawasaki motorcycles by Matthew Richardson is very informative. He has sought out a lot of detail and includes a huge amount of behind the scenes material. My own part of the Green Meanie story was probably at its best in the first of my four-year stand with Kawasaki. I soon discovered that the 500 was not really competitive, but the KR750 was a different matter. Double wins at the North West 200, a Senior TT win and the prestigious MCN Superbike Championship finished a great year for me. Throughout 1977 and 1978 however the 750 fell behind the opposition as the firm were concentrating on the 250/350.

I remember visiting the factory in Japan after winning the Grand Prix in the Netherlands in 1977, and being amazed that all of the racing development for road racing and motorcross was done out of a large wooden shed. Overall, I remember my time with Kawasaki with mixed feelings. There were lots of good moments and being teamed up with the likes of Gregg Hansford and Yvon Duhamel brings back great memories, but I would not be truthful if I did not admit that there was also often frustration that things could have been so much more productive.

Finally, I hope that you will enjoy reading this book, and that when you have finished it you will have a greater appreciation of the important part that Kawasaki has played in the long history of the TT races on the Isle of Man.

Mick Grant
Seven times Isle of Man TT winner

ACKNOWLEDGEMENTS

No book or work such as this can come to fruition without a great deal of support and assistance being shown to the author. First and foremost I must thank Pen & Sword Books Ltd for their continued support for, and faith in, this series. The two other titles which preceded this, *Honda: The Golden Age* and *Yamaha: The New Dawn* very much pave the way for the book which you are about to read. In each case I have tried hard to strike the right balance between technical information and human drama. The latter is in no short supply at an event like the Isle of Man TT, and I must express my heartfelt thanks to TT legend Mick Grant both for the many fascinating insights into the racing world which he has shared with me over the years that we have known each other, and for the support that he has offered in my research. Mick has generously contributed the Foreword, but he also very kindly allowed me to quote from his books *Takin' the Mick,* and *Roadracing* and it is fair to say that this publication could not have been completed without that fulsome and unstinting assistance. Mick also put me in touch with John Cooper, and I would also like to take this opportunity to thank John for his valuable help. Chas Mortimer similarly provided valuable information, and for this I thank him.

Beyond this I must also express my thanks to the late Ken Sprayson, who allowed me access to his wonderful and evocative collection of colour slides from the 1960s and 1970s. Bill Snelling as ever helped me with images from the

Fottofinders archive. Steve Aynsley in Australia kindly offered assistance in locating a photo from his late brother Phil's archive, and granted permission for its use. Paul Ingham kindly supplied a photo from his own collection.

Helen Gibson as ever was enormously helpful with contacts in the racing world, and through her I was able to speak with several former Kawasaki sidecar competitors. In this respect I would like to thank Des Founds for his unstinting assistance in relation to Kawasaki sidecar engines; Richard and Eric Bregazzi provided invaluable information for which I express sincere gratitude, and Alan Warner likewise was a mine of information. Dave Molyneux as always was helpful in providing information about his father John.

Likewise, my thanks go to Simon Crellin at the Isle of Man Government Motorsport Office for assistance with use of the TT trademark.

 Any errors of fact or interpretation are entirely my own.

Matthew Richardson
Douglas, 2025

INTRODUCTION

Kawasaki, the last of the Japanese 'Big Four' manufacturers, arrived on the motorcycle racing scene comparatively late. Kawasaki Heavy Industries (to give the firm its full title) sounds an unlikely name for a leading maker of high-performance motorcycles. Yet it accurately reflects the origins of the long-established Japanese company and its wide-ranging output. Founded as a shipbuilding operation in 1878 by Shozo Kawasaki, the firm initially built large steel hulled ocean-going vessels. In 1886, the Tokyo operation was expanded into Kawasaki Dockyard and by the turn of the century it had embraced other forms of construction and transportation such as bridge sections and railway locomotives. Today, as well as constructing ships, KHI manufactures helicopters, trains, robots and aircraft: an aeronautical department was first formed in 1918, to be renamed in 1937 as the Kawasaki Aircraft Company, and it became a leader in Japan in the field of aircraft design and construction. Yet as a result of this, the company found itself in a difficult situation in the aftermath of the Second World War, when military aircraft production came to an abrupt standstill, leaving it with redundant resources and surplus manpower. It turned instead to producing small petrol engines, which were much needed to help war torn Japan get mobile once again. Unlike that of most other businesses in that country, the company infrastructure was still in relatively good shape after the war. Indeed, the experience that it had gained during the conflict would prove to be useful afterwards. As a result, it continued to grow, and eventually became an industrial giant encompassing almost all forms of heavy engineering, on land, sea and air. Virtually anything industrial, Kawasaki made it.

Although many years passed before the Kawasaki badge appeared on a motorcycle, the company had two-wheeled links in this period, supplying engines for Meihatsu and Meguro, among others. Meguro was one of the few early Japanese motorcycle manufacturers to resurface after the Second World War. Somewhat ironically, the company began by building copies of British Velocette singles, and post-war they made a 500cc twin that was more or less a BSA A7 replica. Kawasaki had already made engines for two-wheelers sold under the Meihatsu name. As early as 1954 it had supplied Meihatsu's 58cc two-stroke unit, but major expansion into motorcycling was to come about in 1961. The aircraft sector of the company oversaw the creation of a new plant for the mass production of motorcycles at Kobe, and the old Meihatsu network was reorganised into Kawasaki Auto Sales. After setting up a motorcycle research offshoot, Kawasaki formed an increasingly close connection with the Meguro Manufacturing Company, the other associated motorcycle manufacturer, before the two companies eventually amalgamated as a result of a buy-out in 1963.

The first motorbike credited as a Kawasaki, an unexceptional 125cc two-stroke single, made its debut two years earlier, but the marque only began to surface as one of the majors in the mid-1960s. A number of British and other riders dabbled with the Kawasaki brand at the Isle of Man TT in the 1960s, 1970s, and 1980s, and the book that you are about to read tries to reflect the achievements of most of them. However, only one racer really made a serious and sustained impression with it, and went as far as to write Kawasaki into the Island's history books, and that competitor was Mick Grant.

Chapter One

FIRST BUT ALSO LAST

The story of the Kawasaki company is in many ways a microcosm for the industrial history of Japan as a whole, featuring as it does the competing influences of imported foreign manufactured goods, set against the growing desire to produce home grown Japanese products; the pressures and needs of war have shaped the direction of the company's output, and the shattering effect of total military defeat in 1945 have also influenced the development of the corporation. Finally, Kawasaki was to benefit from (and indeed contribute to) the Japanese economic miracle of the 1960s, when in common with other industrial entities in Japan it became part of an export drive which captured significant sections of the US and Western European markets. Unlike rival concern Honda, which was established in the post-war years specifically for the purpose of manufacturing motorcycles, the company already had a long history of engineering innovation, in areas far removed from two-wheeled transport.

The origins of the firm in fact go back to 1878, when Shozo Kawasaki established Kawasaki Tsukiji Shipyard in Tokyo. Born in Kagoshima to a kimono merchant, Shozo Kawasaki became a tradesman at the age of 17 in Nagasaki, the only place in Japan which was then open to the West for commerce. When he was 27, he started a shipping business in Osaka, which failed when his only cargo ship sank during a storm. In 1869, he joined a company handling sugar from

Ryukyu (known now as Okinawa Prefecture), which had been established by a Kagoshima samurai. In April 1878, supported by Masayoshi Matsukata, the vice minister of finance, who was from the same province as Kawasaki, he established Kawasaki Tsukiji Shipyard on land borrowed from the government alongside the Sumidagawa River. This shipyard, at Tsukiji Minami-Iizaka-cho (currently Tsukiji 7-Chome, Chūō-ku), Tokyo, was arguably the first such concern in Japan, and marked a major step forward for the nation as a shipbuilder.

Meanwhile in 1893, he became involved in developing new sea routes for the import of sugar from Ryukyu, at the request of the Japanese government's Ministry of Finance. The new sea route that he devised made the import of sugar to the mainland far more efficient. In 1894, he was also appointed executive vice president of the Japan Mail Steam-Powered Shipping Company. Having experienced many sea disasters in his life and career, Kawasaki developed a strong trust in Western ships, mainly because they were more spacious, stable and faster than typical Japanese vessels of this era. At the same time, he became particularly interested in the techniques employed in the modern shipbuilding industry in Europe and America.

Around the same period, the First Sino-Japanese War had started and the shipbuilding industry in Japan as a whole received a major boost. Kawasaki Dockyard Company Ltd as a result enjoyed sudden prosperity. With full order books, Kawasaki was also kept busy in receiving and completing a run of commissions for ship repairs. Now realising the limitations of private management, Kawasaki decided to take the company on to the stock market directly after the close of the war. Eighteen years after it was founded, in 1896, it was incorporated as Kawasaki Dockyard Company Ltd. Then close to 60 years of age, and without an heir old enough to succeed him, Kawasaki nominated Kōjirō Matsukata, the third son of his business benefactor, Masayoshi Matsukata, to be his successor. Kōjirō Matsukata was thus appointed as the first president of the new public company.

Kōjirō Matsukata was born in Satsuma (now part of Kagoshima Prefecture) in 1865. He became a secretary to Japan's prime minister during his father's tenure at the Ministry of Finance, between 1891 and 1892. After being appointed the first president of Kawasaki Dockyard Company Ltd in 1896, the younger Matsukata would hold this position for thirty-two years until 1928. By expanding the business beyond shipping into rolling stock and aircraft, he showed great vision, and by implementing Japan's first eight-hour working day system as well as other measures, he nurtured and grew Kawasaki into a leading heavy industrial company in Japan. On a personal level, Matsukata was also known as a collector of art. The National Museum of Western Art in Tokyo was later to be established around the core of Matsukata's private collection. In addition, the Tokyo National Museum houses his extensive personal collection of Ukiyoe prints.

In 1897, Kawasaki Dockyard completed a cargo-passenger ship, named *Iyomaru* (of 727 gross registered tons), its first ship built after becoming a publicly traded company. During the ten years of private management between 1886 and 1896, the company had built about eighty new ships, including six steel ships such as *Tamamaru* (about 570 gross registered tons). Since the first steel ship was built in Japan in 1890, the shipbuilding industry had rapidly modernised, in doing so moving away from the use of iron to steel. The foundation of Kawasaki Dockyard in many ways marked the beginning of Japan's modern shipbuilding industry.

The company's first dry dock (currently known as No. 1 Dock, at Kobe Shipyard, Hyogo Prefecture) was finished in 1902, and its historic importance was recognised when it was listed as a registered tangible cultural asset of Japan in 1998. Shozo Kawasaki had first realised that the company's shipyard needed a drastic increase in capacity when the Kawasaki Dockyard was established in Kobe city. He planned to construct a dry dock by reclaiming unused land next to the shipyard. In 1892, a structural survey began, and in 1895, boring tests were carried out. After the incorporation of Kawasaki Dockyard, Kōjirō Matsukata continued to pursue the plan.

Construction work was difficult and challenging, due in the main to the extremely weak foundations of the site on the Minatogawa River delta. After a number of failures, a new technique was adopted to harden the underwater foundation by pouring concrete into the basin. Six years later in 1902, the dry dock was completed at last, however it had cost three times as much and taken three times longer than the construction of a similar dock would have done under more favourable conditions. Never the less the new structure when completed was 130 metres in length, by 15.7 meters wide and 5 meters deep, and could accommodate ships of up to 6,000 gross registered tons.

The Kawasaki Dockyard was adjacent to the government-run Kobe railway plant, to the north. Kawasaki's first president, Kōjirō Matsukata, had a desire to further expand into new business areas, and given the location of the dockyard, one especially promising new enterprise would be the manufacture of railway carriages. In 1906, the newly opened Hyogo Works began construction of locomotives, freight and passenger cars as well as steel bridge girders. This same year, the Kawasaki concern first began production of marine steam turbines at its dockyard.

In the early years of the twentieth century, Japan was rapidly becoming a significant naval power. The Imperial Japanese Navy was at this time allied with, and heavily influenced by Britain's Royal Navy. As a result of this influence, around 1901 the Japanese began to think about introducing submarines to their fleet, and it was decided to form a submarine flotilla soon after the start of the Russo-Japanese War. In 1904, five Holland-type boats, known as Submarines No. 1 to 5, were imported from the United States.

At the same time, the Imperial Japanese Navy proposed to build its own submarines in its domestic shipyards. In 1904, it awarded an order for the first two to Kawasaki. Although the navy provided it with plans received from J.P. Holland, the designer of Holland-type submarines, the exact details of the vessels to be built were left to the company to decide. Kawasaki now devoted all of its energies to building submarines that would live up to the navy's expectations, and to demonstrate its capabilities as a shipbuilder to the rest of the world. It invited engineers from the United States to observe the work, as well as continuing to research technical problems even after laying the first keel. In 1906, having overcome many difficulties, Kawasaki completed and delivered the first two such vessels to be built in Japan, Submarines No. 6 and 7, to the navy. This in fact was the ethos which drove Japanese naval thinking in this era – firstly to achieve the assimilation and naturalisation of Western technology into Japanese industry, and then to surpass it.

The Battle of Tsushima, the naval engagement that decided Japan's victory in the Russo-Japanese War, saw the first defeat of a European state by an Asiatic nation in modern times. Japan was a fast-rising power, and the Japanese government now made plans to strengthen its naval forces by increasing domestic shipbuilding capacity, so that its large fleet vessels, all of which were previously manufactured abroad, could now be built in its own shipyards. Whereas private shipyards had previously received government orders for small vessels, such as early destroyers and torpedo boats, they would now also receive orders for major capital ships. Built by Kawasaki Dockyard, the dispatch boat *Yodo* was the first 100-ton warship built by a private shipyard, and was highly regard by naval officials. It marked the beginning of true shipbuilding by private shipyards in Japan.

In 1872, British-made steam locomotives had run for the first time on Japan's inaugural railway line between Shinagawa and Yokohama. In this area also, Japan aspired to reduce its reliance on Western imports and to develop its own domestic industry. Kawasaki had started manufacturing rolling stock in 1907, and just four years later produced its first steam engine, the Tender-type locomotive (2B saturation steam type, No. 6700–6704), for the Ministry of Railways. Its performance was highly acclaimed and the ministry later praised the company, confirming that its locomotive had done even better in tests than those made in foreign countries. Kawasaki would go on to manufacture 3,237 steam locomotives in total until production ceased in 1971, greatly contributing to the development of railways in Japan.

Japan was an ally of Great Britain during the First World War, and Matsukata spent some time in London during the conflict. He was impressed by the use of aeroplanes on the Western Front, and as a result established the aircraft department at the Hyogo Works upon his return to Japan in 1918. Aircraft development had accelerated in the fifteen or so years since the Wright brothers' historic flight, when aeroplanes made from wood and cloth could only travel short distances. Aero engines were becoming increasingly powerful, and wood and canvas would soon give way to stressed steel construction. With the shipping division divided off and independently incorporated as Kawasaki Kisen Kaisha Ltd (K-Line) in 1919, this left the corporation with more resources with which to develop its aviation ambitions, and it signed licensing agreements with Salmson in France. Kawasaki soon began to build licensed French engines as well as planes. Following the example of its rival firm Mitsubishi, Kawasaki accelerated the training of its engineers by seconding them to the military arsenals and to France. But Kawasaki went even further. After hiring a naval officer and sending him to France to acquire advanced aircraft technology, it recruited more than seventy army aircraft technicians directly out of the arsenals. Within forty months, in September 1922, Kawasaki was manufacturing army reconnaissance planes, and established a new aircraft production plant.

Kawasaki completed its first aeroplane at its Hyogo Works shortly after manufacturing started, and conducted test flights in Sohara Village (now known as Kakamigahara City), Gifu Prefecture. The Japanese army found it to be an excellent performer during this series of tests, and as a result adopted it for use as their first military aircraft, giving it the designation Otsu Type 1 surveillance plane. Kawasaki would in total complete the manufacture of about 300 aircraft of this type until 1927. Kawasaki would eventually go on to build Japan's first all-metal aircraft, thereby laying the groundwork for the technological innovations of later decades.

In 1923, the Great Kantō earthquake hit Tokyo, and bridges across the Sumidagawa River collapsed. Kawasaki constructed replacement structures such as the Kiyosubashi Bridge, Shirahigebashi Bridge and Eitaibashi Bridge, which became well known for their elaborate designs. Kawasaki utilised state of the art technology for the construction of these bridges. For example, it adopted high-tensile steel (Ducol steel), made at the company's Hyogo Works, for the first time in Japan for use in the upper cables of the Kiyosubashi, an elegant suspension bridge, and for the lower connections of the Eitaibashi, an enormous steel arch bridge. In this era, Kawasaki received orders from the Earthquake Reconstruction Bureau and other organisations in Japan for twenty-five new bridges in total, including the bridges mentioned above, requiring some 16,000 tons of steel. Kawasaki also constructed the Kachidokibashi Bridge across Sumidagawa River. This leaf-lift (trunnion bascule) bridge was based on a drawbridge in Chicago, which used the same principles of design. The bascules, which hold the bridge centre of 44 meters, can be raised to a maximum of 70°, making large ship traffic possible. However, the bridge no longer opens today, due to new regulations to ease road traffic jams. In 1928, Hyogo Works was separately incorporated as Kawasaki Rolling Stock Manufacturing Company Ltd.

All was not well with the company, however. During the worldwide slump which followed the Wall Street crash, Japan faced recession and new company president Fusajiro Kajima, who had taken over the reins of the firm in 1928, tried to steer it through this crisis. Major organisational changes and personnel shakeups seemed to put the company back on track, but it was not to be and as a result of the recession, on 20 July 1931, the business filed for a restructuring-type bankruptcy. President Kajima died suddenly and in March 1933, Hachisaburo Hirao took over the helm as company president. It was he who largely paved the way to corporate recovery. At the time, the Japanese economy was also showing signs of revival. President Hirao, who had done everything in his power to get the business back on track, eventually took a seat in the House of Peers upon imperial appointment, and in December 1935, Shosuke Itani, the senior managing director, became the fourth president.

In 1918, Kawasaki had started manufacturing trucks at its Hyogo Works to meet the growing social needs of the day. However, production was suspended until 1929, in order to meet the demands of the bridge construction programme. Thereafter the company (Kawasaki Rolling Stock Manufacturing) resumed manufacturing commercial automobiles. In 1931, the prototype of a 1.5-ton truck was completed based on a US deluxe model, and the next year Kawasaki started producing Rokkogo trucks and buses, some of which were delivered to the Ministry of Railways. In 1933, it also began manufacturing high status Rokkogo passenger cars for such customers as the Imperial family. Although the company would stop production of automobiles in 1942 by order of the Department of War, which intended to shift production capacity away from motor vehicles to aeroplanes, Kawasaki had showed itself to be a pioneer of Japan's automobile industry during that early era. Meanwhile in the 1930s the Kawasaki Rolling Stock Manufacturing Company exported a large number of locomotives, passenger coaches and freight cars to China. Among them were the state of the art engines of the day, Pashina-type steam locomotives which pulled the Ajiago Super Express, linking Dalian and Changchun, China. In 1934 a Pashina-type steam locomotive was constructed for the Ajiago Super Express and the number '1,500' was painted on the side, in commemoration of the fact that this was the 1,500th steam locomotive made by Kawasaki. Ominous dark clouds were gathering on the horizon however, and just three years later the Second Sino-Japanese War began. Many historians now see this event as the true beginning of what would become the Second World War.

In 1937 the aircraft division was split off, and incorporated as Kawasaki Aircraft Company Ltd. In 1939, when war was clearly inevitable, the United States blocked aircraft sales (including technology and parts) to Japan. By this time, however, the Japanese industry had completed preparations to shift – under military tutelage – from licensed to indigenous development and from batch to mass production. Seventeen private airframe and ten private engine manufacturers were soon operating at full capability, and were adding new capacity as quickly as possible, Kawasaki being one of the largest of these. It developed the Ki-60 which was intended to be a heavily armed specialised interceptor, with a high wing loading; however there were problems with the weight and handling of this model, and it never went into production. Instead, it evolved into the Ki-61, which was to be a more lightly loaded and armed general-purpose fighter, intended to be used mainly in an offensive, air superiority role at low to medium altitudes. In 1941 the company began production of the Ki-61 *Hien* (Swallow) fighter, one of the most sophisticated aircraft produced by the Empire of Japan during the Second World War. Originally known as the Type 3-1 fighter, the *Hien* was the only liquid-cooled, inline-engine fighter developed in Japan during the conflict. The *Hien* was known for its world-class performance, with a maximum speed of 610kmh and the capability to fly in formation even at an altitude of 10,000 meters. The Ki-61 was designed by Takeo Doi and his deputy Shin Owada in response to a late 1939 tender by the *Koku Hombu* for two fighters, each to be built around the German-designed Daimler-Benz DB-601 engine. Production aircraft would use a Kawasaki licensed version of the DB-601, known in Japan as the Ha-40, which was to be manufactured at its Akashi plant in Hyogo.

When first encountered by Allied forces, the fighter was wrongly assumed to be a Messerschmitt Bf 109 built under licence in Japan, rather than a home-grown design.

The Ki-61 was the last of the aircraft powered by the DB-601 or its foreign derivatives, and it was soon overshadowed by Allied fighters with more powerful engines. By the time it first flew in December 1941, one year after the Italian Macchi C.202's first flight and three years after the first German Bf 109E, the engine was already underpowered compared to the new 1,120kW (1,500hp) inline or 1,491kW (2,000hp) radial engines being developed (and already nearing the mass-production stage) to power the next generation of Allied combat aircraft, such as the American Republic P-47 Thunderbolt. Moreover, the inline Ha-40 engine proved to be an unreliable powerplant, a situation exacerbated in the South Pacific campaign, where high temperatures caused problems with the fuel pumps. The DB-601 engine required precise and sophisticated manufacturing; the Ha-40 was lighter by roughly 30kg (70lb) and required even higher manufacturing standards. Reaching these standards proved difficult for Japanese manufacturers, an issue further complicated as the war went on by the variable quality of materials, fuel, and the lubricants needed to run a sensitive, high-performance engine. The Japanese equivalent of the more powerful DB-605 engine was the Kawasaki Ha-140, which was fitted onto the Type 3 to produce the Ki-61-II high-altitude interceptor.

However, the Ha-140 power plant also had severe reliability problems that were never fully resolved, and around half of the first batch of engines delivered were returned to the factory to be rebuilt. A bombing raid by the United States on 19 January 1945 destroyed the engine factory in Akashi, and 275 Ki-61-II-KAI airframes without engines were subsequently converted to use the available Mitsubishi Ha-112-II radial engine, resulting in the Ki-100. While the Ha-112 solved the production problems encountered with the Ha-140, the new engine still had a major weakness, chiefly a lack of power at altitude. This significantly diminished its ability to intercept high-flying American B-29 Superfortresses relative to that of the Ki-61-II. It became an established tactic of the interceptor squadrons to try to ram the B-29s in order to bring them down. These were not necessarily 'kamikaze' missions however, as in many cases the Japanese fighters were still able to land after having lost part of a wing. In March of the same year the Kobe air raid took a tremendous toll on the company. Ninety facilities, including the shipbuilding factory offices, were burned to the ground. On top of that, most of the head office was damaged in the air raid that occurred in June of the same year. Ultimately following the two atomic bombs at Hiroshima and Nagasaki, and the declaration of war by the Soviet Union, in August 1945 Japan surrendered. Immediately after the war, the United States commissioned a series of reports on the major corporations forming the Japanese aviation industry, and how they had operated during the war. That covering Kawasaki recorded:

> This company occupied the number three place in Japan's aircraft industry. In over-all production it accounted for 17 per cent of the combat air frames and 12 per cent of combat engines manufactured in 1944, the industry's peak year ... Kawasaki, because of its relatively compact organisation, managed to retain financial and management control of its plants. With production centralised in two large permanent plants, and later dispersion chiefly into defunct spinning mill facilities, the company's relative wartime expansion was small ... there was a tendency,

> almost a well-defined policy on the part of the company to keep the government's influence as small as possible. In fact Kawasaki at first was in a position to refuse certain types of work from the government ... Examination of the heavily damaged plants revealed very little of mass-production technique in either engine or air frame manufacture. Kawasaki methods in air-frame manufacture appeared to be those of the prewar, small order, aircraft industry of the United States.[1]

Post-war Japan underwent a series of social and economic reforms implemented under the direction of the General Headquarters of the Allied Powers (GHQ). In October 1945, Kawasaki was designated as a *zaibatsu* company along with Mitsui, Sumitomo, Mitsubishi, and others. The *zaibatsu* were large family-controlled vertical monopolies consisting of a holding company on top, with a wholly-owned banking subsidiary providing finance, and several industrial subsidiaries dominating specific sectors of a market, either solely, or through a number of other subordinate companies. The *zaibatsu* were the heart of economic and industrial activity within the Empire of Japan, and held great influence over Japanese national and foreign policies.

The *Rikken Seiyūkai* political party was regarded as an extension of the Mitsui group, which also had very strong connections with the Imperial Japanese Army. Likewise, the *Rikken Minseitō* was connected to the Mitsubishi group, as was the Imperial Japanese Navy. The following year, President Itani of Kawasaki and most of the management of the company were forced to resign as a result of GHQ's purge. In response, the firm submitted a restructuring plan to the government. The plan which was eventually approved called for the continuation of the Kawasaki corporation, but with the establishment of a second company that was formed by splitting off the steelmaking division. On 7 August 1950, at an ordinary general meeting of shareholders the establishment of the second company was approved, and Kawasaki Steel Corporation was born. Kawasaki now reorganised itself with a focus on the shipbuilding division, with Toshio Tezuka at the helm as its fifth president.

These were difficult times for the company. Japan's aircraft industry, which had mainly manufactured military aeroplanes, was suppressed when the Second World War ended in 1945. Production of aircraft was totally prohibited by the Allies for seven years, until 1952 when the Treaty of Peace with Japan became effective. Even after the prohibition was lifted, the industry faced difficulties in resuming business due to the seven-year break. Technical knowledge had been lost, equipment was not up to date and component suppliers needed to be established. However, in a somewhat ironic development it would be the United States military and the contracts which it placed with Japanese industry (particularly during the Korean War) which laid the technological foundation for the subsequent development of Japanese industry. A decade later, the Keidanren (Japan's Federation of Economic Organisations) and the Japanese Machinery Industry Association concluded that: 'U.S. military special procurement not only revived the defense industry but provided a foothold for the revival of related machinery industries.'[2]

Through licensed production and the demanding product specifications of the US military, Japanese makers learned the fundamentals of standardised parts manufacture, testing standards, and quality control. Manufacturers such as Kawasaki used US military contracts to train their first post-war generation of engineers in the most advanced manufacturing technologies. The spin-offs from defence production may have been most substantial in aircraft, but they pervaded the entire Japanese domestic manufacturing base in what Senga Tetsuya (the unofficial private sector 'minister of defence'), has called the 'invisible development' of Japanese industrial technology.

Kawasaki started designing a four-seat transporter aircraft at Gifu Works, and in 1953 it completed the KAL-1 transport aeroplane. In addition, Kawasaki focused on the development of helicopters at the Akashi Works. In 1952, the company had signed a technical agreement with Bell Aircraft Corporation (now Bell Helicopter Textron) of the United States, and in 1954 completed the Kawasaki-Bell 47D-1 helicopter, the first rotorcraft to be built in Japan. In total Kawasaki manufactured six 47D-1 helicopters for the nation's Ground Self-Defence Force. Overall as a result of the Korean War, the international balance of payments in the country as a whole improved. Japanese industry boomed again, mainly due to the increase in special procurements by the US military, but also as a result of growth in ordinary exports.

Once Kawasaki's third floating dock was completed in June 1953, the volume of ship repair work doubled in a very short space of time. Simultaneously, the steel structure division had just finished constructing penstocks and dam gates for the Sakuma Power Station, and was also awarded various bridge contracts. The company now constructed a number of steel frames, including those for Koshien Stadium's large infield roof, nicknamed the Iron Umbrella, as well as the Hanshin and Sankei Kaikan Buildings in Osaka City. A hugely significant year for the company was 1969, when Kawasaki Dockyard, Kawasaki Rolling Stock Manufacturing and Kawasaki Aircraft merged once again to become Kawasaki Heavy Industries Ltd. In the 1960s, at the beginning of the era of massive Japanese economic growth, large-scale mergers between companies were becoming commonplace, strengthening as they did their international competitiveness. This accelerated consolidation was seen in various industries across Japan. Under these circumstances, Masashi Isano, president of Kawasaki Dockyard, conceived the idea of creating a single great Kawasaki enterprise by merging all the major group companies. This was based on his long-held dream to develop the company into a comprehensive heavy industrial enterprise, providing products for use on land, at sea, and in the air, which first president Kōjirō Matsukata, had envisioned in the past.

The presidents of the three companies – Isano of Kawasaki Dockyard, Masao Ueda of Kawasaki Rolling Stock Manufacturing and Kiyoshi Yotsumoto of Kawasaki Aircraft – all shared the desire for a greater Kawasaki, and signed a merger agreement on 19 March 1968, following discussion and negotiation. On 1 April 1969, Kawasaki Dockyard officially acquired the two companies, and adopted the new company name Kawasaki Heavy Industries Ltd (it should be noted however that in Japanese characters, Kawasaki Dockyard Company Ltd had already changed its name to Kawasaki Heavy Industries Ltd in 1937. However, its English language name remained Kawasaki Dockyard until the date of the merger of the three companies). Kawasaki Heavy Industries started with about 26,000 employees, paid-in capital of 28 billion yen, and anticipated first-year sales of 200 billion yen. Isano was named president, and Ueda and Yotsumoto were elected executive vice presidents. Also 1969, as if to demonstrate the company's leading role in increasing technological development around the world, it developed the Kawasaki-Unimate 2,000, the first Japanese-made industrial robot. Kawasaki regarded the design and production of labour-saving machines and systems as an important mission, and became Japan's pioneer in the industrial robotics field. In 1968, the company (still as Kawasaki Aircraft) had entered into a technical agreement with Unimation Incorporated, a US company specialising in industrial robots, and began development work.

Indeed, from the perspective of Kawasaki's racing heritage, it was also Kawasaki Aircraft which was the most significant of the three arms of the company, because it was from this branch that the firm's first motorcycles sprang. As early as the end of the 1940s, Kawasaki's management began laying the groundwork for its foray into motorcycle production. In 1949, aircraft engineers at the Kawasaki Industries plant in Takatsuki began designing the company's first motorcycle engine, an air-cooled, four-stroke, one-cylinder, overhead-valve, 148cc machine, which they dubbed the KE, for 'Kawasaki Engine'. The prototype was completed in 1952, and Kawasaki began manufacturing the design in 1953. Having set its sights on the motorcycle market, Kawasaki was clearly going to be a powerful competitor. The wartime experience earned while producing the Daimler-Benz 601-A aircraft engine was its principal technological advantage over firms that had produced nothing but motorcycles throughout their existence. During the early 1960s, Kawasaki Aircraft also realised that they could make more money with large-capacity motorcycles than their rivals were doing with smaller ones. While these big-engined machines did not cost significantly more to build than smaller models, they did carry a much larger price tag. Their first effort was the W1. It was essentially a 650cc copy of the British BSA-A10, and it did not sell well. Perhaps since it was a first effort, potential buyers simply decided to purchase the real thing (unlike today, at that time there were many new and competitive

BSAs on the market). Following the Kawasaki W series, Japan's largest motorcycle of the day, which initiated the big bike boom, the company introduced an epoch-making new model, the H1 (two-stroke, three-cylinder, 498cc) in 1969. The company had forged ahead in the US market in the late 1960s. Motorcycle sales subsidiaries were set up in Chicago in 1966 and in New Jersey the next year. In 1968, the US arm Kawasaki Motors Corporation, USA (KMC) was established as a company, and it aggressively promoted sales across the continent. In addition to strengthening its sales network, the company would introduce successful new motorcycles and after releasing the H1 in 1969, it followed this up with the Z1 in 1972, which would make Kawasaki a household name in the US.

After a nearly a decade of the big bike end of the motorcycle industry being dominated by the British manufacturers, Kawasaki took everyone by surprise by launching in 1969 its first triple-cylinder model. The 500cc Kawasaki H1 Mach III had an air-cooled, three-cylinder two-stroke engine. There were two exhaust pipes on the right side of the bike and one on the left and while most other manufacturers had been developing four-stroke engines, Kawasaki took a different direction and came up with its triple two-stroke. In that era, it was European makers who mainly dominated the US market for large motorcycles, with firms like Triumph and BSA particularly successful. However, exports of Japanese motorcycles with large engine displacements were expected to follow the general trend at the time and to grow dramatically. Predictably, the success of the H1 confirmed Kawasaki's big bike reputation and led to a commanding position in the US market. Among the outstanding H1's unique attributes were awesome power and high performance, an exhaust roar typical of the three-cylinder models, which came out of the asymmetrically set expansion chambers (two on the right, one on the left), and two-tone colouring of white and blue.

In 1972, the company unveiled Japan's largest motorcycle of the day, the Kawasaki Z1, featuring an air-cooled, four-stroke, four-cylinder, 903cc, double overhead camshaft motor, which represented Kawasaki's first foray into the world of four-stroke engines. Previously this had largely been the domain of rivals Honda, but Kawasaki set out to challenge them with a state of the art, unique design. Early in the development stage it acquired the code-name of 'New York Steak' because from the outset the Z1 promised to become a 'mouth-watering motorcycle,' winning overwhelming popularity among customers and critics alike immediately after its introduction. It became a long-term bestseller and the Z1, the pioneer of Superbike models, not only solidified Kawasaki's reputation as a leader in large capacity motorcycles, but remains deeply engraved in the public conscience as one of the most iconic designs produced to date. Back in Japan, through its 1972 merger with Kisha Seizo Company Ltd, the firm became Japan's leader in the rolling stock industry. That same year, it also formed Kawaju Reinetsu Service Company Ltd, the operations of which further expanded its interests into the field of municipal refuse incineration. The twentieth century had ushered in incredible technological advances, and Kawasaki foresaw the need to apply advanced technologies and engineering expertise to large-scale projects worldwide.

Meanwhile, in order to expand its consumer goods business, Kawasaki sought to develop a new product, other than motorcycles, to be powered by a gasoline engine. In 1971, management decided to enter the marine recreational product field and a marine project team was formed at the company.

As an example of the innovative thinking going on at the time, during team discussions, the concept of a new product gradually took shape. This was a creation in a completely new category, which would enable people to enjoy waterskiing, a popular marine sport of the day, by themselves, without a boat. This would become the basic concept of the Jet Ski watercraft. In 1973, at Akashi Works, Kawasaki developed a brand new product (development code: WSAA) by installing in a water craft a two-stroke, two-cylinder, 398cc engine design based on those used for snowmobiles. The product was named the Jet Ski, and this became a registered trademark of Kawasaki. After obtaining a positive response from trial sales in the US, the company began mass production. In 1975, Jet Ski production was shifted to the Lincoln Plant, Nebraska, and full-scale manufacturing of the JS400 commenced. Initially the focus was on the US market and it was not until 1980 that Kawasaki actually started to sell Jet Ski watercraft in its home country of Japan.

In that era, the US the market was also unquestionably the one in which demand for motorcycles was strongest. Therefore, in 1974, KMC established a new motorcycle factory in Lincoln, Nebraska, which was the first US manufacturing site established by any of the Japanese motorcycle or automobile makers. In January 1975, the new plant started producing the KZ series motorcycles, and in the same year also began producing Jet Ski watercraft. The KMC Lincoln Plant formed a new subsidiary, Kawasaki Motors Manufacturing Corporation, USA (KMM) in 1981. Later, KMM would go on to establish a further factory in Maryville, Missouri in addition to the Lincoln Plant, and would see the manufacture of a wide range of products such as motorcycles, ATVs, Jet Ski watercraft, general purpose gasoline engines, industrial robots and rolling stock.

Only in the mid-1970s did the firm really come to see racing as the shop window in which it could display its impressively powerful triple cylinder and other motorcycles. For a company with such a long history of engineering innovation, Kawasaki were comparative late-comers to this arena, but they had seen the glory (and over the counter sales) which it had brought to Japanese rivals Honda, Suzuki and Yamaha. For all three, racing had been the gateway into firstly European and latterly US markets. Whilst Kawasaki was arguably ahead of all three rivals in terms of the latter, being the first Japanese company to actually begin production on US soil, they were none the less wise enough to see where a successful foray into racing might still take them.

Chapter Two

GOING GREEN 1966–1973

The entry of Kawasaki into the world of Grand Prix motorcycle racing was cautious and hesitant. Despite the size and impressive history of the company, they were a long way behind their Japanese rivals Honda, Yamaha and Suzuki. Indeed, these three were several years ahead of Kawasaki in terms of practical experience and machine development. In particular, the other firms had also all taken the important step of recruiting a stable of Western professional riders, who could exploit their machinery to its best potential.

Kawasaki initially had only one such overseas rider. Born in London in 1940, Englishman Dave Simmonds had ridden little-known lightweight Tohatsu motorcycles in the races of the mid-1960s. These years however were dominated firstly by Honda, and latterly by them in competition with Suzuki and Yamaha. When Simmonds switched to Honda machinery, in 1965 he won the ACU British Road Racing Star, forerunner to the British Championship. This brought him to the attention of Kawasaki, at this time still a relatively unknown brand in the world of motorcycles, who were eager to grab a share of the glory currently being fought over by the other three Japanese manufacturers. Kawasaki had found that their air-cooled 125cc machine was unreliable, and so redesigned it with water cooling. However they were still not confident that it would be more dependable, and so sent their only test rider/racer Toshio Fujii (a former Suzuki Grand Prix competitor) to the Isle of Man TT to try it out.

Unfortunately, Fujii was involved in a fatal crash during practice, in September 1966 (the races being delayed that year by the National Union of Seamen's strike). Having fallen heavily at Cruickshank's Corner, he was taken to Ramsey Cottage Hospital and though initially thought not to be badly injured, he later died. Derbyshire rider John 'Moon Eyes' Cooper had shared lodgings with Fujii, and the two had become great friends as a result of the Japanese competitor's bubbly personality and infectious laugh. Cooper was deeply affected by his death, even more so when he returned to their digs to find his possessions still set out in the room as he had left them. Thus, it was as a result of this tragic event that it would fall to Simmonds to make Kawasaki's race debut appearance at the Isle of Man TT.

Later that same month he flew to Tokyo, with a contract from Kawasaki to ride in the end of season Japanese Grand Prix that year, a traditional means by which a Japanese factory could have a look at a prospective new rider. Although he was squeezed out of a podium finish by the gaggle of Hondas and Suzukis which dominated the race, he had none the less done enough to return the investment made in him by Kawasaki; however, the firm did not yet consider their chances against Honda and the other factories to be strong enough to go to the expense of sending a squad of mechanics and managers half way around the world, in order to engage in a full-scale World Championship campaign. Simmonds then came up with a compromise proposal, that they should lend him the bike and that he should do all of the mechanical work on it himself. Kawasaki were still unconvinced, and insisted that he undergo a training course at their factory. At this point they realised that Simmonds was more than capable of the work, so they agreed to the deal. He came back to the UK with the bike, and a box of spares including two crankshafts, four pistons and a few piston rings, and from then on, he would carry their banner in 1967 and 1968 in pursuit of a world title. In 1967 he struggled valiantly with both a 125cc machine and a 250cc steed, as well as a machine for 350cc races, but he was constantly hampered by repeated piston failures. In that year's Junior TT the latter machine failed to complete the race, but it was far from being the finished article. It was basically a works-prepared 250cc Production racer, which had been fitted with bigger bore barrels and larger pistons to bring it up to 338cc.

Despite a number of top six finishes that season, including two fourth places on the Isle of Man, in the Lightweight and Ultra-Lightweight races, Simmonds failed to break the grip of the likes of Hailwood at Honda or Phil Read at Yamaha, who at that time had a stranglehold on the motorcycle World Championship races. Never the less, his finish just outside the podium in the Lightweight TT aboard the newly released A1R caught the attention of the racing public. The same race saw Liverpool motorcycle dealer Bill Smith finish fifth with his Kawasaki, and John Cooper come home in twenty-fifth place aboard a 250cc A1R machine. This latter example had been imported to Britain by two enthusiastic RAF servicemen who were stationed in the Far East, as this was before Kawasaki machines were actually being officially sold in the UK. Northamptonshire enthusiast and sponsor Peter Chapman had put them in touch with Cooper, who remembered that the machine had enormous potential:

> The two lads who had brought the bike over put a big tyre on the back wheel. In Practice it expanded with the heat and it wore a hole in the oil tank, which meant that I fell off at Governors. It was a lovely bike and it was bloody

> quick. I could have won that race with it. When I set off in the race I had a high number, so I set off late, towards the back of the field, but I passed loads of people. Peter Chapman and some others who were signalling for me were waiting for me at Ramsey hairpin, but they weren't expecting me to come round so quickly, so they weren't ready for me! They missed me, then they buggered off so I had no signals. I think I could have won that race, were it not for the fact that I came into the pits and a marshal pushed down on the seat and accidently pushed the oil cut off at the same time! The oil tank was at the back of the seat. So the bike eventually seized up, and I had to push it a long way back in to finish, it seized at Signpost. I don't know what happened to the bike after that TT, I'm guessing the two lads who had brought it over might have sold it.[1]

Interest in the *Samurai*, the sports roadster on which the 250cc racer was based, was greatly increased by the success of Simmonds at the TT, as well as his final standing of tenth in the 1967 250cc World Championship. The racer was very similar to the road machine, the chief difference being in the engine compartment, where the racer employed narrower piston rings. It also had slightly altered port timing on the barrels and longer opening periods on the discs. The balance holes in the flywheel were plugged with alloy, and separate float chamber carburettors were employed, with the carburettor section cut away. The racer had a six-plate clutch rather than the five-plate on the road bike. In addition, the primary drive of the race machine was by spur gears, whilst on the roadster these were helical. The gear ratios in the five-speed box were also slightly altered. On the front wheel a larger diameter, twin-hub double-leading shoe brake was fitted, together with racing exhausts, modified seat and of course a fibre-glass fairing. The *Samurai* (A1) would be updated in 1969 with a redesign of the fuel tank and seat, and a new colour for the front forks and headlight housing. The instruments were now to be separate from the headlights. The model set the pattern for Kawasaki's reputation for high performance motorcycles, and its acceleration was exceptional. The frame was also strong and durable, and it made for excellent handling.

The following year it was rumoured that Kawasaki would make a full-scale assault on the World Championships, this time with a properly organised and manned Grand Prix team, but it never materialised. Instead, they were content to let Simmonds continue to battle on, largely alone, for he never was awarded a full factory contract. This time around things were less impressive, for in 1968 he failed to even finish aboard his two Kawasaki machines at the Isle of Man TT. If they were yet to find a place on the podium, they were none the less increasing numerically, for the 1968 Lightweight race also saw the entry of Kawasaki-mounted Tony Godfrey, once a Yamaha teamster until a serious accident almost ended his career, and of Ian Veitch, one of the ever-present New Zealand contingent at the TT, who had previously been a 350cc champion in his homeland and brought his 250cc Kawasaki with him to the Isle of Man. Sadly, Veitch was to be killed in an accident at Ballagarey. Liverpool motorcycle dealer Bill Smith also participated in this event, his finish in sixth place being the best out of the half dozen Kawasaki machines which participated in this race. It was almost a repeat of the previous year's Lightweight outing in which Smith had finished fifth on the Kawasaki of Gerald Brown, a Ford dealer and major racing sponsor from Rugeley in Staffordshire. Kawasaki had also continued to dabble in

350cc racing – in late 1968 they had released the A7R, a fully-fledged racer rather than a modified roadster, but only a limited number ever reached the British market, those that did being imported by Reads of Leytonstone.

There was hardly any more support on the table for Simmonds in 1969, though Kawasaki did manage to supply him with an updated version of the KR1 machine along with a few spare parts. None the less, this season he was especially confident, as in 1969, the sport's governing body the FIM changed its regulations in an effort to reduce spiralling costs in motorcycle racing. Both 125 and 250cc machines would now be limited to two cylinders and six-speed transmissions. This regulation change caused the dominant Yamaha and Suzuki factories to immediately withdraw their teams from Grand Prix racing. Simmonds' wife Julie later remembered: 'He felt that 1969 would be the year he would win the world championship. He'd done a lot of work on the machine, and without the factory competition of Yamaha and Suzuki, was confident from the start of the season.'[2]

As a virtual privateer contesting the World Championships, Simmonds stood apart from some of the better financed riders, and certainly from the remaining factory teams. He worked largely on his own, his race headquarters being the awning of his Bailey caravan, which doubled as his workshop. Very often he would work late into the night under the glare of an electric light, doing all of his own race preparation and set up. By now however he had ironed out many of the reliability problems inherent in the KR1. At the second round of the season, Hockenheim, he scored Kawasaki's first Grand Prix win. In the third round, the Isle of Man TT, he proved that this was not a fluke, again taking first place on the 125cc in the Ultra Lightweight TT (even though his results in the Lightweight and Junior races that year were poor).

Though Simmonds was heavily tipped to win the Ultra Lightweight race, after topping the practice leaderboard and being clocked as the fastest 125cc through the Highlander speed trap at 115.8mph, it was still not without a series of dramatic incidents. The first of these came when he stopped to fix a loose left plug cable in the first lap. He told reporters afterwards: 'I thought it was all over when my left plug lead came off at Alpine Cottage.'[3]

He momentarily misdiagnosed the problem, and feared that it was something much more serious and which would terminate his race chances: 'I thought the engine was seizing and grabbed the clutch.'[4]

With the plug lead fixed and back on the road once more, further drama came for Simmonds at Handley's Corner: 'I slid right across the road when I hit a patch of cement dust on the exit.'[5]

For a short time this let John Ringwood (MZ) into the lead, but Simmonds quickly regained it. In a race that was characterised by a high rate of attrition, rider after rider dropped out with mechanical trouble, but Simmonds clung on to take the win. With no one to really push him, his 91.08mph race average and fastest lap at 92.46mph were well down on the records set the previous year by battling Yamaha team mates Phil Read and Bill Ivy. Even so, he could not afford to nurse his water-cooled, eight-speed engine, because unless he kept it revving in the 12,000 to 14,000rpm range it was prone to oil a plug. He was buoyed by the encouragement of the crowds lining the course, but couldn't wave back to them as he was still keeping a precautionary finger or two on the clutch lever, just in case of a seizure. With signal stations at his pits and the Bungalow, Simmonds thought he would be well signposted, but in the event he didn't need them, his fans around the course left him in no doubt as to how well he was doing. (Signalling in the Simmonds camp, it was noted, was very much a family affair, with assistance being provided by wife Julie, father-in-law Bill Boddice of sidecar TT fame, and future sidecar TT star brother-in-law Mick Boddice.) The Kawasaki finished the race quite clean and in perfect fettle, the only problem being that the engine was discovered to have run a little on the rich side when it was stripped down and examined in the scrutineers' tent afterwards.

His run of success in 125cc racing continued, and Simmonds claimed the world title for this class at the end of the season, the first for Kawasaki. The company was ecstatic and at the end of the year they staged a celebration for Simmonds in Paris, this being attended by a number of high-level figures from the company hierarchy in Japan. Because a rule change would prevent the use of the eight-speed gear box in the following season, they provided him with a new six-speed cluster, but paradoxically this was also the end of their support. After this great achievement they abruptly lost interest in the 125cc racer. There was to be no further development of the model, and as if to underline this, all of the jigs used for its construction in Japan were deliberately destroyed.

In those days, Kawasaki were proud of their dark red and white livery, their machines winning the nickname 'red tanked racers' as a result. That would change in 1970 with the first appearance on the Isle of Man of a lime green colour scheme, something Kawasaki would stick with for the remainder of the decade. The change in the traditional colour pattern had first come about at the Daytona 200 in 1969. That year, the company sent out the five best riders they could get on their new A7RA bikes – which for the first time ever were painted in the now iconic bright green.

Until then, the colour green was actually considered very bad luck on racetracks, and widely avoided due to superstitious beliefs about failing parts and fatal accidents. However, Yoji Hamawaki, the then president of Kawasaki, decided to not play it safe with the usual reds, blues, and yellows, but to take a risk for the struggling company: he rechristened the brand's so-called 'power research racing team' into 'team green'. The competition laughed at them, but was taken by surprise when Hamawaki's provocative, rebellious move to stand out paid off and actually resulted in a winning streak that year at Daytona – followed by many more after. Success bred success and in the process their motorcycles would earn a new nickname: 'Green Meanies' probably after the 'Blue Meanie' characters in the Beatles film *Yellow Submarine*. Back in 1969 the neon lime green colour was mixed by custom painter Molly Sanders, using three parts green and one part yellow. To this day, the mixture and tone of the shade have only slightly changed and it is mostly assigned the equally eye-catching pantone paint code 777.

In spite of Dave Simmonds' World Championship win in the 125cc class in 1969, Kawasaki had made little impact on the bigger classes of the international Grand Prix scene. That all changed in 1970 when the factory made available a racing H1R version of its fearsome 500cc three-cylinder two-stroke roadster, the Mach III or H1. Claimed to produce 75bhp, the H1R race engine was carried in a tubular steel duplex loop frame equipped (initially) with drum brakes at both ends, the front being a double-sided TLS unit. Following a good showing at Daytona in March, the H1R was well represented on the grid when the European Grand Prix programme commenced in May. H1R riders Bill Smith, Martin Carney and Christian Ravel all finished on the podium during the year but the best performer was New Zealander Ginger

Molloy, who scored four runner-up places to finish second in the World Championship behind MV Agusta's Giacomo Agostini. The model was reviewed by David Dixon in *Motor Cycle* in July 1970. He noted the awesome power that the machine possessed:

> I tweaked the twist grip just a mite too sharply. The instant response lifted the front wheel [and] I shot to the rear so violently that the seat back rest broke off. That's the sort of acceleration punched out by the 500cc three-cylinder Kawasaki H1R, the most powerful over-the-counter racer ever offered for sale. Getting the best out of the 75 bhp is an acquired art and that broken seat episode … is misleading. Power delivery is nothing like so fierce as on, say the factory 250cc Yamaha four – or even the 350cc TR2 Yamaha twin. From 6,000 rpm the Kawasaki's urge starts flowing and around 6,500 makes a businesslike lunge for the 7,000 mark. Because power delivery is so much silkier it lacks the dramatic front wheel pawing the air zip of the TR2. But, by tweaking the twist grip hard with the revs at about 7,000 rpm in low gear, the wheel will lift alright …[6]

However, he also quickly became aware of what was universally regarded as the Achilles' heel of the machine, its instability under certain conditions:

> Exciting speed – and exciting handling! Very stable under straight line acceleration and on smooth corners, the Kawasaki had a mind of its own on bumpy bends … it is difficult to pinpoint the cause but my guess is that it is primarily wrong suspension characteristics. And of course, the high mounting of the engine – well above

> wheel spindle level – is no help. The width of the engine makes a highish mounting unavoidable. But it could, in fact, be a bit lower, while retaining enough cornering clearance, if the bulbous exhaust system could be housed elsewhere than under the frame cradle tubes.[7]

Dixon concluded that the type's greatest asset was its acceleration, and the excessive twitching could be overcome to a degree by entering a corner more slowly and with less bank, and by using this fearsome acceleration to pull out of it. Unlike some other Japanese racing motorcycles, racing Kawasakis were only ever produced in very limited numbers, and were usually only available to works teams and supported riders. There were always fewer Kawasakis on the grids than other makes, but their distinctive green colouring tended to make them stand out.

In the Isle of Man, Bill Smith rode an H1R to third place in the 1970 Senior TT, a position he only achieved when he managed to pass Australian Jack Findlay (Seeley) on the sixth and final lap. That year the TT was run in heatwave conditions, and molten tar was a problem on some sections of the Mountain Course. All in all, it was an eventful ride, as Smith recounted:

> From the start the Kawasaki was 1,000 revs down. Then, later in the race, it tightened up twice – at the Highlander when I was doing about 140mph and as I came out of Creg-ny-Baa. And on the last lap the box carrying the battery broke away and I finished with it held on by the wires and waving in the breeze …[8]

Smith gave a more expansive account of this ride in his 2021 autobiography:

> The race was a nightmare for me for various reasons. We fitted the bike with a huge 7.5 gallon tank made by good friend Bill Jakeman. He also fitted a 1.5 gallon tank in the rear seat reservoir and connected it to the main tank by plastic tubing. This gave me the nine gallon capacity I needed to do five laps non-stop. The extra weight made the Kawasaki handle really badly at high speeds though, which I found out with the awful tank down Bray Hill on the first lap.
>
> Then, going into Ramsey Hairpin on lap two, the clutch lever broke under braking. A three cylinder bike of two stroke manufacture with no clutch was a real problem. The Kawasaki was quick but a real handful. On the fourth lap, both the battery and the extra fuel tank came adrift causing another headache. Then, as I was struggling even to finish the race and coming down from Creg-ny-Baa the bike started to weave badly from side to side. I should have retired at Hillberry, but my pig-headedness kept me going.
>
> At the finish I looked at my rear wheel and found that 16 spokes had disappeared. No wonder it was weaving and frightening me to death. When we stripped the engine for the post-race examination in the pit [we saw] that the centre piston was developing a hole in its crown. I realised I was very lucky to complete the race, becoming the first two stroke to finish the Senior TT in 50 years. What a race!![9]

Still campaigning his ageing 125cc, Simmonds dropped to fourth place in the 1970 World Championship due to improved competition from riders Dieter Braun (Suzuki), Ángel Nieto (Derbi) and Börje Jansson (Maico) but still managed to win the Finnish Grand Prix and scored two second place finishes in the Dutch and Belgian Grands Prix. Simmonds finished sixth in the 1971 125cc World Championship, with one win at the German Grand Prix at the Hockenheim ring. With his spare parts supply now dwindling, any success that Simmonds achieved was now purely down to his ability as an engineer, rather than support from the factory.

Although he did not ride on the Isle of Man in 1971, elsewhere he competed in the premier 500cc class with a Kawasaki H1R. Like the roadster it was based on the H1R had poor road handling characteristics; indeed it was far from being the best handling machine in its class, so Simmonds had his example rebuilt around a Ken Sprayson designed frame. This was lower, stiffer and lighter and it greatly improved the machine's handling. The result was a transformation – he first proved to be competitive by winning the pre-season invitational 500cc Mettet Grand Prix, then finished second to Giacomo Agostini and the dominant MV Agusta at the Finnish Grand Prix, followed by third places in Holland and Italy.

Simmonds scored Kawasaki's first premier-class Grand Prix win (and his own first 500cc class victory) at the season ending Spanish Grand Prix at Jarama, when Agostini sat out the race after already winning the championship. Simmonds ended up fourth in the 500cc World Championship despite missing four rounds. Another area of Simmonds' influence about this time is less well known. Around the Grands Prix paddocks, he had become friendly with an American mechanic named Randy Hall, who was wielding the spanners for Yamaha hero Rod Gould. After two seasons of successful racing in Europe, helping Gould to a World Championship title in the process, in 1971 Hall headed back across the Atlantic to become the first competition manager for the recently established Kawasaki Motors Corporation racing team in the United States. Much of the knowledge that Hall had picked up about the secrets of Kawasaki tuning had come from Simmonds, and this would feed into the burgeoning success of the US team. Hall commented later, 'Dave gave me some good input on springs and damping characteristics and other things that he did to improve the handling and performance on the H1R that he had raced in 1970.'[10]

In 1972, seven years after first his first appearance on the 125cc Kawasaki, Simmonds would race the now obsolete bike to a remarkable third place at the Dutch TT at Assen. He might have gone on to even greater things, were it not for the fact that he was tragically killed in a freak accident later in the same year. At a race meeting near Paris, Australian rider Jack Findlay's caravan had caught fire. Mistakenly believing that Findlay was trapped, Simmonds went inside to try to rescue him, only for a gas canister to explode engulfing him in flames, and leaving him fatally injured. From then on, the Kawasaki banner would be carried by larger engine machines, the H1 and its derivatives and successors.

Like all crankcase-scavenged two-strokes, the H1 had an all rolling bearing crankshaft with six main ball bearings and four seals. These were modern times, so there was no messy mixing of oil and fuel; a tiny three-outlet metering pump, located above the crank's primary pinion, varied the oil supply from a small tank to each cylinder according to throttle opening. To better preserve the engine, these pumps were factory-set to produce thick smoke at full throttle. Oil was supplied to three crankcase drillings, each supplying oil to one main bearing of each cylinder. On the crank wheel facing this bearing was screwed an oil pick-up ring with rubber lips. The oil it collected from the main bearing's overflow entered one end of that cylinder's drilled crankpin, emerging through a radial hole in the centre of the con-rod's big-end needle bearing roller track at Top Dead Centre.

Among many H1 owners, inevitably, there came the claim that, 'this centre cylinder right here, it runs too hot.' That was not usually the case on a properly set up engine, which ran fine on all three. In fact, on the H1R road racer, the centre cylinder always ended up jetted leaner than the outer ones. The reason for this was that 120° Triples do not shake vertically, but they do have a strong rocking couple. In fact, the crank moves just like a double-bladed kayak paddle. That means that its centre cylinder pretty much sits still, while the number one and number three cylinders whip around in orbits. That, by slightly frothing the fuel in their carb float bowls, made them run a couple of jet sizes leaner than the centre cylinder. Because the H1 engine and chassis were fairly heavy in relation to piston mass, this vibration was not intolerable. But when privateers lightened the chassis, so its rocking couple moved it around a lot more. Gradually this was addressed by the factory, and the bike began to show some promise just as the 500cc racing class was coming to an end. The H1 quickly acquired the reputation of evil handling but a simple test could usually isolate the cause. By removing the rear suspension units, the springs could be popped off and stroking the dampers up and down would show if there was equal damping. In some cases, a stock damper could lose all of its oil in a few miles. Yet the reputation persisted, as if the H1's chassis was not a mere technical construction, but rather a malevolent entity bent on destroying its user. Because engines in that era were mounted far back, wheelies (intentional or otherwise) were also easy with the power of the H1. Yet there was plenty of steel in the chassis and a pair of Konis or Girlings would make for a rideable suspension package, certainly better than that with one damper working and the other empty of damper oil.

With the arrival of the water-cooled Suzuki and Yamaha two-stroke fours, not to mention the latest development of the four-stroke MV Agusta, Kawasaki's air-cooled triple was simply outclassed. The factory did build a water-cooled 500cc triple that appeared in 1975, the H1RW that works rider Mick Grant would put to good use in the British events, including winning the Isle of Man Senior TT in 1975. Delivering 88bhp at 9,500rpm they were raced in several Grands Prix that year, proving a little underpowered and suffering from poor reliability, meaning their participation in World Championship events was almost at an end. Only three water-cooled versions of the 500cc Kawasaki were built in total, aside from that raced by Mick Grant, the others were campaigned by Barry Ditchburn and Canadian Yvon Duhamel, with Grant's 1975 Isle of Man Senior TT and North West 200 victories being their only real successes.

Kawasaki introduced the more powerful 750cc H2 initially as a roadgoing machine, from September 1971. It was produced as a direct result of the success of the H1, and was greeted with acclaim by the motorcycle press. When *Motor Cycle Mechanics* stated in December 1972 that it sounded like a load of empty tin cans on a string being dragged down the road, the comment was a purely tongue-in-cheek reference to its typical two-stroke rattle. The magazine was more serious when it stated that:

> Mechanical noise or not, [the] power unit coupled with a five-speed gearbox is really remarkable in the way it catapults you from a standing start to 100 miles an hour in around 12 seconds! Fast and hairy … this machine certainly is unless you keep a very strong rein over your right twistgrip hand. It is not a machine for the nervous or those who have just passed their riding test. It needs a really experienced rider to use and enjoy the full power available from the three 250cc pots and even then, on the

> odd occasion, it is possible to arrive at the situation where you wonder who is in control … you or the machine … Unless the power is kept turned on to keep the bike taut you can expect twitching and snaking at both front and rear ends which although not uncontrollable, definitely gives that heart in the mouth feeling to all but the bravest riders.[11]

The magazine was effusive about the engine, which it described as very tractable; the power it said came in smoothly over the rev range, and the motor lacked the sudden surge of smaller Kawasaki triples. Its only real concern was the fuel consumption of the machine, which grew exponentially as the rider increased speed, never the less it ended by stating: 'But as a superbike, the H2 is definitely very super and if you want this kind of performance, then you must pay for it!'[12]

In the early 1970s, Formula 750 was widely regarded as the world's most exciting motorcycle race series, with the jewel in the crown being the AMA's Daytona 200. One of the key rules of this formula was that it was based upon production engines. Thus it was only a matter of time before Kawasaki produced their own 'factory special' version of the machine, but in the meantime they invited the racing fraternity to do some research and development for them. A manual was distributed detailing how to convert the H2 to race specification, by modifying off the shelf roadster components and using additional parts like the dry clutch and race gearbox from the H1R catalogue. Likewise, non-standard exhausts could be made by the enthusiast or mechanic from drawings supplied by the factory, all of which could then be mounted in the 500cc competition chassis. With the growing popularity of 750cc racing in the early 1970s, several privateers followed the instructions. Most however ended up being disappointed with a machine which suffered badly from vibration, which was only marginally faster on acceleration than a 500cc, and certainly no faster on top end speed. Using a stock frame, a machine could be built which might be reasonably competitive in Production racing, but for a purebred factory machine it was back to the drawing board for Kawasaki.

In response, they speeded up development of the H2R which, though it shared the 748cc roadster's overall format, including its 71 x 63mm bore and stroke, was a full race specification engine in a scaled-up version of the H1R chassis. It was still air-cooled, even though the advantages of water cooling were by now well-proven. Weighing in at 143kg and producing over 100bhp at 9,000rpm, only around thirty-five examples of the H2R were ever built between 1971 and 1974. They achieved worldwide success – in the United States in the hands of Yvon Duhamel and Gary Nixon, and in Australia in the hands of Ron Toombs and Gregg Hansford.

Persuading a two-stroke engine to last 400 miles at racing speeds was the driving force in developing a water-cooled version of the machine, which would be known as the KR750. Development of this machine was codenamed Project 602, and the engine of the KR750 owed little to its H2R predecessor. The new motor was more 'square', now having a longer stroke at 68 x 68.63mm, which gave a capacity of 747cc. The ports were twisted clockwise on the cylinder axes, in order to stagger and overlap adjacent transfer passages, so that the inclined cylinders, now unhindered by the finning required in the air-cooled version, could be packed together more closely. This enabled Kawasaki engineers to reduce the crankshaft length by 19mm when compared to the H2R. Thus, they were able to minimise the overall width of the engine for better aerodynamics. The crank now sported full-circle flywheels to replace the bob-weights of the H2R, and had the generator for its Kokusan CDI on the left and a pair of skew gears on the right. A six-speed gearbox replaced the five-speeder of the H2R, but it retained the dry twenty-four-plate clutch. The inner gear drove the water pump, the outer one both the tachometer and a separate oil pump. This supplied force-fed lubrication to each crankpin from the oil tank under the seat, thereby extending crank life by up to 1,000 miles. The single-ring pistons were mounted on slender rods with needle rollers at both ends, and the combustion chambers had wide 12mm squish bands matching the contours of the domed pistons, thereby increasing compression. In its original form the engine developed 120bhp, though by the end of its career this had been improved to nearer 128bhp.

The motor was fixed by rubber engine mounts in order to prevent the crankcases from cracking, in a new, stiff tubular steel chassis with six tubes bracing the steering head assembly. The original swingarm was of box section construction and fitted with two Girling shock absorbers. Some riders subsequently modified this, or exchanged it for one of a variety of monoshock versions. Seven spoke magnesium Morris wheels were fitted as standard. Overall the machine was narrower, and arguably more nimble, than its main rival the square-four Suzuki RG700 and significantly more so than an inline Yamaha TZ750. If it lacked power when compared with these machines, then it made up for this by being lighter and was arguably the best overall package, with water-cooling adding the reliability that was missing in the H2R. Thus having started initially some way behind their rivals Honda, Yamaha and Suzuki, Kawasaki had refused to be intimidated by their competitors' domination of the racing scene, and in spite of the apparent stranglehold that these three had on the production and marketing of motorcycles worldwide, they still saw a future there for themselves. Having concentrated initially on the smaller capacity motors, Kawasaki engineers had now come up with a big-engined machine that was probably two years ahead of anything that their competitors had in this class. In the right hands it would prove to be an awesome weapon, and would go on to take race victory after race victory in North America, Australia, and Europe. For their campaign on the British racing scene, and particularly at the Isle of Man TT, it was essential that the company found a rider who brought to the table the right mix of skill, experience and commitment, if they were to race, and more importantly to win, at the toughest racing circuit in the world.

Chapter Three

BREAKTHROUGH 1974–1975

With a revolutionary machine that was now streets ahead of their rivals, the only missing piece of the puzzle for Kawasaki at this point was a rider who could really do justice to it. For their British campaign the company found such a man in a competitor who had learned his trade through long and diligent graft, and who now was beginning to prove himself as one of the breakthrough riders for the 1970s at the TT. That man was Mick Grant, son of a miner from Yorkshire who had first tackled the Isle of Man's Mountain Course at the 1969 Manx Grand Prix, and had latterly been an occasional member of the John Player Norton team. He soon started to make a name for himself, with his trademark helmet emblazoned with the large letters 'JL' in tribute to an early and formative sponsor, Jim Lee. Grant's other trade mark, the distinctive racing number 10, was not yet exclusively his, but soon would be. Grant was reluctant to call himself a roads specialist, and he had more than his share of success on short circuits, but there is no doubt that he had a special affinity with the Isle of Man TT. In partnership with Kawasaki, he would go on to create some of the most exciting moments in the long history of that event.

Mick Grant's first contact with Kawasaki machinery came at the 1972 TT, when he was persuaded to ride an air-cooled triple in the Senior race, by his then sponsors, Padgetts of Batley. The firm had a tie up with John Durrance from the then UK importer, Agrati Sales. Grant remembered it as a huge wide thing, the 500cc engine making it scarcely any quicker than a 350cc Yamaha at the time. Never the less he managed to finish third, in a race that was dominated by Giacomo Agostini. The weather for that event was initially awful, and it was postponed by two and a half hours as spectators shivered whilst watching rain drops splash into puddles. However, the local forecast proved correct, and by the time the race started at 4.00pm the improvement was dramatic. Within three laps the track was drying, and the main problem became one of flies. Grant's thirsty machine forced him to make two pit stops as against one for his opponents, but he was none the less glad of the opportunity to clean dead insects from his visor each time. He remembered that at this time the Kawasaki name was not generally well regarded in the racing paddock:

> At the time when I was riding for Padgetts, for the Senior race I had got the option of either the Kawasaki, which I didn't favour because it wasn't a particularly nice looking thing, or an over bored 350 Yamaha – that would have been a 354 – and in fact I wanted to ride the Yamaha, but Peter Padgett and John Durrance more or less pushed me into riding the Kawasaki which was not really what I wanted, but as it happened it worked out well. At the time Yamaha was the be all and end all. When I rode for Padgetts before that, you just opened up a crate took the 250 or 350 Yamaha out, you took the Yokohama tyres off it, put Dunlops on it, changed the jets in the carburettor, and you'd got a bike you could win the British championship with, or even go Grand Prix racing with. So for Kawasaki to come in with a hotch potch thing … [later] I was back at the factory in Japan, Kawasaki, and when you looked at it they'd just got a

> big wooden shed, and although Kawasaki as a company is massive, motorcycles were only a very small part of it. At that time they did all of the competition bikes out of this wooden building, they did trials, motorcross, and road racing. Considering the small number of people compared to say Honda, what they actually achieved over the years was unbelievable.[1]

The following year Grant track tested a Kawasaki for *Motor Cycle News*, this being the race bike then used by Percy Tait, which was based on the 750cc H2 Kawasaki roadster. He recalled that the bike didn't handle well but the engine was impressive, with lots of power available. At the same time, he was riding on and off for Stan Shenton, who ran Boyers of Bromley, one of the UK's biggest Kawasaki dealerships in that era. Shenton's family had held a Triumph franchise since 1927, but it was a sign of the times that after twenty years in the motorcycle trade, he had switched to the Japanese firm as Triumph tottered towards receivership. Up to this point, Kawasaki had never given any serious consideration to supporting racing in Britain, but all that changed in 1974 with the establishment of the wholly owned subsidiary Kawasaki Motors (UK) Ltd. This was initially under the direction of Japanese engineer Michio (Mick) Uchida as managing director and Kit Kitayama as director. Later, they were joined by British businessman John Norman. The company operated in its early stages from the Holiday Inn, Marble Arch, before transferring to its first permanent HQ at Staines, Middlesex.

Uchida for his part was also a graduate of Japanese business school, and had joined the Meguro Manufacturing Company in 1959, which was when he became involved with motorcycles for the first time. When Meguro and Kawasaki merged in 1961 he became manager of the latter's domestic sales subsidiary. He had experience of – and interest in – racing from his early days in Japan when he helped to organise events at the Suzuka track. Newly appointed British director and general manager Norman had spent five years with Raleigh Cycles and then for eleven years from 1962 had assisted in setting up Honda as the first major Japanese motorcycle and car importer in the UK, gaining deep knowledge of the motorcycle industry. For almost a year he had been UK sales manager for BMW but left that role to join Kawasaki. In the US market, Kawasaki had already seen how a successful racing team could boost sales, helping them to capture 14 per cent of the market in the United States in just two years.

Any ideas that Kawasaki UK were about to dive straight into British and European racing were sadly misplaced however, as at this time Britain was in the grip of a serious economic crisis. This was the era of the three-day week and the directors often had to work by candle light as power cuts became the norm. Initially their racing ambitions were modest, and they looked to dealer-backed riders to give them success. Norman admitted that it was a bold step – with black outs and economic restrictions they already had a lot on their plate, but they had support from the industrial giant of a parent company in Japan, who recognised that results would not necessarily come over night, and who saw their investment in Britain as a long term venture. The British directors Michio Uchida and John Norman now approached Stan Shenton regarding the formation of a semi-official racing team. Shenton supplied the required specialist knowledge and experience, as well as the contacts in the racing world. (In later years, even after Stan had stepped back from race management, and the Kawasaki competitive effort moved away from the Boyer team, the Shenton influence would remain, with Stan's son Stuart doing duty as one of the factory squad mechanics.) Norman was quoted in the press as saying:

> Our aim was to provide direct support through an established race sponsor and Stan Shenton offered the perfect blend of experience and ability for the purpose. An association such as this will allow us to plan our 1975 programme in greater detail and we are all looking forward to a successful season.[2]

Around the same time that Shenton was forming his new team, Grant had been offered a Yamaha works ride at the TT through Danny Keaney, who was the Dublin-based Irish importer for that marque. He turned it down however, as he had a feeling that the Kawasaki squad was going places and had greater long-term potential, and over time it proved to be the right decision. For the 1974 TT, Stan set Mick up with one of the same H2 based 750cc triples that he had previously track tested. In fact, it was a 1973 specification H2R which had come from the factory race shop in Japan. Indicative of its transitional nature was the fact that although the rear wheel was wire-spoked, the front wheel was made of magnesium alloy. In practice Grant managed a lap at 105mph. With his wrist still in plaster from an earlier get-off at Brands Hatch, in the Formula 750 race on the Island the Kawasaki proved to be a handful for Mick, far more so than the British bikes that he was also riding around this time; the situation was not helped by the fact that the race was run in the rain, and no one at this time was producing a suitable wet weather tyre for a machine of this sort; Grant was clocked through the speed trap at 161mph, but he encountered massive wheelspin, forcing him to back off, and he struggled home in seventeenth place to collect the only bronze replica of his career. Indeed, he went so slowly that he actually oiled a plug, as his revs were too low, and had to come into the pits to get it changed. Never the less, an indication of the direction in which the wind was now blowing came in the Production TT that year. Although Mick famously carried off the laurels in that event aboard the Triumph 'Slippery Sam,' the 500cc category within the race was won by Keith Martin aboard a Kawasaki H1E Mach III triple (entered by importers Agrati of Nottingham, and sponsored by *Motor Cycle Mechanics* magazine). At the same time, the 26-year-old sales manager from Biggin Hill in Kent set the fastest lap and a new lap record for this category.

The *Motor Cycle Mechanics* team had first entered a Kawasaki 500cc H1B for the Production race two years previously with Terry Grotefeld, but after insufficient preparation, that machine went out on the first lap with an engine seizure. After a good deal of trial and error, they eventually got it running very well, so much so in fact that it proved to be extremely reliable. After a long race, all the mechanics had to do was strip the top end, check the piston rings for wear, reset the ignition timing, change the chain and rear tyre and it was ready for its next meeting. Keith Martin had joined them to race the H1B during the 1973 season. He took to it like a duck to water and although he criticised the handling slightly because of rear end twitching, he showed tremendous promise by finishing third in that year's Production TT. After putting the H1B out to grass, the team were lucky enough to get their hands on the first of the new 500 H1E models to come into the United Kingdom.

The new version had a different exhaust system, a longer rear swinging arm and the engine was rubber mounted to reduce the amount of high-frequency vibration which had previously caused a number of exhaust pipe failures. The team made modifications to the rear wheel size, changed the suspension units, and fitted clip-on handle bars, a racing tank, seat and fairing. The most extraordinary thing, that many people later refused to believe, was that the engine was absolutely dead standard. *Motor Cycle Mechanics* editor Charles Deane observed:

> Power output has never been a problem, mainly because in standard trim the three-cylinder motor is claimed to develop around 60 brake horsepower. Without any tuning whatsoever, it is possible to gear the machine up to give a maximum speed in the region of 130 miles-an-hour, which for a bog-standard roadster is no mean performance … What modifications have we made? Well, first and foremost was the rebuilding of the wheels to replace the 18-inch rear with a 19-inch WM3 alloy rim. Then of course we swapped suspension units to fit good old British Girling dampers. Dunlop TT100s, 3.60 on the front and 4.10 on the rear, are a must for extra grip and long wear life … up until now we always used NGK plugs and Renolds racing chain, but with offers of bonus cash for a TT win, we used Champion plugs and Regina racing chain on the Island.[3]

They ran it for about 35 miles on a test track, before stripping it just to check that there were no high spots or scoring on pistons, and after easing the 'tongues' which protrude down into the inlet ports, where they had been scoring the rear of the pistons, they rebuilt the engine and timed the ignition. With the team now having converted the H1E to full Production racing spec, and having incorporated all that they had learned about the foibles of the Kawasaki triple over the past two seasons, Keith was ready to go – the machine and his leathers in the company's trademark matching green and white livery.

With only 35 miles under its belt the engine was still fairly tight, but the four laps of practice showed that it had great potential. Martin felt that its handling was now much improved, and he was holding the bike flat out through corners like Hillberry where before on the earlier model he had to roll off the power, because of the rear end weaving. Clearly the longer swinging arm had improved matters here. On the day of the race Keith's second kick start meant that he was about eight or ninth away from the line, but as he later said: 'The acceleration of the Kawasaki is phenomenal and by Quarter Bridge a mile or so from the start I had caught the leader, Danny Shimmin, and passed him on the straight towards Braddan Bridge.'[4]

By the time Martin reached Ballacraine just over 7 miles out he had an advantage of over twelve seconds and by the Mountain, where *Motor Cycle Mechanics* had two signal points (one at the Gooseneck, the other at the Bungalow) he had thirty seconds in hand. Safe in the knowledge that he had a comfortable lead, Martin rolled off the power early going into the corners but piled it on down the straights. The result was that from a standing start he broke Stan Woods' existing lap record and held a lead of thirty five seconds over the second placed man, Alan Rogers aboard a Triumph. Martin slowed the pace a little for the second lap and when he came in to the depots to refuel he had only a twenty eight second advantage. This meant that Rogers flew past the pits just as Martin was preparing to leave. The fact that he was ten seconds down on the leader at Ballacraine compelled him to push harder once again, and by the end of the Sulby Straight the sheer power of the Kawasaki had put Martin back in control once more. At the end of the third lap, he crossed the line six seconds ahead of Rogers who was trying everything he knew in order to stay with the green machine. Taking no chances, Martin really wound the Kawasaki up and left the Triumph behind; his flying lap set a new record and he finished thirty seconds ahead of second placed man Rogers. He said after the race that his machine had behaved perfectly except for slight brake fade in the closing stages, when he took things easy; were it not for this his speed might have been even faster.

It was an emphatic performance, underlined by the fact that the Kawasaki also set a new race record for this four-lap event. This groundbreaking victory, and Martin's domination of this fiercely competitive class, were both telling portents for the future. The machine was clocked at a maximum speed of 127mph through the *Motor Cycle* speed trap at the Highlander, and there might have been even greater reason to celebrate the following day were it not for an unfortunate mishap; Martin and the *Motor Cycle Mechanics* machine were entered for the Senior TT, but toward the end of the Sulby Straight the track was covered with oil and petrol from a bike which had crashed. He saw the warning flags, sat up from under the fairing, and touched his brakes. It was enough to send him flying down the road at about 120mph. Rider and machine parted company and both slid for about 200 yards before coming to rest, fortunately it was a straight part of the course so Keith avoided coming into contact with a brick wall, and was able to walk away with just cuts and bruises.

The Mach III had by now undergone significant changes and improvements since it was first introduced by Kawasaki. Braking, handling and useable power had all been improved. The better handling was as a result of the introduction of newly designed hydraulically damped telescopic front forks, and also by slightly altering the position of thc motor in the frame. An adjustable hydraulic steering damper had also been fitted in addition to the standard friction damper in the steering head. This had the effect of eliminating the peculiar weaving action which had been a feature of the earlier versions. The suspension was also considerably harder than on the early Mach III, and this also helped in cutting out the wallowing tendency of the bike when travelling through high-speed corners. This gave the model a 'tight' racing machine feel, but at the cost of making the rider aware of every bump and dip in the road. The twin-leading shoe brakes of the early variants had also been replaced by an 11.5 inch hydraulic single disc unit, which now gave excellent braking. Although both Martin's machine and his leathers were in the bright lime green colour that would soon become a very familiar sight at the TT, Martin himself was usually a Suzuki rider and it would not be him that would make the colour famous; in fact he would go on to ride for Benelli. As an aside, it is worth noting that there was perhaps no more ardent Kawasaki campaigner in the 500cc Production TT races of this era than was Bill Milne, a motor mechanic of Cardenden, Fife. He entered a Mach III each year between 1971 and 1974, with a best finish of sixth place.

The 1974 Production race featured another uncommon machine which was a portent of things to come. In the 1,000cc category *Motor Cycle* newspaper entered a standard Kawasaki Z1 900-4, ridden by Derek Loan. Even though it was virtually straight from the crate – the whole point of this class – Loan took the machine out in the first night of Practice and achieved a lap of 82.24mph, as well as being clocked through the Highlander speed trap at 132mph, on just the original Japanese tyres. His biggest problem was the front brake, still a single disc as the second unit for the other fork leg had not arrived in time. Dunlop racing tyres, as recommended by the factory, were soon fitted; they were 3.50–4.50 x 19 inch front and 3.50–4.50 x 18 inch rear KR83 types. The brakes had failed when the fluid started to boil and froth, but this was cured when racing specification brake juice was used after the first session. Problems with the handling persisted none the less, and despite trying different fork oils the weaving remained a concern throughout Practice. Loan told reporters: 'The bike still wobbles and weaves under power, so an attempt was made to locate a steering damper.'[5]

None could be found however, until the team bumped into some staff from Shenco, the Kawasaki dealers in Ramsey. They had one spare they said, but would have to go back to the shop to get it. Some hours later it transpired that it had been sold, but undeterred they collared a passing 500cc Kawasaki triple rider, and borrowed his! On the day of the race itself, Loan would obtain only a bronze replica for seventeenth place, but that hardly reflected the sheer guts and determination he had shown in trying to control the unruly beast for four gruelling laps. He told journalists afterwards:

> I got a good start and I was about fifth going down Bray Hill. The first lap wasn't so bad because I had some brakes at least. I'd grown used to the handling in practice. Wherever I had to knock it off, then open up again, a weaving motion set in. But as long as I kept on the power it was fairly predictable in most places. I must have had the oddest line of all through Greeba, though. It was quite enjoyable through Laurel Bank and Glen Helen. There was this bird sunbathing in her bra out at the Gooseneck. I nearly went into the wall. She'd

> disappeared by the time I came round again. It was weaving about a bit but it was quite controllable. The front brake became more or less redundant at the start of the second lap. Anyone at Quarter Bridge would have seen that! The rear brake, thank goodness, always seemed to be there when I desperately needed it. When the bike was upright the engine braking was really useful – in fact, by the end of the race, it was essential. The motor never missed a beat. Not once. Not even a cough. When I stopped it was still ticking over. But the back tyre was shot when we finished. I was taking Bray more or less flat in fourth. It was going down the hill all right and it was all right at the bottom. But coming out of the dip it was getting into a sideways weave and I could have been in real trouble. I overshot at the pits at the end of lap two. I just didn't realise how much the front brake had faded, with roadster pads and only a single disc. Once I got the pit stop out of the way I felt quite relaxed. There weren't too many people out on the track, and I like being on my own. The crowd loved every minute of the bike's antics. Going past the grandstand at the start of the fourth lap, the bike went all over the place. I had to stand on the footrests and give it a good talking to. I was up on the rests at Sulby and Rhen Cullen as well, and I was having to knock it off all the time at St Ninians because it was going out of control on the bumps.[6]

If the machine's handling was poor, then the performance of the engine was outstanding. It was clocked at 132mph again past the Highlander at 8,800rpm in top gear, and it accelerated faster than a Yamaha TZ350 coming out of the Gooseneck – in fact Loan would have overtaken it if there had been more room to do so on the road. Fans were waving and clapping on the Mountain on the last lap but as he was climbing flat out in fifth, the top of the brake fluid reservoir came off and the contents went all over his visor. Everything was just a blur after that and he had no front brake at all. He looked at the rev counter in disbelief, because he thought that this instrument had disintegrated.

By now the effort of wrestling the mighty machine was beginning to take its toll and he was beginning to feel tired. Hillberry and Signpost were challenging to say the least and he had to go down through the gears in order to slow down enough. Apart from a bit of a wobble, he managed just to negotiate the turn at Creg-ny-Baa. The bike's chain had also taken a battering and there were 3 inches of slack in it at the end of the race. Overall, the fact that a machine straight out of the crate, and with a newcomer in the saddle, could turn in a performance like this was a testament to the engineering skill with which it was originally designed and built. This race dealt the Boyer team an unexpected and heavy blow however, in that rider Dave Nixon from Ashford in Kent was tragically killed on the second lap, riding a Triumph. Stan Shenton knew Nixon of old, as he was his workshop foreman and had previously raced Triumphs for him. Shenton had recently been in negotiation with him to become a Kawasaki rider, and had the tragedy not occurred it was fully expected that he would turn out for the Boyer squad at the next year's TT.

Indeed, rumours were now circulating in the paddocks of a major factory push from Kawasaki that was coming the following year. Mick Grant decided to stick with the Boyer H2 for the remainder of the season, and despite some engine blow ups he managed to impress the company hierarchy with some new lap records and a win at Snetterton in Norfolk.

Right: Shozo Kawasaki, who founded the company which bears his name, in 1878. (Public Domain)

Below: A destroyer built for the Imperial Japanese Navy being launched from a Tokyo shipyard in 1926. (Library of Congress)

Grant lands the Boyer Kawasaki at Ballaugh Bridge, 1974 TT. (Courtesy of Mick Grant)

Mick Grant and Barry Ditchburn at the press launch for Kawasaki's 1975 campaign. (Courtesy of Mick Grant)

Barry Ditchburn in Kawasaki leathers, 1975. (Public Domain)

Mick and Carol Grant at home with the Classic TT Trophy, October 1977.
(Courtesy of Mick Grant)

Mick and Carol Grant in the paddock after victory in the 1978 Classic TT. (Courtesy of Mick Grant)

Above: Grant with the Classic TT trophy at a Kawasaki press event, 1978. Kawasaki UK director Michio Uchida (right) and Mr Akimoto, a director from headquarters in Japan. (Courtesy of Mick Grant)

Left: Grant with the Jimmy Simpson Trophy for fastest lap of the meeting, with ACU representative Mr L.Jackson, 1978. (Courtesy of Mick Grant)

TT success translated into showroom sales, as this 1978 newspaper advert testifies. (Author's Collection)

The rider's view of the clocks on the 1978 KR750. The machine redlined at 9,000 rpm. (Author's Collection)

STOURBRIDGE
News

Just Champion!

Stourbridge company secretary Warwick Newman became part of the Isle of Man TT folklore by winning the 1,000 cc sidecar championship. Together with his "Chairman" Eddie Yarker, Newman lapped the famous 37½ mile circuit at 104 mph to win the RAC Trophy.

Above: Geoff Johnson in the 1984 Production TT, the first win anywhere in the world for the Kawasaki Ninja. (Fottofinders Bikesport Archives)

Left: 1986 Sidecar TT Champion Warwick Newman with the RAC Trophy, awarded for most points over the two legs. (Courtesy of Stourbridge News)

In November of that year he was signed up as a factory rider for the forthcoming 1975 season, alongside Barry Ditchburn. Grant remembered:

> My trouble up to then – and I guess others have suffered in the same way – was that I had worn so many colours and had ridden such a variety of machines. Although I was reasonably popular, I wasn't as recognisable as I was later when I was associated with Kawasaki. I was desperately keen to be associated with one particular marque instead of being a Jack-of-all-bikes.[7]

He and the Kawasaki team would go on to form a mutually beneficial partnership:

> Well, from 1975 I had a formal racing contract which lasted four years which gave tremendous security. Of course it was always my ambition to make a living out of racing, but there were so many people vying for rides a contract with a factory team was like gold dust, just like it is now in fact. I have to say it was the best time in my racing career, the bikes, the competition with other riders and playing a part in establishing Kawasaki as a name in the UK bike market were all equally stimulating and important.
>
> It has to be said that there were some people at Kawasaki in the very early days that did not fully understand the need to go racing, but that soon changed when we not only won MCN bike of the year several times in a row, but also sold lots of race bikes as well. Remember, this was a time when manufacturers would produce runs of bespoke racing bikes to sell as there was less emphasis on production based racing back then.

> I was in Yorkshire and the bikes were prepared and stored in Bromley, Kent at Boyers run by Team Manager, Stan Shenton. There were few gentlemen riders like Hailwood, but mostly it were lads who had some knowledge of fixing up bikes themselves and so working on the bikes or making suggestions for changes and upgrades was sort of second nature. As Kawasaki Motors UK became established after taking over from Agrati, I tried to do as much as I could racing and promotional wise, I had a great relationship with the UK Kawasaki MD, Mr Uchida. In fact he still stands out as one of the most memorable and impressive figures during my Kawasaki career.[8]

In October 1974, the FIM revised its homologation requirements for the Formula 750 world series, dropping the total number of machines that it required to be produced from 200 to 25. This allowed Kawasaki to finally come up with a pure racing version of their biggest triple-cylinder machine. Racing manager Misao Yurikusa and development chief Kazuhito Yoshida had plans for a motorcycle of this nature back in 1973, but these were thwarted at the time by economics and homologation requirements. After the green light was given in October, development proceeded quickly in order to get it ready for the forthcoming season. However there was a mix-up at Kawasaki headquarters in Japan, which initially misinterpreted the FIM rules to mean that only twenty-five engines were required rather than twenty-five complete motorcycles. As a result, the engines (in particular the gearboxes) were at first under developed. The new model was designated KR750 (code named Project 602) and the only similarity between the old 750cc H2R and the new KR750 was that they were both 750cc triple-cylinder two-stroke machines with the primary drive on the right-hand side. Among the myriad differences, the most obvious ones were that the KR750 had a six-speed gearbox, instead of the older bike's five, and the dry clutch had two more clutch discs. A water pump was built into the magnesium right-hand clutch cover as part of the change to water cooling.

At the heart of the KR750 was a piston-port two-stroke three-cylinder engine which owed little to its predecessors. The liquid-cooled aluminium cylinders were arranged so as to provide larger transfer ports, and close cylinder spacing. The over square H2R engine dimensions became square, at 68 x 68mm, and although the longer stroke increased piston speed, it simultaneously enlarged the port area. Despite liquid cooling, there still remained a problem with overheating and it was important to try to keep the engine temperature below 70°C for best power. The most obvious difference between the KR750 and its predecessor was in terms of width. It was noticeably less wide due to a reduction in the length of the crankshaft by 19mm. The factory claimed that the crankshaft would last for 1,300km but in fact initially this was the Achilles' heel of the machine and team Boyer would sometimes find that cranks would fail after as little as 100km. The chassis was lighter and better-handling than that of the H2R. It featured an updated rubber engine mounting system, and a lightweight box-section swingarm. It was found that the machine was often able to match the acceleration of the rival Yamaha TZ750, because of its lighter weight. Unfortunately, there had not been time for enough of the track testing of this and the smaller KR250 twin, the two new models under development, and more time was needed to fully progress their reliability and performance. This meant that the racing season would have to also serve as a development year, in full view of the public and the press.

It was a gutsy decision by Kawasaki to go ahead on this basis but it also showed how committed the factory was to seeing these new KR models on the track – and, furthermore, to making them into winners.

After their victory in the Thruxton 400-mile race at the end of 1974, Kawasaki Heavy Industries, and particularly Misao Yurikusa (senior manager of the motorcycle division in Japan), were so pleased with them that team Boyer Kawasaki received full factory support for 1975. This included four KR750s, five KR250s, and two H1RWs. Ken Suzuki, formerly of Tohatsu and Bridgestone, joined the team to liaise directly with the factory. The British KR750s came from Japan with rough cast unported cylinders, these being finished off by team Boyer mechanic Nigel Everett. The machines also originally came with experimental aluminium brakes, but it was found that the heat generated by racing conditions was enough to melt them, and so they were changed instead to a set of stainless-steel discs. A pair of Girling shock absorbers were also fitted. Everett was Grant's personal mechanic, and had joined him earlier that season when he was barely out of school, but already had valuable experience gained at Mick Wheeler's workshop in his native Whitney, near Oxford. Everett worked with Grant throughout the 1970s and was to be an integral part of the Kawasaki effort in the coming years. The Yorkshireman remembered of him:

> What mattered … was that he was never less than 100% behind me. His strength wasn't tuning. It was being unbelievably quick and thorough with the spanners. Once I was lined up on the … grid when it started raining heavily. In the time the other teams had just about managed to change wheels, Nigel had whipped in a set

> of different yokes as well. It barely seemed possible, but I not only had the best set up of any rider in the race, but was absolutely confident the job had been done right.[9]

In February 1975, at simultaneous press conferences in Tokyo, Los Angeles and London, Kawasaki senior managers announced their plans for the coming season. Their targets were the 250 and 500cc World Championships, the Formula 750 series (not yet a World Championship class), and the British Superbike Championship. After years of using machines derived from roadsters, the bikes for all three classes would at last be purpose built. Kawasaki were putting their money where their mouth was and they clearly meant business. Particularly impressive was the KR250 twin, but the H1RW and KR750 triples also had a great deal of promise. In the early part of the season the brittle gearbox proved itself to be the racing Kawasaki's fatal weakness, but this was soon corrected and the factory had a completely redesigned and re-engineered gearbox available to the UK team in time for the start of the British racing calendar that year. Grant recalled:

> The 750 was a brilliant piece of engineering. In 1975 it was a year ahead of its time; by 1978 it was two years behind. Any 750 two-stroke [by then] needed four cylinders to obtain the necessary horsepower … I compared it with the John Player Nortons which had bad gearboxes from the first day they were raced to the last, if the reports I read were right. It didn't impress me that Kawasaki gear boxes were spitting bits out, but I was impressed that the factory was doing something about it and that – in spite of its massive size – it was adaptable enough to sort out this problem. They were a new team aiming to set a

> new image and I was going to grow with them. It wasn't merely a case of having to follow in the shoes of another rider.[10]

Grant was aware of the success that Canadian rider Yvon Duhamel had already enjoyed with the air-cooled version of the Kawasaki in the United States the previous year, so he was confident that the KR750 would be a winner. It was the lightest big racing machine in the world, and had the edge on the once all-conquering Suzuki triple. The bike's main weakness was its unreliability through crankshaft failure over long distances, though this was gradually sorted out. For Barry Ditchburn, who was teamed with Grant for 1975, it was his first works ride after eight years of privateer racing. Born in Northfleet, Kent in 1949, Ditchburn started out with a 500cc Triumph engine in a Norton frame, later upgrading it to a 650cc power unit. When the Yamahas became prevalent in the early 1970s he switched to these, riding for a time for renowned sponsor Ted Broad. In order to make ends meet he had been working part time in his father's steel fabrication factory, and remembered that at the end of the 1974 season:

> Stan Shenton, manager of the Boyer Kawasaki team asked me to partner Mick Grant on his 750 in the Thruxton 400 miler, but Ted said I would be riding his Yamaha so I turned the offer down. Two weeks later Ted said he wouldn't go to Thruxton after all, but when I rang Stan to see if the ride was still open he told me Kork Ballington had taken it. It looked as if I was out of a ride altogether, but a week later Stan rang back to say that Mick was going to America instead of Thruxton, and would I like to partner Kork. I did, and we won it from the second lap on, which was the best day's work I ever did, because all

> Kawasaki's chiefs were there, and it led to the works ride the following year.[11]

He was a rider with no shortage of natural talent, inherited in part at least from his father Harry who was a big name in grass track racing at Brands Hatch in the 1940s, also appearing at the 1947 Manx Grand Prix as well as numerous trials and scrambling events. A magazine article from the mid-1970s observed that little was known about the inner man beneath the quietly determined outer crust. Ditchburn largely kept his thoughts to himself and had never courted publicity. Some people misinterpreted his introverted nature for sullenness, and claimed that he appeared cheerless and even miserable in public. However, the truth was that his glassy stare and silent indifference to the crowds around the team Kawasaki camp were the result of a trance that he slipped into before racing. While his mind traced the lines around every bend of the circuit, he relived every bump and slide of practice in a detailed mental re-examination of his performance. At times like this, Ditchburn was in a world of his own. He admitted: 'I'm on Cloud 9, deep in thought about the bike, the start, and which bend I have to try harder on – until someone speaks to me and I have to come back to earth.'[12]

On the start line, when the flag dropped and the revs screamed as thousands of brake horsepower let rip all around him, Ditchburn's feet – as well as his wheels – were firmly on the ground. He explained that he didn't take unnecessary risks and rarely crashed: 'I'll admit I'm a coward. If the bike is not going right, or something doesn't feel spot on I won't stick my neck out, and I'll be happy to settle for second or third spot rather than chance crashing and finishing nowhere at all.'[13]

Whatever talent he had inherited from his father had been honed and improved in long hours at racing circuits, and whilst he was now in the top tier of British road racers he maintained that it was the love of racing that kept him going, and that he would do it for no reward if he had to:

> I don't race for the money – though it plays a vital part now, and I don't do it for the glory or publicity that winning can bring. The personal satisfaction I get out of riding as hard and as fast as I can is all I need to make the effort and risks worthwhile. Obviously everyone races to prove that they are faster than anybody else on that particular day and it is a fantastic feeling to win, whether it is a vital championship round or a programme filler event.[14]

He explained that being a works rider did not mean that you could sit back and put your feet up – whilst it was true that the physical side of racing was made much easier with bikes, mechanics and transport provided, the psychological pressures were much greater. There were some days that he did not even feel like sitting on a motorcycle, but as a factory rider he had to race just the same.

There was a good deal of speculation in the motorcycling press and among the race-going public about who was the Kawasaki team's number one rider, and how deep the rivalry between the two men ran. Grant for his part believed that it was not necessary for two team mates to be friends in order for them to work successfully together; indeed, successful sportsmen thrive on competition, and having an equally ambitious team-mate on identical machinery will tend to produce a highly competitive racer. He recalls:

> 'Ditch' and I formed a friendship during the Kawasaki team days and I often heard first hand about the rivalry

> that develops between two riders in the same team. To bc fair, the moans were mostly from 'Ditch' but his comments were never malicious ... Ditchburn in the Kawasaki days ... they were super. People always thought we were at each other's throats and we weren't. There was a situation occasionally and there were people in the team who stirred things up but when we went on trips to the continent we'd laugh from start to finish. Ditch was always good company.[15]

In the run up to the 1975 TT, Grant fired a warning shot across the bows of the opposition with an outstanding performance at the North West 200 in early May. He scored a double victory in the 500 and 750cc classes at the Portrush circuit, clearly underlining what the Kawasakis were now capable of. In the former class in particular he brought the new water-cooled triple home nearly half a minute ahead of his closest rival, Tony Rutter. This however belied the fact that the team were still having problems with the 500cc machine, Boyer chief mechanic Rod Scivyer (himself an ex-British Champion) remembering:

> The Achillies heel was the crank and the disturbing habit of pistons seizing for no apparent reason. I know a lot of two strokes had that habit but this one was a joke. At one time we inherited a large box of pistons from the USA team and we had to go through the lot trying to find a fit which didn't seize. In the end we resorted to measuring a set which had been run in our motor and had not seized and I spent endless hours at the lathe changing the shape of new ones in the hope that it would cure the problem. Needless to say it met with only limited success. The cranks broke with alarming regularity. In Sweden in

> '75 we spent, Nigel Everett and myself, almost the entire practice time rebuilding the motors and eventually were down to one spare crank which we had to fit to Mick's engine the night before the race. This one of course had to be different, it was about 25mm too long on one end. The only thing for it was to saw the end off. We worked well into the night, with regular forays into the paddock to scrounge new saw blades. I have to say, at this point, that Mick was absolutely brilliant, making regular trips to and from the team hotel with food, drink and encouragement. This was obviously a task well below the status of the team management who of course were never seen during the whole time (bitter, no not me). The race followed its normal course with first Ditchburn and then Mick retiring.[16]

At the 1975 TT, in Practice the team got off to a good start. Scivyer had assistance not just from Everett but also Ken Suzuki who carried out liaison with the factory in Japan over engine development, and Hideyoshi Kosuge who was over on a three-week working holiday from Japan. On the 750cc, which was massively over geared, Grant managed 105mph on the first time out. By Wednesday he had achieved 106.95mph, the fastest ever TT lap up to that point. Incredibly this was done on a Dunlop slick rear tyre that had already done the North West 200 and the King of Brands races on Whit Monday. Things weren't as smooth as they seemed, however. Grant told reporters:

> When we brought the 750 here it was a camel, it handled so badly, it was set up for the North-West 200 which is very smooth compared to the Isle of Man. But with longer rear suspension units and softer springs, it's

> OK now. But this is the fantastic thing about the TT – you have to fit the bike to the circuit and not the other way round as happens everywhere else now, and you get the satisfaction of trying really hard to ride properly here. You never know if you've done it at the absolute.[17]

On paper he also should have been the hot favourite on the 500cc machine, but he had little time to practice on it. Scivyer remembered:

> The I.O.M that year was a joke, apart from Mick winning the 500. It all started when team management decided that they would not take the transporters to the island. Instead we were to use a borrowed Transit which had been arranged, more of that later!!! Before we went Ken Suzuki and myself decided to try and modify an engine and exhaust system which would provide a bit more top end for the island. We duly completed it, but with no time left in which to test. Team management decided that it was a waste of time and space to take it but relented when we argued that at the very least it was a complete set of spares and off we went.
>
> Practice went as expected with the 500 destroying itself at all too regular intervals, until it was obvious we would run out of power plants. Two more engines were brought over from Kawasaki and these were interesting beasts. Mick's first experience of these engines was to discover that the gearbox of the first one had a reversed selector, instead of up for up it was up for down. We replaced it whilst it was sorted and this was where things got really dangerous. The gearbox of the second engine had been assembled in such a way that the gears went thus 1st, 2nd, 3rd, 4th, 6th, 5th. As you can well

> imagine Mick's first trip down Bray Hill was somewhat interesting. Well after all that, they both failed and we were left with the unknown quantity, the motor we hadn't run. Mick was all for giving it a go, but there was no more practice. We fitted it and took it to Jurby and Nigel and I ran it up and down for what seemed like forever, until Mick turned up. He gave it a run and pronounced himself well pleased as it actually had a power band. Having ridden with the standard engine I knew what he meant, it was like riding a fast road bike.[18]

As if the team had not had enough problems already with engines, there was a further element to complicate matters; the good old ACU, still in the dark ages, had a ruling that on the start line of a race, the engine of a motorcycle had to be switched off. Getting away quickly from the flag was always the key to success in a TT race, but the H1RW could be tricky to start at the best of times. The clutch action was rather stiff, so it was quite hard to catch the engine as it fired and a knack was needed in order to match throttle opening to engine speed. Any 1970s Grand Prix push start was challenging for the rider, but the ACU ruling meant that a water-cooled machine like the 500cc Kawasaki would be stone cold, after twenty minutes of waiting for the flag to drop. This was a recipe for disaster, as the organisers were effectively inviting engine seizures. The morning of the 1975 Senior TT was damp, and it was a fairly typical Manx day, not exactly raining but dull and dreary. As Grant slowed down for Quarter Bridge on the first lap, the engine predictably seized. At this part of the course, the crowd know if a competitor has got it wrong often before the rider themself does, and he remembered ruefully that they started moving back from the barriers. Somehow he managed to get the machine under control and coasted for a distance, firmly believing that his chances in the race were now over. Never the less, shortly afterwards he decided to let out the clutch, and the engine rattled into life on two cylinders. He remembered later: 'I thought, "well I'm not walking back, I'll ride round and do a lap, and if it wrecks it, it wrecks it." I kept going and I think the 500 revved at around 11,000 and I never went above 8,500 for the first lap. I just rode it steady.'[19]

However, to his surprise a pit signal told him that he was now actually on the leader board. Plenty of other riders were evidently also having engine problems that day. As he continued to lap, the heat seeped into the third cylinder and the machine came back on song. Grant brought it home for the win, a full thirty seconds ahead of second placed man John Williams. Ditchburn finished in twentieth place. After the race, Grant was interviewed by Manx Radio's Peter Kneale, and told him that:

> The conditions were sort of half and half really. Part of the course was excellent and the rest of the course was very bad – very wet, and certainly on the second lap, very bad mist on the Mountain. The average speed [of over 100mph] surprises me actually. On the first lap, just after May Hill I was as near as dammit off it, but after that, no problems. After getting this one in the bag I feel very confident about [Friday's race], I just hope its dry. I'm not particularly bothered by the wet, actually, but when you're getting 750 machines and 500s that are very fast, the tyre problem is very important, and the worst possible situation you can get is a circuit that is sort of half and half. We've got tyres for the wet and for the dry, but in between its very difficult.[20]

Scivyer had his own memories of the 1975 Senior – and the aftermath:

> Well that was that. Of course it seized, at Quarter Bridge on the first lap, but Mick caught it, rolled for a while, dropped the clutch and it never missed a beat for the rest of the race. Needless to say the management thought they had done a wonderful job and immediately decamped to the nearest watering hole to soak up the plaudits of the hangers on and journos leaving Nigel and myself to load up that Transit. Again Mick being Mick, came back to find out where we were and invited Nigel and myself to dine with him and Carol at his hotel that night.[21]

The 500cc machine which delivered Kawasaki's first Senior TT win would in due course be presented by Kawasaki management to Lord Montague, for exhibition at the National Motor Museum at Beaulieu, Hampshire. However, after a number of years on display, it was looking somewhat dilapidated; it was subsequently refurbished by mechanic Nigel Everett, and is still to be found at the museum. Grant remembered:

> It wasn't a good bike, it was no quicker in a straight line than a 350 Yamaha and quite a bit bigger. Of course we did a few other Grands Prix on it and it was totally outclassed, but I've got photographs of myself and Geoff Duke handing over the bike on behalf of Kawasaki to Lord Beaulieu and the trust. I saw the bike again when we did a promotional day down at Beulieu about 25 years ago and it was in an awful state, there had been kids jumping all over it, so Nigel restored it.[22]

Although the 500cc Senior was still a Grand Prix event, and Grant had delivered Kawasaki's only second ever win at this level, by this point in time the big race at the TT was undoubtedly Friday's Open Classic. The race carried no World Championship points but instead had the biggest prize pot in TT history up to that time – £1,500 for the winner, and Grant looked hot favourite to win. With a challenge from the Yamaha machines, which would need only one fuel stop to his two, Grant would need to pull something special out of the bag. He had an idea that he might encounter transmission problems with the bike, and so his plan was to go all out at the start, and to break the opposition in the first couple of laps. If he could gain an advantage of twenty seconds or more early on, this would also offset his disadvantage in terms of pit stops.

The morning of the Classic race brought the Kawasaki team drama and excitement even before a wheel had been turned in anger – though it was of the wrong kind altogether. It was discovered that Grant had locked his keys in his car the night before, and staying as he was outside of Douglas it looked like he might not even make the start. Luckily a wire coat hanger was deployed to get the door open and all was well. From the clutch start onward, the Yorkshireman was in irrepressible form. In the early stages of the first lap, his speed was no better than that of the 750cc Yamaha of Percy Tait, but as he powered the machine through the more twisting sections of the course Grant began to turn on the pressure. After 17 miles, at Ballaugh, he was six seconds faster than John Williams' 350cc Yamaha.

Tommy Robb at the Ballacraine commentary box reported that unofficially, from Ballacraine to Ballacraine, Grant had logged a speed of 108.77mph on the first circuit of the race, which equalled Mike Hailwood's eight-year-old lap record. This of course had been set during his epic battle with Agostini, in the 1967 Senior. The crowd at the

Grandstand was agog with excitement when the Kawasaki came in for a pitstop – it was a quick fuel dump lasting just fifteen seconds, before Grant was away again. There was drama now as he slowed down and came into the hairpin at Governor's Dip, and he remembered: 'I'd set the steering damper very stiff so I couldn't turn the handlebars far enough and had to foot it.'[23]

However it was not enough to cause a serious problem, and he grabbed the headlines at the end of his second lap when he set a new outright lap record of 109.82mph. In the process, he had overturned Hailwood's long standing milestone – indeed he was twelve seconds inside it. Hailwood himself was in the press box at the Grandstand that day in 1975, and when news came over the Tannoy that Grant had broken his record, he muttered, 'the bastard.' Mick later went on to pay tribute to the maestro by saying that of all the accolades he had received during his long career, that back handed compliment was undoubtedly the greatest. At the time, however, he recalls that it meant very little. Noting the clapping and cheering of the crowd, he was somewhat bemused and wondered why people were getting so excited over the small matter of a lap record falling. Only in retrospect did its significance become apparent.

The Kawasaki however could not keep up the blistering pace, and a broken chain put Grant out at the Gooseneck whilst he was leading on lap three. The Mountain Course was so bumpy that the suspension was working to full capacity all of the time. When the back wheel is off the road, engine revs shoot up. When the wheel hits the road again the wheel centre can be going twice as fast as the road speed, which puts tremendous strain on all the mechanical components and the tyres. The weakest link is generally the chain, and this is the part which is most likely to break under the stress. On a dead-level short circuit, the bike would not be subjected to such strain, which is one of the reasons that the Mountain Course is widely considered to be the toughest in the world. As he stomped down the hill towards the nearest marshal's hut, a scream from behind made Grant pause and turn – an unlucky fan had jumped over the wall to grab the broken chain as a souvenir, only to discover that it was still red hot! Rod Scivyer remembered another amusing incident from this race:

> The aforementioned Transit had all the signs of a hastily swept out chicken coup. It was forever breaking down, and on its last trip, to pick up the stranded 750 which had thrown its chain during the race, it broke down once too often. A pickup full of marshals on their way back to Douglas offered us and the bike a lift back and the Transit was duly deposited where it belonged, in the ditch just up the road from the Gooseneck.[24]

Ditchburn also retired in the Classic race on the second works Kawasaki, floored by a leaking petrol tank at Keppel Gate. For Grant it was the bitterest of disappointments. The race had been his for the taking, if only the chain not given out. His new lap record was of little consolation when first place would have meant the richest prize in TT history, as the cheque would have been worth around £11,500 in current terms. Later on however, in a more reflective mood Grant thought again about taking Hailwood's long standing lap record. He had beaten it using modern race tyres, disc brakes, and on a bike that he absolutely loved. Hailwood by contrast had set it on a bike with drum brakes, 'wooden tyres' as he called them, and aboard a machine that he hated. It really should not have taken eight years to better it, but it underlined even more what a great rider Hailwood really was.

Grant also retired in the 250cc Lightweight race at the 1975 TT, which was hardly surprising. After paddling the machine off the grid, he had lost more than his twenty seconds starting advantage over next man on the road Derek Chatterton by the time the leaders reached Ballaugh, 17 miles out, on the first lap. After a further 20 comparatively sluggish miles, Grant pulled into his pit reporting too little acceleration and too much heat, and decided to call it a morning. The KR250 tandem twin had been flown in from Japan for him to ride just before the meeting started. He had previously ridden the machine at an early season race in Ontario, Canada and the vibration that it produced was so bad that it actually shook loose its exhaust pipes on that occasion. Development in the factory race shop had so far done little to resolve the problem. However, after its initial disappointing results, the type would go on to be one of the most successful of Kawasaki's designs, and indeed eventually it was almost unbeatable. Although an early prototype was exhibited at the Amsterdam Motorcycle Show in 1970, Ken Yoshida was the engineer who had eventually been tasked with the responsibility of undertaking the practical design of this new 250cc racing engine, which had first begun to take shape in 1973. Kawasaki had always liked the rotary valve-type of inlet control, but realised from experience with the 250cc A1R racer that the normal across the frame type of twin with a direct crankcase induction engine was inevitably going to be too wide. It would be too difficult to optimise the handling and reduce the bike's frontal area, without restricting the airflow into the carburettors. Ken therefore designed an inline twin-cylinder engine and correctly realised that, by offsetting the crankshafts by just 16mm, he could overlap the rotary valves and shorten the length of the unit.

Also by putting the two crankshafts as close together as possible, the design would reduce the pitch-line velocity of the coupling gears. In an engine capable of 12,000rpm, the pitch-line velocity of these coupling gears was in a very critical speed range. Water-cooling was necessary because of the inline design, and to obtain the maximum performance. To keep the engine weight down, the crankcases and rotary valve covers would be cast in magnesium. A special type of ball bearing would be used on the crankshaft main bearings and these had two wedge shaped nylon rings around their outer diameter, that were designed to slightly crush when the two halves of the crankcases were bolted together. This design would help to keep the roller-type main bearings in place in the relatively soft magnesium cases. The design also offered the option of phasing the crankshafts with either a 180° firing order, or as a 360° twin-cylinder firing as a 'big single'. This would prove to be a valuable design option as the development of the KR250 proceeded.

Design goals that were set by the company specified that the engine should be capable of 240bhp per litre, which would equate to 60bhp for 250cc, and that the motorcycle would have a dry weight of less than 100kg (220lb). The neat little engine of the KR250 was very much Ken Yoshida's baby, with another engineer in the racing department, Nagato Sato, being assigned the job of doing the detailed design drawings. Ken's inline twin basic design was extremely advanced for this time period, particularly with the proven high-performance rotary valve-type inlet system that Kawasaki favoured. The finished engine design was very close to that as originally envisaged in late 1973.

It featured 'square' cylinder dimensions of a 54mm bore by 54.4mm stroke and came with a seven-speed gearbox. Two 32mm Mikuni carburettors (later increased to 34mm) were mounted at a slight upward angle on the left-hand side of the engine, while the water pump, the Kokusan Magneto CDI ignition and multi-disc clutch were located on the right-hand side. The cylinder head and the separate cylinder block were each cast in aluminium as 'one-piece' units for the twin-cylinder engine, and the cylinder bores were coated using the ELEX process. The cylinders had three large transfer ports and a single exhaust port without a bridge. Each piston featured a single ring. There was a great deal of experimental and testing work carried out by Ken Yoshida and his staff on the phasing of the two individual crankshafts. On the plus side of the 360° phasing (with the pistons going up and down together) was the fact that it eliminated almost all vibration. The torque output would fluctuate like that of a single-cylinder engine, but as first proven in dirt track racing, and later in road racing, in this set up the rear traction was noticeably improved and provided a harder acceleration out of the corner.

On the negative side, this 360° phasing created a huge load on the crankshaft main bearings and crankcases, especially as the lightweight magnesium crankcases did not have the strength and hardness that aluminium crankcases would have had. On the plus side of a 180° phasing (with the pistons alternately going up and down) the torque output was very even and the load on the crankshaft main bearings and crankcase was greatly reduced. The smoother and lower torque peaks would allow a smaller clutch and the transmission could be lighter. So at this time, the concern over the lessened impact on main bearings and crankcase was the deciding factor which lead to the use of the 180° phasing, despite the vibration that this would produce. It was also noted that push-starting the KR250 with the 180° phasing would be a lot easier than with 360° phasing. This was another important factor to consider, because most Grand Prix races at that time were dead motor starts, requiring an easy to push and a quick-starting motorcycle.

One of the primary design goals was to keep the weight of the engine and total motorcycle as light as possible. To accomplish that, as well as the crankcases and rotary valve covers, the primary drive cover and carburettors were also originally cast in magnesium. However, duration testing showed some problems with using magnesium for the crankcases, so after some analysis over the weight savings versus performance and durability, the crankcases were changed to aluminium. In line with the lightweight design theme, the front and rear brake discs were aluminium with a sprayed steel coating. The single front brake calliper on the right-hand fork was cast into the Kawasaki designed and made aluminium fork sliders.

Kawasaki used a one-piece fork with cast-in brake calliper design early in 1975, but as the season progressed and the KR250 got faster, better brakes would be required and the company went back to the more conventional set-up that permitted the fitting of stronger callipers and bigger discs. Another early problem which was encountered with the KR250 was overheating, which in turn was leading to loss of power. The oil was heating up to well over the optimum operating temperature of 80°C, and indeed in some cases the oil got so hot that it actually melted the plastic rings around the crankshaft bearings. Using a lighter grade oil offered a temporary solution, but Ken Yoshida liaised closely with the Kawasaki Heavy Industries race shop to come up with a more durable solution. Initially they shipped new drive gears for the water pump which would push more coolant through the radiator. Eventually a redesigned water pump and thicker radiator would go some way towards resolving the overheating problem. Like their bigger KR750 brothers, all twenty-five KR250 motorcycles which were produced to comply with homologation rules were fitted with Koni suspension units and Morris Mag wheels. Grant remembered the machine's designer fondly:

> Yoshida was the most amazing engineer you could wish to meet. I remember him with hand grinding tools grinding scrolls inside the gears and they looked as if it had been done on a machine. I remember he wanted a timing disc, and he got some scraps of aluminium out of the back of his workshop – he made a timing disc and it looked like something that had been bought from a shop. Absolutely brilliant. You had that much trust in the guy [as a result].[25]

Later, Kawasaki would reverse the phasing of the cylinders and this simple expedient would have the effect of transforming the performance of the machine. It eliminated the vibration problem in an instant, and made the 250cc into a race winner. Nagato Sato began to redesign the engine in 1974, reverting to an earlier feature of rotary intake valves. With rotary valves the peak power was similar to that of a piston-port design, but there was considerable gain across the powerband. Grant's assessment of the 250cc saga was that more than mere mechanical considerations were involved:

> it was hard to understand why Kawasaki had even built it at all. Why bother if they weren't going to give it a proper run? I suspect there must have been some political conflict high up in the company because there's no doubt at all that it could have been dominating world championships two years earlier than it did. The 1975 250's main problem

> was that its pistons were 180 degrees out on its two geared crankshafts, which caused the most horrendous vibration, By the time it made its belated grand prix appearance two years later, the pistons rose and fell together and it was an altogether smoother and better engine. The 500, on the other hand, was always pretty hopeless. It was significantly heavier than a Yamaha twin and didn't handle half so well, yet despite an extra 150cc it seemed to have only a marginal speed advantage.[26]

Even though he had first raced on the Isle of Man in 1968, a year before Mick Grant, Ditchburn had only been there a handful of times. He was never truly happy riding the TT course, and 1975 would be his last appearance on the Island. He recalled later that the PR side of being a factory racer was not for him: 'I was always happy to stay out of the limelight and in those days we just didn't know enough about suspension and chassis set up. If it wasn't right we just rode around a problem.'[27]

Ditchburn may have disliked the Isle of Man, but he made up for it with a win at the annual post-TT meeting at Mallory Park. Grant scored a second place here and this together with his win at Scarborough saw him leading the British Superbike Championship, a title that he would go on to win that year, with Ditchburn a close second. It had been a spectacular debut season for Kawasaki, and the KR750 had swept all before it. For Grant, his success in 1975 meant that he was now perceived as the team's number one rider (by the hierarchy in Japan, certainly). As a result, he usually got first access to anything that was new or experimental from the factory. On the face of it this might have given him an advantage over team mate Ditchburn, but in fact it was a mixed blessing. If the new part worked well, then it would certainly give Grant an edge, but more often than not he would waste valuable practice time on something that ultimately was not going to work.

Overall, for Mick Grant the 1975 season had been one that he would come to look back on as one of the best in his career; from setting new records at the North West 200 and taking victory and lap records at the TT, he went on to take the MCN British Superbike crown, beating a certain Barry Sheene in the process. For the coming 1976 season, the world (or at least Great Britain) should have been at Kawasaki's feet, but it was not to be so. In fact, it was worldwide problems that were almost their undoing. These included the severe recession caused by the oil crisis following the Yom Kippur War in the Middle East, and they would contribute to that year being one of the toughest and most disappointing that team green would experience in their 1970s racing campaign.

Chapter Four

ALSO RANS 1976

In Britain the early part of 1976 was dominated by the economic depression caused by the international oil crisis. Arab petroleum producing nations had decided to retaliate against Western nations which had supported Israel in the Yom Kippur War, by cutting back on oil exports. This had created an artificial shortage which in turn sent inflation spiralling upwards, and led to economic turmoil. As a result there was some speculation in the press as to whether Kawasaki would actually even compete that year. Despite the team's 1975 success, a general cutback for 1976 almost saw an end to the British racing programme, until increased financial support came from akill new sponsor, in the form of Hodge Finance Ltd, who also provided hire purchase agreements for the company's chain of dealers. As the achievements of the Boyer Kawasaki team had been so impressive in Britain during 1975, the Kawasaki hierarchy expected them to do even better during 1976. As Stan Shenton ruefully observed, the previous year they had been too successful for their own good. Without the prospect of the latest engine parts from Japan, indeed without the benefit of basic spares in the early part of the season, the British team did whatever they could to improve performance. They worked on the handling characteristics of the bikes, and had Girling produce new gas-pressurised shock absorbers to help with this. Unfortunately, internal divisions were also developing within the team, as Grant remembered:

> We negotiated contracts for 1976 individually, and sometime in 1976 I was out for a meal with Barry Ditchburn, and he let slip that the contract money that he had got was quite a bit more than I was getting, and I had done all the winning in 1975. That was the beginning of the end of a good relationship with Stan Shenton. As a peace offering John Norman, who was MD of Kawasaki at the time, and who was always against racing – he would have rather spent the money on a budget for marketing bikes directly – gave me one of the race bikes.[1]

The root cause of this discontent within the team lay in the fact that Ditchburn had been approached by Suzuki GB in the off season, and offered a contract to ride for them. He turned it down to stick with Kawasaki, but was savvy enough to do so only once they had agreed to match the Suzuki offer. This however had unexpected consequences for team dynamics. Kawasaki team management should have handled the matter with more acumen, because in spite of Norman's attempt to pour oil on troubled waters, the incident did much to poison future relations within the Kawasaki UK camp.

In the previous season the KR750 had taken all before it, and in theory with a winter of improvements it should have been on even better form, but the early outings that year the machine showed a worrying tendency to seize, particularly over long distances. If it made it to the latter stages of a race, the crank was likely to fail. Most of the failures were big-end or main bearing failures, so it was obvious that the crankshaft couldn't cope with the punishment to which it was being subjected. To try to counter this, Kawasaki brought the rev ceiling down from 11,000rpm to 9,500rpm which although it did not entirely cure the problem, made the engines slightly more dependable than before. Grant remembered:

> Well, for the start, there were no electronics or data logging and the like. We had the bike and that was it. In their day the air-cooled 750cc H2R and the later water-cooled KR750's were really competitive. We had three engine specs from what you might call mild to wild. They were never much trouble and despite being simple piston ported two strokes they never 'nipped up' like some of the small 'strokers' I'd ridden. That said the cranks did have a short life and you had to make sure they were changed according to their service limits. For short races we never had any issues, but long races on the stage three motor were more of a gamble as you might say. The bike went like a rocket, but remember rockets also go bang, so we did live on the edge a bit when we used the most powerful motors.[2]

Grant only rarely used the top stage of tune. The motorcycle was simply too difficult to control, and it proved impossible to get the power to the ground out of corners with this set up. Most of the time he used the middle state of tune. The 1976 500cc machine meanwhile was basically an H1RW with various minor modifications. These included forks and front brakes borrowed from the KR750. The 1976 TT however would turn out to be a disappointment for Grant and for Kawasaki. For one thing, the opposition, chiefly John Williams who was mounted on 500 and 750cc factory Suzukis, would turn out to be a lot stronger. The ACU once again proved itself to be living in the past, when they made another attempt to turn back the clock. This time they were proposing to ban slicks on the Island, despite the fact that there was ample and growing evidence to show that treaded tyres simply couldn't cope with the power and speed of the big bikes by the mid-1970s.

That year Grant arrived on the Island too late for Monday practice, so did not see the circuit until 5.30am on the Tuesday. He took out the 500cc machine but conditions were terrible – it was raining and visibility was poor, though he was credited with the fastest lap of the day at a lowly 85mph. In the afternoon session he took out the 750cc and did a lap at 104mph. This was the fastest speed set for this class, but Charlie Williams exceeded it on his 350cc Yamaha which was an ominous portent. It was an eventful session for Grant, as he first swallowed a fly at Quarter Bridge, then his screen was broken at Glentramman by flying stones. Coming round the last of the three bends at the thirty-second milestone and approaching Windy Corner Mick also killed a bird, 'of the feathered type, of course', he quickly assured reporters. After this Grant took out the 500cc once more, but had only made it as far as Kirk Michael when the big ends failed. The engine was revving to 11,500rpm in its maximum state of tune, so the team reduced this slightly so that it peaked at 10,500rpm. Wednesday of Practice Week was spent at Jurby airfield experimenting with the 250cc machine and running in a brand new 500cc engine. Nigel Everett ran it with his hand constantly hovering over the clutch lever, and Grant reckoned he saw a look of relief on his face when the mechanic said that it was run in enough.

Wednesday evening practice saw Grant achieve one of his ambitions – something that he had never admitted in public beforehand – to be the first rider to lap the Island at 110mph. Before he went out that evening he was actually apprehensive in case John Williams should achieve the milestone first on his Suzuki, but in the event he was seventeen seconds faster than Williams; the only problem came after the session, when scrutineers could not find the Kawasaki's drain plug! Grant managed the achievement on the same 750cc machine that he had won the Superbike race aboard at Brands Hatch two days earlier. The bike was fitted with a Dunlop slick on the rear and a cut slick on the front. He was particularly satisfied with the time, give than this was only his number two bike! Later in the week the number one bike arrived, in transit from the French Grand Prix. Although it was more powerful in terms of sheer horsepower, it remained to be seen whether that would actually be an advantage or not at a circuit like the TT. The successful outing with the 750cc was followed by anti-climax when Grant went to go out with the 500cc machine; the practice session was almost over for solos when he got to the line, and officials curtly told him that he was four seconds too late to start. Even Grant's protests that he wouldn't get in the way of the sidecars fell on deaf ears! Overall he performed well in practice, and even after setting the new unofficial lap record of 110mph, Grant later upped this to 112mph. At the end of Practice Week, Grant wrote of the situation in his weekly newspaper column:

> Perhaps in the 500cc race I wouldn't mind a rainy day because although the 500 is really nice to ride and a good handler, it's down on speed and doesn't give anything like the power of the Suzuki fours. It also seems a shame that I'm going to have to refuel twice. If Mike Hailwood was right when he said that 70bhp was the ideal amount for the TT circuit, then the few horse power I have in excess of this shouldn't be an embarrassment.[3]

The 1976 Senior TT was billed as a showdown between Grant (setting off as number one) and John Williams (immediately behind him as number two). By Ballacraine on lap one, John Williams was first on the road. Grant arrived just behind him but Williams had already opened up a gap of twelve seconds. By Ballaugh Bridge, Grant was seen glancing over his left shoulder, and shortly afterwards he pulled in. He subsequently restarted, but was way off the lead and was reported to be tussling with mid-fielders. His engine finally seized at Black Hut, and he toured in to retire at the end of the lap. Despite what he wrote in his column, it is fair to say that he never truly got to grips with the strange handling characteristics of the hotchpotch 500cc machine, which were further compounded by the extra-large fuel tank that it was fitted with that year. Suzuki rider Stan Woods later told Grant that he thought the Kawasaki was going sideways when it passed him at School House! It proved his point however that on the Isle of Man, good handling was more important than pure horse power alone. This, as it turned out, would be the last appearance of a Kawasaki factory 500cc machine at the TT during the 1970s. Although there was talk in Japan of developing a new machine for this class, it would not actually materialise until the beginning of the next decade.

The KR250 again was a disappointment. A modified engine had arrived a week before the TT but Grant could complete only one lap in the race before the machine overheated. During 1976 Sato would complete the redesign of the engine, and the new model would make its debut at the end of season Japanese Grand Prix that year. Within the engine the two crankshafts were now phased at 360°, cancelling the forces at mid-stroke, overcoming the earlier vibration problem and giving a wider spread of power (from 6,000rpm). A new low drag Kokusan ignition system fired both spark plugs simultaneously. Another change was to the rotary valves, the previous steel type now being replaced by a thicker fibre (1mm) with less drag. Flame-sprayed aluminium valve covers replaced the wear-prone magnesium type, and with

34mm carburettors, the power was now around 55bhp at 12,500rpm. A six-speed gearbox was now standardised, but the most important development was to the chassis. Designed by Kinuo (Cowboy) Hiramatsu, the basic duplex cradle was conventional, though lighter and smaller than before. It featured a Uni-Track mono-shock rear suspension. The swingarm was constructed of steel tubing, with a bell crank providing a 2:1 leverage ratio on the upright Koni shock absorber. The swingarm also featured a lower brace, and the rear axle rode on eccentric adjusters. There was a single front disc brake, with the twin-piston Kawasaki calliper no longer cast as part of the still skinny 36mm front fork. Hiramatsu also redesigned the fairing, the front now being angled to generate down-thrust on the front wheel at high speed. These developments saw the weight increase to 104kg, but this was still lighter than its main rivals.

The International Classic TT was held on the final Saturday of Race Week, because of bad weather on the Friday. Again, a clash between John Williams and Mick Grant was expected, and the latter was feeling confident. Occasionally, he recalled, he would get an overwhelming sensation that he was going to win a race, although this occasion was to prove that the premonition could not always be relied upon. Predictably both men made fast getaways from the line; Grant's was especially spectacular – riding this time as his trademark number ten he was some way down the grid, but pulled a wheelie and a half as he roared away past the Grandstand at the start of the race. Gremlins struck again however as clutch trouble became apparent, a problem which had begun really in the first hundred yards of the race, when the plates began to disintegrate shortly after leaving the starter's flag. Grant hoped at first that it was just oil on the plates and if so, they might begin to grip again as they got hot. This proved not to be the case and Grant pulled in at Ballacraine hoping to make adjustments. He asked spectators if they had any tools, but the crowd just stared goggled eyed with amazement, and none were forthcoming. After chatting to marshals below the commentary box, he wheeled the machine across to the pub. There, pulling the motorcycle back under compression, he managed to restart the engine. Travelling Marshal Albert Moule held him back until there was a safe gap, and then Grant joined the race once more – one minute and twenty seconds down. As he reached Doran's Bend and Laurel Bank he fancied that the clutch might be improving. However it began to deteriorate again in third and fourth gears, and he later retired. He remembered:

> I'm not being big headed, but I could have won that race at whatever speed I wanted, except the clutch went, which never ever happened. I think that it was adjusted wrongly and right from the start the clutch slipped so I only got one lap in. And I had no 500 so that was my '76 TT over with, but in practice I had put the unofficial lap record up by a couple of miles an hour so I knew that it was within my grasp.[4]

After a particularly disappointing visit to the Isle of Man, Grant had to console himself with the only award that he took away from the Island that year, a watch presented to him by Bulova (the timing sponsors) and worth a princely £100! After the highs of 1975, the 1976 season overall turned out to be a low point for Kawasaki. If anything positive was to come of it, however, it was perhaps that it underlined the fact that under-investment in development translated very clearly into poorer performance on the race track. There was some light at the end of the tunnel, because for the coming year new machinery was promised by the Kawasaki factory in Japan.

The 1976 TT was significant for other reasons, however. After boycotts, endless arguments over safety, and a long battle, the FIM had finally decided to withdraw Grand Prix status from the event. That year would be the final one in which points gained on the Island could count towards a world title. It was a meeting filled with intense emotion. The uncertainty about the future of the TT hung heavy in the air, but those riders who had no wish to be there had already walked away long ago. When interviewed in the paddock after the races had finished, competitor after competitor asserted his intention to return the following year. More than one claimed that you could not truly call yourself a world champion if you had not raced on the Isle of Man. As Stan Shenton pointed out in an interview, in 1974, 1975 and 1976 Kawasaki had been practically the only works team present on the Island. For the TT organisers, the commitment that Kawasaki UK – with the 1975 British Superbike Champion in Mick Grant – would be back next year was exactly the shot in the arm that they needed. In spite of the loss of Grand Prix status, some of the best racing of the 1970s was still to come, and the credibility that the presence of Kawasaki lent to the event did much to secure its future.

Chapter Five

BOUNCING BACK 1977

After the disappointments of 1976, in the following year Kawasaki were determined to do better. For the 1977 racing season there was a new model KR750, this being the lighter 602L. The 602L was the final version of the KR750, and weight reduction extended to magnesium crankcases and an aluminium clutch. The dry weight was now 136kg and other developments included a larger radiator to overcome earlier cooling problems, and a new ignition system that fired all three cylinders simultaneously, 120° apart. The cylinders now had an unbridged exhaust port along with four transfer ports. To isolate the 38mm carburettors from vibration these were mounted on the chassis and connected to the inlet ports with soft rubber boots. There were new rear mounted brake callipers and a combined front wheel bearing and disc mounting. The rear axle was now mounted in eccentric adjusters, a cantilever brace stabilised the swingarm, and the shock absorbers were more laid down. Handling had been improved, weight reduced and braking improved. Yet even with this development the 602L was initially outclassed by the Yamaha TZ750, and generally the new model was not as successful as Kawasaki had anticipated. It was now becoming apparent that the days of the three cylinder machine were numbered, as they could no longer deliver the same power as their four cylinder rivals. Grant remembered:

> In 1975 and 1976 the 750 Kawasaki was the best bike out there, especially in 1975. The Yamaha wasn't as good, the

> Suzuki wasn't as good. By the time it got to 1977 they were catching up. So from '77, and '78 we were actually dropping back, and the reason we were dropping back was in spite of the fact that in 1977 they brought a new engine out, which was less unreliable. 1975 and 1976 it was a high revving engine at 11,000 rpm. It used to break crankshafts. The FIM World Championship races were 100 miles, and the cranks would do normally do about 90, so it didn't work well. So for 1977 and 1978 they brought the revs down to 9000 rpm. They slowed the timing down, made it a lot beefier engine with much more torque, much bigger exhaust pipes to compensate, and it did make it a lot nicer bike to ride. But Yamaha and Suzuki were marching on, and in '77 and '78 we were going down hill. The reason for that, as I mentioned earlier, was that the Kawasaki racing department was actually quite small, and they could only do so much. I think they had realised the potential of the 250 and 350 Grand Prix bikes, so instead of developing the 750 they were concentrating on making these work.[1]

Finance also continued to be a source of friction within the Kawasaki UK setup. The original deal was that Grant would be paid a fee by the team, plus any prize money that he won and also the start money for each meeting, which he negotiated himself with the race organisers. By this time Grant was probably the best-known motorcycle racer in Britain, after Barry Sheene, so this could at times be a substantial amount of money. However, for 1977 team management proposed a new arrangement, whereby they would negotiate the start money on his behalf and pay him a fixed fee. He went along with it but soon regretted the decision, as he began to realise that they would never bargain as hard on his behalf as he would for himself. Grant visited the Isle of Man in early May in order to check over the course and familiarise himself with the alterations which had taken place over the previous year, particularly those at Union Mills, where the entrance to the village had been widened. That summer, Kawasaki were looking to the Island to give them a much needed morale boost.

Grant and the Green Meanies came to the 1977 TT in the midst of a season which had so far delivered mixed blessings. The latest version of the KR750 looked impressive, but a series of annoying technical glitches had marred its results in European meetings; there were early season disappointments at both Imola where Grant was sidelined with ignition problems, and in the prestigious Moto Journal 200 at the Paul Ricard circuit in France he was holding fifth place when he ran out of fuel. At the following meeting in Spain there was also a poor showing, and in the Transatlantic Match Race Series back in the United Kingdom its performance had been mediocre. By the time of the North West 200 in early May, however, things were improving and Grant took victory in the 750cc race at that event. Big news at the TT that year was the arrival of Honda Britain, the first 'official' appearance by a Honda squad on the Island since 1967. With them as a rider was former competitor Phil Read, also returning after an absence of five years. Grant came back with a witty one liner when a journalist asked him if Read would pose a threat. 'Pose, yes. Threat, no!' was the reply. Controversial and outspoken at the best of times, Read's previous comments about the TT meant that he needed police protection on occasions, but Grant was also grabbing his own share of the headlines. In practice the big Kawasaki was clocked through a speed trap on the drop to Brandish at 191mph. This was so astonishing that many at the time refused to believe it, and questioned the accuracy of the timing equipment. Grant however thought that it was credible. For him it was the fastest part of the course, coming off the Mountain and with a following wind. At the time the Kawasaki was regularly clocked on the banking at Daytona at over 180mph, so with the higher gearing used at the TT, a speed in excess of 190mph was definitely within the reach of the bike.

Grant sat out the Senior TT as the 500cc machine had finally been put out to grass by Kawasaki, but this year the 250cc model was also starting to show some promise. Grant never missed an opportunity to extol the virtues of this machine to the Kawasaki hierarchy whenever the opportunity presented itself. To his mind, with the ongoing effects of the oil crisis on the price of petrol, the days were numbered for big engine motorcycles. John Norman was more hesitant however, telling reporters that there was as yet no long term plans for the 250cc: 'We will see how Mick and Barry [Ditchburn] fare and then take stock of the situation. Obviously we want to make an impression on the Grand Prix scene with a view to making a proper entry into the championship in 1978.'[2]

Grant had not had an opportunity to ride the newly redesigned model until mid-season at the French Grand Prix. He immediately felt at home on the bike – he had made his name on 250s and 350s and always loved the feeling of precision which came from riding the smaller types. In practice for the TT the team worked hard on set-up, and had it running well. If it could endure the rigours of the Mountain Course then a win was a distinct possibility in the Junior race, but on the way to the starting grid with minutes to go before the flag dropped, it sprang a coolant leak. Although the fault was spotted and hurriedly fixed, it meant that Grant had to start with a stone-cold engine. The bike spluttered down Bray Hill on one cylinder. He stopped at Braddan to check the plug leads, which made no difference, and the machine was clearly experiencing carburettor trouble. At one point it appeared that Grant would have to retire, and although the misfire had cleared by Ballacraine, by the Bungalow his signals were telling him that he was already ninety seconds down on Charlie Williams. He wrote in his weekly *Motor Cycle* newspaper column afterwards:

> Even if the bike had been on full song from the word go it would have been a job and a half to have beaten Charlie on the sort of form he was showing. But it would have been nice to have a go! As it was, it was an impossible task, and only the chalk-written complaints on the blackboard of my signalling post at the Gooseneck provided any cheer in an otherwise disappointing race.[3]

There was more to this than purely a misfiring engine, however. Grant was the first to admit that unlike riders such as Joey Dunlop or Mike Hailwood, throughout his career he had struggled to adapt his riding style straight away when changing from one machine to another for different races. When aboard the smaller machine, many corners had to be taken flat out without changing down through the gears as was the case with a big 750cc, something he often found difficult. Charlie went on to win, with Grant taking a disappointing seventh place, which hardly reflected the capability of the machine. He reflected ruefully:

> I've got a weakness. I could ride 250s and 350s quick around the Island. I could ride 750s quick. I couldn't do both together. Most people could but I couldn't. Everyone expected me to win on the Kawasaki because I'd just been winning Grands Prix on it and Stan Shenton for

> sure felt that I was just not bothered, but nothing could be further from the truth. Places like Rhencullen where on a 750 you come down one gear for it. On a 250 in 1974 I was doing that flat out and Glen Vine on a 750 you come down one gear. I couldn't help it I was coming down one gear on a 250 and you've got to keep it flat. I just couldn't acclimatise to it, so the net result was I finished seventh.[4]

In some regard, however, Grant was being unduly hard on himself with this assessment. Tests have proved that in a disc valve engine like that of the Kawasaki 250cc twin, carburation is far more critical than that on a piston-controlled model such as Kawasaki's 750cc triple. The latter could go from a 540 main jet down to a 460 with no risk of misfire at the top or bottom end. But with a needle only two sizes out on the rotary induction two-stroke, the machine would not run cleanly. Grant himself observed that if it was not set up correctly, the twin would accelerate like an old bus. To get it right required barometers and gauges for measuring the moisture in the atmosphere, as well as a keen eye on the weather. On the Isle of Man it was particularly difficult to get right, because of the changes in air pressure at different parts of the course. A skilled Japanese factory technician might have been able to get it set up correctly, but the Kawasaki UK operation just did not have the necessary capability.

The 750cc however showed the most promise following the astonishing performance in practice – if only the raw power which it was capable of producing could be contained, and did not work against it as had happened before. Grant thought that keeping the front wheel down as it roared away from the start line might be a problem; as it turned out it wasn't, but excessive wheelspin was. He remembered:

> Much was made in the early Seventies of tyres not being able to cope with the sheer power of the new breed of big two strokes. It wasn't half so dangerous, but the same was true – and for much longer – of chains. They, too, struggled to cope with 100-plus horsepower over long races. So in the Classic TT any problem was likely to be with the chain, which had sidelined us in both previous years. True enough, despite adjusting it during both pit stops, by the final lap it was jumping the sprockets again.[5]

What had been expected to be a three-way fight in the Open Classic turned into a two-man battle, after Phil Read came off during an unofficial practice the previous evening, and was unable to start the race. That left Mick Grant and John Williams as the main contenders. Grant set off from the line as number six, with a wheelie as usual as he passed the Grandstand. There was much drama at Ballacraine, as first Tom Herron misjudged the bend and ran up the slip road. As he was desperately trying to turn around and rejoin the race, a few seconds later Grant made the same mistake and, leaving his braking too late, ran off the course at the same spot. He quickly restarted but John Williams had also had problems, and Grant managed to stay ahead of him on the road. Coming through Ballaugh, Grant was on his own, having now fought his way through the field to the front. He made a slight mistake when he changed up rather too soon, but even so had increased his lead by the Bungalow. The roads were dry but conditions were gusty on the Mountain, which threatened to bring lap times down. Never the less Grant had set an opening lap of over 112mph from a standing start, with an unofficial time showing as 20 minutes and 12.4 seconds back to the Grandstand. The rest of the field were chasing hard however, but this only served to push Grant on, and the second lap was the fastest ever up to that time. He had averaged 121.62mph from the start to Ballacraine.

The big Kawasaki wheelied on the exit from Ramsey Hairpin, on his way to the Bungalow. He went through the speed trap just below the Creg-ny-Baa at 191mph on his way to the record lap. John Williams by now was out of the race, and Grant continued to increase his lead. With the possibility of the chain breaking a serious consideration, Grant had planned to build up a forty-second advantage in the first three laps, then come in for adjustment to the links and rear sprocket. As arranged he came in for fuel at the end of lap three. With plenty of time in hand it was a leisurely pit stop, the mechanic Nigel Everett using the quick filler to refuel the tank, before turning his attention to the 101-link Regina chain. He made the adjustment, then the rider was away again. Grant was making it look easy, as if he was out for a Sunday ride, but by lap five the chain was slackening again. Grant remembered that as he approached the Mountain section he was worried sick that the chain would break, and in the same place that it had done so in 1975. In his words he handled the throttle with a touch like a midwife's; without this care, he concluded, the chain would undoubtedly have gone. By lap six he held a commanding lead, through Charlie Williams was working hard to try to close the gap. Grant wrote at the time:

> The only real moment in the entire race came at the top of Barregaroo which I had been struggling with all practice. I suddenly found myself in the right hand gutter at the top of the hill [and] that's just where you don't want to be. Definitely too close for comfort! John Williams, and later Bill Smith, told me they were taking Bray Hill flat out in top on their five hundreds. I tried it in fifth instead of fourth and went through 15mph faster.[6]

Many people heard the commentator at the Bungalow say that the bike sounded out of tune, and that Grant was looking down at his engine as if there was something wrong with it – there wasn't, but it was his way of letting the fans who were waving at him all around the course know that there was still a long way to go to the flag. It had a similar effect upon his wife and pit crew waiting at the Grandstand, which included Eddy Fenwick who had been a spanner man with sidecar legend Mac Hobson. Carol Grant however had issues of her own to contend with. Shortly after the race started an overzealous official told her that the pit board which she was using was larger than the 2-foot-square ACU regulation, and that her husband would be disqualified as a result. Strangely it was the same pit board that she had been using all week, and no one else had seemed to notice or care up to this point. A compromise was reached whereby Grant would not be disqualified if Carol switched to using a regulation sized board for the remainder of the race. The only problem was that Mick was unaware of all this, and was puzzled as to why his wife had suddenly stopped signalling whilst she looked for a smaller board. Was divorce on the cards? He continues:

> It was an anxious lap, but by then all I needed to do was finish. The race was in the bag. My biggest moment had actually come on the opening lap when the rear brake disappeared going into Ballacraine and I almost joined Tommy Robb in the commentary box. Luckily the brake came back, allowing me to lead from start to finish, with a new race record, 110.76 mph. Along the way I'd broken the outright lap record on the opening lap, extending it to 112.77 mph on the second. Chain worries aside it was a textbook race ... it was a pretty good cashbook race, too. One of the effects of the TT losing its GP status

> was that, at long last, the organisers had to find another reason for persuading riders to go to the Island. The obvious answer was money, which even the dimmest jockey can understand. Yet although being paid what you considered your worth was important to all the top TT riders, money was never the motivation during a race. Winning was. That year, though, there was a subtle difference, since a new prize money formula paid us for our position at the end of each lap, rather than in final results. So every time I passed the pits I thought, 'Ching! That's another £1,000. Nice.' I was almost disappointed when the chequered flag went out and the gravy train came to an end – except that I ended the race £6,000 better off. I'd have cashed it in, though (well, maybe some of it) for a 250cc win. I still thought the little tandem twin was Kawasaki's best shot.[7]

As Grant pushed the Kawasaki back along the pit lane, with a sea of arms reaching out to offer him congratulations, he was initially disappointed to hear Manx Radio commentator Peter Kneale broadcasting over the loudspeakers a speed of only 110.76mph, but he soon discovered the true facts – that was just his average for the race. His fastest lap of 112.77mph had not only given him once more the absolute lap record – it had put him and Kawasaki firmly back in the headlines for all the right reasons. After the race, talking to journalists Mick commented: 'From the fourth lap on I daren't rev the engine to more than 7,000 rpm for fear of snapping the chain, but it's a chassis problem really. The engine moves about in the frame putting an impossible strain on the chain.'[8]

In fact, later events would disprove this theory – when the team tried remounting the engine so that it moved less frequently, the chain problems persisted – but speaking to Peter Kneale on the day Grant continued:

> I was relieved and delighted [to have won] believe me ... at the fuel stop I knew we'd have to adjust the chain, which we did ok, no problem, but then it went again on the fifth lap and on the last lap over the Mountain, I was petrified, I thought that it was going to break at any minute, but it didn't, good old Regina! Apart from that there were no problems at all … the conditions were very good but I'm surprised we went quite as quick as that, after the second lap I didn't press on too hard, to use Phil [Read]'s phrase I was cruising a little bit![9]

He added later: 'I never make predictions because you appear such a fool if you're wrong, but I did say that someone would have to do a 112mph lap to win.'[10]

After the TT that year, team manager Stan Shenton tried to downplay the importance of the milestone to the company, stating that chasing new lap records was not any deliberate part of their policy:

> Of course you can't ignore the possibility of a record with Mick Grant at a place like the Isle of Man, for he is now probably one of the most experienced riders in the Isle of Man, so with a machine which is reasonably reliable, it is always more than a possibility that he will do well there. The TT course is very much a knowledge course and a rider without the course knowledge, even if he has the fastest bike in the world, is not going to do any good. But the object of the exercise, so far as I am concerned, is to win races. Ideally that should be done at the slowest possible speed … and, if you can finish one second ahead of the

> man behind, that's all you need to do. Going deliberately for a lap record could put you out of the reckoning for winning the race because the rider could crash or break something on the machine by over-driving it.[11]

It was hardly a ringing endorsement of Grant's achievement on the Island, and it hinted further at the worsening personal relationships within the team. None the less after the TT a lot of the problems with the KR750 seemed to have been ironed out, and Kawasaki's fortunes in the British Superbike Championship also began to improve. Grant won at Scarborough and Brands Hatch to finish second in the championship overall. The improvements which the factory had made to the machine had managed to keep it competitive but in this dog-eat-dog world, the other big Japanese manufacturers were also developing their engines and frames year on year. For how much longer could Kawasaki continue to dominate the big bike races on the Isle of Man?

Chapter Six

LAP OF THE GODS 1978

The 1978 TT is rightly remembered as one of the most dramatic meetings of the decade, if indeed not the modern era. As well as boasting the cream of 1970s racing talent, Kawasaki at this time were at their peak, and – if the weather held – it promised a feast for racing fans. The firm had previously set the outright lap record on the Isle of Man, one of the most prestigious achievements in motorcycle sport, and the question on every race fan's mind was could they defend it from the relentless onward march of Suzuki and Yamaha (joined once again this year by a team from the resurgent Honda Britain). In the event, not only would Kawasaki defend the title of fastest machine on the Isle of Man, but in the capable hands of Grant they would actually go on to raise the bar.

At Kawasaki UK racing, Barry Ditchburn had now departed to be replaced by South African rider Kork Ballington. Grant enjoyed a good relationship with Ballington, but he was alone in competing at the Isle of Man as the focus of the latter was not the TT, but Grands Prix. Stan Shenton and Ken Suzuki were still the main team principles. Grant's relationship with Shenton however was by now at a low ebb, and the atmosphere within the squad was tense. Finance was also still an issue, and the previous year John Norman had admitted that the cost of the team Kawasaki race programme was horrendous. He stated at the same time that there would be no thought given to running the team on a similar basis to rivals Suzuki GB, where individual riders were allowed a much freer hand in terms of personal sponsorship. For him it was all about raising brand awareness. Norman believed that racing was a means to an end, to create maximum exposure for the Kawasaki brand. For this reason, he insisted that Kawasaki machines would never arrive on the start line painted in different colours each season. The distinctive lime Green Meanie image had taken time to create, and it was important. Having said that, in 1978 he was not above rebranding the outfit as team Kawasaki Life. This move was in many ways typical of the often dysfunctional set-up within the organisation, in as much as when Kawasaki UK signed the sponsorship agreement with the Italian firm of Life International helmets, they did so without first consulting their riders. For Grant it was particularly galling as he already had a private sponsorship deal with Nava helmets which suited him very well, and he had no desire to swap to Life. He tells us:

> For 1978 I wasn't best pleased when I found out that Shenton had done a deal with Life helmets for a helmet that I didn't feel comfortable with. It just wasn't a nice helmet, it wasn't a nice fit, and I remember there was one shot of me coming over the start line and the helmet is half way up my face and I'm looking over the bottom bit of it. It was a ridiculous thing, and the comical bit of it was I don't think Kawasaki ever got any money for it. [It was] a typical Italian company that said we'll give you whatever, and then never came up with it! I think they went bust in the end.[1]

When Grant refurbished his 1978 Kawasaki racer a few years later, and had the fairing resprayed, he vented his feelings by taking the opportunity to excise any reference to Life helmets that had previously been present. The blue stripe that had been added to the green and white livery as part of the abortive sponsorship deal was also expunged at the same time.

For this season there was a new KR250 and a larger KR350, with engine developments including smaller, steel-caged needle roller bearings replacing the left side brass caged ball main bearings, and there was an aluminium box-section swingarm along with a more aerodynamic seat unit. The swingarm retained the Uni-Trak linkage, and the chrome-molybdenum tubular frame and non-adjustable forks were also retained from the previous version. The KR350 was very similar to the 250, with a bore increase to 64mm giving a cylinder capacity of 349.9cc. The clutch was strengthened, and the carburettor size increased to a Mikuni VM36SS. The claimed power rose to 75bhp at 11,800rpm. However, with many components such as the crankshaft and main bearing shared with the 250, failure of these constituent parts was more likely to be a problem than in the less powerful machine, and indeed during practice for the 1978 TT races the machine would be dogged by persistent seizures.

Grant remembered that in a way, smaller bikes were harder to ride on the Isle of Man because on them the corners could be taken flat out. Whilst it was possible on a 750cc to rush up to corners then brake, creep round them and blast away again down the straights, with a 250cc the objective was to keep it flat-out all the time. On a machine of this type, after each bend the rider should be working out the right approach for the next one, in order to ride the most efficient racing line. By the 1970s, riding a 250 was much like an old Matchless G50 and for him personally, success in the smaller classes gave him if anything more individual satisfaction, because of the skill needed to ride them fast. Switching from one style of racing to another was difficult however, and here riders like American Pat Hennen had an advantage. He was only competing on 500 and 750cc machines, so the racing line for each was broadly the same. Grant by contrast had a 250 and 350cc machine which counted as one class, and a 750cc machine which required a completely different style and approach. In the run up to the 1978 TT he added:

> The 500cc race was won with a 110mph fastest lap last year and I shall be interested to see how fast my 350cc Kawasaki will go in the Senior race this year. I have not raced a 350 in the Island since 1974 when I finished second on Gerald Brown's Yamaha. I'm looking forward to the 250 and 350 rides because, as I said before, I will be able to get on the classic TT lines. Places like the 32nd and 33rd milestone where it's possible to get in a tight fast line, a place like Milntown which to me is not a separate corner but part of a two-mile section that takes you to School House Corner. Get one part wrong and the whole lot's wrong. These sections may look like a three penny bit – that dates me a bit I suppose – but when it comes to racing it has to be one smooth line.[2]

Monday of Race Week saw the Senior TT. In spite of Grant's hopes for it, the 350cc twin cylinder machine had predictably seized a piston at Ballaspur, leaving Suzuki-mounted Tom Herron to take the win, and Mick to walk back down the road to Ballacraine. In the 250cc Junior race, Grant's luck again deserted him on lap three when his machine ran out of fuel on the Mountain. The pit crew were baffled, as mechanic Jim Fitzgerald remarked: 'In practice we tested and found that the machine needed six and a half litres per lap. So we put in enough for three laps and then a one gallon cushion on top of that.'[3]

At first glance it was a puzzling situation, because on the face of it, it meant that that the 250 was more of a gas-guzzler than its much bigger cousin the 750, which had an extra cylinder to feed. However the truth was that one of the mechanics had simply miscalculated the amount of fuel that was needed. In many ways it was typical of the dysfunctional nature of the team by this stage, and it was not the first – or last – time that Grant would be denied a finish by an unnecessary technical problem caused by lack of attention to detail.

The year 1978 as a whole saw the continuing battle between Kawasaki and Yamaha in the big bike category begin to turn in the latter's favour. It was widely acknowledged that the design of the KR750 was now three years out of date. However, there were still to be fireworks aplenty in the 1978 Classic TT – still remembered as one of the greatest ever races some forty-six years later. The interest in this event had been building year on year and 1978 promised an outstanding field – the cream of late 1970s road racing talent in fact. John Williams again on his Suzuki, Mike Hailwood (who had also returned to the TT) on a factory prepared Yamaha, and privateer Tom Herron (also on a Yamaha) who had already won the Senior earlier that week. A young Joey Dunlop, at only his second TT, also lined up on the grid. With them was Grant, on an updated version of the previous year's 750cc Kawasaki triple.

That year's KR750 was a water-cooled two-stroke, three-cylinder machine, first introduced in 1977 but improved upon for 1978. The inline three-cylinder motor featured magnesium crankcases, rather than the more normal aluminium ones, which was bending the rules slightly at the time, whilst the exhaust exited via two hand-crafted pipes on the left, and one to the right. With a race-standard right foot gear change, it achieved 128bhp at 9,500rpm, though the power really started to kick in at about 6,500rpm. Grant remembered that for 80 per cent of the time on the Isle of Man, he did not take it beyond 8,500rpm. If he had taken the machine to maximum revs in every gear, it would actually have been 3mph slower, because there would have been too much power for him to handle. There were places where he would change gear at 8,000rpm, nowhere near the top of the power band, and it would pull nice and softly. In this manner he could tip into a bend, change up and still be accelerating. If he had been going to 9,500rpm on the same corner and giving it stick, the back end would have been bucking. The machine's biggest advantage over its main rivals was still the fact that it was relatively light, giving a good power to weight ratio.

Neat oil went into the big ends via an oil pump, whilst a 32:1 petrol/oil mix went into the fuel tank. However, with oil being splashed about by the big ends, the effective burnt oil ratio was around 25:1. As with all two-strokes, getting the jetting right was crucial. For the TT the carburettors would be set up at Jurby, which was close to sea level, but there was a 2,000 foot variation in height between this and the summit of the Mountain section of the course. It was therefore a fine line between achieving maximum performance and seizing the engine. If the mechanics erred too much on the side of caution the machine would be sluggish on the Mountain section, though some caution was necessary in order to actually finish a race because if the carburettor jetting was too high, the machine had a tendency to seize at the end of Sulby Straight. It was a problem, observed team manager Stan Shenton tersely, that was unique to the Isle of Man and could only be addressed once there. He added:

> On a course like the Isle of Man it is also vital for the rider to get behind the fairing and be streamlined. He has to keep out of the wind and often we raise the screen height. The Isle of Man is a particularly long circuit and a lot of it is taken at very high speed over long periods of time.

> You're probably flat out for four or five minutes at a time, against only seconds on a short circuit, so it is important for the rider to keep out of the wind. Because of this it is desirable to have a screen which gives clear vision without distortion.[4]

The 750's seven-spoke magnesium Morris wheels were originally fitted with twin front 296mm aluminium brake discs and a similar 235mm rear disc, but this latter item was replaced by Kawasaki UK with cast iron rear brakes, which were better suited for racing conditions as they did not melt when hot. Another modification was pure Grant – a half tennis ball secured inside the fairing below the Perspex screen, containing a damp sponge. Grant had once accidentally removed all the tear-offs from his visor at once, and now reasoned that if that should happen again and a large insect should splatter itself on the visor during a race, he could at least slow down and clean it with one hand, which would be safer than racing at speed with limited visibility. Slick tyre technology was in its infancy in the mid-1970s and although Grant went out in the race with a slick on the rear, he still opted for a treaded tyre on the front. The riding position was pure 1970s. The rider sat low down, wedged between the high seat back behind and the petrol tank in front. With his neat riding style, Grant liked to lean with the bike on corners, though the high footrests, positioned as they were more to get them out of the way of the exhausts than to prevent contact with the road, tended to make it difficult to leap or lean off the bike, in the style which Sheene had made so fashionable in that decade. Fellow rider Alan Cathcart wrote:

> I remember [Mick] … as he screamed the Kawasaki past me down into Windy Corner, in 1978 TT practice,

> cranking it over to the right with that unmistakable style, ensconced in the bike without hanging off or allowing his knee to skim the tarmac through what is one of the TT's most short circuitesque corners.[5]

Grant was acutely aware that the weakness which had bedevilled the big Kawasaki on previous outings was the chain, and this year he was taking no chances. During Practice Week he had arranged to meet Vic Doyle of Renold and Mr Villa of Regina at Jurby airfield, and told them that he would use whichever of their products stood up the best to some intensive testing. After thrashing both makes up and down the airfield for half an hour, he was amazed to find that Renold had come up with something that this time could really go the distance – the company had managed to produce a new lubricant which did not break down as the chain got hot. Under testing their chain had not stretched at all, and neither would it do so in the big event at the TT in this era which was the end of Race Week finale, the Open Classic. Sponsored by one of Britain's biggest soft drinks makers at this time, it carried probably the richest prize fund in British motorcycle racing. Mick's remarks at the time betray something of the embarrassment that he felt as a result of the let-down earlier in the week, but also his determination to deliver the goods when it really mattered:

> It's a good job I thrive on pressure, because before the Schweppes Open Classic TT I had more butterflies in my tummy than in any other race this year. Till then the week had been so bad I knew I had to pull something big out of the bag to make everyone's efforts worthwhile. On Monday the 350 Kawasaki hit mechanical problems early on and on Wednesday the 250 machine simply ran

> out of petrol on the third lap; just how or why we do not know. The mechanics assure me that there was enough fuel in the tank at the start of the race to last me three laps and I have no reason to disbelieve them. But the tank ran dry on the Mountain and that meant the little twin was thirstier than my 750, which is hard to swallow. But all that misfortune can be forgotten after the second Classic win in succession.[6]

Later on, he remembered that the event was promoted in the media as a clash between the old master and the new pretender:

> The Classic was billed as a showdown between Mike [Hailwood] and me and, though you generally ignore that sort of hype, I was as fascinated as anyone else by how we'd compare. At the time I had Brian Richards with a signal board at Laurel Bank, which allowed me to get my positions from the commentary post at Ballacraine (it later moved to Glen Helen). As I reached there on the first lap of the Classic, it read 'P1 +0' to Hailwood.[7]

It was, Grant observed ruefully, now becoming an interesting race. On the first lap, Hailwood and Grant were level on time. Hailwood had won the Formula 1 race earlier in the week aboard the Sports Motorcycles Ducati, and was hotly expected to win this outing as well, but this time he was Yamaha-mounted, and the machine was not in the same league as the Ducati. It lost a piston on that first lap, and he was forced to retire. The Yamaha of Tom Herron also developed mechanical problems, and he too fell by the wayside. Only John Williams now presented a serious challenge to Grant, but his 500cc Suzuki RG500 was no match for the bigger engined Kawasaki.

The leader on the ground was Joey Dunlop but Grant passed him at the Bungalow, so he now headed the field both on the road and on time. On his second lap, Grant shattered the outright lap record once again, setting a blistering speed of 114.33mph. His first lap was fast, but a standing start cost him for or five seconds, and the bike had a full tank of fuel, which lost a few more. With the second, he had a flying start and finish, 30 per cent less fuel and he was by now into the swing of the race so it was hardly surprising that this was the quickest. On the third lap he would be slowing down to approach the pits for fuel, and on the fourth he again would have a standing start and a full tank of fuel. By the fifth and sixth laps, he would be thinking about preserving the engine in order to finish the race, or maybe coming in for an additional top up of fuel. He continued:

> It was a hard race and the last few miles were mental torture. After the mid-race fuel stop Nigel Everett, my mechanic, worked out there would be very little left at the end of the race if I didn't stop again. Thanks to a complicated system and the help and co-operation of many people, Kawasaki team manager Stan Shenton out at the Gooseneck was requested to give me a sign on the fifth lap telling me to stop for gas.[8]

But what Stan and everyone else in the pit didn't know however was that, for Grant, on the fourth lap the drama had really begun. As he approached Ballacraine, he became aware of a problem with the back brake. During Practice Week, Grant had had the engine remounted in a new frame made by Ken Sprayson and Ron Williams of Maxton engineering. As the motor was now held more firmly, there was more vibration than usual, and this eventually caused the brake master cylinder to work itself free of the chassis. As he braked coming into the sharp right hander, Grant could feel the cylinder dangling by his left foot. He believed however that he could still hold it safely with his boot, and prevent it from becoming entangled in the chain or catching the wheel – he took a long look whilst out on a straight part of the circuit just to be certain of that. As he later told a post-race press conference, he toyed with the idea of pulling into the pits, but the risk here was that the scrutineers might not let him go out again if he did. Even if he raced on, the fear was that having no rear brake would affect his performance: 'My heart sank because I thought John Williams would be able to catch me. I had to assume a speed that would keep me out of danger but still be quick enough to keep a distance between me and John.'[9]

The rod holding the offending brake cylinder broke completely during the fifth lap and it actually fell off at Parliament Square, but Grant raced on, leaving the bemused Ramsey marshals to pick it up from the road. Fortunately, he was not black flagged for having a dangerous machine. The real conundrum now was what to do about fuel. There was one more pit stop due, but Grant gambled on the fact that he would have enough in the tank to complete the final lap without pulling in, and he eased off the pace slightly to give himself more of a chance. Mechanic Nigel Everett was ready at the Grandstand, fully expecting the rider to come in, but Grant sailed past at 160mph, remembering later:

> Out of the corner of my eye, I could see Nigel stood trembling with this big fuel can and his mouth wide open as I went through flat out in fifth gear. It was comical to see the vacant look on his face. After the race, we found there was a litre and a half left in the tank, which was a bit too close for comfort. I know there was a question of

> me being black flagged and it had been reported around the circuit that something was dangling down, but I think common sense prevailed. No top rider ... will do anything daft, and that includes me. Had I been black flagged I think I might even have carried on, knowing it wasn't dangerous, and argued about it afterwards. It tickled me pink to get safely round at 112 mph without a back brake. It won't be in the record books, but it pleased me to know I could tour round at 112 mph in that state.[10]

Another less well-known problem which dogged Grant throughout the race was an issue with the shock absorbers. He remembered afterwards:

> It was the most bizarre thing ever. It still beggars belief to be honest. We'd got the bike right, we knew we were going to have a dingdong race but the bike was absolutely perfect. I never looked at the bike again, because you have lots of other things to think about. So I set off down Bray Hill; even though in those days the suspension wasn't as good as we have today it just got really bumpy on the run into Ramsey. In practice it had been OK, but now it was kicking me out of the seat. I'm thinking, 'What the hell has happened here?' anyway, eventually when I got back I found out that Girling had convinced Nigel to put these gas units on. Well gas units, I know now, on the compression stroke can jack solid and it was kicking me out of the seat. Although I managed with it, I wasn't best pleased when I got back. To this day I don't know why it happened. They definitely shouldn't have done it.[11]

As the race ended it was Grant first, followed by John Williams and Alex George. Having pocketed the eye-watering cash prize that accompanied this victory, canny Yorkshireman Grant did not forget to collect on another, albeit smaller side wager that he had arranged with another veteran TT campaigner:

> The money for winning the Classic TT was very welcome but it wasn't the only cash I won in the race. Earlier, Formula Three world champion Bill Smith had bet me I would not catch him on the first lap until after Ramsey. I asked him for a sporting chance and suggested the Bungalow. We compromised at the Gooseneck as the winning post in our private duel. The wager was for £50 and I waved as I passed Bill at the top of Begarrow. But you know what motor cycle dealers are like. After the race he offered me 40-per-cent discount for cash and gave me £30.[12]

The new experimental compound which Renold chains had been developing had proved itself to be better able to withstand the rigours of the TT course, and the power of the big bikes. It was the first time that Grant had used this make since it let him down in the 1975 Classic, but the chain had gone the distance this time without stretching at all. After enduring so much drama and indeed danger out on the course, Grant was embarrassed when he dislocated a finger opening the victory champagne! Writing in his regular newspaper column, he concluded:

> Finally, just a word about the 114mph. I am pleased to be back in the record books as the fastest man round the Island but I sometimes think that the press worries too much about record laps at the TT rather than [focussing] on a man winning a race. It's the first past the post that counts and any record laps on a circuit are just a bonus.[13]

Sadly, despite delivery of a new lap record and a prestigious race victory in this, the 100th anniversary year of the company, this great TT win was to be the swansong for Grant's relationship with Kawasaki. The incident with the brake cylinder led to tensions with the team management who were unhappy that Grant had modified the frame, and also implied that the failure was caused by one of his mechanics who had forgotten to screw the cylinder up tightly. For his part, Grant was dismayed to learn of this, commenting later: 'I couldn't see why there had to be any questions asked. We'd done the job which was required, won the big race and set a new lap record as well. How it was achieved should not have mattered as long as it didn't involve cheating.'[14]

Always the smallest of the Japanese manufacturers, the company's limited resources in terms of facilities and manpower, together with the distraction provided by the simultaneous development of the KR250 and 350 twin models, meant that the KR750 was never fully developed as it could have been, and this was another reason for Grant's growing disillusion. The early success which Kawasaki achieved in 1975 had also discouraged them from putting in the effort required to stay on top in the following years. What had started out as a revolutionary and highly advanced machine was ultimately superseded, as rivals Suzuki and Yamaha regained their advantage.

There were also other wider issues developing within the team. Grant felt afterwards that he was at the peak of his abilities at this time, and a World Championship was realistically achievable, were it not for the fact that Shenton had teamed him with a new mechanic with whom he did not gel. Race after race resulted in frustrating (and often avoidable) mechanical failures. After an otherwise disappointing season, Grant was by now ready to part ways with Kawasaki if the company did not come up with a redesigned engine that could keep pace with the big bike competition. By the end of 1978, for him the fun of riding for Kawasaki had gone. Yet Grant was of the opinion that if things hadn't been so sour there on a personal level, he probably would have stayed. He really wanted Kawasaki to bring out a new 500cc machine, and yet the irony was that when they eventually brought out the 500 that Kork Ballington rode in Grands Prix in the early 1980s, Grant felt that it was not a particularly good bike, and that Ballington did well to get the results that he did on it. By September 1978 there was speculation that if Barry Sheene moved into car racing as he had hinted that he would, then Grant might be offered the resulting vacant seat at Herron Suzuki. It must have been a tempting prospect, and he was quoted in the press as saying: 'I must have something competitive for the big bike classes, the 500cc and 750cc, next season and I must leave myself open to offers.'[15]

In the event it was not Suzuki who came up with the most attractive offer for the 1979 season, but Honda. The company had been out of top flight motorcycle competition for more than a decade and the package that they now offered Mick was an attractive one. It included the latest Honda machinery for the TT, and the chance to travel to Japan to participate in the development of Honda's NR (New Racer) project, through which they planned a triumphant return to 500cc Grand Prix racing. Grant recalled:

> At the time I was making my decision to sign for Honda, I don't think Kawasaki thought I'd leave. When I did break the news, I think they were very surprised. Obviously, we had our ups and downs, but over the four years I reckon it was a very good partnership. The 750 was a fabulous machine to ride. It may not have been the quickest or the

> best handling bike in racing, but the memories made me sad to see the end of our partnership. If Kawasaki had produced the machines to continue the challenge, I would have thought seriously about staying.[16]

Grant went on to have more TT success with other marques, and the 750cc machine passed into the hands of former Kawasaki team mate Barry Ditchburn, who campaigned it in 1979. However when Kawasaki allowed Ditchburn to keep it at the end of that season, Grant was able to buy it from him. He retained the 1978 Classic TT winning Kawasaki as part of his personal collection for many years, lovingly maintaining and caring for it, until in 2024 it passed into the hands of a collector in the United States. The machine is still in running order, although Mick was always careful to impose an 8,500rpm rev limit on those few apart from himself whom he allowed to ride it, in deference to the forty-year-old crank. Never the less he had fond memories of a machine which was well-suited to the undulating Mountain Course:

> What made the Kawasaki so good in the Island was the fact that it had power low down and so instead of going round on the back wheel for a lot of the time under fierce acceleration it would pull nice and steadily all the time. You could always change gear well below maximum revs.[17]

With an impressive competition history, an iconic rider and a pedigree as an exceptionally rare works racer, being one of only a handful built by the factory, the 1978 Grant Kawasaki 750 is also unquestionably one of the greatest ever TT motorcycles, and represents the pinnacle of Kawasaki's achievement on the Island in that decade. Aside from its TT performance, it is arguably among the greatest solo machines of the 1970s British racing scene, also having a host of other competitive achievements to its name. It was almost joined in the Grant historic racing stable by another of the Green Meanies, had it not been for an accidental slip of the tongue, as he recounts:

> Despite jumping ship, I came agonisingly close to getting an accidental farewell bonus from Kawasaki. The KR750s had spent the previous season at my home in Lepton, where Nigel had looked after them. At the end of the season Nigel took two of them down to Bromley in the van, telling the team he'd be back the following week with the other one.
>
> 'What other one?' they asked. If we'd kept our mouths shut we could have kept it and they'd have been none the wiser.[18]

Mick Grant remains one of those few successful TT riders who it can be legitimately said have put more into the TT than they got out of it. His greatest achievement is perhaps not measured in race wins but in the fact that for some twenty-five years he was able to make a successful living as a professional motorcycle racer. It is important to state however that for him it was not about the money. Such was his love for the sport that he would have done it for nothing, if he could have. Yet in doing what he did he helped to make the Kawasaki brand a household name, certainly in the United Kingdom, and he played more than his fair part in keeping the TT alive at a critical time, when many people questioned whether it still had a future without Grand Prix status. As for Kawasaki themselves, few in Britain could argue with the company when they claimed that through racing, the brand's following in this country had grown year by year. The green and white team livery was instantly recognisable and even where victory was lacking, the team had earned both respect and support through their commitment and the ferocity of their challenge at virtually every important motorcycle meeting.

The TT was evolving and changing however, and the late 1970s had seen the flourishing of the Formula 1 class on the Isle of Man. The event was part of a World Championship series, and had been granted to the TT organisers by the sport's governing body, the FIM, to soften the blow of the loss of Grand Prix status. It catered for four-stroke motors from 600 to 1,000cc, and was immediately attractive to the Japanese factories as a shop window for their big engine machines. In 1978 Scottish rider Ian Richards finished third in the Formula 1 TT aboard a P&M (Peckett and McNab) framed Kawasaki Z1000, constructed by legendary frame-builder Richard Peckett. The partnership was formed in 1975 when Peckett and Peter McNab (who had worked together at Dresda Autos) began designing and building bike frames together, as well as modifying existing ones. Starting in Twickenham, they soon moved to an industrial estate in Brentford as the business grew. Their first frame was raced by Richard in 1976, and he started winning regularly on it the following year. As well as obtaining good race results for himself, the reputation of the company began to grow when other riders began to have success on them, as well as Richard's podium place on the Isle of Man. Their frames were now attracting attention across the British racing scene among privateers and the smaller teams, and later that year an as yet unknown Kiwi named Graeme 'Croz' Crosby made an impression on one, whilst acting as a replacement for an injured rider at a UK short circuit race. He was luke-warm about the machine however, remembering: 'I'd look at bikes like the P&Ms which were nice but they didn't have that feral-ness ... The English set their bikes up traditionally, so they didn't have that ability to flick left and right.'[19]

Racing fans adored Crosby for his speed on the track, and his devil may care antics off it. He was the first to arrive at any party (indeed he would probably be the one to start it) and usually the last to leave. The following year, 1979 saw his first appearance at the TT. The up and coming New Zealander entered two races at that year's meeting aboard a Moriwaki tuned machine. Mamoru Moriwaki had founded Moriwaki Engineering in Suzuka City, Japan in 1973, and he became best known for his work in modifying engines and constructing frames for the Kawasaki Z1. Crosby and co-rider Tony Hatton had first ridden for Moriwaki at the 1978 Suzuka 8 Hours race, the most prestigious event on the Japanese domestic calendar, where they finished in third place. Many years later he recalled this debut, and the Moriwaki Kawasaki:

> I could not believe how fast and stable it was. First time out I was two seconds under the lap record. The bike was a real cracker. Tony Hatton and I then rode the bike in the 1978 Suzuka eight-hour race and finished in third position, despite Tony running out of gas and having to push it back to the pit area. We had a ball. The bike formed the building block for my attack on the UK racing scene in '79 and I stuck a similar one on pole for the Suzuka race in that year too.[20]

His bikes had also been successfully raced in the Australian Superbike Championships in the late 1970s by Crosby, and this led to a continuing association between the two. Moriwaki's reputation continued to be enhanced when Crosby and Akitaka Tomie qualified a Moriwaki Kawasaki on pole position at the 1979 Suzuka 8 Hours, ahead of all the major factory racing

Above: The Kawasaki Ki 61, the most advanced Japanese fighter plane of the Second World War, and the only one with an inline liquid cooled engine. (Public Domain)

Below: Bill Smith in the 1968 Lightweight TT. (Fottofinders Bikesport Archives)

Above: The 250cc Kawasaki used in the 1968 Lightweight TT by New Zealander Ian Veitch. (Courtesy of Paul Ingham)

Below: Dave Simmonds (on ground) before the 1969 Ultra Lightweight TT. Brother-in-law Mick Boddice sits on the bike. This would be Kawasaki's first TT win. (Courtesy of Ken Sprayson)

Above: The start of the 1969 Lightweight TT. Kel Carruthers (Benelli) no 1, Dave Simmonds (Kawasaki) no 2. At this time the famous green livery was still a year in the future. (Courtesy of Ken Sprayson)

Right: Bill Smith aboard a Kawasaki, in the now familiar green paint scheme, after the 1970 Senior TT. He finished third. (Courtesy of Ken Sprayson)

Above: Keith Martin aboard the Kawasaki Mach III on which he won the 1974 500cc Production TT. (Fottofinders Bikesport Archives)

Below: Mick Grant aboard the Boyer Kawasaki 750, 1974 TT. (Author's Collection)

Above left: The 1975 Kawasaki Christmas card. Aboard the Reindeer are Grant, Ditchburn, and chief mechanic Rod Scivyer. John Norman of Kawasaki UK and race team boss Stan Shenton stand to the side. (Courtesy of Mick Grant)

Above right: Mick Grant in the 1975 Senior, the width of the machine evident from this angle. (Vic Barnes)

Below: Grant in the 1976 Senior. The 500cc H1-RW featured a 750 front end and oversized fuel tank, which made for difficult handling. (Fottofinders Bikesport Archives)

Above: Grant airborne at Ballaugh, 1977 Classic TT. (Courtesy of Mick Grant)

Below: Mick Grant in the 1978 Junior TT. (Courtesy of Manx National Heritage PG/14641/70)

Right: A close-up of the 1978 750cc machine shows the blue line added to the fairing design through the abortive deal with Life helmets. (Author's Collection)

Below: The 1978 Grant KR750 as it appears today. After acquiring it, Grant removed any reference to Life helmets from the fairing. (Author's Collection)

Above: Graeme Crosby, 1979 Formula 1 TT aboard the Moriwaki Kawasaki. (Fottofinders Bikesport Archives)

Below: George Oates and John Molyneux, Kawasaki powered at the 1977 TT. (Courtesy of Dave Molyneux)

teams. It would be something of an understatement to say that the genial New Zealander's impact on the UK racing scene in 1979 caused a stir. At a time when a full body kit fairing and clip-on handlebars were considered essential elements for a racing motorcycle, his was a bike wearing normal handlebars, ridden by an unknown from 'down under' sitting in an upright position, that immediately had the measure of the home-grown stars. Only a motocross machine winning the Senior TT would have caused more of a stir. Crosby explained the rationale of the machine later:

> We only had the high bars because we were aiming towards the new Daytona Superbike race and because proddie [production-based] racing was big at home – all clanging handlebars, scraping side covers and lots of crashes, that's what the audience liked. [21]

He also admitted that he had a great deal of affection for the Japanese marque:

> I have got a lot of feeling for Kawasaki because they are a smaller concern with a smaller number of machines being raced that immediately gives a positive identity for a rider. They just do not seem to realise the strong position they have in racing because they also have a solid background in this branch of the sport having always produced successful racing machines. They gave me identity through the high bar machine.[22]

Initially he had not intended to contest a full season of the British TT Formula 1 Championship in 1979; in fact, he had come over from New Zealand with the Isle of Man TT as the main item on his agenda. Newcomers are usually expected to compete at the Manx Grand Prix before tackling the TT proper, but a letter written on his behalf by Mike Hailwood, who had seen him ride in New Zealand and Australia, got Croz a direct entry into the main event. He recalled:

> I'd always wanted to do the TT, it's an icon race. I didn't feel it'd be too dangerous because I'd always been street riding and street racing. It was Mike Hailwood who helped us get a start. He was living in New Zealand and used to watch a few races. I was just a hairy-assed kid, but we used to go to his place, talk about the TT and spill red wine all over the carpets, much to his wife's dismay.[23]

His Isle of Man debut was just as astonishing as his Suzuka performance. The naturally talented New Zealander brought his Moriwaki Kawasaki home in fourth place in the Formula 1 race at an average speed of 107.39mph. The yellow and blue 120bhp Z1000 was a wolf in (rather grubby) sheep's clothing. It looked tatty but in fact was as fast as the latest Honda 1,000cc machines. Both engine and chassis were the handiwork of Moriwaki, the former had been strengthened with Z650 valve buckets, replacing the stock tappets, and solid cam chain tensioners, replacing the standard auto tensioners. The carbs were 31mm Keihin smooth bores, ignition was by a total loss system and the crank end was sawn off for additional ground clearance. The chassis had also been tweaked and strengthened, and included revised geometry, Z650 triple clamps, lengthened Moriwaki swingarm and Kayaba racing forks and shocks. Ironically, one of the established riders who Croz outpaced in that race was the very same Hailwood who had given him a reference, now making his farewell appearance. In the opinion of *Motor Cycle News*, Croz was the sensation of the event. The newspaper described the way in which he appeared to be a lonely figure as his carved his way through the field under a Manx sky heavy with cloud; he overtook riders right, left and centre, despite the fact that his foot slipped off an oily footrest several times, after his engine breather came adrift. Unfortunately, bad luck struck in the Classic TT, his bike expiring on the mountain with a holed piston.

The swansong for Kawasaki UK's involvement in racing on the Isle of Man in this era came at the 1980 250cc Junior TT. There was no factory team actually present at this event, but they did provide Kent's Chas Mortimer with a twin-cylinder Grand Prix machine which had previously been campaigned on short circuits by Kork Ballington. Mortimer had a long association with the TT having previously ridden Yamaha machinery through much of the 1970s, and had five wins to his credit at this point. Of the Kawasaki he remembered:

> The bike was not good around the TT course, as we discovered. It was built for Grand Prix racing and in every practice session that we went out in something broke. It was just too flimsy for the TT course. On the very first practice session going down Bray Hill, at Ago's Leap the front wheel came down and the steering damper came away, it pulled the bracket out of the frame and I got into a huge tank slapper. After that we had a broken exhaust pipe, broken exhaust pipe bracket, and so on. All through the week we just couldn't get the set up right either and, in the end, it was no quicker than a [Yamaha] TZ250.[24]

During the race itself, it was a fuel stop on lap three which ended Mortimer's hopes on the works Kawasaki, after he got up to third position before pulling in, just three seconds behind second place man Steve Tonkin. During his pit stop a fault in the refuelling gear forced the valve of the refuelling nozzle and the side valve on the tank to stay open, with disastrous effects. Mortimer was splashed with petrol and frantically wiped his visor while his helpless crew sprayed everyone in the close vicinity. He set off again, but fuel was still pouring out of the tank and beginning to burn his skin. He was finally forced to pull in and retire at Quarter Bridge. At the time, he had not expected the machine to complete the race, but on reflection he felt that were it not for the fuel mishap it might well have finished, as it was now running much better than in practice.

If it was the end of the road for Grand Prix-based motorcycles at the TT, then this was more than compensated for by the increasing Kawasaki involvement with the Formula 1 race, with machines typically now entered by small dealer-based teams or similar. In 1980, Oxford Fairings entered three Kawasakis. That ridden by Les Burgan from Meriden in Warwickshire was a previous year's model. It featured a pressed together crankshaft which had been argon arc welded to prevent it slipping out of alignment under the extra stresses of racing components. It also included Yoshimura Bonneville camshafts and Yoshimura single compression ring slipper pistons for less piston to cylinder friction. The cylinder head was ported and underwent valve seat modifications by sidecar grass tracker and tuner Paul Pinfold from Coventry.

A total loss Boyer ignition system was fitted, and this required battery recharge after each race. The gearbox was a Kawasaki close ratio racing unit and the exhaust system was by Peckett and McNab, as were the frame and fairing. Spondon 38mm forks were fitted at the front whilst at the back were Girling gas rear shocks. The front brakes were 'borrowed' from a TZ750 Yamaha, whilst the wheels were CMA. In 1980 the rules for this class were slightly updated to allow upgraded carburettors as well as extra engine tuning and custom exhausts. Before the TT Burgan's machine was test-ridden by *Motor Cycle Mechanics* features editor Brian Crichton, who pronounced himself impressed with the smooth and strong power delivery from the four-cylinder engine, which was capable of delivering 95bhp at the back wheel. He continued:

> It would have been reasonable to anticipate the motor to have a very tight power band. Instead it pulled well from 3,000–10,000 on the Smiths magnetic rev counter with best power available from 5,000–8,000rpm. The machine's phenomenal acceleration … took a lot of getting used to, as did the high footrest riding position, and reversed gear lever and hence reversed gear change pattern. An error in this department was swiftly pointed out by the back wheel trying to overtake the front! Settling down to get used to the machine involved a lot of initial over-reaction. Because the acceleration felt so much more pronounced than on a standard 1,000cc road bike I was shutting off too early for the corner and over braking with a lot of rear wheel hop as a result. The riding picture became clearer as I relied almost totally on the front anchors and engine braking to slow the machine down and stayed put in the seat rather than try to slide from one side to the other.
>
> It was amazing to find that first gear could be used to exit [very tight corners] without wheel slip or wheelies. This flexible machine felt safe, secure and swift. The ride was hard but the handling was rock steady and the more that was asked of it, it seemed the more there was in hand. Suddenly there were no straights any more. The extra speed, handling and ground clearance available meant that corners were cranked into earlier and the machine had to be kept over as the power drifted it out of a corner. It was definitely a test of formula fun from Formula One.[25]

There was also a huge surge in interest in production-based racing at the TT, which really took off at the start of the 1980s. The revived Production TT was now a highlight of the Race Week schedule, and all of the 'Big Four' Japanese factories keenly contested the three-lap event on the Island. Kawasaki machines continued to finish in top six positions in production-based classes on the Isle of Man for the much of the early part of the decade, with a highlight being North Yorkshire rider Geoff Johnson's win in the 1984 Production 1,500 TT (Open Class), also setting a new lap and race record in the process, with a GPZ900R; born in 1952 in Richmond, Johnson made his living as a bus driver in the early days before coming to prominence at his local tracks including Croft. He soon became a professional rider; remembered as a straight-talking and suave Yorkshireman with an eye for a good deal and a pay packet to suit, in the paddocks he was affectionately nicknamed 'moneybags'.

The GPZ900R was the first of the famous Ninja line of racing motorcycles, indeed Johnson's machine was the first Ninja anywhere in the world to achieve a major race win, only weeks after the model was launched in the United States. Like its predecessor the Z1, the model had a long gestation period, Kawasaki having realised in the late 1970s that the Z series was coming to the end of its life span. In a time before computer testing, each element was assessed on road and track, which necessitated a long lead-in time. The Ninja was developed in secret over six years, and was a revolutionary design, being Kawasaki's and the world's first motorcycle equipped with a sixteen-valve liquid-cooled inline four-cylinder engine. The 908cc four-cylinder engine was smaller in capacity than most of its rivals, but made up for this through higher revs; it delivered 115bhp, making it the first stock road bike to exceed 150mph. Although prior to its design, Kawasaki had envisioned producing a sub-litre engine that would be the successor to the Z1, they can have had no idea how wildly successful it would be. Although its steel frame, 16-inch front and 18-inch rear wheels, air suspension, and anti-dive forks were fairly standard at that time, and water cooling and four-valve heads were not new, the GPZ was the first with both in an inline design. Putting the cam chain on the end of the engine helped to keep it narrow. This slimmer, compact engine was also mounted lower in the frame, without compromising ground clearance, which brought the centre of gravity down and allowed it to take Japanese superbike performance to a new level. The GPZ900R was famously featured in the 1986 movie *Top Gun,* being ridden by the character of 'Maveric' (played by Tom Cruise) and thus became something of a cultural icon. At the same time, it set a new standard for the Japanese motorcycle industry as a whole.

The machine ridden by Johnson was owned and sponsored by Kawasaki dealer Mike Grainger of GT Motorcycles, and its story begins in late 1983. It was then that Grainger received a phone call from Manchester based bike tuner, Barry Gannon. The long and short of the call was that Barry wanted Mike to provide Johnson with a Honda VF1000RR for the 1984 Production TT. Being a solely a Kawasaki dealer, Mike was unable to supply a Honda, but instead offered to lend Geoff one of the all new Kawasaki GPZ900s that were due to arrive in the UK at the start of the new year. A deal was agreed and when the new GPZ hit the shores of Britain in May of 1984, Mike registered a bike and clocked up 1,000 miles on the road, in a bid to help run it in ahead of the TT.

The bike was then shipped off to Barry Gannon and prepped to the prevailing production rules. In a clever, yet legal modification to the bike, the concentric was turned around on the rear wheel in order to gain the bike more rear ride height.

The tyres were changed to 150/18 profile Metzelers, which also helped raise ride height, while giving the bike a smaller contact patch in a straight line, thus saving fuel, reducing friction and increasing the gearing. The bike was ready and so was Geoff, even though he'd not had chance to practice on the machine. A number of the new GPZ900s had been entered into the Production class and they were soon taking the island by storm, topping the time sheets and blowing the opposition out of the water during Practice Week.

Geoff had yet to win a TT, but confident with the package underneath him, there was no better a time for him to pursue that elusive first victory. With the start of the 1984 Production TT under way, history was being made as Geoff fought his way to the head of the field, battling off challenges from fellow GPZ mounted rider Barry Woodland, who had initially pulled away from the drop of the clutch with a twenty-one second lead, while the established stars, the likes of Steve Parrish and Mick Grant, trailed the leaders. Johnson was touching speeds approaching 151mph through the traps, whilst Woodland hit trouble when he overshot his pit for a refuelling stop, losing over a minute. He also had problems with overheating – the water in his machine's cooling system boiled, and the indicator went off the temperature dial, forcing him to slow down. Geoff managed to hammer home a convincing win over the three-lap-affair, with a record race speed of 105.28mph. Barry Woodland finished second and Howard Selby, who was also racing a GPZ, completing the podium. At the end of the race Johnson told reporters that it was a:

> Perfect ride. Not so quick up the Mountain on the last lap. Only a few slides, particularly where the sun had begun to melt the tar. My moment was at Brandish, where I made the spectators lift their legs over the bank in a hurry when

> I ran wide. This race shows that on equal bikes, I can hold my own with anyone.[26]

Following examination in Parc Ferme however, Barry Woodland's Kawasaki was suspended from the results for an infringement of the rules; as all of the first three machines home were of the same model, it gave the scrutineers an opportunity to look at them side by side, and the result was revealing. Chief scrutineer Eddie Carter later commented: 'There were three bikes, so we did a comparison. We found a difference in the texture in the ports [on Woodland's machine].'[27]

Woodland told the scrutineers that the head had been changed under warranty because swarfe had scored the camshaft bearings; as the heads were in short supply in the UK at the time Kawasaki's Randall Thomas, who was on the Island to help the scrutineers with technical aid, had one flown in from the Continent. Despite the head still having black paint in the ports, the slight difference in finish was enough to catch the attention of the technical inspectors. Carter continued: 'We are not sure what condition the latest heads are supplied in for warranty claims.'[28]

Woodland for his part admitted to feeling depressed at the development:

> I can't dispute it, the tracts feel smoother, though they're still painted. I got annoyed when they measured the ports and said they were 0.02mm larger. That's nothing. Randall says the head is standard so it must be OK. From my point of view I fixed it up for a friend to buy the bike at trade from Kawasaki through dealers Motorcycle HQ near Heathrow. I'm just sick that some people seemed to be looking to make an example of somebody to show how tough they were.[29]

He lodged a protest at his exclusion with the ACU at the prize presentation that evening, and the result was in doubt for several days pending an investigation by chief scrutineer Carter. The following week he took a trip to Kawasaki's Slough base to compare the cylinder head with those of the stock models there. After this, it was deemed to be illegal through having a modified inlet porting, even though the head had been taken from factory stock, and Woodland was thus disqualified from the results. This had the outcome of promoting Honda rider Peter Linden up into third place, robbing Kawasaki of a Grand Slam. Despite this setback, the Kawasaki hierarchy still had plenty of reason to party, as Jack Gow had now also been promoted up to fifth, meaning they still had three GPZ finishers inside the top five.

Second placed rider in this race, Howard Selby, was from North Berwick. He had been involved in the auto industry since leaving school and had gained experience over the years in both cars and motorbikes. He spent ten years working locally as a mechanic, before becoming a professional racing motorcyclist. With a passion for the sport, he competed in many competitions across Europe with a number of accolades under his belt including winning the Scottish Championship three times, reaching the top three in the British Championships and achieving success at the Isle of Man TT races. He would go on to become the European 600cc Supersport Champion in 1990. Throughout his career building and tuning his own engines was one of his specialities. He told reporters after the race: 'I was worried about the fuel situation on the last lap. I got a sweat on when the gauge went to "E" but there turned out to be plenty of juice left.'[30]

After Johnson's victory Grainger continued to ride the winning bike on the road for a time, and also using it at several sprints, before retiring it as its significance became more widely appreciated. The machine now remains on long term display at Grainger's Exeter showroom. He remembered some years later: 'Geoff was not simply a sponsored rider but a very close friend; [it was] an historic win that was to become a cornerstone of the Ninja legend.'[31]

He went on:

> We saw a chance and took it ... Geoff Johnson was reckoned to be one of the best riders of the time racing production bikes, so we taped over the indicator lenses, took the main stand off for more ground clearance and did any modifications that were allowed under the rules.[32]

To win a TT on a machine which has been built specifically for the race is hard enough, but Johnson's achievement was all the greater on a bike which had come straight from the showroom, and is a testament to the fact that Kawasaki got the design of the Ninja right from the outset. Initially it was branded as 'Ninja' in the American market only (another option was the title 'Panther' but history will show that the correct decision was taken). Soon the evocative name that conjured up an image of cutting-edge performance had spread across the globe, and the name 'Ninja' is now attached to many Kawasaki machines. The iconic GPZ900R was the predecessor of today's fast, big-capacity sport bikes, adding technology from the race track to a street bike in a way that hadn't been witnessed before. The simple explanation for its success was that the GPZ was designed from the outset to not only be monumentally powerful, but to cradle that power in a slim, light, strong and compact rolling chassis. For that reason its all-new engine was water-cooled with a cam drive on the right-hand side of the cylinder for extreme narrowness. It was also helped by the fact that it boasted state of the art suspension, brakes and aerodynamics.

In the same event the following year Bill Simpson's was the highest placed Kawasaki, just 3.8 seconds behind winner Geoff Johnson (who had now switched to Honda machinery). The weather that day was variable, with pouring rain in Ramsey and sun at Ballacraine, but the Production TT turned out to be the most exciting event in Race Week. Every class was tight, and each road bike was a handful to ride at race speeds. At the beginning the Honda and Kawasaki were neck and neck; indeed Johnson had been dicing for second place with Selby, his rival from the previous year; he later told reporters that he felt if he passed Selby too early in the race, it would be to his advantage, but by lap three he was slowing him down on corners, and decided to pull the pin. In fact, Selby's Kawasaki had the speed advantage over the Honda in a straight line, but lacked acceleration out of the bends; by the end of three laps, the latter machine had come out on top. The race had the look of a Kawasaki benefit however, with machines from that factory filling seven of the top ten places. Simpson's late charge was slowed in the last few miles when he became involved in a dice on the road with fourth-place man Dennis Ireland. Simpson was a motorcycle dealer from Dumfries, a top-level racer who won five Scottish Championships and took a joint TT win with Chas Mortimer in the punishing ten-lap Production TT of 1976. He was a gifted engineer to boot.

The GPZ900R was so well made that it was later sold alongside newer, much more advanced Kawasaki models that emerged from the Japanese manufacturer. Indeed, it remained in production in Japan until 2003. The development of the Ninja was the third instance in which Kawasaki engineers had broken the mould for high performance road-going motorcycles, following as it did in the tyre tracks of first the

Mach III, and latterly the Z1. The contribution of these three iconic models, and their racing derivatives, to the history of the Isle of Man TT races cannot be over stated.

By 1986, Suzuki had regained some of the ground it had lost, and the Production A race that year was dominated by their machinery. There was some joy for Kawasaki however in the Production class C event in which Gary Padgett and Malcolm Wheeler fought a breathtaking duel for supremacy. This class, for 250–400cc two-strokes and 401–600cc four-strokes, was new to the TT in 1986, and veteran Wheeler was mounted aboard a Kawasaki GPZ600R. This Kawasaki model (also named the Ninja 600) was the one that really kicked off the 600cc sports bike sector, also known as the 'Supersport' class in racing. Although it shared a number of features with its bigger 900cc brother, the Ninja 600 was far from being simply a scaled-down version of it, and was very much a motorcycle in its own right. The GPZ600R was launched in 1985 and was the first of a new breed. It featured a 592cc four-stroke, liquid-cooled, inline four, sixteen-valve engine making a claimed 75bhp – an engine configuration now synonymous with the 600cc sports bike class. The bottom half of the motor came virtually straight off the air-cooled GPZ550, but from the cylinders up it was all new, and with liquid cooling and four valves per cylinder added to the mix. The 550 unit had actually been very successful in Production racing; it had an exceptional reputation for reliability and many tuners claimed that this was one of the toughest engines that Kawasaki ever built. The new liquid-cooled unit continued this bullet-proof reputation. A well-designed fairing also helped it to obtain impressive top speed numbers, although power delivery was flat and uninspiring below 8,000rpm, and the little rush that took place from there on up to 11,000rpm was too little too late to be really exciting. The seating position was very racy, with the low bars a long reach beyond the fuel tank and a seat well dished down behind the fuel tank. Sixteen-inch wheels were all the rage at the time, and despite the bike being quite low and the engine fairly wide, Kawasaki had managed to equip it with good cornering clearance. In an echo of the earlier KR750, for the first two years of its existence the GPZ600R had the field pretty much to its self as rivals struggled to compete, however it was a victim of its own success as thereafter Honda, Yamaha and Suzuki came back with improved Supersport models of their own.

In the race, having started together on the roads, Padgett edged away from Wheeler initially to lead by 4.6 seconds at the end of the first lap, when they both pitted for fuel. That allowed Steve Linsdell to take control to the tune of 5.2 seconds by the end of lap two. However, he had to slow to conserve fuel and this in turn allowed Padgett and Wheeler, who had now closed back up, to go head to head over the final lap; they now fought out a short-circuit-type battle, swapping the lead a couple of times on the last run home; at Hillberry, with just a couple of miles to go, Wheeler passed Padgett and stole his line on the way out of the bend. He thought that he had the race in the bag at that point, but Padgett was having none of that. He made up ground through Cronk-ny-Mona and then managed to out-brake Wheeler at Signpost. Wheeler had no answer to this in the few tricky corners which remained between Signpost and the finish line, and at the flag the Padgett's Suzuki held just a one-second advantage over Wheeler's Kawasaki after 113.19 miles of racing. Padgett told reporters after the race that Wheeler was like a shadow just behind him for much of the distance, one moment on his right, the next on his left. For the Kawasaki rider, his maiden victory still eluded him. He told journalists, 'When I finally win one, I'll pack it in.'[33]

The race marked the conclusion of an astonishing twenty-year spell in which Kawasaki had gone from being almost unknown at the Isle of Man TT, to being one of the most eye-catching and technically brilliant manufacturers to compete there. As one rider commented, there were always fewer Kawasakis on the grid, and that alone set them apart from the other makes; but aside from this they were true innovators, who never simply copied what the other Japanese factories were doing. Instead, they sought their own path, and aimed to produce engines that were bigger, faster and better than anything else that the opposition had. It is fair to say that some of the greatest moments in TT history were provided by the machines in green, and those who rode them.

Chapter Seven

SIDECAR SUNSET 1973–1986

Although the Kawasaki brand is synonymous with solo racing in the 1970s, it is an often overlooked fact that the marque also powered sidecar outfits at the Isle of Man TT in this era. The crucial difference between the two however was that in sidecar racing there was little or no direct influence from the factory hierarchy in Japan; nor was there every any sort of official team. Development work was firmly in the hands of private individuals or at best small independent engineering works. Whilst it would certainly be fair to say that the Yamaha TZ engine was the weapon of choice for most sidecar drivers at the TT from the early 1970s onward, at the same time a small though significant minority pioneered the use of Kawasaki 900cc engines during the same period. One of the first to switch to the marque was Birmingham rider Mick Boddice who used Kawasaki power at the TT in 1973; he remembered that at the time, the BSA motors that had been his mainstay in the 1960s were coming to the end of their life, but a family connection led him to an innovative new power source:

> Dave Simmonds was my brother-in-law. He only rode his H1R once, at Brands, it handled so badly. So, there was this Kawasaki engine lying about, and I did reasonably well on that. But it wasn't really a good sidecar motor, though more powerful than most things.[1]

The 500cc triple-cylinder motor allowed Boddice (with passenger Kenny Williams in the chair) to achieve a highly creditable fourth place in the 1973 750cc sidecar TT. At first he was a lone voice, but by 1976 with the increase in capacity of the sidecar class at the Isle of Man TT from 750 to 1,000cc, others also began to take up this make of engine. On the street bike scene things were also evolving rapidly, and as road bikes were the main source of powerplants for sidecar outfits at this time, that change was bound to be reflected at the TT. From the late 1960s Kawasaki had been developing a four-cylinder four-stroke 750cc machine. Production of the resulting Z1 had begun in 1972 but in order to stay ahead of rivals Honda, the displacement had now been increased to 903cc. The Z1 was hailed later as the world's first superbike. It was arguably the most significant model that Kawasaki has ever made, and it was to be the bike that changed the company's whole direction as far as production road-going motorcycles were concerned. It was air-cooled, and was the first production motorcycle to feature double overhead camshafts. It had full instrumentation and an electric start, produced 82bhp and had a maximum speed of 130 to 132mph. The bike was noted for its smoothness, steady acceleration and stability, though it was heavy at 542lbs. It was not long before this engine and its successors began to appear in numbers on race tracks. In 1976 the Z1 was replaced by the Z900, widely acknowledged as the most powerful road bike then available. Manx competitors George Oates and John Molyneux were Kawasaki powered in both 1976 and 1977, having purchased a brand new Z1 road bike specifically to obtain the engine. At this time, the main advantage of the Kawasaki over its Yamaha rival was an economic one. The Kawasaki was around a third of the price of its fellow Japanese competitor, with a new Yamaha TZ750 engine coming in at around £3,000 (almost £20,000 in current terms). All of the set up and preparation work on the engine was carried out by Molyneux, whose day job was as a mechanic. The results obtained by the Oates/Molyneux pairing in 1976 were disappointing but the Sidecar A race in the following year's TT saw them bring their home-built 900cc machine back in seventh place, arguably the best result for a Kawasaki engined outfit in this era. Oates, from Ballamodha, Isle of Man and Molyneux from Jurby (also on the Island) would be forced to retire in Race B with fuel pump trouble. Both sadly died in a racing accident later that year, at the Ulster Grand Prix.

Between 1979 and 1980 another Manx driver, Eric Bregazzi, and his passenger Jimmy Creer made use of Kawasaki power at the TT, the former remembering of the big Z900 four-strokes:

> The Kawasaki was a good, robust engine. I wished I'd never switched to Yamaha, going from four strokes to two strokes, it was a disaster. I wish I'd never done that. All we did it for was to gain a few miles an hour. I wished I still had the Kawasaki, the Yamaha was more of a headache. I had the Kawasaki up to a really high spec. I had a close ratio box for it, it was Yoshimura, full cams, everything, high compression pistons. I used Yoshimura tuning parts, which you could add to a standard engine if you could get the bits. I got Boyer ignition on it, that was good, it did away with the points thing because that was electronic, I had two batteries in parallel, that gave me more ignition power so it would last for the three laps. Then I decided to go Moriwaki because we got in with [Graeme] Crosby and all that lot. It's only a marketing thing this stuff, they're all much of a muchness, there was Yoshimura, there was Moriwaki, and there was something else. Action Fours was cams, some gave you a massive lift but they weren't as tractable. That thing was like a turbine, it was great, it had loads of torque. I could take my hands off going up to Ballahutchin, I just used to let it float it was steering so

> well, and it was only a homemade frame. Keith Griffin welded it all up. The engine came out of a road bike, a Z9. You had to get different gaskets, and pistons, it was quite an expensive job in those days. But it was reliable. I used to run it on Castrol R, and I used to change the oil twice a year, that was all. The Yamahas were a couple of miles an hour faster, and yet there were a couple of guys on Kawasakis that were doing very well.[2]

Mamoru Moriwaki's work on Kawasaki engines had been brought to widespread attention of the TT fraternity following Greame Crosby's outstanding debut performance aboard one of his machines in 1979. However some sidecar racers felt that, if anything the Moriwaki engines, capable of producing up to 135bhp, were actually too powerful for their purposes. Moriwaki's father-in-law was Hideo 'Pops' Yoshimura, who after Second World War service as an aircraft mechanic, set up a business tuning motorcycle engines. In 1971, he moved his enterprise to Los Angeles at the beginning of the four-cylinder superbike era. In 1976 the AMA introduced a racing class for production based bikes and Yoshimura established himself by entering fast, reliable Kawasaki Z1 bikes. He soon gained a reputation as an excellent motorcycle tuner, and with his over the counter parts available to racers everywhere who had the budget, he and his son-in-law were the go-to suppliers for performance upgrades. Bregazzi meanwhile remembered that the biggest drawback of the Kawasaki engine in sidecar use was its weight, but its advantage was not only the fact it was cheaper to buy than a Yamaha TZ motor, it was also significantly more cost effective to run:

> There was a fellow who got round at just over 100mph I think on a Kawasaki. The Yamahas were also a lot

lighter, [but] that thing I had, you went down Bray Hill, you nearly went through the bottom. It was heavy, it was a hell of a lump. The frame was made from T45 [steel tubing] which was cold drawn seamless, and was gas welded up. The engine was so heavy that it was a two-man job to lift it. That's why I had a little winch to haul it up, that was so I could position it where I was building the tubes round, and you could just have it suspended there or sitting there, or lift it up or take it down. The reason I got a Kawasaki was me and Artie Oates were clanking away on the Beezers [BSA engines], and Artie was the first to get a Kawasaki. He was lucky enough to get one from 'Sooty' Sutcliffe who had a fully tuned Z900, it was a 1,000cc in a special frame, he used to win up at Jurby Road Circuit and places like that, and he sold it. George Oates got one too, and there was then three of us on Kawasakis. You could come across them in breakers' yards and get bits off them. We upgraded every year. The Kawasaki had no weakness, it was bulletproof, even when tuned, it was just fantastic, but of course they were big and heavy and clumsy. You had Ireson and the other fellows on two-strokes, and me and Jimmy had ambitions that we were as good as them, as you do when you are young! We decided to go to Yamaha to get up to 100 mph, but it wasn't as easy as that! After a few years of that we had run out of money; the Kawasaki didn't cost anything, once you had the bits, you didn't have to refresh them, you just put S and S springs in them. You could get the cylinder heads all done, but I'm not even sure that I ever did that, [or] maybe use bigger valves. I got my Moriwaki cam from a dealer in the south of England. You could get a close ratio box from Kawasaki, that wasn't any

> special part it was just another part, and it only cost us £400 or something like that.[3]

By this time, around a quarter of the field at the Isle of Man TT were using the marque. Among them was Cheshire driver Des Founds who raced long wheelbase Formula 1 sidecars on the Island between 1981 and 1983. His first outfit was a Rumble Kawasaki GS1000. He built his own chassis and engines and remembered:

> Quite a lot of people used the Kawasakis because they were easy to pick up from scrap dealers and tuning parts from the States were available. They were a strong engine, especially the Z900 which was bored to 998cc as the limit for TT was 1,000cc. Quite a lot of guys used them in long chassis where the engine was in the back not like today where F2 must have the engine in front of the driver … when it was going through it was bloody quick. The secret was not to rev it too high but I was always hard on engines as I wanted to win a TT. They were successful in other hands but not the front runners, I know this as I built quite a few for my competitors whilst mine blew up. These large engines were mostly dry sumped so that you could lay them down a bit in the chassis. [I] loved every minute of it.[4]

He continued:

> I raced a long chassis in the island with the Kawasaki motor in, I've got to say it was the most comfortable bike I've ever ridden at the TT. Quite noisy I'm told but I suppose it's because for 70 % of the time you're flat out. Most of the tuning parts ie – cams, pistons, conrods came

> from the States. The engine in the rear was good for grip and you could use a lot more tyre sizes that were available back then. The only thing with a long chassis was that you were always trying to get your passenger to give you more traction on the front of the bike because the rear had lots of traction due to the engine and passenger in that area, usually meant the passenger climbed over your back to get forward. I had some good rides with the big engines … Happy days and no pressure in the TT paddock, in fact it was more of a family thing with the sidecar brigade. You could borrow most parts and engines from your competitors.[5]

Among those fellow competitors were newcomers Johnnie Rutherford and Barry Wallace, both Scots, whose outfit number seventy-eight was entered by T.B. Oliver Motorcycles of Hawick. Kawasaki powered, they used a largely standard engine for practice and a Moriwaki-tuned 'short circuit' engine for the race. One of their two mechanics kept a diary of their TT campaign in 1981, and described Race A:

> The starter's flag eventually dropped and Johnnie and Barry pushed off. The engine fired with no trouble and so they had started their first lap of the TT. Ian and I settled down in the pits surrounded by tools and spare wheels. They weren't needed. The race turned out as uneventfully as the practice (for no.78 anyway), with Johnnie and Barry circulating like clockwork, all three laps being close to 27m 30s ... Jock Taylor, Derek Bayley and Mick Boddice had all finished and were on the rostrum while Johnnie and Barry were still racing. I know it's not likely that they would put in a 10 minute lap, and so win, but they might at least have waited until everyone had finished!

> In the finisher's enclosure there was much back-slapping and congratulations. Johnnie said that he felt much better than in practice, more relaxed and less tired. I got the impression that Barry knew the circuit much better now, and this helped Johnnie a lot. Apparently the race was just like the practice. Jock Taylor came past at Kirk Michael, but they saw very little of anyone else.[6]

The team had shared space in Douglas taxi-owner Jimmy Stoddart's large garage with three other crews, and it turned out that Johnnie and Barry, who would have been pleased just to finish in this their first race, had done better than any of the others, coming thirty-third out of forty who finished. The machine however had received a severe battering from the bumpy course, much as it had in practice week:

> We all felt quite pleased with ourselves. However, we came back to earth when, on checking the bike over, we found two more bad cracks on the frame and another leak in the petrol tank. So we resigned ourselves to completely stripping the bike yet again. Other than another oil and filter change, the engine, thank God, needed no attention.[7]

Their experience demonstrated that whatever damage the course could inflict on the sidecar frame, the engine proved itself to be robust. When the morning of the second sidecar race dawned wet and miserable, it seemed likely that the event would be postponed, or at least delayed. The cancellation of the Senior in the morning seemed to confirm the prognosis, but by the afternoon things on the weather front were improving and it was announced that sidecars would leave the start line at 3.00pm, just half an hour later than scheduled.

This time, Rutherford and Wallace found that the clutch would not free off properly; one of their mechanics had made life hard for them by over filling the oil in the device, resulting in severe clutch drag. With the outfits soon to assemble on the starting grid, there was no time to remove the drain plug and let the oil out. With help from some other mechanics, they push started the machine in second gear, and aimed to get the engine as hot as possible before the flag dropped. As the minutes ticked by on the grid there was concern among the pit crew that the motor would cool down too much, and become impossible for one man to push start on his own. As it transpired, when they were signalled away Barry pushed for all he was worth and the engine spluttered into life. For the remainder of the race the motor proved as reliable as in the previous outing, and the duo circulated without incident.

Kawasaki released the new Z1000J for 1981 and these improved engines formed the basis of the factory endurance racers. Now with larger (magnesium-bodied) Mikuni 34mm carburettors, a revised combustion chamber and valve angle, as well as larger valves, these engines proved outstandingly reliable. KHI three-ring forged 69.99mm pistons provided a maximum allowable 1,015cc and the compression ratio was a moderate 10.2:1. The standard pressed up crankshaft was lightened by 25 per cent by removing material from the counterweights, and there were special tapers on the crankshaft to run the ignition on the left and alternator on the right. To reduce detonation, and overcome the difficulty of inferior racing fuel, twin spark plug ignition was employed.

In 1986 Stourbridge driver and trainee accountant Warwick Newman became sidecar champion at the TT, despite not winning either of the two legs. He first appeared on the Isle of Man in 1981 with a Kawasaki K1 powerplant in his outfit. After a brief switch to Yamaha, his most successful TT came after a return to the famous green livery. His passenger in the early years, Alan Warner, remembered:

> He advertised in *Motor Cycle News* that he was looking for a passenger for the Southern 100. I answered the ad and I flew over to the Isle of Man from Gatwick to take part in that race. We did our first TT together in '81, and every year we got a replica, we were always up there, we were getting quicker and quicker. Warwick was everybody's mate, a really nice guy. We were the stereotypical sidecar crew. He was short and stout whereas I'm six foot two. He did the books for Cradley Heath Kawasaki and that was how he got in with them. He used to buy the engines from scrap, then we used to put new crank cases on from Cradley – they used to crack because we were putting too much power through them.
>
> The Kawasaki was a beast after Warwick started having the motors done by Phil Manzano, I'm not sure how he got in with him, but he used to tune the motors for the Dutch drag racer Henk Vink. The cams were so wild in the Kawasaki that it used to spit the shims out. Well Phil Manzano redesigned the engine with the buckets upside down and it stopped the cams kicking the shims out. He contacted Kawasaki in Japan about this, and when they designed the 650 engine they incorporated this change. The other thing he did was start spot welding the crankshafts. Everybody had trouble with crankshafts because they were just pressed up, and the cranks used to spin slightly and knocked out the valves. In fact this was a normal mod for most people in drag racing – and drag racing was one of the toughest ways to develop an

engine – but it meant that in a sidecar our motors were virtually un-burstable. Phil asked Warwick 'What do you want?' in terms of mods and he said 'everything'! Phil was a bit of a recluse. Warwick used to meet him at motorway service stations to pick up the engines. I think he didn't want people going to his workshop. To my knowledge no one else had their engines done by him, though at the TT of course people generally didn't discuss that, they kept quiet about it.

Even now people still talk about that bike. We were among the last people still using four strokes. The main advantage that we had was that because I was tall, on the start line I held the engine cover and the wheel arch. He held it on the brake then jumped on whilst I slipped onto the passenger platform. We went off the line like a train. We would always be in the first group into the first corner and hold the lesser Yams on the straights but couldn't touch them through the corners due to the weight of the motor. It was just too big, it weighed about eight stone. There were two levels really, the top boys had the Yams and then there was us.

Things started to change when they brought out the 1,015 engine. That was a pain because Warwick had previously just had the 900s bored out to 1,000cc. With the new engine he had to get new 900 barrels put in, and then bore these out to 900cc. Warwick wouldn't cheat but I think that a few others probably did run 1,015s. In the late 80s they opened it up anyway, so it didn't matter if your engine was over 1,000cc. They were happy times, a lot of people remember it as a happy time.[8]

Phil Manzano, of Tenterden, Kent was at the cutting edge of Z1 headwork in the 1970s; highly respected, he was widely regarded as Britain's best cylinder head porter at the time. After he was made redundant by his employer Letraset in 1970, he went into business building and repairing motorcycle engines, as he remembered it so that he could practice his hobby all day long. Other competitors remembered that Newman's 998cc outfit could certainly move, but that he had to wrestle with it at times. The 1986 Sidecar A event was a great race and there would have been no happier men on the Isle of Man on the night which followed than Lowry Burton and Pat Cushnahan, who earlier had just won their first TT. Carrickfergus man Burton had previously been runner up, but had never had the pleasure of being the winner and was absolutely delighted. Newman and the Cradley Heath Kawasaki had certainly given them a run for their money, however. After being passed and left for dead on the first lap by the West Midlands driver, Burton and Cushnahan went on to take control of the first sidecar race in dominant style on their 750cc Yamaha powered outfit. On the first lap they were lying in sixth position behind Dick Greasly, Dave Hallam, Warwick Newman, Nigel Rollason and Dennis King. By the second lap their blue and white outfit was in front and had a one second advantage over Hallam at Ballaugh after a lap at 105.90mph. The Irish men went on from strength to strength after hitting the front, stretching their lead on the third lap to thirteen and a half seconds by Ballacraine from Hallam in second place and Newman third. Burton eased the pace slightly on the last lap to make sure there would be no problem of running out of petrol and by Ballaugh held a ten second advantage over Hallam, who was leading on the road, with Newman still holding third. Hallam ran into a spot of bother with his engine between Ballaugh and the Bungalow which let the race leader Burton through to lead on the road. At the finish Lowry Burton and Pat Cushnahan held a forty-seven second lead over the second place crew of Warwick Newman and Eddie Yarker, with Mick Burcombe and Parker third. In Race B the Cradley Heath Kawasaki supported duo of Newman and Yarker finished third, giving them victory overall across both legs and taking home the RAC trophy, which was awarded to the winner of the two race sidecar TT Championship.

What really sounded the death nell for the big Kawasaki engine in three-wheeled racing around the Island was the sudden change in regulations which the ACU brought to the sidecar TT in 1990. Indeed the rules for sidecars were effectively rewritten overnight, with the event going now solely to Formula 2 class. The change was prompted by the generally poor state of sidecars at that time. Outfits were being built for 500 and 750cc two-stroke engines, which were tiny motors. They were quite lightweight, and initially intended for Grand Prix use. Riders were then buying those bikes second hand, and adapting them to fit a cost-effective engine to go TT racing with. This would usually be a 1,000cc Suzuki, Kawasaki, or Honda, big four-strokes which were nearly double the weight of the engine that the chassis was originally designed to carry. As a result, accidents were happening with increasing frequency; frames were breaking, and racers were losing their lives because the general state of the outfits was so poor. In the end the ACU had to be seen to do something. The machines at the TT weren't getting any faster, they were just getting more dangerous. So, the organisers thought that if they changed the rules, people would have to build new bikes, and build them suited to the engines they were actually going to use. The specification for TT sidecars was reduced almost overnight from 1,000cc down to Formula 2 regulations, which was 350cc. Competitors could also ride a 600cc four-stroke in Formula 2 as they can today, but those engines were so old fashioned and heavy in those days that they simply were not competitive, indeed many manufacturers, Kawasaki included, did not even make a 600cc engine that was suitable for racing at that time. Kawasaki would not make a return to the sidecar TT until Dave Molyneux (son of John Molyneux) brought them success in the second decade of the twenty-first century.

NOTES

Chapter One: First But Also Last

1. United States Strategic Bombing Survey, *Corporation Report No. IV Kawasaki Aircraft Industries Inc*, Washington, 1947, p.1
2. Richard J. Samuels, *Rich Nation, Strong Army*, London, 1994, p.141

Chapter Two: Going Green 1966–1973

1. John Cooper, conversation with author
2. Peter Carrick, *The Story of Kawasaki Motorcycles*, Cambridge, 1978, p.9
3. *Motor Cycle News*, 18 June 1969
4. Op cit
5. Op cit
6. *Motor Cycle*, 22 July 1970
7. Op cit
8. *Motor Cycle*, 17 June 1970
9. Bill Smith, *Bill at Ballaugh*, NL, 2021, p.44
10. *Classic Racer*, 7 June 2020
11. *Motor Cycle Mechanics*, December 1972, p.39
12. *Motor Cycle Mechanics*, December 1972, p.40

Chapter Three: Breakthrough 1974–1975

1. Mick Grant, conversation with author
2. *Esher News and Mail*, 2 May 1974

3. *Motor Cycle Mechanics*, August 1974
4. Op cit
5. *Motor Cycle*, 8 June 1974
6. *Motor Cycle*, 15 June 1974
7. Mick Grant, *Roadracing*, London, 1979, p.88
8. https://kawasakinewsuk.blogspot.com/2012/
9. Mick Grant, *Takin' the Mick*, Yeovil, 2012, p.120
10. Mick Grant, *Roadracing*, p.87
11. *Motor Cycle Mechanics*, March 1977
12. Op cit
13. Op cit
14. Op cit
15. *Classic Racer*, Spring 1987, p.33
16. *Autosport Forum*, 12 December 2009
17. *Motor Cycle*, 7 June 1975
18. *Autosport Forum*, 12 December 2009
19. Mick Grant, conversation with author
20. *The Story of the 1975 TT*, Stanley Schofield Productions, author's transcript
21. *Autosport Forum*, 12 December 2009
22. Mick Grant, conversation with author
23. Peter Carrick, *The Story of Kawasaki Motorcycles*, p.113
24. *Autosport Forum*, 12 December 2009
25. Mick Grant, conversation with author
26. Mick Grant, *Takin' the Mick*, p.156
27. Ian Falloon, *Kawasaki Racers*, Yeovil, 2002, p.64

Chapter Four: Also Rans 1976

1. Mick Grant, conversation with author
2. https://kawasakinewsuk.blogspot.com/2012/
3. *Motor Cycle*, 12 June 1976
4. Mick Grant, conversation with author

Chapter Five: Bouncing Back 1977

1. Mick Grant, conversation with author
2. 1977 TT Programme, p.41
3. *Motor Cycle*, 18 June 1977
4. Mick Grant, conversation with author
5. Mick Grant, *Takin' the Mick*, p.154
6. *Motor Cycle*, 18 June 1977
7. Mick Grant, *Takin' the Mick*, p.154
8. *Motor Cycle*, 25 June 1977
9. *The Story of the 1977 TT*, Stanley Schofield Productions, author's transcript
10. Mick Grant, *Roadracing*, p.106
11. Peter Carrick, *The Story of Kawasaki Motorcycles*, p.114

Chapter Six: Lap of the Gods 1978

1. Mick Grant, conversation with author
2. *Motor Cycle Racing*, June 1978, p.51
3. *Motor Cycle News*, 14 June 1978
4. Peter Carrick, *The Story of Kawasaki Motorcycles*, p.115
5. *Classic Racer*, November 2002, p.64
6. *Motor Cycle*, 17 June 1978
7. Grant, *Takin' the Mick*, p.149
8. *Motor Cycle*, 17 June 1978
9. Grant, *Roadracing*, p.108
10. Op cit
11. Mick Grant, conversation with author
12. *Motor Cycle*, 17 June 1978
13. Op cit
14. Grant, *Roadracing*, p.108
15. *Daily Mirror*, 1 September 1978
16. Grant, *Roadracing*, p.86
17. *Motorcycle Racing*, June 1979, p.21
18. Grant, *Takin' the Mick*, p.177

19. Mat Oxley, *The Fast Stuff*, Sparkford, 2013, p.389
20. *Classic Racer*, March/April 2010
21. Oxley, p.389
22. 1980 TT Programme, p.70
23. Op cit
24. Chas Mortimer, conversation with author
25. 1980 TT Programme, p.57
26. *Motor Cycle News*, 13 June 1984
27. *Motorcycling Weekly*, 12 June 1984
28. Op cit
29. Op cit
30. *Motor Cycle News*, 13 June 1984
31. https://www.ttwebsite.com/
32. *Motor Cycle News*, 24 November 2014
33. *Motor Cycle News*, 11 June 1986

Chapter Seven: Sidecar Sunset 1973–1986

1. *Classic Racer*, 16 April 2019
2. Eric Bregazzi, recorded interview courtesy of Richard Bregazzi
3. Op cit
4. Des Founds, conversation with author
5. Op cit
6. *Motorcycle Sport*, October 1981, p.519
7. Op cit
8. Alan Warner, conversation with author

BIBLIOGRAPHY

Alexander, Jeffrey W., *Japan's Motorcycle Wars*, Vancouver, 2008

Carrick, Peter, *The Story of Kawasaki Motorcycles*, Cambridge, 1978

Cathcart, Alan, *Kawasaki H1-R*, NL, 2020

Falloon, Ian, *Kawasaki Racers: Road-racing Motorcycles From 1965 to the Present Day*, Yeovil, 2002

Grant, Mick, *Roadracing*, London, 1979

Grant, Mick, *Takin' the Mick*, Yeovil, 2012

Oxley, Mat, *The Fast Stuff: Twenty Years of Top Bike Racing Tales From the World's Maddest Motorsport*, Sparkford, 2013

Richardson, Matthew, *TT Titans*, Barnsley, 2018

Samuels, Richard J., *'Rich Nation, Strong Army' National Security and the Technological Transformation of Japan*, London, 1994

Smith, Bill, *Bill at Ballaugh*, NL, 2021

United States Strategic Bombing Survey, *Corporation Report No. IV Kawasaki Aircraft Industries Inc*, Washington, 1947

Walker, Mick, *Mick Walker's Japanese Grand Prix Racing Motorcycles*, Low Fell, 2002

Walker, Mick, *Mick Walker's Japanese Production Racing Motorcycles*, Low Fell, 2003

Walker, Mick, *Performance Motorcycles*, Hoo, Rochester, 2001

West, Phil, *Superbikes: Machines of Dreams*, New York, 2013

INDEX

SUNK BY A U-BOAT, ATTACKED BY KAMIKAZES

MEMOIRS OF A WAR AT SEA

JOHN MARSDEN

PEN & SWORD MARITIME

First published in Great Britain in 2024 by
PEN AND SWORD MARITIME
an imprint of
Pen and Sword Books Ltd
Yorkshire – Philadelphia

ISBN 978 1 03610 858 8

A CIP record for this book is available from the British Library

Typeset in Times New Roman 11/13.5 by
SJmagic DESIGN SERVICES, India.
Printed and bound in the UK by CPI Group (UK) Ltd.

Pen & Sword Books Ltd incorporates the imprints of Pen & Sword
Archaeology, Atlas, Aviation, Battleground, Discovery,
Family History, History, Maritime, Military, Naval, Politics, Railways,
Select, Social History, Transport, True Crime, Claymore Press,
Frontline Books, Leo Cooper, Praetorian Press, Remember When,
Seaforth Publishing and Wharncliffe.

For a complete list of Pen & Sword titles please contact
PEN & SWORD BOOKS LIMITED
George House, Units 12 & 13, Beevor Street, Off Pontefract Road,
Barnsley, South Yorkshire, S71 1HN, England
E-mail: enquiries@pen-and-sword.co.uk
Website: www.pen-and-sword.co.uk

or

PEN AND SWORD BOOKS
1950 Lawrence Rd, Havertown, PA 19083, USA
E-mail: uspen-and-sword@casematepublishers.com
Website: www.penandswordbooks.com

FSC
www.fsc.org
MIX
Paper | Supporting responsible forestry
FSC® C013604

Contents

Acknowledgements

The making of this story was the coming together of the tale of one man's experiences during the Second World War, and the official record of the conflict. When I first sat down with my father to embark upon the project it became clear that, although his memory of events seemed clear enough, the fog of time had obscured the sequencing of his experiences, though happily not to any great extent. Though he retained a lot of the detail of the actions and operations he witnessed at first hand, he was understandably ignorant of the wider picture and of the overall context of the war in terms of strategies and tactics. This meant that, as an author, there were two main tasks for me to come to grips with in order to craft a comprehensive, coherent and accurately sequenced version of it all. That is, I realised that I would have to embark on a quest for substantiating documental evidence amongst the Admiralty Papers in the National Archives, as well as conduct a search for photographic evidence from a number of sources. The former I hoped would add to the accuracy and context of my father's account, the latter to the immediacy of his experiences. Happily, my expectations regarding the actual existence of these two elements were far exceeded, so my first acknowledgements must go to the archivists at The National Archives in Kew and the Merseyside Maritime Museum in Liverpool, my father's home town, for their unstinting efforts in preserving the documental and photographic records of the conflict.

The Battle of the Atlantic was the longest battle of the war if not of all time, and the resulting statistics of human and material losses were staggering, as were the logistics of allied and enemy efforts to maintain their opposing efforts. Most if not all of this enormous data pool has been, and continues to be, pored over by various archival institutions who have, as a result of their untiring spirit, produced clear and comprehensive data sets detailing the scale of it all, some of which they have magnanimously placed in the public domain. As a result many an historian has benefited hugely from online access to the resources put together by the likes of Arnold Hague (convoyweb.org.uk), uboat.net, naval–history.net and warsailors.com. So, I would like to express my deepest gratitude to the unsparing efforts of bodies such as those just mentioned and others like them; without whom anyone hoping to access the details of the Atlantic struggle would face some challenging research demands.

Having put together an early draft of my story, and not feeling sure of its merit, I turned to an old friend, Tony Campbell, for help, asking him to have a look at the prototype document and comment upon it. Being the gentleman that he is, he clawed his way through what I now consider to have been a pretty raw manuscript, and provided me with some feedback which was always gently phrased (he should have been a little harsher) but helpful when reading between the lines. After taking it all in Tony's words gave me pause for thought, allowing me to restructure and strengthen the story, thus making the task of coming up with a more viable working draft much easier than it otherwise might have been. So, for his help and patience, I will always owe him a debt of gratitude.

With a somewhat improved draft I then decided to ask one of my cousins, Chris Corrigan, to assess its strengths and weaknesses. Being a relative Chris was a little more, direct, should I say, in his analysis of my work; and in addressing the issues he raised I think I managed to make some further improvements to the structure of the story.

When I felt that my efforts were finally beginning to pay off, I considered it would be a good idea to take soundings from two acquaintances whom I thought might be able to provide me with a measure of tangential advice on the content of my maturing project. With that in mind I asked David Hush whose father had served aboard the escort carrier HMS *Striker* during the war, a sister ship to my father's HMS *Empress*, to compare his father's memoirs with those of mine. David's father did, in fact, put some of his wartime experiences down on paper for the benefit of his descendants, and it seems he was also happy to talk about the war in the presence of his growing family during the post war years. So, my brief to David was to compare the timbre of his father's story with that of mine and let me know his thoughts. My second collaborator at this stage was Sean Doyle, a veteran of the Falklands War who I thought might be able to assess those parts of my father's story relating to the attitudes and actions of men belonging to a close–knit military unit in a wartime setting and to compare his own experiences with those I have attempted to echo in my writing. After reading my manuscript both David and Sean seemed to think there was some merit in my efforts, to the extent that, allowing for their natural politeness, I felt confident that it was time to go to press. So, I must give thanks to both for taking the trouble to read my story and provide me with some encouraging feedback.

Finally, I must express my deepest thanks to Mr. Matthew Canti, son of Dr Gordon Canti who served in the capacity of doctor/surgeon to Johnnie

Walker's Second Support Group. Assigned to HMS *Wren*, Dr. Canti was allowed the possession of a stills camera for the main purpose of recording the effects of wounds, disease and surgical procedures relating to his work. However, when the appropriate circumstances arose during actions at sea, Dr. Canti sometimes felt the need to capture them on film, and the results of his on–the–spot photography are spectacular, as the reader will see.

Many of Dr. Canti's pictures are available to view via access to the photography collections at the Maritime Museum, National Museums Liverpool, however, during the course of a warm–hearted meeting with Matthew, he granted me permission to make a selection from his father's collection to include in the publication of my story, for which I am eternally grateful.

Introduction

The story of the two world wars of the twentieth century has been written almost exclusively by professional historians and by participants from the Armed Forces drawn mainly from the officer class. It is to be lamented that there are so few accounts of events written by those who served amongst the lower ranks and experienced the fighting at first hand. Culturally, those who were not considered suitable for the officer corps were drawn mainly from the working classes, many of them having completed their state education at the age of fourteen during the years leading up to the Second World War. It was mainly as a result of the differences in educational background between these two groups that there exists today just a handful of well–known biographies relating to the two great conflicts against Germany and her allies, which have sprung from 'the ordinary soldier'. One such is Frank Richards' *Old Soldiers Never Die*, in which the author tells us of his time as a signaller serving on the Western Front with the Royal Welch Fusiliers. But even this remarkable piece of work would have been lost to us had Richards not presented his manuscript to one of his old commanding officers, Robert Graves, during the 1920s. Graves, recognising the value of Richards' work, used his influence to have it published, and at the last count some nine editions of it have appeared since it first rolled off the presses in 1933. It is still in print today; a testimony to Graves's insight and to the allure that a story written by a member of the lower ranks holds for many readers keen to understand what the First World War was really like for the 'ordinary' man.

It was with Frank Richards' example in mind that I decided some years ago to record my father's wartime experiences via a series of conversations, some of which I recorded on tape for later scrutiny, others I simply took down on paper as we conversed; in fact quite a few were actually conducted over the telephone. My intention was to compile them in a formalised, contextual and chronological fashion, once I had corroborated what he had told me via references to archive material, as well as other literary and historic sources; the hope being that the final product might be considered as something worth placing in the public domain.

Like Richards, my father was not an officer, neither, during his time in service, did he attain the rank of NCO. He was a stoker, pure and simple, in the Royal Navy, and saw action against the U–boats during the convoy battles in the north Atlantic during 1943 and 1944 until his ship, HMS *Woodpecker*, was torpedoed and sunk in February of the latter year. Thankfully, there was no loss of life amongst her crew; all were rescued and delivered safely home aboard ships of the Royal Navy and the Royal Canadian Navy.

When my father returned to sea after a period of so-called rest and recuperation in the remote Scottish Highlands, it would be as a member of the crew aboard the escort carrier, HMS *Empress*; a ship he joined during the autumn of 1944 as she readied herself for assignment to the East Indies Fleet. It was in that theatre that he was to experience action against Japanese forces right up to the end of hostilities, and it would not be until December 1945 that he returned to a war–shattered Britain.

Unavoidably, my father's account of the events in which he participated left many a gap to be filled; that task I attempted to accomplish via reference to the Admiralty papers held in The National Archives at Kew, as well as other historical texts. Data from those same sources also provided for a good measure of corroboration and verification for many of the seemingly unimportant minutiae of my father's tale. It was this correlation between the spoken word and the official records that was to provide me with a measure of confidence in his recall, as I combed through the archival documentation.

The approach I took with any relevant official data I uncovered was twofold: in a few instances I wove it into my father's narrative in order to include more of the historical detail and context surrounding his story, but most of it, together with accompanying technical data, I have embedded in the story, distinguishing it from my father's narrative by using the full width of the page, while my father's narrative is expressed in indented text.

I must confess that, on occasion, my father's version of events was at variance with some of the archive content. For instance, when describing a tragic accident which took place on the flight deck of HMS *Empress* in July 1945, he insisted that there were two resulting fatalities, when only one was recorded in the ship's log. With regard to another incident, he insisted that the pilot and crew from an aircraft belonging to one of the escort carriers, *Activity* or *Nairana*, he couldn't say which, were lost when their Swordfish crashed whilst attempting to land on the flight deck. At the time, both carriers were accompanying Commander 'Johnny' Walker's Second Support Group during an Atlantic patrol in February 1944, but no such fatal incident was recorded in the log of either. Some crash–landings are recorded in those documents, but no aircrew fatalities are mentioned, however further research was to provide confirmation of my father's assertions, as will be seen. In other words, his recall sometimes captured the fine detail missed by some of the official documentation.

One final thing I must stress to the reader is that, whilst writing this story, I attempted to mimic my father's vernacular as closely as possible. However, in the interests of injecting an element of flow and readability into his narrative, I have in some places been less than one hundred per cent faithful to his manner of expression, but the essence, authenticity and veracity of his experiences will, I hope, shine through in the general rendering.

Preface

This is not a story of endless and continuous action at sea; for instance, it contains tales about weeks spent in basic training, the boredom of barracks life whilst awaiting a ship posting, and of a six–month stay at a naval rest and recuperation facility in the Scottish Highlands. Neither is it a story about strategies, war production figures, mobilisation of industry and the forging of alliances. In essence, it is a story about the smallest cogs in the complex machine of industrialised warfare: the ordinary civilian–soldier. In the protagonist's case it is a story about jimmy–the–ones, button–tossers, the Jack Dusty and the Peggy; of rum rats, tots, sippers and gulpers; of boiler cleans, arrestor gear and catapult maintenance and much else. In essence it describes the mundane backdrop to the war and how, during short, intense periods of action, that unexciting canvas can be torn to shreds in a life–or–death struggle. There is tragedy, of course, but there is humour and an unassuming heroism combined with examples of humanity, stoicism and the hope for a better life when peace was finally to return.

When researching stories of this nature, it is almost inevitable to come across a number of coincidental details, usually of a fairly trivial complexion, and in many cases meaningful only to the researcher. But in some instances a coincidence might be of interest to a wider audience, and in my case I think I can list two of this type which I came across. The first applied to *U–202*, the first U–boat sunk by Walker's newly formed Second Support Group in June 1943. At that time she was captained by Gunter Poser who had succeeded *Kptlt*. Hans–Heinz Linder in September 1942. Under Linder's command, *U–202* suffered a narrow escape from destruction when she was depth–charged whilst attempting to penetrate the Straits of Gibraltar in December 1941. Some readers of this story may well recall the famous film, *Das Boot*, written and directed by Wolfgang Petersen in 1985. If so, they will know that the U–boat depicted in the movie suffered just such an ordeal, and after surviving a nerve-shredding experience during which his boat lay lifeless for many hours on the ocean floor its captain, played by Jurgen Prochnow, managed, via the completion of a number of running repairs, to bring her to the surface. Once safe from his pursuers he called out from his bridge atop the conning tower the English words, 'Not yet! Not yet!' in defiance of the Royal Navy ships from whose grasp he had just managed to escape.

After completing some deeper research, I am now quite sure that this minor detail was an indirect reference to the Second Support Group (in fact, I am sure I have seen a version of the film in which the words uttered by Prochnow were, 'Not yet, Mr. Woodpecker! Not yet!'). In either case, the words strongly suggest that Petersen's character in the role of U–boat captain, although strongly based upon the experiences of *Kptlt.* Heinrich Lehmann-Willenbrock of *U–96*,[1] also incorporated some influence from Linder's experiences during the war; hence the reference to his Gibraltar Straits experience in the film.[2] There is further evidence to support this supposition, in that Linder had joined Willenbrock in *U–96* whilst undergoing his U–boat commander's training course, accompanying him on sea patrols between January and March 1941; and it would seem that the two men maintained contact with each other until Linder's death, which came about as a result of a Russian air–raid on the German U–boat base in Libau, Latvia, on 10 September 1944, where he was by then in command of a training school for U–boat crew.[3] This was exactly the fate which befell Petersen's character in the film. The coincidence here is the fact that HMS *Woodpecker* was credited with the destruction of Linder's old boat, *U–202*, sunk on 2 June 1943. Willenbrock, the commander of U–96, survived the war and went on to write, *The Patrols of U–96 in World War II*, which gave rise to *Das Boot*. There, I thought, ended the thread of coincidence which seemed to run through the histories of Willenbrock and *Woodpecker*, until I discovered that, after *U–256* sank *Woodpecker* whilst under the command of *Kptlt* Wilhelm Brauel in February 1944, she was to spend her final operational weeks under the command of Willenbrock!

The second, and somewhat less tenuous coincidence, concerns the fate of *U–264*, the last of six U–boats to be sunk by the Second Support Group during Walker's famous patrol of February 1944. HMS *Woodpecker* played a direct part in the sinking of *U–264* and helped rescue her crew, all of whom survived. At the time her captain was *Kptlt.* Hartwig Looks who, years later, appeared in an interview he gave as a contribution to ITV's landmark documentary series of the 1970s, *The World at War*, in which he described the famous convoy battle fought between the U–boats and the Allied escort forces protecting convoy ONS 5 in April/May 1943. Whilst speaking with my father one day, I played a recording of Looks' interview to him, pausing it at a convenient point to ask him if he recognized the speaker. Obviously, he did not, and it may be that Looks was picked up by a ship other than *Woodpecker* when his boat was sunk by Walker's ships. However, the expression on his face when I explained who it was on the screen was both a joy and a surprise to behold. A recording of Looks' interview is now held by the Imperial War Museum. If I may indulge the reader's patience a little longer this coincidence may be stretched a little further in that, during February 1943, Looks, in *U–264*, was shadowing a German blockade runner, *Hohenfriedberg*, whilst she was being chased down by the British cruiser, HMS *Sussex*. Rather than surrender their vessel the German crew decided to scuttle her, but before *Sussex* turned away, Looks managed to fire a salvo of six torpedoes at her, all of which missed their mark. The U–boat captain then surfaced and rescued the whole of the crew belonging to the German merchantman. Late in the war Marsden was to witness a Japanese kamikaze attack upon *Sussex* – which she also survived.

Chapter 1

The Liverpool blitz

The narrative constructed during the production of this story was strongly driven by the answers given to me in response to questions I posed to my father during a number of conversations. The talks took place over an extended period and came in several forms: some were face to face affairs, during which I took notes or recorded what was said on cassette tape. Others were conducted over the telephone, with notes being made contemporaneously. On checking my records I found that our earliest talk took place in 2004, and that the final conversation occurred some six years later. The script I followed when driving the conversations had a chronological element to it, in that I tried to take my father through his experiences from the day the war broke out until he was de–mobbed and began to reconstruct his life on civvy street, as he would have put it.

The end–product of our interactions was a surprisingly coherent and roughly time-ordered set of notes which formed the bones of what follows, but I was still left with the task of adding flesh to the skeleton. This was done by checking official records at The National Archives, and performing a comprehensive search through the various on-line sources of Second World War material relating to the Atlantic and Indian Ocean theatres, as well as by reading a number of personal stories written by participants in the Battle of the Atlantic and some post–war compilations by historians. All of which had to be woven into the story that follows. Having taken such a twin–pronged approach, I have attempted to distinguish between comment and commentary by indenting the blocks of text representing my father's comment, and leaving my own commentary to occupy the full width of the page.

Finally, the important part. The nature by which I harvested my father's story meant that the raw transcripts of our question–and–answer sessions had to be recrafted to produce an ordered, coherent and comprehensible story; and this should become apparent when reading what follows in that it is clearly not a verbatim reproduction of my father's speech. However, having faithfully preserved the fact or essence of what he said, there was a need to convert his raw narrative into something which is, I hope, more easily readable. In doing so I have tried as hard as I could to preserve my father's lexicon and vernacular, but in some places these are tinged with my own style where needs must. However, I feel the overriding importance of the story revolves around my father's description of events in which he took part, and of his post–fact thoughts about his wartime experiences as a whole; all of which are faithfully reproduced herein.

> The wartime experiences I am about to describe were, to a greater or lesser extent, common to many of the lower ranks who served in the forces during the last war. I am not claiming any special credit for my war service, there were others who made a bigger contribution than me and whose stories will never be told, but if there was one thing in common amongst us all, it was that we accepted what we were asked to do, and went about it with the will to see it through. The majority were never looking for any glory for what they did, and when the war was over, all that they wanted to do was to return home to their family and friends and settle into a way of life they hoped might offer themselves and their children something better than what had gone before.
>
> My story covers only the war years and the first eighteen months or so that followed, but I will begin by giving a short summary of the early years of my life, in the hope that it will describe a background and way of life common to many of my class and generation.
>
> I was born in the city of Liverpool on 9 June 1923, and became one of four surviving brothers and five sisters. One of my brothers, a twin to my younger brother, Patrick, died in infancy shortly after he was born. At the age of five I went to St Joseph's Primary School in Rose Place before moving on, aged eleven, to Bishop Goss Secondary School in Cazeneau Street. The education I received was, I suppose, basic by modern standards, and I left school at the age of fourteen to find my first job with a firm of local builders.
>
> My ambition was to take up an apprenticeship before reaching my sixteenth birthday and to begin to learn the trade of joiner or carpenter. Traditionally, when they began their working life, boys of fourteen and fifteen were expected to swallow their pride and be prepared to do any of the chores demanded of them by foremen and tradesmen whilst working at a factory, shipyard or construction site. It was only after many months of fetching and carrying that they would be accepted into a trade as an apprentice. In my case, after two

years of what was really nothing more than skivvying while hoping for a chance to become indentured, I could sense that my hopes of learning a skill would not be fulfilled. Others lucky enough to have family or friends in certain trades were always promoted ahead of me; so, rather than continue with the low pay, poor prospects and manual labour of being a builder's mate, I decided, at the age of seventeen, to look for something else.

Over the next two years I had several jobs, but the one I persevered with longest was that of a loader aboard a brewer's dray which travelled the streets of Liverpool six days a week, delivering barrels of beer to the city's public houses owned by Bass's brewery. It was heavy work but I enjoyed being out amongst the bustle of the city streets I knew so well.

By the time I was eighteen the opportunity of taking up a trade had passed me by, but at least I had avoided serious injury, or worse, during the working days of my early teens; a fate which was not unknown amongst boys under the age of fifteen or sixteen. However I did come close to disaster on my way to work one day, when I fell from the platform of Liverpool's Central station straight into the path of the train I was waiting to catch. Somehow, I managed to keep my wits about me after falling onto the rails, and calmly rolled away from the track, pressing my frame up against the platform wall as the train rolled to a stop beside me. Above me I could hear the shouts of the people, 'He's dead. He's got to be dead,' they were calling, as I lay out of sight beneath them totally unharmed. For the short duration of that incident I kept telling myself to 'keep a cool head,' while I lay there waiting for the train to move on. If I had panicked, it would almost certainly have been the end of me; and it was this kind of self–control in the face of danger that was to stand me in good stead in years to come. Once I was sure that I had survived I called to the people above, telling them that I was uninjured, and once the train had pulled away they helped me climb up onto the platform.

My father, after whom I was named, worked in the horse–drawn haulage business while I was growing up, earning the best part of his living by transporting cargo between the docks that lined the River Mersey and the goods yards, markets and warehouses which at that time were scattered around the old city centre. Liverpool was a busy sea port between the wars, and although that did not always mean full employment for its population of nearly one million, there was usually opportunity available for those who really wanted it.

My mother, Mary, took work in the Liverpool fish market whenever it was available, and on those days her eldest daughter and namesake took on the job of looking after her younger brothers and sisters, myself included. It was a duty she began to take on at the age of ten or eleven.

For many years, before the time my elder sisters were married and left home, all eleven of us lived in a three–bedroom tenement at Thurlow House, off Scotland Road, close to the city centre. During that time I shared a bedroom, and sometimes a bed, with my three brothers. My five sisters shared the third bedroom while they were all living at the family home. Such arrangements were nothing unusual in those days, when families were large and housing was in short supply. However, this story is the story of the seven years of my life that coincided with the Second World War and the early months of peacetime, so it will now begin in earnest on the day that war broke out.

The declaration of war against Germany came not long after I had turned sixteen, that is on Sunday 3 September 1939, and I heard the news as I walked home from mass at St. Joseph's parish church on that unforgettable morning. The news did not come as a surprise, the newspapers and radio had been covering the situation and reporting on Chamberlain's visits to Germany where, we were led to believe, he did all that he could to avoid another war. During those days it was said that he was just playing for time in order to give the country a chance to arm itself for the war that everyone was expecting, but wanted to avoid.

As the word that we were in a state of war with Germany spread around the streets in the Scotland Road area of the city, I wanted to see how people would react to it. Many of those in the neighbourhood had lived through the first war, and a good proportion of the men had served in France and Belgium. So, I thought I would be able to see from their reactions how they felt about the idea of another war, and by doing so I might be able to get an idea about the situation the country was now in.

From what I can remember, most people had a clear look of worry on their face as they heard the news. There was certainly no cheering about the thought of what was going to come, in fact, there seemed to be some sense of fear in the air. Maybe it was the amount of bustle, unusual on a Sunday morning in those days, that has stayed in my mind, but the atmosphere felt a bit different that day; people were scurrying about, gathering in little groups to hear news from one another, and to tell what they knew to their friends and neighbours in turn.

Of course, I was a teenager then, as were my friends and my brothers, and we were going to be affected by the war; many of us would have to join the forces and we knew it. Maybe it was that, and the mix of excitement and fear that filled our minds, which made us a bit giddy! We were going to be fighting the Germans again, and there were many like my father whose memories of the first war were still fresh. If anybody understood the situation we were in, it was them, and they were uncomfortable about what might come.

Throughout my childhood I came to know that those who had served in the First World War would never speak about their experiences. It was the way that generation coped with their memories for the rest of their life. Like my father, many of them also bore the scars and disabilities that came from their war service. Being a haulier meant that he served in the Army Transport Corps as a driver. I know he went to France in 1915, and was wounded in the closing stages of the war in 1918, but that is it. As a result of his injuries he was discharged from the Army a few weeks before the war ended. He had few words for me when I arrived home full of beans on that Sunday morning, but I could see the worry on his face. 'You're only sixteen, lad,' he said, 'it'll be two years before they can call you up, and you never know, it might all be over by then.' I said nothing, but hoped he would be wrong. I was excited; I felt that I was at the beginning of something that was going to carry me along to who knew where. I did not really want it to end before I had my chance of adventure. The idea of the air raids that were soon to come had hardly entered my head, and my ignorance was soon to be shattered.

Shortly after one of the earliest raids on Liverpool had taken place, one which had concentrated on the river front, my father was sent to load his wagon at Brunswick Dock, and it was there where he saw some of the damage caused by the bombs.[1] He told me how an old barge that had been hit was lying half submerged in the dock and how, in the background, many of the dock warehouses had been badly damaged by direct hits. As we spoke that evening he shared some thoughts with me. 'These are just light raids,' he said, 'they're only testing the city's defences; and they'll get heavier once they know they can get through.' But the Germans were losing aircraft. One day, the wreckage of a Junkers bomber was put on show at St George's Hall on Lime Street.[2] My father's prediction of heavier raids came true as time moved on through 1940 and into the spring of 1941, when they came to a peak in an eight–day blitz during May of that year.

The first really heavy raids on Liverpool happened in December 1940 and January 1941, and they were to claim the life of two of my young relatives. The early news we got after the big raid of late December 1940 was that all of my family had survived, but we found out later that one of my cousins, Christina, aged fifteen, had been killed in the neighbourhood of Blackstock Street when a bomb exploded close to the entrance of the local air–raid shelter.[3] It was said that it had smashed through five stories of a tenement block before ricocheting towards the shelter, where it exploded, killing many of those inside. There were hundreds of casualties across the city that night, and the death of Christina came less than two years after she lost a younger brother, William, who died of illness at the age of seven just before the outbreak of the war.

One of the January raids claimed the life of my young nephew, Tommy Dickens, my sister Kitty's only child at that time. He was suffering from diphtheria and had been admitted to Walton Hospital just after Christmas. We were told that, when the air raid began, there was some panic when the patients and doctors were evacuated from the wards and taken to the shelters. Tommy was left behind in the confusion. He could not call out to anyone, and being hardly visible in the blackout he was left behind. Once the all–clear was sounded and the doctors had returned to the ward they found him dead, lying on the floor close to his bed. It was said that, while he was trying to escape, he must have pulled the tubes from his throat which allowed him to breathe and suffocated. He was just two or three years old. We were all shaken by the loss, he was my parents' first grandson, and at that time my only nephew. It was some ten years before Kitty had her second child.

Of my immediate family all except my elder brother, Jim, were in Liverpool during the big blitz that followed in May 1941, and all of them experienced the terror of the raids, which went on for eight consecutive nights. I was approaching my eighteenth birthday at the time and willing to take a chance to make a few bob whenever the opportunity arose. Before he left home Jim used to work on the docks, and when he went away he left his docker's registration book with me, the second–eldest boy in the family. It was as good as a passport to work in the port in those days and while I had it I was, for all intents and purposes, a registered dock worker.

One evening during that May blitz my brother–in–law, John Connolly, another Liverpool stevedore, called at my parents' house and talked me into me to accompanying him on a night shift at Huskisson Dock. We were either mad or desperate for money even to consider the offer of work that night, but after weighing it up we set off determined to get a good night's pay.

There were two ships at the quayside when we arrived at the dock, both of them waiting to be loaded with ammunition.[4] Once we had been signed on for the night we were told to work a half shift from seven o'clock until eleven o'clock, but at that point our courage began to desert us and we became unsure about accepting the job. My brother–in–law had already worked some shifts while the bombers were overhead and, pausing for a moment to think about it, he felt he might be pushing his luck this time, so certain was he that the Germans would be back once darkness fell. Nervous and unsure, we were on the verge of walking away, but in the end we geed each other up and decided to get on with it.

All was well as we began the work of loading the holds of one of the freighters. After an hour or so had passed, with the work going along smoothly, we began to think we might finish the shift before the Germans made their appearance. It was not until we were having our first tea break, at about nine o'clock, that the air raid warnings sounded. The bombers must have come very close to the docks before they were detected; I say this because the first bombs began to fall almost in time with the sounding of the sirens. The ship we were working on was by then heavily loaded with explosives, so we did not need to think twice, it was a case of getting away from the docks and into an air raid shelter as fast as we could. I gathered up my things, and after making sure that my brother–in–law was with me, I made my way away from the quayside. As I passed through the dock gates I was surprised at the lack of panic amongst the rest of the men, who had all come to the same conclusion as me and my brother–in–law and decided to make for safety. Some had broken into a steady trot away from the dock, but most were calmly striding away as though they had just finished a normal shift.

Once on the streets I could see that there were incendiary bombs lying everywhere. The carriageway known as the Dock Road was already strewn with them and they were continuing to rain down. I noticed that they did not burst into flame until they hit the ground, and when they did they exploded in a shower of sparks. They were, for want of a better description, just like over–sized sparklers, about eighteen inches long and three inches in diameter. But the impact they made when they hit the ground or nearby buildings was enough to allow them to smash through the slate roof of a house before bursting into flames inside the loft. Showers of them fell as the first wave of bombers passed over. The following waves then began to pass overhead, no doubt using the fires as a marker for the bomb aimers, and began to drop their bombs. I cannot say that I was frightened by it all, in fact I felt a bit excited at the sense of danger I experienced, and I could see the men of the National Fire Service (NFS) and the Air Raid Precautions (ARP) wardens dashing about trying to douse the flames from the incendiaries as I headed away from the river. Sometimes I had to skirt around the fire bombs as I went along, and wherever I found a pile of sandbags standing at the kerb, I would throw some of them onto the incendiaries in an attempt to smother the flames. I suppose it was my way of doing something, rather than just stand there taking whatever the Germans wanted to throw at us.

Due to the damage being done to the town as the raid went on, many of the water mains had been burst, causing a loss of pressure at the fire hydrants that were dotted around the city, which meant that the Fire Brigade's hoses were virtually useless. I can remember coming up to one fireman who was just standing there, in the middle of the road, watching the fires blaze around him as the tears rolled down his cheeks. He did not even notice me as I passed him, and as I continued with my escape from the danger area I could see that the overhead railway which ran for much of the length of the docks had taken a number of direct hits.

The raid went on, and the number of explosions I could hear as we dashed from street corner to street corner was increasing all the time, so much so that it was sometimes difficult to tell the difference between the explosions of the bombs and the firing of the anti–aircraft guns positioned around the docks. There was quite a lot of red–hot shrapnel falling to the ground by this time, but during it all I had managed to keep close to my brother–in–law; we were heading towards Boundary Street by the shortest possible route as we skirted around burning buildings and bomb craters, keeping close to the walls as if they could give us a bit of protection. All around us, apart from places where fires were burning, it was pitch dark due to the blackout, and we had to struggle to discover a safe route that would take us further away from the river, as it was there where the bombers seemed to be focussing most of their attention. All the time, as we went carefully on our way, I was afraid that I might stumble into a crater, invisible in the darkness of the blackout and the smoke from the many fires around us.

The noise was deafening. I could not tell how close to us the bombs were falling, but thankfully it was never so close that I felt any of the blast as they exploded. Then there was the sound they made as they came down towards the ground. My mind was trying to make sense of it all. I can still picture the beams of the searchlights going up through the smoke, searching for the bombers. Fascinating though it was, I did not feel like standing and staring at the sight of it for more than a few seconds, I was too keen to get away from what was clearly the main target area for the bombers and find shelter.

As we put more distance between ourselves and the docks, I eventually became separated from my brother–in–law as the chaos around us increased. It would have made no sense to try and find him, as it would only have exposed me to a risk of death or injury, so I decided to go on alone. I found out later that he had been ordered into an air raid shelter by the ARP wardens, where he was forced to sit out the rest of the raid. My main concern, once I found myself alone, became that of trying to reach the house of my eldest sister, Mary, in Queen Anne Place. It was her husband, John, that I had been with, and in my ignorance of his situation I was sure he too would be trying to get to the family home. I was desperate to make sure that my sister and two young nieces, Teresa and Marie, were safe.

Fires were blazing everywhere now, completely out of control, they threw a reddish light onto the broken buildings and picked out the uniformed men whose duty it was to remain on the streets as they went about their job; be it shepherding people to the shelters or helping to fight the flames. On and on I went, and when I finally got to the air raid shelter in Queen Anne Place, I made my way down into the cubicles to find Mary and her children safe and well. I spent a little time with them, trying to reassure them that they were safe where they were and that they would just have to stay there until the raid was over. Once the all–clear was sounded everything would be alright, I said. I do not know if my words had any effect; they were obviously shaken by what they had seen and heard that night. Luckily, the tenement where they lived was not hit, which meant that, for another day at least, they still had a home to return to once the bombers were gone. With my mind a little more at ease I decided it was time for me to make my way, via Holly Street and Christian Street, to my mother's home at Thurlow House. The building was part of a large complex of tenements consisting of five and six storey flats, each one having a front door that opened onto a shared landing which ran the length of the block.

It was a short journey, only half a mile or so, and the worst of the bombing seemed to be over as I emerged from the air–raid shelter into the dark, smoke–filled night. As I made my way other people were beginning to come out of their shelters, stepping warily into the streets, and I soon got news from a neighbour that my mother had refused to go to the local shelter when the raid began. On hearing that, I quickened my pace towards home and was relieved to find her safe and well when I finally reached the flat. Nevertheless, she was clearly shaken, and she had had a lucky escape. One of the tenement blocks, the only one still under construction at the time and less than fifty yards from the block where we lived, had been badly damaged by a big explosion from what I think was a land mine.[5] The blast had caused a lot of damage to some of the other blocks on the complex, which meant that the occupants, including my own family, had to be moved to temporary accommodation while their homes were being repaired.

On the day following the raid I got news that the ship we had been loading in Huskisson Dock had been hit by the bombs. The local newspapers reported that, after she was hit, the ammunition in her hold exploded with such a force that pieces of wreckage were found hundreds of yards away from the dock. The damage to the dock and the nearby warehouses was so great that it made them unusable for many months. In fact, I do not think the dock was used again until the end of the war.

After my escape from what would have been certain death at Huskisson Dock that night, the air raids carried on for the remainder of the week; there was some rest during the hours of daylight, followed by a return to the terror and chaos after dark. Two nights later, as the fires burned all over the city, there was no sign of the fire brigade attempting to bring them under control. There was a big police presence on the streets to deter looters, especially after dark, and I can remember asking one of them why there was no sign of the firemen. 'I don't know,' he replied, 'the place will just have to burn.' After walking away, I realised that the water mains had still not been repaired, as such it was impossible to get water to the fire pumps. But within a few days, things began to improve. Heavy machinery was brought in capable of pumping water directly from the river to the stand–pipes that had been erected around the city, with that the fires were quickly put out and the work of recovery was soon underway.

The centre of the city suffered a lot in the May bombing, but the destruction was worst in Bootle due to its proximity to the docks. It was said that, of the twenty–one thousand homes in the town, about seventeen thousand had been destroyed or severely damaged. Many people were left homeless as a result.

At the end of the eight–day blitz the city began to come to life again, but there was a lot of work to be done before things could return to anything like normality. Fires that had been burning for days had to be put out, unsafe buildings had to be pulled down, roads and streets to be cleared of rubble, craters filled, water, gas and electricity supplies reconnected, people re–housed and a thousand other things. Most of all, the port had to be brought back into operation. Huskisson Dock was written off; it was considered beyond repair – in the short term at least. It made more sense to concentrate efforts on sites that had suffered less severely. On a positive note, there was plenty of employment for those who wanted it. For those who were homeless; and for those whose houses had been damaged to the extent that they had no cooking facilities, mobile canteens were set up to provide free tea and sandwiches.

Between the end of the blitz in May 1941 and volunteering to serve with the Navy about six months later, I was able to take advantage of the labour shortage to find a number of temporary jobs. In one of them I worked as a labourer at a warehouse owned by Bibby, a local soap manufacturer. It had been badly damaged during the bombing, and I was paid four pounds fifteen shillings a week to salvage the white flesh, or copra as it is known, from thousands of shelled coconuts; it was lying scattered around the ruined buildings, unfit for its intended purpose. Once it was bagged, loaded onto trucks and taken away to another plant, it was processed to produce oil – according to what I was told at the time.

Chapter 2

Answering the call; life in barracks

Summer 1941, and the time was fast approaching at which I could expect to be called up. It had been decided that everyone who volunteered before being called up would be allowed to choose which of the three services they wanted to join. For quite a few months I had been thinking about joining the RAF, imagining it would give me a chance to fly. I had somehow convinced myself that most of those in the Air Force would get such an opportunity; I was really excited about the thought of flight and keen to see what it was like, but to this day I have never experienced it, and I fear it is something that will pass me by.

A friend of mine, Frank Sweeny, knowing about my hopes, made some early enquiries and found out that the RAF was recruiting men who they thought might make good rear gunners. Since hearing about it he had gotten it into his head that it would be a great thing to do. If only he had known what he would have been letting himself in for! Nevertheless, by telling me about it he convinced me that I should go with him when he went to volunteer, and one day, in our ignorance, we made our way to the recruitment station at Renshaw Hall in the centre of Liverpool. All three branches of the forces had offices in the building.

When we arrived we headed straight for the RAF desks and spoke to the recruiting sergeant. We told him about our eagerness to fly, and explained that the idea of becoming a rear gunner was something we would like to know more about. Once we had had our say he began by explaining the recruitment process to us, but we were soon disappointed when he said that the first thing we had to do was to sit a test. Not too keen on the idea, I pleaded with him to allow me to sign up without going through with such a thing, explaining that I had hardly had occasion to pick up a pen during the four years that had passed since I left school; but my words fell upon deaf ears. We were taken to a room, each handed an examination paper and told to get on with it.

As I sat down and began to read through the paper, the first thing that caught my eye was the section on questions in mathematics, some of them requiring an understanding of algebra. During my school days just the sound of that strange word had always filled me with fear, not that I ever received any lessons in it. It was hopeless. I looked at the sums containing xs and ys and a smattering of other squiggles which I later found out to be letters from the Greek alphabet, and decided it was not worth attempting the exam, as I would only make a fool of myself. At that I left the desk I had been sitting at and handed in my blank paper. I stepped outside and waited for a while, and it was not long before Frank reappeared from the room. He, like me, could make neither head nor tail of many the questions and had walked out. That test, although we could never have imagined it at the time, probably saved our lives. Casualty rates amongst RAF rear gunners were very high.

We were then faced with a choice between service with the Army or the Navy, and neither of us was willing to entertain the idea of joining the Army. We reckoned that service in the Navy would, if nothing else, offer us regular meals and a comfortable bed every night. Army life, we knew, could be a bit less predictable. Happily, the selection process for the Navy was a completely different affair to that of the RAF. The interviewer simply gave us a list of the possible roles on offer and asked us to choose which of them we might like to take up on entering the service: stoker, signaller, able seaman, etc. Once we had made our choice we were asked to give our name and address. We were then told we could leave the building and wait for our call up papers which, said the interviewer, would be sent out in due course. I had opted for the role of stoker, imagining it would give me an opportunity to learn something of a technical nature which might serve me well once the war was over. Frank plumped for able seaman.

When I arrived home from the recruitment office with the news that I had signed up to join the Navy, I did not get much of a response from the family members who I shared it with. It was only my father who commented, saying that he thought it was a mistake to risk being caught up in an action at sea. 'There's no back door,' he said. I suppose I could understand his reasoning after what he had been through in France during the first war. He had not been a front–line soldier, but the infantry were not the only ones who faced the threat of death or injury. A few months before the war ended he was seriously wounded and sent home. As a result of his injuries, he was left with quite a bad disability that affected him for the rest of his life. Despite his experiences in France, he still felt that service in the Army, rather than the Navy, would increase my chances of survival. 'A soldier can always leg it if he has to,' he said.

Our papers arrived within six weeks. Frank was to go off to Lowestoft to train as a seaman; I was to be sent to HMS *Duke*, a basic training camp in Great Malvern near the city of Worcester. It was a new building, recently opened with the intention of it becoming a training school for officers serving in the peace–time Royal Navy. When war was declared it became a reception centre for ordinary recruits.

The time was soon to arrive for me to report to camp, and on the day that I left home for Worcestershire I could see the concern on my mother's face. She had watched my father go off to war in 1915, leaving her alone with two young daughters. When he returned he was not the man he used to be. She had also lost a brother in the fighting; he died in a hospital in Egypt and was buried somewhere near Alexandria. She never got to visit the cemetery, it seemed a million miles away, but she knew the price of war. After saying my goodbyes, I took my call–up papers to Lime Street station, together with my instructions to report to the Redcaps on duty there. Once my documents had been inspected I was given a train pass for travel to Bristol. My adventure had begun and it would take me across the world to places I could only have dreamt of while growing up in Liverpool.

During my first day at HMS *Duke*, 4 November 1941, all new recruits were told to report to the assembly hall, where we were given a talk by a senior officer. He read out what was, in effect, a general list of what was expected of us: things we could do and things that it might be better for us not to do during our basic training. On the following day we received our uniforms and things began to take on a more military appearance.

We were soon introduced to a physical training instructor who made it clear that, during the coming six weeks, we were going to discover just how fit we were. This gave some of us pause for thought; we had all heard stories of how tough the forces could be with fresh recruits and now it was just a matter of time before we found out if we were up to it. However, it transpired that the first few days of training consisted mainly of drilling on the parade ground, which most of us found to be more tiresome than tiring. We were marched time and again up and down the square for most of the day, every day; but some hours of the week were set aside for exercising in the gym. Even then it was all fairly easy; the instructors taking us through a programme of general fitness training which seemed to have the unexpected aim of getting the whole of the cadre through the course. Then, one day, about three weeks into the training period, we were all sent on an eleven–mile cross country run. Nobody fell out, a detail which might surprise people, but most young men of that era were naturally fit; many of them were already some years into their working life by the time they reached their eighteenth birthday. Almost all would have done some heavy manual work during that time, and if they did not do the modern–day thing of running a few miles once or twice a week, they would certainly walk that distance every day on their journey to and from work, and much more besides.

I should mention that we did not sleep in hammocks during our time at *Duke*. Instead, we were each given a single bed of which there were six to a dormitory. It was not meant to be that way, of course, at least not for the ordinary ratings. We were just lucky enough to have been sent to a place that was going to become an Admiralty administration centre, as such the accommodation had been designed for officers. I could not complain, it meant that I had a bed of my own for just about the first time in my life, what a luxury! Unfortunately, those first six weeks at Great Malvern turned out to be the best I was to experience during the whole of my time in the Navy when it came to accommodation; after that it was more or less all downhill from the day I left Worcestershire.

At *Duke* the trainee seamen were given a lot of rifle practice; the stokers much less. During my first lesson I was issued with a .22 rifle for practice shooting on the indoor range, where we were each handed five rounds of ammunition and told to fire at targets placed about thirty yards away. Our supervisor was a qualified instructor who told us to aim slightly below the centre of the target, as the bullets tended to hit a spot just above the point of aim. 'If you want to hit the bull, aim at six o'clock,' was his catchphrase. With my five rounds I managed one bull's eye, one hit in the ring surrounding it and three more hits in the outer rings. We were ordered to lie down while firing, and can I remember thinking to myself that we could all have done much better if the instructor not been so much of a distraction. He was always barking out orders while he paced up and down behind us, kicking our ankles as he went and telling us to keep our feet further apart.

One day during the following week, I was included in a group of about fifteen recruits who were considered to have done well on the indoor range. Being regarded as potential sharpshooters we were taken to the outdoor range and this time we were given the real thing, the Lee Enfield .303 rifle. Once again we would be firing five rounds of ammunition and, if anything, received an even rougher manhandling than that of the previous week. This time the targets were set at a range of one hundred to one hundred and fifty yards, and it was made clear to everyone that safety on the range was of paramount concern. We were not handed our weapon until we were laid down in position; a clip of five rounds was then given to each man and we were shown how to load the rifle. It was a cold, early winter's day, and with the instructors continually shouting at us and prodding our chests and legs with the toe of their boot, all they succeeded in doing was to break our concentration and impress nobody but themselves. Unhappy at the harassment, I decided simply to fire off all five rounds as fast as I could in order to get it over with. I did not even take the trouble to find out how good or bad my shooting had been. As far as I was concerned, that was that, when it came to shooting practice, and the only other occasion on which I had cause to handle a rifle was on a day during Warship Week in Gloucester.[1] This was a week dedicated to raising money from the public as a contribution towards the cost of building new warships. On the day I refer to, I was sent off to take part in a parade through the town. I took my place in the ranks, and while the majority of the recruits were marched along the streets, others carried buckets into which the public was encouraged to drop whatever loose change they had. The day almost ended in disaster for me. Once the parade was over, I went into Woolworths for a cup of tea, and after enjoying my little refreshment I walked off leaving my rifle standing against the wall next to the table I had been sitting at. Luckily, but a good time later, I realised what I had done and dashed back to Woolies to rescue it. Had I lost it I would have been presented with a bill for seventeen pounds to pay for a replacement.

I do not think we lost a single recruit through absconding during those first six weeks of basic training, which would have been an easy thing to do if anybody had wanted to slip away. If anything, most of the lads seemed to enjoy their time at Great Malvern, the food was good, the level of hygiene good, the dormitories were heated and the sleeping arrangements were divine. Most of us had never had it so good!

When our basic training came to an end we were allocated to naval barracks in various parts of the country. I was posted to HMS *Drake* at Plymouth, others went to Chatham, some to Lowestoft. We had been given no training in seamanship before we left Great Malvern, something that surprised me, but apart from that I had no complaints to make about my introduction to service life. On my final day at *Duke* I was given a train pass and instructed to report to North Road station in Plymouth together with others from the cadre. When we arrived at our destination we were immediately gathered together on the station platform, loaded aboard a covered lorry and driven to the base.

One of the first things that struck me as we entered the barracks at Devonport was the contrast they made with the facilities at HMS *Duke*. In comparison, *Drake* seemed a much older place; it had also suffered as a result of recent German air raids and a lot of the damage was still to be repaired. On the whole, it was a gloomy and unwelcoming sight.

On climbing down from the lorry, all new arrivals were sent to a room in which the floor space was divided into a number of separate living areas, each partitioned from its neighbouring areas by rows of tall, steel lockers, and it was as we were allocated to a particular partition of the room, that we were each assigned a personal space in one of the lockers and told to store our kit there. We were then issued with a hammock; a novelty we had to get used to quickly and something most of us managed without too much trouble. Once you had learned the knack of how to sling it, using two of the vertical posts located amongst the lockers as its stays, it was secure enough to lie in. Nevertheless, after hoisting yourself into your canvas there was always the chance of falling out onto the floor. This happened to some in the early days and it never failed to raise a laugh amongst those who witnessed the painful landing. All considered, one could not, by any stretch of the imagination, describe the accommodation at the barracks as being good, and if anyone had even classified it as being basic, they may well have found themselves accused of exaggerating.

I could sense that I was not going to enjoy my stay at Devonport. It was grim, ill lit and unwelcoming, and as a result of its depressing atmosphere I soon became keen to get away to sea. Happily, I was given the impression that I would not have to wait very long for my opportunity, but this did not turn out to be the case.

During our first three weeks at *Drake*, we were trained in fire–fighting by members of the London Fire Brigade (LFB) who were stationed at the base. The barracks, as I have mentioned, had been the target for a number of air raids and it had been decided that we, the latest cadre to arrive, once trained how to tackle fires, would make a useful reinforcement for the London firemen if the need arose before we went to sea. Apart from the time we spent with the LFB, the rest of our daily routine was fairly relaxed during those first few weeks. There was a non–stop stream of new recruits coming into the barracks to replace those who were posted to ships, and the arrival of the newcomers always provided some distraction for us during our hours of association, as we checked for the presence of any acquaintances from home.

Once our training in fire–fighting was finished, my cadre was sent to HMS *Raleigh* at Torpoint on the west bank of the River Tamar, opposite Devonport. Close to the town there was an oil storage depot where twenty–eight huge tanks held a reserve store of fuel oil for the ships of the Navy. Each had a large number painted on its side (one to twenty–eight). Within sight of the storage tanks there was a watch tower, and to get to the observation cabin at the top of it you had to climb a sixty–foot ladder. Inside the cabin, which was constructed of steel plating, there was a telephone connected to a command post on the ground. If ever there was an air raid, some of the men would have been told to man the little shelter so that they could tell the command post where any fires were breaking out within the depot – that was if they were not roasted alive in the meantime.

Now that we were considered to be expert fire fighters, something we achieved in a very short time, we were taught how to the operate the Dennis pumps that were held on standby at the depot. These were large water pumps mounted on twin–wheeled bogies so that they could be easily hauled into place when tackling fires. The regular practice drills we were required to carry out with these machines always gave us a welcome opportunity for some competition, and as such were carried out with great enthusiasm. By the time we had mastered them we could complete a whole drill in less than two minutes.

By the end of our stay at the fuel depot we had been at Torpoint for a full four months, and as we prepared to return to Devonport we were told that, before going to sea, we would be offered the chance to choose between serving aboard one of the Navy's big ships or a posting to a smaller craft. We were also told to make the best of our remaining time together, as we would soon be split up and posted to our ships in a piecemeal fashion and may never see each other again. In the meantime, having become experts in fire–fighting, as they put it, we would be expected to pass our skills on to the new drafts as they arrived at the base to replace those of us sent away.

By the time we returned to Devonport I had been in the Navy for about six months, which meant I was entitled to some home leave. Shortly before receiving my pass, I was one of five recruits from the cadre to be offered the chance to volunteer for service with the Navy's motor torpedo boat flotillas (MTBs). It was an offer we were all keen to accept.

According to the mixture of rumour, news and gossip which circulated the base at Devonport, the Navy had begun a big ship building programme, and as a result the number of MTBs being brought into service was expected to rise quickly due to their short construction time. The bigger ships would begin to appear sometime later, but at least the shipyards seemed finally to be getting to grips with the reality of the country's situation. It was said that the time needed to build a frigate, though much less than what it had been in peacetime, was still about four months. MTBs on the other hand could be built in a matter of weeks. But before receiving my posting to an MTB flotilla, I left the base for my two weeks home leave, and by the time I returned to Devonport I found that I had missed the boat; literally. My four friends had taken their opportunity and joined the little boats while I was in Liverpool.

Each of them required two stokers and my pals had been paired off; each pair being assigned to a different boat. They were already on active service before my leave was over, and it was extremely annoying for me, knowing that I had now to settle into the routine of barracks life once more. About two years later, while on shore leave, I met up with one of the four. He was on the run at that time having jumped ship, but I shared a few drinks with him as I was still keen to know what it was like to be on the MTBs. The idea of taking on the German E–boats in the channel, which is how I saw it, had gripped my imagination at the time I volunteered to join them. My friend, however, was more interested in pouring out his heart to me about the breakup of his marriage which, he said, was the reason he had 'skated.' It was the last time I ever saw him.

In spite of the fact that I was in the middle of my training to become a stoker, I was once again sent to HMS *Raleigh* together with others from my cadre who, like me, were still waiting to be sent to sea. We were, as warned, given the task of training naval ratings in fire–fighting. The men sent to join us were recruits who had signed up as able seamen, so it seemed as though the Navy had finally realised that training its stokers to fight fires would mean that their skills might not be put to best use. Personally, I felt the whole experience had been a complete waste of my time.

After five weeks of working as an instructor I became completely disillusioned with the way in which my life in the Navy was going, and I decided to make my feelings known. I spoke to one of the officers at the base and made the point that I had not joined up to be a fire–fighter, stressing as much as I could that I just wanted to finish my training and go to sea as a stoker as soon as possible. At first it seemed as though my actions were about to be rewarded; within a week I was released from my instructor's post and sent back to Devonport, but nothing much happened after that. Sadly a ship posting never materialised, and more meaningless duties at the barracks came my way. I should say at this point, purely as a matter of interest, that during basic training my pay was one pound and eight shillings a week. Once qualified as a stoker I would receive an extra seven shillings a week, which would take my weekly pay to one pound and fifteen shillings. From this it was easy to see that qualification was being deliberately withheld from so many as a deliberate act; it was simply a money–saving game for the Navy.

Shortly after returning to *Drake* I was assigned for a period of several weeks to the dirty and uncomfortable work of boiler cleaning. It was genuine stoker's work, so although still less than happy, I decided just to get on with it, hoping that I would soon be sent to sea. As the warships came in, the trainee stokers were sent aboard to carry out this unpopular chore, and it went on for week after week, resulting in a demoralisation amongst my comrades which soon became apparent. We became a bit narky; short–tempered, and we soon began to complain about our food and accommodation. These were things we had been willing to accept at first, because we regarded them as temporary evils in the life of every recruit, but we were now becoming seasoned hands and we felt we were ready for the chance to go to sea. The waiting, the frustration and the boredom of killing time ashore were getting harder to stomach, and to give more justification for the change in our attitude, it must be said that the living conditions at the barracks were nothing short of a disgrace. There was no linoleum on the dormitory floors; bare wooden boards were the standard, and these were cleaned by just swilling them with buckets of water before sweeping it away with a yard brush. For the most part the furniture consisted of old, knocked about three–piece suites, the stuffing of which was lousy, but there were no plain wooden chairs which would have allowed you to sit down for a while without running the risk of being bitten or infested by bugs. At one time, as a means of easing the overcrowding in the accommodation blocks, some of us were moved from the base to a bomb–damaged church and ordered to sleep on the floor. They were dark days. But life was not entirely without its lighter side, and one incident that happened about that time has stayed with me ever since. I still have a chuckle whenever I think about it, and as is the case with so many funny stories, its roots lay in drink.

All new arrivals at the barracks, so long as they had been signed–in before 11:30 on the day and were past their twentieth birthday, qualified for a daily tot of rum served just before lunch. The barracks accommodation at *Drake* was divided into what were called messes. There were about three hundred men to a mess, and a mess seemed to be treated by the base administrators as an indicator for the volume required when it came to dispensing rum around the site. It would arrive at 11:30 in a large dixie carried, as always, by some of the old salts at the base, all of whom had a long–cultivated taste for the liquor. They were known as 'rum rats' and they were experts in making sure that no sailor in the mess ever received his daily tot in full measure. Once everyone bar themselves had been served, the savings would remain in the dixie to be used to top up their own ration.

With the dixie sitting on a large table in the centre of the mess, one of the rum rats would pull out a book in which were listed the names of all those qualifying for a tot that day. Another of the rats would call out the men by name, while a third stood by the dixie holding the standard measure at the ready, which amounted to about a quarter of a gill. On being called forward a sailor would hold out his mess tin to receive his ration. It was at this point where you needed to be ready to spot the tricks used to deny you your full tot. There might be a ha'penny lying in the bottom of the measure; a thumb might be placed on the lip of the measure with its tip displacing a small amount of rum; the measure might be held at a slight tilt so that it would be not quite full when it was tipped into the mess tin; and so on.

On the day in question, one of the new men stepped forward before his name was called and demanded his tot. At first this caused a lot of confusion amongst the rum rats; it was as though it was something they had never seen before. They looked at each other, not quite knowing what to do next. At the end of the pause the rat holding the register of names asked the new man who he was, and a name was given in reply. The register was then carefully scanned by the bookkeeper, with the result that the newcomer was told that he was not listed. He was then told to report to the quarterdeck to get his ration there. At that the new man left, but he soon reappeared, insisting that he should receive his rum in the mess. The rum rats would have none of it. They refused point blank to serve him. At this the man's anger boiled over; he lifted the dixie from the table and yelled out that, if there was to be no rum for him, there would be none for anybody else in the mess. At that point, before the stunned rum rats could react, he flung the container, contents and all, across the floor. The resulting scenes had to be seen to be believed. Men were on their knees, some licking and slurping at the floor boards, others were trying to scoop up what they could with anything that came to hand. Within seconds punches were being thrown and furniture knocked over as almost all those present in the mess became involved in the brawl. Luckily there were no officers present to witness the scene, which in the end fizzled out once everybody had let off enough steam.

Each night in the mess, between 20:00 and 21:00, the men would find out what their duties were for the following day; it was usually a killick who brought the news. He would enter carrying a bundle of chits; these were strips of paper about one inch wide and a foot in length, all bound together in a book resembling a wad of raffle tickets. Written on the paper slips were the details of a man's next assignment, usually in type but with hand written notes where needed. The chits were of two kinds: one for giving the men a task at the barracks, the other to inform them that they had been drafted to a ship. There was a chit each night for every man in the mess.

One night, after receiving so many duty chits over the previous months, I finally received a draft. I was detailed to report to HMS *Carlisle*, a cruiser which was berthed in Devonport, and I cannot say I was unhappy at the thought of leaving base. Next morning I gathered my belongings, packed them into my kitbag, took down my hammock, rolled and tied it, picked up my small brown suitcase and set off to find my new home. But once I got aboard it soon became clear to me that *Carlisle* was a very unhappy ship. There was no sign of the kind of welcome usually given to the new arrivals at the barracks; in fact, there was no greeting at all from any of my new shipmates. It was easy to see that morale amongst the crew was very low, and it gave me a very uneasy feeling. After reporting to the forecastle as a replacement stoker, I was escorted to the boiler room by another matelot. He was quite open about the fact that he was what we termed a 'skate,' a man who had previously jumped ship and had been tracked down and returned to the Navy. The usual punishment for this offence was a ninety–day sentence served in a naval prison, and in some cases, before a man's sentence was up, the naval prison service would deliver him to a ship which was about to sail on a long voyage, usually to the Far East.

This was the first time I had spent any amount of time in the close presence of a skate, but I had seen many of them enter the barracks when being returned to the service. At Devonport they would arrive on trains which pulled directly into a siding within the walls of the base. All of them would be in handcuffs, and after being taken off the train they would be marched straight onto their ship by an escort of Royal Marines. Once they were aboard, the marines would post a guard on the gangway to make sure there were no easy opportunities for escape before the ship cast off. I felt uneasy in the man's company, he was unfriendly, untalkative, a bit distant and moody.

After inspecting the boiler room I went to look for a place where I could stow my kit and sling my hammock. As I was settling in one of the crew came up to me and made it clear that he would prefer it if I found somewhere else to sleep, insisting he had already claimed the space I was about to use. As I looked around for another berth I began to get a better idea of the state of things aboard the cruiser. At one point I overheard a group of men plotting to throw other members of the crew overboard during the next voyage. At that I decided I would be better off if I went ashore for the night, so I got cleaned up, shaved and dressed, and set off to find a YMCA, or something similar, where I could spend my nights after coming off duty until the day we sailed. I just did not fancy the thought of spending a night aboard *Carlisle,* and I felt it was just my luck that I was the only man from the barracks who had been posted to the ship; it only added to my sense of loneliness.

Suddenly my luck changed. When I returned to the ship next morning, the chief stoker sent for me and told me to report to the forecastle. It was there where I was told that I was no longer needed and that I had to return to barracks. I had been drafted to *Carlisle* to replace one of the stokers who had been complaining of what he said was appendicitis, but after being admitted to Stonehouse Hospital he was examined and passed fit to return to duty. He had been faking it in an attempt to avoid sailing with *Carlisle* on her next voyage – and I could not blame him.

I spent another two or three weeks at Devonport before I received a second draft, and it was during that time I met up with an old pal from home. The two of us would sometimes take a trip into Plymouth to have a few pints together. One time we had a bit too much to drink, and when I returned to *Drake* I could not find my hammock. Instead of upsetting those who were sleeping nearby by fumbling about in search of my kit, I decided to sleep on one of the old sofas that lay around the mess; it was a bad decision. By the time I woke up I was infested with bugs, and it made me feel so bad that

I reported to the sick bay. The medical staff ordered me to remove all my clothing and take it to the de–lousing facility, where high pressure steam jets were used to sterilise it. It was only after I had taken a long, hot bath and put on my freshly cleaned clothes that I felt better. But the whole incident was enough to make my morale sink even further. A few days later I was given a second draft, this time to a destroyer, HMS *Fernie*. She was stationed at Sheerness and was at that time attached to the Russian convoys.[2] I had heard a lot about the conditions when making the runs to Murmansk, but by that time, as far as I was concerned, one ship was as good as any. I had had enough of barracks life and I was just happy to be leaving. It was mid–March 1943.

On the following day I was given my train pass and set off to join *Fernie*, but I was about to have another lucky escape; lucky in the sense that it saved me from making what Churchill called 'the worst journey in the world,' a trip to Archangel or Murmansk. The medical condition which saved me might have been triggered during my train journey to Sheerness. For most of the trip I sat near an open window, which meant the smoke and soot coming from the engine would get into the compartment from time to time. By the time I arrived at my destination I could already feel that I had the beginnings of an infection in one of my eyes. After leaving the train I asked someone at the station for directions, and found my way to the jetty where I waited for a transfer to the ship. After about an hour and a half spent on the cold, lonely pier, a liberty boat appeared and pulled alongside. I spoke with the skipper and told him that I was a draft for *Fernie*. I then scrambled aboard and we set off towards the ship, which was anchored in the sound.

Within four hours of going aboard I was called to the sick bay to undergo a medical examination, and the ship's doctor quickly diagnosed my worsening eye infection, which was confirmed by the presence of swollen glands. It was enough to have me struck from the crew. The medic explained that he could not risk putting to sea with anyone who was not one hundred per cent fit. Once in the northern seas, he said, life was so hard that there would be little time to spend treating the sick. I was soon returned to shore.

On my return to *Drake* I reported to the administration office, and once I explained why I had been relieved from duty there were some strong words for those considered responsible for having sent an unfit man to sail with the Russian convoys; the more so as I had been given a medical examination at Devonport on the day before I left and was passed fit for the posting. Totally demoralised by losing yet another chance of going to sea, I settled back into the routine of barracks life wondering if I would ever get to serve aboard ship before the war was over.

One of the most monotonous things about life at *Drake* were the fire drills, which were carried out almost every week. Checks were made to ensure that the fire buckets were full of sand; that everyone knew where the buckets were standing; that the men knew what to do when the fire alarm sounded; that fire escapes were kept clear, and so on. The base authorities were paranoid about these drills, and to be fair the barracks had suffered during the air raids on Plymouth in 1941. On those occasions the fire–fighting had been for real and many lessons were learned. As such, everyone was expected to take the drills seriously.

During one particular drill myself and five others were placed under the supervision of a chief stoker, a man who was well known for the sharp way in which he spoke whenever he addressed anyone of a lower rank. It was said that he tended almost to bark at the people under him, rather than talk to them. We were going to take part in an emergency drill to test our reactions to an alarm indicating that a fire had broken out in the attic. Directly beneath the attic space concerned was the snooker room, a place where men would get together for a bit of relaxation while off duty. So, the scene was set for a piece of pure slapstick comedy – with audience.

Having been told about our drill we waited for the sound of the practice alarm, and when it went off we sprinted away to tackle the 'blaze'. In order to get into the loft where the fire was supposed to be burning we had to find ourselves a ladder, so we scurried about in search of one, trying to look concerned. We were doing our best to take things seriously enough to keep chief stoker happy. Once we found a ladder we carried it off at the double, with the chief stoker running ahead shouting, 'Fire! Fire!' as we burst in on the occupants of the snooker room. In no time at all the loft door was pushed open, the ladder run up; and with me at the foot of it holding it steady, three of the party climbed up into the loft with the shouts of the chief ringing in their ears. They had not long been in the attic before he began bawling at the top of his voice to, 'Come down! Come down!' One of the men up above was an acquaintance of mine from home. I knew he was a bit short–tempered, and as I could feel that he was getting very agitated by the non–stop shouting of the chief, I began to wonder just how long it would be before he flipped. As he was waiting his turn to come down the ladder his anger began to boil up, and he started shouting back at the chief, telling him to 'shut up', but his words had no effect, the chief continued shouting as though he was in a trance. At that he lost control of himself and slid down the ladder, one foot on each side bar, and as he sped past him he landed the chief an almighty blow on the head with the torch he was carrying. At the sight of all this commotion, the men who had been playing cards or snooker before we arrived were now looking on in amazement, and when the chief's head resounded to the thump it received, they were in fits of laughter as they watched him stagger about the room, half senseless and just about managing to stay on his feet.

As his head began to clear the chief pulled himself together and began to make threats to his assailant, who claimed he was only trying to recover his balance by flinging out his arm as he slid down the ladder. When it was all over we continued to break into fits of laughter whenever we thought about it. On the following morning, when our tormentor returned to assign us to new duties, he made such a comical sight that we just about managed to contain ourselves. Overnight, such a lump had risen upon his skull that his cap would not sit straight upon his head. Luckily nobody was placed on a charge because of what had happened, but it was the last fire drill I can remember being asked to take part in whilst in barracks, as I was about to be given my long–awaited posting to a ship.

Characters the likes of my acquaintance from home, the man referred to above, were by no means uncommon in the Navy. I had the pleasure of meeting another of his kind when my path crossed with that of a man by the name of Gleeson, who came from either Bradford or Blackpool, I cannot remember which. I will refer to him as Brad Gleeson to avoid any confusion, as he was no relation to my long–time friend, Frank Gleeson from Liverpool, to whom I will refer once more at a later point in this story. Brad had an unfortunate knack of getting himself into scrapes, even in the most unlikely circumstances. At some time before the war he had earned his living in the boxing ring, and was what some people might describe as being 'a bit of a rough diamond.' One of his favourite sayings was that he would do anything for anyone, so long as they spoke to him nicely. However, I could not help but hear the hint of menace in his voice whenever I heard him repeat those words.

I first met him when he moved into barracks after serving a ninety–day stint in the lock–up; he was assigned the locker next to mine. As a result of being constantly in trouble he had not had any home leave for about eighteen months by the time I met him, and on this, his most recent release, he had been promised that, so long as he kept his nose clean for two weeks, he would be rewarded with two weeks home leave, and he was determined, so he said, to stay out of trouble at all costs.

After spending his first five days in the mess in a contented frame of mind he began to get frustrated at being cooped up all day, so he came up with the idea that we should go to the cinema in Plymouth. He seemed serious about avoiding the pubs, so I agreed to go with him and suggested that we ask for a free gangway on the day. This was a way by which men could leave barracks at a time later than five o'clock in the evening without going through the trouble of submitting to a proper dress inspection. The checking of your appearance was something that applied to everybody who was going on formal leave, and before being allowed off the base you had to present yourself in full uniform, including lanyard, for inspection by an officer. I could never be bothered with having to go through the rigmarole of dressing up, so I always requested a free gangway whenever I wanted to go anywhere of an evening, and tended to leave barracks at about seven or eight o'clock.

Brad thought my idea was a good one, and when the chosen evening arrived I went off to get ready once I had finished work. He had told me earlier that a pal of his was in the Strong Box (they had become pals during his last spell there) and that, after paying him a visit, he would return to meet me before we both went into town. The reason for wanting to visit the Strong Box, he said, was to take a couple of 'tiddy oggies' to his old cell mate as, he said, the food in the lock up was 'not of the highest quality.'[3]

Once dressed and ready to go out I waited in the mess for Brad to reappear, but time passed by and there was no sign of him, so I decided to take a walk towards the gaol to see if I could find him. As I stepped out of the building, there he was, close to the doorway, minus his collar, and looking a bit of a mess. He was surrounded by an escort under which he was being marched off. When he noticed me he asked his gaolers to stop so he could have a word with me. When he spoke he explained that, after buying two tiddy oggies in the canteen, he had made his way to the Strong Box. On reaching the cells the PO on duty asked him what he wanted, and he had replied that he was fetching a couple of pasties for his pal. On hearing this the PO refused to let him in. There was then a heated exchange, explained Brad, during which he 'snapped' and gave the PO 'a bit of a pasting.' At this he was overpowered by the rest of the guard, and after a struggle he was now in the process of being marched off for questioning. It was the last I saw of him. There are some fellows who just cannot be tamed, and I would place Brad amongst them. I finally left Devonport a few days later.

The new year was now well underway, and during the months of January, February and March of 1943, *Drake* became a very miserable place. During those long, dark days of winter the gloominess of our quarters was made worse by the fact that they were lit almost everywhere by dim, forty–watt bulbs, many of which had long given up the ghost and were waiting to be replaced. One night after finishing my duties I decided to take a bath, and so dim was it in the ablutions block that, both during and after I had run the bath water, I did not notice the filthy state of the tub I was about to use. In complete ignorance I climbed in, and as I began to wash myself I noticed the presence of a greasy, clinging scum all over my body. It must have been stuck to the sides of the bath, invisible in the half–light of the block, and had mixed with the water as the tub had slowly filled. It was too late to get out and avoid the worst of it, as I was already covered in slime. It was clear to me that, either there was nobody assigned to regular cleaning duties in the toilet block, or that I had suffered the bad luck of using a bath tub which somebody had left in a terrible state. I gingerly hauled myself up out of the filthy water, but by then the scum and slime were clinging to the hair on my head and legs. At that moment the duty officer appeared, so I called him over and made him aware of the state I was in. He hardly seemed bothered by it and did nothing to help me. I was left to clean myself as best I could, but I was not going to try another of the baths in the block, so I was left with the only option of a long rinse under a cold–water tap; there was nothing else for it. After an uncomfortable twenty minutes or so I managed to remove most, if not all, of the disgusting slime from my body, but it hardly mattered. I felt so uncomfortable about the whole experience that it was a long time before I could put my mind to ease.

The whole question of personal hygiene appeared to be ignored at Devonport. Many of the old, enamelled hand basins which were in daily use were punctured and leaky, and would not hold any reasonable amount of water for any length of time. It was nothing short of a disgrace. It seemed to me that the one and only thing that was ever taken seriously as regards the general health of the ratings was the ever–present threat of tuberculosis. Nobody was ever allowed to join a ship until they had reported for a chest x–ray. There were also regular health checks at the x–ray unit for all those in barracks who had not had an x–ray during the previous six months. Once it had been taken and analysed the result was recorded in your pay book, which was then stamped to confirm the date of the procedure.

There were two particular offices at *Drake*; they bore the names, DF01 and DF02, and it was there where those responsible for writing up the draft chits were housed. I had been at Devonport for sixteen months by this time, still waiting for a ship, so I decided to take things into my own hands by paying a visit to the chit writers and pleading my case for a ship transfer as soon as possible. I was asked if I had any preferences for a posting, and in desperation to escape from barracks life I told them I was willing to consider anything they had to offer. 'Rest assured,' I was told, 'and just make sure you are present in your mess when the killick appears with the draft and duty chits this evening.' I returned to the mess for what seemed like an endless wait. When the killick finally arrived I could not contain myself, and on approaching him, for I could not wait to see what he had for me, he became aware of my presence and told me that he had been instructed to send me along to DF02.

I was at the office door in a flash, and it was there where I was delighted to hear that they had found me a draft. I was to join HMS *Woodpecker*, a Bird–class sloop.[4] 'Are you a Scouse, by any chance?' asked the officer in charge, to which I replied, 'Yes.' 'Then you might be happy to know that she's stationed at Liverpool,' he said. He must have noticed the expression that began to spread across my face, as he then asked me if I felt it to be a suitable posting. I replied that it was – very much so! I was beside myself at that point in the interview and it really must have shown. He then told me that my happiness might be further increased, as he was in the process of confirming two weeks leave for me!

Alas, the two weeks leave did not materialise, as information later arrived to the effect that *Woodpecker*, then berthed in Gladstone Dock, would be sailing in five days' time. I was to leave for Liverpool straight away. Eighteen months had passed since the day I arrived at Great Malvern to start basic training.

Chapter 3

My first days aboard HMS *Woodpecker*

With my train pass in my pocket I travelled to Plymouth North Road station, caught the one o'clock train to Liverpool and arrived a little after midnight with orders to report aboard HMS *Woodpecker* without delay. When the train pulled into Lime Street, I gathered up the awkward load of my suitcase, kit bag and hammock, stepped out of the carriage and made my way out of the station onto the city–centre streets where I caught a tram to Gladstone Dock. Before climbing aboard I took a glance along Lime Street towards Commutation Row, just beyond which was the entrance to Gerard Gardens, a block of tenements belonging to the scheme of corporation flats where my family lived. I imagined them all, sitting around the fireplace, unaware of my presence just a few hundred yards away. For all I knew this might be the last time I would be so close to them; if things were to go badly for me, I would not be the only sailor to be lost at sea on his first trip.

It was my first visit to Liverpool for quite a few months, and it seemed as though the city had not suffered too much in the meantime. Air raids were then a thing of the past, I do not think there had been any for almost two years, but the damage caused in the spring of 1941 was still everywhere to be seen. As the tram trundled along the empty streets I began to wonder if I might still get an opportunity to see my family before we sailed, and with my mind drifting I was suddenly brought back to myself when the driver called the stop for Gladstone Dock, which was just a short walk from the halt where I was dropped off. On arrival at the dockyard I showed my pass to the policemen on guard duty at the dock gate and was allowed through. It was late April 1943.

Of the six ships that were about to make up the new Second Support Group, five were berthed at Liverpool, the fifth, HMS *Starling* was, I think, at Belfast or Londonderry. She was captained by the famous Johnny Walker, who was about to take command of the group. The ships were in dock for refuelling and preparation before setting out on what would be their first patrol as a single group. *Woodpecker* was the latest ship to join Walker's flotilla.

Once in the dockyard I lugged my belongings along the quayside, checking the names of the ships as I went, and it was almost an hour past midnight by the time I caught my first sight of *Woodpecker* lying at her berth. I can still remember seeing the quartermaster standing at the top of the gangway as I approached him up the steep climb under the weight of my kit. When I reached the spot where he was waiting, I showed him my papers and was told to come aboard to seek out the coxswain's office. After a brief talk, the cox led me along to the stokers' mess where more introductions were made before he left me to settle in, having given me instructions to report back to him on the morning of the following day.

Some of the crew were still on leave, which meant there were plenty of vacant spaces around the mess which I could claim as my berth. But I was keen to avoid a repetition of the kind of welcome I received aboard *Carlisle*, so I found myself a decent spot and, after a quick check with those present to make sure nobody objected to me being there, I slung my hammock and stored my belongings close by as best as I could. That done, I settled down to my first night aboard my new ship. On the following day, I received a message requesting me to report to the chief stoker rather than the coxswain. This was to be another friendly encounter during which the chief explained to me the basics of life aboard ship whilst at sea. There were two watches; let me call them Red and Blue, and each rating was assigned to one or the other which, in effect, meant that most of those aboard the ship were divided into two separate crews. It was the Navy's way of ensuring the twenty-four hour manning and operation of its ships.

The atmosphere aboard *Woodpecker* could hardly have been more different to that aboard *Carlisle*. There was a happy, confident manner amongst the crew, a lot of laughing and joking, and it did not take long for me to begin to feel happy in my new surroundings. Many of the men were from my home town, some from Manchester, some from St Helens and others from Scotland. By talking to them during that first day aboard *Woodpecker* I found out that, just before

> being assigned to the Second Support Group, she had completed an escort patrol during which she had been with a convoy on its way New York.[1] On her return journey she had picked up a homeward bound convoy.[2] Both crossings, it was said, were completed with no sign of the Germans.

The return trip to Canada and the United States just mentioned was *Woodpecker*'s first active patrol after being commissioned. The convoys referred to by Marsden were ON 164, an outward–bound convoy for New York which left Liverpool on 1 February 1943 and arrived in New York on 19 February 1943. No ships were listed as lost due to enemy action. The inward–bound convoy from New York to the UK was SC 120, which left on 13 February 1943 and arrived in Liverpool on 5 March 1943; again, no ships were listed as lost due to enemy action.

At first glance it would seem that, from the arrival date of ON 164 in New York, and the departure date from New York of SC 120, *Woodpecker* could not have been with the return convoy. However, escorts did not always stay with a convoy all the way into its port of destination. On some occasions they would rendezvous with outbound convoys a few days after their sailing date, leaving the inbound convoy to complete its voyage under modified escort cover.

After the successful completion of her Atlantic crossing *Woodpecker* took part in a second patrol, shepherding the dual convoy KMF 11 & WS 28. This left the Clyde on 15 March 1943 en route to Algiers. Later, its two component convoys split at a position west of Gibraltar; WS 28 making for Freetown, Sierra Leone, where it arrived on 27 March, whilst KMF 11 continued towards Algiers, arriving on 23 March.[3] It was there where *Woodpecker* stopped to refuel, after which she joined the escorts of a convoy making the return trip to the UK; this was convoy MKF 11, an inward–bound convoy from Bone, North Africa, which left on 26th March 1943 and arrived on the Clyde on 5 April 1943. No ships were listed as lost due to enemy action.[4]

There were no encounters with U–boats on either passage, but the port of Algiers was attacked by Italian aircraft not long after the incoming convoy arrived. It was after she had completed this Mediterranean patrol that *Woodpecker* was transferred to Johnny Walker's Second Support Group.[5]

> During the final two days before sailing with *Woodpecker* on what was to be her first patrol as part of the Second Support Group, I was introduced to the system of canteen messing, and I will now provide an example of how it worked. All hands were allowed one shilling and nine pence per day for messing. The mess money from

all the different messes was collected on a regular basis and handed over to a man who went by the title of the 'Jack Dusty.' It was he who took on the job of buying provisions for the ship's crew. He was responsible for the purchase of food and other necessities as well as various extras, some of which could be sold to members of the crew, with any profits being returned to the mess funds. A book was kept by each mess, and each week the men were asked to list the food or dishes they would like to have served at the galley during the coming seven days. Any members of the mess who enjoyed cooking, and had the confidence that they could satisfy the standards demanded by their shipmates, could volunteer for the task of assisting the cook while off watch.

From memory the different messes aboard *Woodpecker* were organised as follows: the ASDIC mess with about seven men; the stokers' mess with about thirty; the seamen's mess with about one hundred and twenty and the officers' mess with about fifteen. *Starling*, being the Group Commander's ship, carried extra officers and specialists.

While his ship was in port the Jack Dusty, with his weekly purse, had the freedom to buy supplies as and where he pleased. *Woodpecker*'s 'Dusty' preferred the local markets, especially when buying fresh fruit and vegetables. He could commission a Navy services lorry whenever he planned a visit to the stalls, and to judge by the quantity and quality of the fresh supplies he returned with during my first few days aboard, it seemed that, in the port of Liverpool at least, there was no great shortage of necessities during the early months of 1943. On the other hand rationed items, such as bacon, eggs and butter, were far less easy to find; oranges, for example, were very difficult if not impossible to come by. The messing system allowed for monthly accounts to be presented and this avoided any suspicion that the funds held by the Jack Dusty might be going astray.

As a matter of interest the oldest man in the mess was known as the 'Peggy', and with his knowledge of the world's sea ports he could usually be relied upon for advice regarding the best places to visit during a run ashore.

I am often asked about the daily rum ration issued to naval ratings in those days, and here is what I usually have to say about it: Firstly, in its raw state it was something similar to a thin syrup; in other words a bit heavy, which meant that it was watered down in the ratio of one, two or three parts of water to one of rum. If you think of the amount served in what is called a double measure of spirits at a public house (about one sixth of a gill) then you would be close to imagining the volume of a tot of rum.

The official drill was enforced aboard the Navy's big ships, which meant that the men had to drink their rum ration in the presence of an officer. This was done to prevent them storing away their tots until they had built up a decent volume of spirits, which they might then sell to their shipmates or drink themselves in the space of a few hours in order to get tipsy. Aboard the small ships the routine was more relaxed, the men were allowed to take their measure of rum to the dinner table and drink it at their leisure. That is not to say that everyone could be trusted not to hoard their rations. When the men were about to begin a period of shore leave, some would secretly store away several days' rations in a larger container with the aim of going ashore with what was termed a 'good starter.' I will confess to having done this myself on one occasion, when I used an old brylcreem jar as a makeshift hip flask.

Having accumulated a supply of rum you had to solve the problem of how to get it ashore without it being discovered. Many were the methods used to achieve this. The most common was that of putting on a pair of long socks when dressing to go ashore. These came up to about calf height on the legs, and into the top of one of them you could insert your 'flask'. The baggy sailors' trousers we wore would ensure that there was no visible bulge on the leg; no outward sign that might be spotted as you passed the guard on your way out of the dockyard. All of this was not without its risks; if you were caught it was considered to be a serious breach of the rules, and the punishment could be anything up to ninety days in a naval prison or in a military wing contained within a civilian prison. But I can say that I never saw anyone brought up for that particular offence.

Finally, the day came to sail on my first patrol. It was also to be the first patrol of the Second Support Group, and we left Liverpool bound for Londonderry or Belfast (my memory is not clear as to which) where we were to team up with *Starling*. On the way we were re–directed to Larne where we berthed for two days. Once *Starling* joined us the group was complete: *Starling, Woodpecker, Wildgoose, Wren, Kite and Cygne*t. And after leaving the port of Larne we assembled off the Irish coast and headed westward into the Atlantic. It was May 1943.

Chapter 4

My first taste of action

> I do not think we were ever with a convoy during the first two weeks at sea in the Atlantic, which meant that all I could ever gaze upon was the empty ocean, and it made me think that we might well be wasting our time. It was difficult to believe the U–boats were here, and even if they were, how would we know, and how could we find them? It seemed impossible they were out there, maybe even watching us. It all made me think that the odds must have been firmly in favour of the Germans in this game.

Marsden's early thoughts were somewhat naive, of course. The U–boat was not the perfect fighting vessel he imagined it to be; it had its limitations. It could not remain submerged for long periods and it could move only at low speed whilst below the surface. It also had to communicate with other U–boats at sea and with its base in mainland Europe; all of which allowed its radio messages to be intercepted by Allied ships, as well as land–based listening stations, thus giving away its position. Enemy transmissions could also be decoded, and when British intelligence was successful in breaking a code, it sometimes allowed the Admiralty to marshal its anti–submarine forces in such a manner as to offer a material threat to imminent U–boat operations in the Atlantic. Even during engagements at sea, once a U–boat had made an attack on Allied shipping its close presence was necessarily revealed, which meant that well organised, local escort forces could mount swift counter attacks. The U–boats had also to navigate to and from their bases on the French Atlantic coast at the beginning and end of their patrols, and could thus be intercepted whilst traversing the Bay of Biscay before disappearing into the vastness of the North Atlantic, or when re–emerging from the open seas on their homeward voyage. Of course, the greatest threat to Doenitz's boats would eventually come from the air, but during the U–boat war the allies were slow to exploit the advantages provided by air cover, air reconnaissance and air search and destroy tactics. The problem was two–fold: a lack of aircraft in the face of competing claims for their use in other theatres;

and in the early days of the Atlantic struggle, a lack of range amongst the few aircraft types assigned to the U–boat war. That said, the U–boat was still more vulnerable to destruction than it might seem to be at first glance, especially by the spring of 1943, as Marsden was about to learn. At that time, the ships of the Second Support Group were some several hundred miles west of Ireland with the ocean seemingly to themselves, when suddenly the alarm was sounded calling all hands to action stations. The technical teams, on continuous surveillance at their ASDIC screens and radio detection units, had picked up a radio message being transmitted by a U–boat located somewhere on the surface not too far distant from Walker's ships. The excitement of Marsden's first chase had begun.

> Whenever a U–boat was detected by one of our ships, it would hoist a black pennant to alert the other ships of the group. Knowing there was a U–boat somewhere near, the rest of them would try to pick it up. Obviously, as we closed in, it would usually detect us and try to escape, but with Walker in charge its chances were not good. So long as we could keep a ping on it, we could keep depth charging it until we either sank it or forced it to come up.
>
> An attacking ship could drop anything up to about twenty depth charges when going for the kill, but to keep a tight pattern it would have to slow down as the charges were dropped over the stern. This meant that as soon as the last of the charges was rolled into the sea, she had to go to full throttle to get clear of the explosions. Once all the charges had exploded down below, a look out was kept for any signs of wreckage coming to the surface. During this chase it became clear that the first attack had failed, so the next ship was ordered to move in and the whole procedure was repeated. The second attempt on the U–boat also ended with no signs of success. I cannot remember which of the sloops made the first attacks on this occasion; it may have been *Wildgoose* and *Starling*.
>
> The attacks continued as we kept a ping on the U–boat, the sloops being positioned and repositioned before they attacked, and after each set of underwater explosions there was a halt while the sea was scanned for signs of wreckage or oil slicks. In this, the first hunt of a U–boat I took part in, the depth charge attacks were repeated time after time for about sixteen hours. Walker was not a man to give up.
>
> Over such a long time the usual changing of the watches would continue aboard the ships in the chase. For example, during this

hunt I would spend anything up to four hours at a time working in the boiler room as the action went on, taking my rest when relieved at the end of each watch. After my relief had taken over on one occasion, I was surprised to be ordered to take my place at the stern of the ship to help the men at the depth charge racks. It was hard work. Each of them weighed about four hundredweight and they had to be manhandled onto the racks. It was from these that the charges were rolled into the sea. The depth at which a charge would explode was controlled by the setting of a fuse, and Walker would sometimes tell the attacking ship what the settings should be. The fuses were then primed by one of the ship's electricians in the lead–up to an attacking run.

The visible effect of the underwater explosions at the surface depended on the depth at which charges were set to go off. If they were set to shallow, the explosions could be heard and they would be followed almost immediately by a huge water spout when the blast reached the surface. If the charges went off at greater depths you could not hear them, and sometimes the only sign that they had exploded was a kind of sudden jolt across the surface of the water, as though the sea sprang up a bit before falling back, giving off a wispy spray.

The hunt went on into the night, and my earlier thoughts about how we could be sure that we had found the enemy below began to run through my mind once more. I was having doubts as to whether it had all been real or just a bit of a wild–goose chase. Then, at about eleven o'clock, Walker signalled to all the ships in the group, telling them to stagger the time at which the usual midnight change of watch took place. Some ships were to make the change at 23:30, the rest at 00:30. There was to be no changeover at 24:00. The U–boat had to surface because its sea batteries would have been running low, and Walker wanted all his ships on full stand–by close to the stroke of midnight. His thinking was that, in trying to escape, the U–boat skipper would surface at that moment and try to take advantage of the change of watch which he would have known was about to take place at that time. In doing so he might gain a few minutes and get off a few rounds from his deck–gun at the ships surrounding him. If luck was on his side, the panic amongst them might give him a chance to make a dash for it on the surface under cover of dark. U–boats could make a speed of only five knots or so when submerged, but they could match the escorts on the surface, where they could use their powerful diesel engines.

As the night wore on there was a growing sense of tension amongst the crew of *Woodpecker*. Had the last sixteen hours or so been a complete waste of time; were we just chasing shadows? The moment of truth was near and everyone was ready.

The U–boat broke surface almost on the stroke of midnight and began to make a run for it. Some of its crew scrambled from the conning tower looking as though they were about to man the four–inch gun on its deck. The response was incredible. Star shells were launched, bursting over the whole scene and leaving the U–boat completely exposed. Walker's ships then opened up with a tremendous amount of fire. The German crew put up a brave struggle in their attempt to get away, but after their boat had taken many hits it began slowly to sink. It seemed that the skipper might have opened the sea cocks to scuttle it, and I think he was the last man to leave when he jumped into the sea. As soon as the U–boat had disappeared, the job of picking up survivors began. It was not easy to find them in the dark, but we stuck to it as best we could under the light from the star shells which were bursting above the spot where she had gone down.

Once a rescue ship had been nominated and was ready to make a trawl towards the U–boatmen, scrambling nets were lowered over her side. These reached down into the water, and as the sloop slowly closed on them, the survivors took hold of the netting as best they could and hauled themselves up out of the swell into the arms of the matelots standing at the gunwales. Many of them were pulled from the sea in this way during the first pass, and further trawls were made until it was certain that all who were in the water had been rescued. If any of the U–boatmen were too weak to save themselves, or showed any signs of injury, our sailors would sometimes climb down to the rescue. I never saw a single German survivor being left to his fate. The action had lasted about thirty minutes, the rescue mission maybe about an hour.

Several survivors were eventually picked up, but there were certain rules which had to be followed when rescuing German seamen, or any other survivors, from the sea. First and foremost our ships were officially forbidden to stop; which is not to say that they never broke that particular rule. Sometimes a ship would, if it

> was considered safe enough, come to a stop to make sure that men were not left behind. However, a ship slowing down to a stop in order to pull survivors from the sea would make an easy target for a U–boat skipper, and some of them might have been ruthless enough to sink a ship attempting to rescue their comrades. The action just described took place in early June of 1943.

The U–boat referred to here was *U–202*. It was sunk by ships of the Second Support Group after being depth charged to the surface and destroyed by gunfire on 2/6/43 at location 56.12N, 39.52W. There were 30 survivors from its crew of 48.[1]

High frequency direction finder sets (HF/DF) were used by RN anti–submarine (A/S) forces to detect radio traffic from U–boats and determine their bearing from the listener. The sets did not provide an estimation of range, though some writers point out that on occasions when two escorts were listening–in they could, by triangulation, make a rough calculation of the distance to the target. Others claim that an experienced operator could estimate the range by analysing the differing strength of signal in each node of the detector aerial.

Although he did not know it at the time, Marsden had almost certainly witnessed some of Walker's 'creeping attacks' as so clearly explained by Donald Macintyre in his own story of the war in the Atlantic. In essence, Walker developed this tactic as a means of overcoming what was a limitation of the ASDIC system. The ASDIC 'ping' was generated from a transmitter fitted to the underside of the hull of an A/S warship, and it emitted the sound in the form of a conical beam whose circular base travelled ahead of the emitting ship on a downward trajectory, expanding its circumference as it travelled through the water. Any submarine caught in this beam would cause the sound wave to be reflected towards the receiver part of the ASDIC apparatus, also located on the hull of the A/S sloop. This would provide the range and bearing of the U–boat from the attacking ship which, in the optimum configuration, would by then be travelling astern of the U–boat, following its course and all the time closing upon it. The problem with the system was that, as the sloop got closer to the U–boat, it would inevitably drop out of the sloop's conical-shaped sound beam. The deeper the U–boat the sooner it would disappear from the sloop's ASDIC screens.

As a sloop approached the U–boat its skipper would be keeping a keen eye on what his hydrophones were telling him about its position above, and as it closed in he would know roughly when a salvo of depth charges was about to be released. At that point he would change course to avoid them, and this would happen at about the same time as his U–boat would vanish from the sloop's ASDIC screen as the sonar cone passed over it. Walker realised this and decided that the best way to overcome the problem would be for the sloop in contact with the U–boat to remain well astern of it as it followed its prey, thus keeping it in its conical ASDIC beam. It would then call on one of the sloops on standby to switch off its ASDIC and move slowly in between it (the sloop in contact) and the spot on the surface beneath which the U–boat lay. With the speed of the second sloop kept to the minimum required to gain slowly on the U–boat, its approach might not be heard by its captain, thus causing him to maintain his depth and course. The sloop in contact would then wait until the second sloop was almost directly above the U–boat. It was at that point when it would signal the second sloop to begin dropping its depth charge pattern, which should then explode in close proximity to the target.[2]

Of course, only two sloops were required to carry out a creeping attack, but with another on standby, ready to move in and launch a second attack, the momentum of a hunt could be kept up. U–boats were sturdily built, and a 500 lb. depth charge would have to explode within about 20 feet of one to sink it directly. Most U–boats were sunk due to an accumulation of damage inflicted upon them by several depth charge salvoes, and it would sometimes require something in excess of a hundred depth charges to destroy one.

U–202 was under attack for some fourteen hours before being forced to surface. During her attempts to shrug off Walker's ships she discharged no less than 76 submarine bubble targets (SBTs). These were sonar decoys of compressed air fired from the torpedo tubes in an effort to confuse the hunter's ASDICs system. *U–202* was sunk at the end of what was to be her 9th patrol. During her operational life under the command of Captain Linder (first six patrols) and Captain Poser (last three patrols) she claimed to have sunk nine merchant vessels with an approximate combined tonnage of 50,000 tons, and to have damaged four others, all between 27 August 1941 and 23 February 1943.[3]

During her final patrol under Hans–Heinz Linder in June 1942, her mission was to land a party of four saboteurs on Long Island, New Jersey; something she succeeded in doing, though not without mishap. Whilst placing the men ashore the tide fell, leaving her stranded on a sandbank. Well within view of the shore she would have been discovered had it not been for the heavy mist which enveloped her at the time, and she was eventually forced to dump most of her fuel before being re–floated when the tide returned.

On her fourth patrol, which took place in mid–December 1941, Linder attempted to take her into the Mediterranean, but she was discovered by a Wellington bomber of the RAF as she approached the Straits of Gibraltar on the surface during the night of 17/18 December. Four bombs were dropped, the explosions from which damaged her engines, and she was forced to sit on the sea bottom in 50 fathoms of water until they were repaired, allowing her to surface and return to Brest.

As a point of interest, it was Linder's act of sitting *U–202* on the sea floor in the Straits of Gibraltar which was depicted in the famous German film, '*Das Boot*'. Linder was killed on 10 September 1944 during a Russian air raid on Libau, Latvia – as depicted in '*Das Boot*'.

It was in the early morning of 1 June 1943 that *U–202* surfaced to make a lengthy radio signal, which was detected by *Starling* and *Wildgoose*. By triangulation of the two bearings, her range was calculated at some 30 miles before the pursuit began.

Almost twenty–four hours later, after having survived some 150 close–proximity depth charge detonations, and leaking at both stem and stern with some four tons of sea water in her bilges, she was forced to surface due to her batteries and air being almost exhausted. Of the eighteen men who died in the ensuing fire fight with Walker's ships, some were killed whilst swimming in the water when *Starling* passed along her starboard side and dropped a shallow pattern of depth charges. Others were killed by gunfire. At the time of her sinking she was captained by Gunter Poser. He survived the action just described.[4]

> With our first success behind us, and by that I mean the first kill made by the Second Support Group, we continued with the patrol. After several hours sailing it was announced over the tannoy that we were in contact with a convoy, but I do not remember if we actually had it in sight at the time. When we eventually caught up with it, we made some sweeps to be sure there were no U–boats shadowing the merchantmen; that done we closed up on them, as it was decided that we would refuel from one of the oil tankers amongst them. The oiler was stationed near the centre of the convoy which, I suppose, was a way of making it less of an easy target for the U–boats. The group was about to carry out its first mid–Atlantic refuelling since it was formed. So, taking it in turns, the ships picked a way through the freighters and came alongside the oiler from which they were going to refuel.
>
> Refuelling at sea was a nasty, filthy and dangerous job, as I was about to find out. I had just come off watch as *Woodpecker* was pulling alongside her oiler, and as I was completely ignorant of what I was about to experience, I volunteered to assist in the work. When I reported to the forecastle to tell them of my willingness to

> lend a hand, they seemed very pleased to hear it and advised me to find the officer in charge of the operation for instructions.

The convoy referred to above was HX 241, an inward–bound convoy from New York which sailed from the US on 25 May 1943 and arrived in Liverpool on 10 June.[5] No ships were listed as lost due to enemy action.[6] Arnold Hague lists the following escort oilers as being part of HX 241: the *Kaia Knudsen*, the *Saintonge* and the *Esso Nashville*. Escort oilers were introduced to the convoy system during 1943 to give the allied escorts, especially the support groups, greater range at sea.[7]

As far as the risks of oiling at sea were concerned, it must be said that two men were lost overboard whilst ships of the SSG were refuelling in the North Atlantic on the night of 9/10 February 1944, some ten months after the occasion described above. It would seem that the casualties may have come from the oiler(s) involved in the operation, rather than the escorts, as there are no RN casualties from Walker's ships listed for the dates given.[8] Unfortunately, Alan Burn, the source of the story, does not give the name(s) of the men, nor the ships from which they were lost.[9]

> Once *Woodpecker* had got into position, the operation began when a seaman hurled a coiled rope across to the tanker that was stationed alongside and no more than fifty feet from us. A large, heavy hose was then hauled across to *Woodpecker* from the oiler, and once it was connected to one of our fuel tanks the refuelling began. It was my job to keep a check on the oil level in the receiving tank as the pumping was going on. To get a reading I was given a gauge which was really no more than a giant dipstick. I had to keep dipping it into the tank and lifting it out again, checking the oil mark, wiping it clean and repeating until the oil level came up to the 'full' mark on the gauge. Once that happened, I would call out to the supervisor and the feeder hose would be raised and swung away, showering me with stinking oil drops as it went. The tank was then sealed and the whole thing repeated for each of the empty fuel tanks. It was a real test of stamina to keep going, and each time I raised the giant dipstick from a fuel tank I was spattered with oil specks before I could wipe it clean. By the time the job was only half finished I had already made up my mind that I would not be volunteering to do it ever again. As usual when at sea there was a stiff breeze blowing, and as the work went on it generated a heavy swell, as

well as a thick spray of sea water that kept blowing along the decks making the job even more uncomfortable.

It might be instructive if I explain that, while refuelling at sea, the responsibility for keeping a ship level in the water falls on the shoulders of the chief stoker. During a voyage, the oil in a fuel tank is burned by the ship's boilers until it becomes empty, and at that point it is filled with sea water in order to maintain ballast. In the meantime, the fuel supply for the engine room is switched to the next tank, and so on. This meant that, before a tank could be refilled, the sea water had first to be emptied, and the ship's sea pumps were employed for that. A Bird–class sloop had eight separate fuel tanks; four along the port side and four along the starboard.

Being a strike force the Second Support Group did not, as a rule, stay close to a convoy. Our job was to find and sink U–boats before they had a chance to attack the merchantmen, and this meant we could be on patrol several miles away from a convoy as we searched for enemy submarines. If the group detected a U–boat we would keep up the attack until we sank it or it somehow managed to escape, in the meantime the convoy would sail on under the protection of its close escorts, which stayed with it for most of its Atlantic crossing.

Sometimes we would take up position some miles ahead of a convoy, and with the group steaming forward with each ship a mile or so abreast of the ones next to it, the search would be on for any U–boats forming up in the path of the oncoming merchantmen. Like this, the group could sweep a lane about five miles wide clear of enemy U–boats. Any German skipper realising that he was in the path of the sloops would probably slip away as soon as he could, in order to avoid being detected. Sometimes the group would receive signals from the Admiralty telling it of the possibility that U–boats were operating in its area, and when this happened Walker would head for the position in the hope of catching them.

Once the refuelling was complete the group stayed with the convoy as it made its way towards the UK, and on reaching home waters we returned to Liverpool where we docked on 9 June 1943; the day of my twentieth birthday. Happily, I was allowed home on alternate nights while the ship was being prepared for its next patrol, and when my birthday was marked by my being called out for my first daily tot of rum at 11:30 that morning, it was agreed to allow the arrangement to begin on our first night in port.

As we entered the Mersey that morning *Woodpecker* headed for her berth in Gladstone dock, and because word of our success had gone ahead of our arrival, there was a small group of newspaper reporters on the quayside waiting to talk to any members of the crew who were willing to discuss what had happened. The pressmen were keen to find out how the sinking of the U–boat had been achieved, but I do not think any of the ratings could tell them much.

Arriving home that evening I found there was something of a family gathering underway, at which my mother, father and elder sister Kitty were present, to name but a few. At one point during the evening they presented me with a gold signet ring to mark the occasion; it is something I have worn until this day.

With the ship in Liverpool, I was provided with a lot of opportunity to mix with family and friends, such as on the day of my twentieth birthday as just related. I was not due any formal home leave, but on most days, whenever I was off watch and given permission to leave the ship, I would catch a tram at the stop outside the dock and be home in less than half an hour. I was quite full of myself after my first experiences at sea, but I cannot say that my family members showed much interest in my adventures. When thinking about it, I suppose that was hardly surprising. As far as they were concerned, I had been in the Navy for almost two years and there was nothing unusual, certainly in their minds, about sailors going to sea. After taking all of this into account I thought it best to keep my thoughts to myself, rather than risk becoming the butt of a bit of ridicule. After about a week's rest and recuperation in Liverpool the group set sail once more. This time we would be heading for the Bay of Biscay.

By mid-1942, the Bay of Biscay had become a busy transit area for the U–boats. By then the Germans had established bases at the French Atlantic ports of Lorient, Brest, St Nazaire, La Rochelle and Bordeaux, in order to give them direct access to the Atlantic. The availability of the French ports provided Doenitz with an alternative to his original submarine bases in the Baltic, and they provided him with great advantages in that his U-boats would no longer be forced to use mainly the northern route, via the North Sea, in order to enter the Atlantic. Using the French ports would mean great savings in fuel in reaching the Mid–Atlantic, as well as allowing the crews' provisions to be consumed whilst mainly in the battle area, rather than in transit to and from it, as would be the case if operating out of the Baltic. In other words, after the conquest of France, the German U-boat fleet was able to both reach its zone of operation quickly and remain there longer than it could before the seizure of the bases listed above. However, the Bay of Biscay was within easy striking distance from the British ports dotted along the south coast of England, as well as the concentration of military air bases in that same region. With its naval and air forces growing in strength and quality as the war went on, the RAF and Royal Navy were developing the kind of capabilities to make transit of the Bay a very risky affair for the U–boats. Such was the thinking behind the Biscay campaign of mid-1943, when a series of air and sea offensives was conceived as a way of restricting U–boat access to the North Atlantic. The key to success was to be the development of close air/sea cooperation between the Navy and the aircraft of RAF Coastal Command, a tactic that was still in its infancy, but with great potential should it be proved viable. Walker's Second Support Group, conceived and trained as an A/S strike force, was the ideal naval formation for both the strategy and tactics about to be deployed in Biscay.

Operation Musketry, First Biscay Patrol: 17–30 June 1943

The Bay of Biscay was to become a regular hunting ground for the Second Support Group during the Bay Offensive of June, July and August 1943. Sometimes, when they sailed into its southern waters, they would get close enough to the Spanish coast to observe it with the aid of binoculars.

The Royal Navy was determined not to allow the U–boats the freedom of the Bay of Biscay whilst navigating between the open Atlantic and their bases in France. In fact, the Admiralty demanded a free hand to deal with the U–boats in Biscay waters; the gloves were most determinedly off in this fight, and nothing would be allowed to interfere with the offensive against Doenitz's fleet. In confirmation of this, and to emphasise that there would be no distraction from the main task of destroying U–boats, all neutral shipping was made aware that the Admiralty considered the Bay of Biscay to be a war zone. Accordingly, all countries were advised that their ships would be in danger of being sunk by the Royal Navy if they were suspected of running the blockade of German occupied Europe, or of lending any assistance, such as the provision of intelligence, to the enemy. Walker, if he did not know already, was made aware of just how serious the Admiralty had become in its determination to apply pressure on the U–boats in Biscay, when orders were issued that suspect vessels were to be 'sunk at sight.'[10] When this was put to Marsden his response was that, if true, then Walker must have been given at least some discretion on implementing them, as we shall see.

On this, Marsden's second trip to sea, the group spent about ten frustrating days in the Bay whilst attempting to obtain some measure of success in the application of the relatively new tactic of a combined air–sea offensive against enemy submarines. Walker had been hoping for at least a modicum of success in coordinating his operations with those of RAF Coastal Command, but it appeared that his efforts on this occasion did not deliver the benefits he was hoping for. During the course of the patrol there was some irregular communication with aircraft flying over the Bay, and on one occasion the group was directed by aircrew to a location where it was claimed a U–boat had been detected on the surface, but all of their efforts went unrewarded; they failed to find any sign of the reported target. In some instances, signals were received from pilots to the effect that they were running low on fuel and were breaking off from a target under observation. In such circumstances Walker never took up the chase.[11]

Another successful A/S commander, Donald Macintyre mentioned above, had many complaints about what he considered to be a half–hearted approach to air–sea operations on the part of the RAF. Having flown as a pilot in the Fleet Air Arm early in his naval career, he was well–qualified to pass judgement. He claimed that the problems with such operations stemmed from the fact that the RAF pilots were poorly trained, if trained at all, to communicate with the Royal Navy and to provide the kind of tactical support they required. The pilots allocated to such tasks as maritime reconnaissance or convoy protection, found them lacking in excitement and glamour and, according to Macintyre, the only time their spirits soared was when they were given the opportunity to attack U–boats on the surface. On such occasions they showed a fearless determination, not to say recklessness, to destroy the enemy, losing several aircraft in the process. In an effort to improve inter–service liaison Macintyre actually accompanied the crew of a Catalina during one of their reconnaissance patrols, and was thoroughly disheartened by the experience.[12]

Nonetheless, the first Biscay patrol made by Walker's ships did not go without its rewards. Two U–boats were sunk, but the RAF was not to be involved in either action. The first was undisputedly a victim of Walker and his ship, *Starling*. From the moment the enemy's presence was detected it was his sloop which commenced the action, reacting quickly to the sonar contact when it first appeared on her ASDIC screens. With the U–boat in close proximity, she closed upon her prey and made her first depth–charge attack before her captain had had time to make a tactical deployment using the rest of his ships. He was in luck on this occasion. It was not long before the U–boat captain decided to throw in the towel and bring his boat to the surface. Unfortunately, there was to be no escape for him and his crew. With his boat wallowing about on the surface, and the crew perhaps making desperate attempts to start her diesel engines, Walker decided to ram. The outcome was that the submarine was sunk with all hands, and that *Starling* sustained severe damage to her bow section as a result of the collision. The U–boat concerned was *U–119*, it was sunk by depth charges and ramming by HMS *Starling* on 24 June 1943 at location 44.59N, 12.24W. There were no survivors from its crew of 57.[13] Marsden's assessment of it all was as follows:

> I could never understand the eagerness of naval captains to take almost any opportunity to ram a U–boat. I always imagined that in doing so there must be a good chance that the ramming ship and the U–boat could become locked together. If a fire then broke out aboard the U–boat, or if its ammunition exploded, then the result could be the loss of the U–boat and the sloop. Alternatively, the sloop could be so badly damaged in the collision that it would sink along with the U–boat. Nothing about the use of this tactic made sense to me. Once a U–boat had been caught on the surface by one of our ships, especially at close range, it did not stand a chance against its four–inch guns, let alone the fire power of two or three sloops. The result of this particular sinking was that *Starling*, once she reached port, was forced to put in to dry dock for repairs. Another U–boat might have been sunk, but to my mind it could have been done without the loss of *Starling*.

In fact, Marsden's assertions were endorsed by some of the naval officers who reviewed and commented upon Walker's report on this patrol into Biscay, one of them making the observation that, 'The only point I would question was *Starling*'s decision to ram the first U–boat. Apart from the damage to *Starling*, which might have been avoided, a golden opportunity for the capture of a complete and almost undamaged U–boat may have been lost.'[14]

Captain Donald Macintyre provided further support for Marsden's concerns when he described how HMS *Harvester* had damaged her propellers when she rammed and sank *U–444*. Unable to make speed, *Harvester* was consequently torpedoed and sunk by *U–432* on the following day. There were several such 'damaged by ramming' incidents during the Battle of the Atlantic.

To be fair to Walker, he did provide an explanation for his decision to ram *U–119* in his report, when he stated that, as the German vessel came to the surface, 'It was observed at this stage that the U–boat remained fully battened down, going slow ahead apparently under control, and no attempt whatever was made to abandon ship. It seemed clear therefore that the enemy had been blown to the surface and was fully capable of diving, accordingly I ordered, "Full ahead both – stand by to ram."'[15]

It is probably best to leave the final comment on his matter to Admiral of the Fleet, Commander–in–Chief, C.N. Forbes, who wrote a footnote to Walker's report:

> 1. …
> 2. This spirited account of successful attacks on two U–boats is self–explanatory and I have nothing to add.
> 3. This was the first occasion of a force of A/S vessels being sent into the Bay of Biscay for the specific purpose of hunting U–boats in cooperation with aircraft of 19 Group. Much valuable experience was gained and on the return of the force to Plymouth a meeting was held at which the necessary modifications to the orders of 'Musketry' were decided.[16]

Marsden continued:

> On the same day that we made the kill just described, a second U–boat was detected, and this one did not give up the fight as easily as the first. I was on watch while *Woodpecker* and the other ships of the group made a number of attacks on this target, so I was unable to observe the action from the decks. When *Woodpecker* went in to carry out a depth charge run, I can remember that the explosions gave all of us in the boiler room quite a shaking. The stress of being aboard a ship when it takes a bit of a pummelling in this way was always a test for the stokers working down below, knowing that the ship was locked down for action stations. In some ways your fate was in your own hands, as the whole ship was relying upon the engine room to provide the power it needed to pull away once a full pattern of charges had been rolled over the stern.
>
> The hunt went on as I continued with my watch, but eventually, after a long struggle, the U–boat was destroyed by depth charges. If I remember correctly, it was *Kite* that got the credit for the kill. There were no survivors to pick up, which meant that two U–boats, together with their full crew, had gone to the bottom within twenty–four hours.

This was *U–449*. It was sunk by depth charges by ships of the Second Support Group on 24 June 1943 at location 45.00N, 11.59W. There were no survivors from its crew of 49.[17]

On completion of this patrol the group returned to Plymouth, where there was to be an inquest into the lack of success experienced during the combined operations the group was taking part in. As a result of the early failures it was said that Walker, rather than give up the struggle, had determined to do all that he could to improve matters. He was rarely to be seen at the dockyards whilst his ships were making ready for their next patrol, instead he was absent, pushing his case for more effort during his meetings with the high command.

Operation Musketry, Second Biscay Patrol: 3–16 July 1943

After a short stay in port the group left Plymouth and set sail for the Bay of Biscay once more, and with *Starling* under repair, Walker was leading in *Wildgoose*. On this occasion there was to be no great excitement. Walker's ships spent about ten frustrating days in the Bay, sweeping a wide expanse of sea in search of an apparently non–existent foe.

> During some of our patrols in the Bay of Biscay we had to go to the rescue of RAF aircrew who had been shot down, sometimes by U–boats, sometimes by German aircraft. We were always told that the Navy had powerful cruiser forces on standby to go into the Bay if the Germans ever brought any of their ships into action against light forces such as the Second Support Group. I think it was during our second patrol in the Bay that we made contact with one of these cruisers when it signalled to Walker the position of a dinghy, aboard which there was an airman waiting to be rescued.[18] Ships such as cruisers were under strict orders not to stop or slow down in order to pick up survivors in the water, so we were expected to investigate. On this occasion *Woodpecker* was ordered to pick up the flyer. We headed for the given position and once there it was not too long before we spotted him, alone in the dinghy. As we closed in a scrambling net was lowered after the airman had signalled to us that he felt able to climb aboard. Once he was safely on deck he told us that he was a sergeant rear–gunner, the only survivor from what I think he said was a Sunderland flying boat. He soon made clear to us his feelings about the crew of the cruiser that had refused to pick him up, and about the time he had spent in his survival dinghy

> since he was spotted. In spite of his complaints he seemed to be in good condition considering his experience, but I was never told how long he had been adrift. He was certainly sea sick, but quite well. The airman remained aboard *Woodpecker* for the remainder of the patrol, and took a keen interest in what he saw before our return to port.

The Report of Proceedings for the patrol which ended on the 16 July contains the following extract:

> '… [HMS] *Bermuda* reports dinghy in water containing air force personnel. *Woodpecker* detached.'

It is later stated that *Woodpecker* re–joined at 07:00 [on 13 July, 1943] with one RAF sergeant aboard. The date and nature of the rescue make it highly likely that the man rescued was Sgt. E Davidson, 1195435, '… rescued by RN ship, Bay of Biscay, 12 July 1943….' He was the only survivor of a Sunderland lost in the Bay of Biscay.[19]

> There was another incident that occurred during this patrol which really set tongues wagging. It all started when we got a signal telling us that an aircraft belonging to RAF Coastal Command had sunk a U–boat in an area towards which we were sailing. It was said that some survivors from her crew had been reported adrift in a dinghy that had been dropped to them by one of the aircraft involved in the sinking of their boat. Walker sailed to pick up the U–boatmen, and it was not long before *Starling* spotted them and pulled alongside. Before hauling them to safety aboard his ship, Walker had insisted that the Germans should give him certain information as the price for their rescue. Apparently, this was a fairly common thing to do under the circumstances, but as far as I am aware no German seamen were ever left to their fate, whether they gave information or not. In this case the men turned a deaf ear to Walker's questions, in fact it was said that they were still full of fight. They were given a final opportunity to give the information we wanted before being hauled aboard *Starling*, which they again refused to take, so Walker ordered the group to sail away and leave them wallowing about in the swell.
>
> Once our ships were out of sight from the U–boatmen, about fifteen miles away, we began to sweep back and forth, and it was

> not long before we began to wonder what might happen to the German sailors. The sea was not rough at the time but there was still an appreciable swell, high enough to make life in an open dinghy pretty uncomfortable. All the time this went on the button–tossers were passing gossip about the situation around the ships.[20] Walker was taking a big risk. Had the men been lost he might well have paid dearly for it, but after standing off for about twenty hours we returned to the area where we knew the dinghy to be and this time, on offering to pick up the U–boatmen in exchange for information, there was no need to ask twice.

This incident took place after the sinking of *U–607* on 13 July 1943 by a Sunderland aircraft of RAF Coastal Command (Sunderland N of 228 Squadron supported by Halifax O of 58 Squadron). After depth–charging and sinking the U–boat, about twenty–five survivors were spotted in the water. The Sunderland dropped a dinghy close to the men, seven of whom managed to reach it and climb aboard.

The following description is taken from the Report of Proceedings for the patrol:

> The distribution of the men on deck when the vessel was sunk was as follows: three men on the quadruple 20 mm. and one supply number; two men on each side of the single 20 mm. guns and one supply number for both; the gunnery officer (Leutnant zur See Gassauer); one hand to clear empty cartridge cases; two hands to hoist ammunition from below decks; one port look–out; one starboard look–out; the Captain; the First and Third Lieutenants and the coxswain. A number of these men are known to have been killed. It was thought that only a small number of men succeeded in escaping from inside the U–boat. None of the men thrown into the water were wearing life jackets and many speedily drowned. A yellow raft was dropped by the Sunderland near the main group of survivors and seven men managed to clamber into it. Of these seven men, four were officers.
>
> The party drifted in the raft throughout the day. The sun was shining fiercely and the men began to suffer from sunburn aggravated by superficial burns from ignited Diesel oil. British aircraft were continually flying over the position. Towards noon vessels of the Second Support Group were sighted and these passed close by the raft without stopping.

> N.I.D. Note: Captain (D) Second Support Group,[21] reported that he reached the scene of the sinking at 1143 on 13 July. He continued: 'By this time there were four aircraft flying round the position, and a considerable amount of oil was seen on the surface, as well as seven disconsolate Huns squatting in a rubber dinghy. With the prospect of a kill in front of me, I could not spare a ship to pick them up and perforce left them to a contemplation of nature while the hunt was on.'
>
> Towards evening the dejected party sighted five Ju.88 aircraft flying in formation at a height of some 10,000 feet. These aircraft passed over the dinghy apparently unaware of its existence. No other incident occurred until rescue.
>
> N.I.D. Note: HMS *Wren* reported that, returning to the area in the early hours of 14 July, the raft was sighted in position 44.50N: 008.50W, at 0400 Zone Time. A whaler was lowered and when it had approached the raft the survivors were asked for the number of their U–boat. This they refused. The whaler immediately put about and the Germans were told, 'No number, no rescue.' This speedily decided the captain to divulge the number and he called the whaler back. The party was picked up at 04:15.

There is a slight divergence between the accounts given by Walker and Marsden, but there was obviously a first contact with the Germans in the raft, followed by a second on the following day, when they were picked up. The German survivors taken aboard by *Wren* are listed in the Report of Proceedings relating to the patrol.[22]

Walker's hopes for this patrol had been dashed. He had been hoping for a greater degree of success in the war against the U–boats through the coordinated help of RAF Coastal Command, but despite his efforts expectations had once again been frustrated. There had been some good communication with aircraft flying over the Bay, and the group was sometimes directed by various aircrew to a location where it was claimed a U–boat had been detected on the surface, but all came to nothing. As had happened on the previous patrol, his exertions to establish a close and successful working relationship with the airmen went mostly unrewarded; he never found any sign of the reported targets. As the group returned to Plymouth in mid–July with nothing to show for its recent efforts, all of those involved, including the men of Coastal Command, it was said, were feeling quite deflated. Perhaps, after their first two patrols, Walker's men were beginning to expect success against the enemy every time they put to sea. However, it would seem that there had at least been some improvement in the communication between RAF Coastal Command and the Second Support Group, according to Walker's remarks in the Report of Proceedings:

> An amazing feature of this patrol was the large number of sightings received from various sources, in spite of which not one submarine contact was obtained by any ship of the group during the whole period of the patrol. It is pleasing to report that the air cooperation was a tremendous improvement on that experienced during the last trip and was, in fact, of a high standard.[23]

As the group neared home *Woodpecker* was detached to Falmouth.[24]

Operation Musketry, Third Biscay Patrol: 23 July – 6 August 1943

On its next sally from Plymouth the group made sail for a third consecutive patrol in the Bay of Biscay. *Woodpecker* had been resting in Falmouth and sailed from there to join her sister ships. With *Starling* still in dry dock, Captain Walker was aboard *Wildgoose* once again, and from the commencement of the operation he began to coordinate his activities with those of Coastal Command. He was obviously a great believer in the potential benefits of such tactics, and was stubbornly determined that they be put into practice in the Biscay area and improved upon until the results he expected were forthcoming. It would not be long now before his work began to reap some of the rewards it deserved.

By the time it took up station, the group was receiving much clearer intelligence and instruction from the aircrew of the Sunderland flying boats, as well as the Halifax and Liberator bombers operating over the Bay. Of course, Marsden was ignorant of the tactics in detail, but he was willing to venture an illustration as to how he thought things were managed. With a little paraphrasing and the use of a sprinkling of knowledge gleaned from the official records, what he said was probably not too far removed from the following:

> When an aircraft sighted a U–boat on the surface it would signal the group giving us enough information to work out its position, and we would go full speed towards the target. We could be anything up to twenty miles or more from the U–boat, and in the meantime, while waiting for us to arrive, the aircraft would carry out attacks upon it in an attempt to sink or damage it before it could dive. But once a U–boat had dived, it could only do about five knots. This meant that if the aircraft stayed close to where it dived, while we steamed

> towards them, then they could drop flares to indicate the spot. Like this, even if it took us the best part of two hours to arrive, we could still be sure of being close to the target. That being the case there was a good chance it would not escape. Once on the scene it would not be like looking for a needle in a haystack, as we could be sure that we were somewhere near the submerged U–boat, and with a bit of luck we might be able to detect it on the ASDICs equipment. However, our first spot of bother on this patrol did not come from the Germans.

By the summer of 1943, Doenitz had instructed his U–boat captains to remain on the surface whilst traversing the Bay of Biscay, and fight it out with any Allied aircraft which attacked them. He came to this decision after several U–boats had been lost or damaged by diving too late when trying to avoid attacking aircraft. As a result, they subsequently became victims to bombs and depth charges dropped by the aircraft whilst they were still at shallow depth. The rule which accompanied his instructions was that a boat should not to dive unless a depth of 60 to 80 metres could be reached before an attacking aircraft could release its bombs.

The AA armament fitted to the U–boats to allow them to take on the Allied aircraft underwent several evolutions. Initially they carried only 20mm machine guns, which did not stand up well to conditions at sea. The first upgrade was a switch to twin–mounted 37mm or 20mm machine guns. In May 1943 the Germans introduced flak U–boats which carried two quadruple 20mm, one 37mm and two single 20mm guns. In total seven U–boats were converted into flak boats, but under operational conditions they did not provide for the expected level of success, the heavier fittings to the conning tower making them top heavy. In November 1943 the Germans decided to re–convert the flak boats for normal operational use.[25]

During its patrols in Biscay the Second Support Group would take up station in the sea area designated Musketry, which covered a large expanse of the Bay of Biscay. It was roughly delineated as the region lying to the east of a line drawn from the tip of the Brest peninsula to Cape Ortegal in the NW corner of Spain.

Starling was still under repair as the group was readied for its third Biscay patrol, but a new chick, *Woodcock*, had joined the flock which, together with *Woodpecker*, *Wren*, *Wildgoose* and *Kite*, meant that five of Walker's ships sailed south. It was during this patrol that they intercepted a flotilla of Spanish trawlers off Cape Ortegal, and the encounter did not pass without incident.[26]

During the course of the war, it became known that the Spanish were providing aid and intelligence to the enemy. German submarines were operating out of Lorient, St Nazaire, La Rochelle and Bordeaux on the French coast, which meant that they had to cross the Bay of Biscay before they could enter and return from the open seas of the Atlantic. When doing so they tended to hug the north-west coast of Spain before 'turning the corner' into (or out of) the Atlantic, no doubt cruising in Spanish waters and hoping for any protection from attack that this might afford them. It was also known that the U–boats were secretly being allowed to use the facilities at some Spanish ports, usually refuelling and revictualling from German supply ships under cover of darkness. In fact, in his book, Gunter Hessler made mention of the Spanish ports of Las Palmas (Canary Islands), Vigo, El Ferrol and Cadiz, as being amongst those used by German U–boats for re–victualling. In his book on the Atlantic conflict Donald Macintyre named two supply ships which the Germans had based in Las Palmas between 1939 and 1941, as the *Charlotte Schliemann* and the *Corrientes*.[27] So, the scene was set for the taking of a little retribution.

> As the group approached the trawlers they were signalled to stop, but they ignored us and continued to head towards Spain. A shot was put across the bows of one of the boats to convince them that we meant business, and almost immediately a flag was hoisted. It did not mean anything to me, but I expect our signallers were able to understand it. However, the Spaniards still refused to stop, so we had to chase them down. Soon, the slowest trawler was caught by *Wren* and boarded, as were the rest when we caught up with them in turn.[28] *Woodpecker* sent boarding parties onto two of the boats and organised a complete evacuation of their crews to our ship.[29] The transfers were carried out using one of our whalers, and once aboard, a group of about sixteen of the trawlermen was ordered down to the stokers' mess. From there they were taken away in turn for interrogation by our officers.
>
> As the time passed by we became friendly with the Spanish, and the atmosphere was soon a lot more relaxed than it had been. They could see that we meant them no harm, as they were never placed under guard, let alone armed guard, while they were with us. It was not long before we were told to allow them on deck, where things soon began to take on more of a party atmosphere. They had brought some of their fishing catch with them when they were transferred to *Woodpecker*, and when they were given back their property they began to gut the fish, getting it ready for storage or cooking. It was a sight I will never forget. *Woodpecker's* deck soon

looked like an abattoir, literally running with blood as the Spaniards set to work with the fish knives we lent them. I cannot remember with any certainty whether or not the trawler men were giving the fish away, or if our men simply decided to help themselves to it, but I suspect the former was the case, our guests being keen to show their friendliness to us. Either way, the ship's cooks were soon in possession of a large supply of fine, fresh fish.

The Spaniards were aboard for several hours, and after a while, as I became tired of the excitement and activity taking place on the lower deck and down below in the mess, I went onto the upper deck to see how things were going. While I was there, I watched a boarding party leave one of the trawlers and pull like mad to get away from it in their whaler. Once they were clear there was a large explosion aboard the Spanish boat, which soon sank as a result. It was quite clear to me that scuttling charges had been laid in the hold. I began to wonder how the Spaniards would react to this, so I went back to the lower deck to help in case there was any aggression from them. I need not have worried about it; they were terrified. I suppose they thought we were going to take them back to England as prisoners – or worse! Of course, none of the Spaniards were harmed and there was never the slightest intention to mistreat them; and if they knew about the help their country was giving to the German U–boats, then maybe they were able to understand our actions.

Of the seven trawlers we stopped that day, six were sunk with scuttling charges. The seventh boat was spared so that it could be used to ferry the other Spanish crews to a port in Spain, and I could not help but notice that of the seven boats we stopped, it was the oldest and scruffiest of them all that was spared.[30] Of the six that were sunk, some looked to be in fine condition, almost new, and it was a shame to watch the destruction of such good little boats. Once the six trawlers had gone down, all the Spanish sailors were transferred to the seventh boat. They were then given a crate of corned beef, along with other supplies, and we sent them on their way.

As they began to put some distance between themselves and the ships of the group, they seemed to recover some of their spirit. There was a lot of shouting and waving towards us which looked anything but friendly. In response, some of the crew aboard *Woodpecker* tried to get the gunners to point the ship's four–inch guns at them, simply to see what their reaction would be. The idea was not taken up, but I am sure the outcome would have been entertaining.

I was told later that the Spanish trawler men who were taken aboard *Wren* had expressed an interest in joining the Royal Navy in the fight against the Germans. Whether this was a genuine desire to fight the Nazis, or was simply an attempt to make us think they were on our side in order to reduce the chances that they would come to harm at our hands, I do not know. But I suspect the latter would have been the case. All of this took place about a hundred miles off the coast of Spain in late July1943.[31]

After saying our farewells to the Spaniards we carried on with the patrol, and we were soon to see some intense action which seemed to show that things were getting better between ourselves and Coastal Command. Maybe the reason for this was that the RAF crews were now making determined attacks on the U–boats. But an air attack upon a U–boat was sometimes every bit as dangerous to the aircrew as it was to the U–boatmen. In fact, I would say that the submarines were armed with excellent anti–aircraft guns, and as an attacking aircraft would have to come very close to carry out a bomb or depth charge attack on a U–boat, the Germans may well have had the upper hand in the contest. Sunderland flying boats, Halifax and Liberator bombers were being used by Coastal Command, but they were big, slow aircraft, and they must have made good targets for the gunners aboard the U–boats.

By early 1943, Allied A/S aircraft, such as the Sunderland flying boats, were fitted with the ASV (Anti Surface Vessel) Mk III radar, which allowed them to detect U–boats on the surface by using short wave frequencies in the centimetric band, thus superseding the Mk II long wave (1.5m) version, which could be detected by the radar warning system known as METOX carried by the U–boats. To function, the METOX system required the fitting of a large antenna to the conning tower, and when extended this could be detected by the new ASV Mk III radar.

There is an interesting story here: When the Mk III ASV was introduced, the METOX system, being unable to detect short–wave emissions, became ineffective, thus blinding the U–boats to the presence of approaching A/S aircraft. With the new system in operation the Germans became completely mystified as to how the Allied aircraft could detect them – apparently without the use of active radar. They were further confused by a story told to them by a captured RAF airman, who insisted that the RAF no longer used ASV radar. The METOX system aboard the U–boats, he insisted, was a weak emitter of radar, upon which the listening systems aboard the aircraft could home–in.[32] All that aside, the Germans were quick to adopt a form of wide–area defence against the increased threat of air attack as they made their surface crossings of the Bay. They would sail in small groups, usually two or three boats together, and if some or all of them were armed with AA guns it could give them the upper hand in a fight, especially against a Sunderland or a Liberator operating alone. Of course, the danger to the U–boats in adopting these tactics lay in the possibility that surface ships operating in the vicinity would be in contact with the RAF pilots. If that were the case the sloops and frigates would stand a good chance of claiming a high rate of success against the submarines, should they close in quickly and catch them on the surface, or arrive on the scene not long after they had submerged. This was exactly what happened in the next action involving the Second Support Group. In this instance, an aircraft of RAF Coastal Command reported the presence of three U–boats on the surface, at a distance of some ten miles from the group. The airmen, on fixing their position, allowed Walker to calculate a bearing along which to proceed to intercept the enemy.

The U–boats observed were *U–461*, *U–462* and *U–504*. The first two were U–tankers, which were designed to carry supplies of fuel oil to the battle areas in the Atlantic where they would rendezvous with operational U–boats and refuel them. This enabled Doenitz's boats to stay at sea until they had expended all of their torpedoes before returning to base, thus making the sea patrol of each boat much more efficient.

Doentiz's favoured metric for the Battle of the Atlantic was the regular calculation of the number of tonnes of Allied shipping sunk per U–boat, per day. This figure was always improved the longer his boats could stay at sea by not having to cut short their patrols due to a lack of fuel. As such, the U–tankers made a significant contribution to the battle, and were regarded by the Allies as significant prizes. However, there was, perhaps, a subtle calculation to be made. Whilst refuelling the operational boats, the U–tankers tended to hold a fixed position and establish radio contact with their 'calves' in order to guide them to their source of replenishment. Whenever detected, this two–way radio traffic could allow the Allies to stage an ambush at the refuelling positions. In effect, the U–tankers were inadvertently acting as lures to the U–boats which, once gathered around the supply boat, presented magnificent targets for allied aircraft, as will be seen. See, *An Aside*, at the end of Chapter 7, where an example of such an ambush is described.

Returning to the developing action in Biscay: the chase was on, and at about seven miles range HMS *Kite* reported that she had sighted a submarine on the horizon; it was one of the U–tankers referred to above, sometimes described as 'milch cows,' for the German, *milchkuhe*.

> As we steamed towards the U–boats the aircraft, in this case a Sunderland and, I think, a Liberator, were already attacking them. From about seven miles away we opened fire with our four–inch guns. We were now going at full speed towards the action, and as the range got shorter we saw a hit scored by what looked like a third aircraft on a second U–boat which we could now see. The action was becoming hotter, and it was not long before we saw one of the aircraft being hit by the AA fire coming from the U–boats, as a result it soon began to give off smoke as it turned away. At that point the Sunderland returned, dropping bombs or depth charges, which appeared to explode close to one of the U–boats and must have caused it a lot of damage.
>
> As we closed in it was obvious that the second submarine had been sunk by the air attacks. The hit by *Kite*'s gunfire on the first boat as we closed in was confirmed by the pilot of one of the aircraft when he signalled, 'Good finish'.[33] And as the second U–boat disappeared from sight after the Sunderland's attack, it left a number of survivors on the surface.

The first–sighted boat was *U–462*, sunk on 30/7/43 at location 45.33N, 10.58W by depth charges dropped by Halifax S of 502 squadron, and gunfire from ships of the Second Support Group. HMS *Kite* was (part) credited with the kill. There were sixty–four survivors from her crew of sixty–five. In the Report of Proceedings relating to this patrol, the RAF pilots involved in the action actually stated that the gunfire of the ships did not inflict any damage on *U–462*. The airmen claim to have observed all the naval salvoes falling about 500 yards short of the target. This would have been a remarkably consistent undershoot if true, as *Kite* fired 56 rounds, *Wren* 37, *Wildgoose* 16 and *Woodcock* 12.[34]

The second–sighted boat was *U–461*, sunk on 30/7/43 at location 45.33N, 10.48W by the combined actions of a Sunderland (ironically belonging to RAAF squadron 461 with identifier 'U', abbreviated to U/461) operating with RAF Coastal Command, and a United States Navy (USN) Liberator (PBY–4). There were fifteen survivors from her crew of sixty.[35]

Once pulled from the sea and processed, the resulting prisoner interrogation report revealed a doleful tale of the fate awaiting any survivors from merchant ships which had been torpedoed and sunk during the course of the Battle of the Atlantic. Being a tanker/supply vessel, whose role it was to replenish U–boats at sea, the likes of *U–461* would sometimes rendezvous with U–boats which had earlier picked up the skippers of their victims. Lower–ranking sailors or civilian survivors were usually not so fortunate; these were almost always left in their lifeboats to fend for themselves.

In February 1943 *U–461* rendezvoused with a client U–boat, *U–66*, somewhere in the South Atlantic, which had been picking off merchantmen between Trinidad and the Azores. Aboard her was Captain D.M.S. Davis of the SS *St. Margaret* (4,312 tons), sunk on 27 February 1943 in mid–Atlantic, who was given over by the captain of *U–66*, Friedrich Markworth, to *U–461* as a prisoner. There had been several more survivors from the merchantman, including a Polish woman, her daughter and an English woman. However, all three females, together with some forty men, were left to fend for themselves aboard a small lifeboat and two rafts. Luckily, they were spotted by American aircraft on 5 March 1943 and later rescued by the USS *Hobson*.[36]

> The third U–boat had submerged by the time we arrived at the scene. So, the group began a sweep of the area, and it did not take long to find her on the ASDICs. Several depth charge attacks were made against this U–boat over the next few hours. Walker was never a man to let go once he had got his teeth into something, but I think the possibility of a 'hat trick' on the day made him even more determined. This time it was my ship, *Woodpecker*, that would be given the glory of the kill once the U–boat had been sunk. There were no survivors from her crew.[37]
>
> All the time we were engaged in the action against the third U–boat, some of the survivors from the other two were left floundering in the water, as it was out of the question to begin a rescue mission with at least one U–boat known to be close by. Most of our efforts remained focussed on the hunt for her until she was sunk, only then could we turn our minds to anything else. Once the kill was confirmed the task of picking up the German survivors could begin in earnest, though I think *Woodpecker* had already managed to pick up a small group of survivors from the U–boat sunk by the Sunderland.
>
> The U–boatmen still in the water were lucky in that the sea was warm enough to ensure they were in no danger of freezing to death; coupled to that, I think all of them were wearing a Mae West which

was keeping them afloat. Sadly, two of them were unlucky. As my ship went in to pull the Germans from the water, they were signalled to bunch together in order to make things easier, but two of them seemed to drift off together, away from the main group, and began to move towards our stern. The deck at that location on a Bird–class sloop was sometimes only three feet or so above the water, and as the U–boatmen came nearer to us I could see they were in danger. I decided to try and help them, so I made my way to a position at the side of the ship about three or four yards from the stern. I got myself down and clung on with one hand to the base of the safety rail that surrounded the deck, I then reached down as far as I could and tried to pull one of them in. He reached up towards me, but the distance between us was just too much. It was a matter of inches but I could not grip his hand, and I was forced to watch as he and his comrade were sucked under the surface by the vortex from our propellers. The only identifiable remains that came to the surface were fragments of the Mae West they were each wearing. Looking back, I suppose those young German sailors deserved some pity, though not much was expressed by my shipmates. By that time in the war I think it would be fair to say that the feelings shared by most of *Woodpecker*'s crew were that, in war, both sides had to give their all. We were doing our job; they were doing theirs. It was either us or them while the war went on. That was the sad reality of it all.

The rescue mission went on and, once aboard, the prisoners who were not officers were sent to temporary quarters arranged in one of the passages below. While this was going on I noticed that the skipper of one of the U–boats was being detained on the forecastle by one of *Woodpecker*'s officers who had decided to interrogate him on the spot.[38] This had all the makings of an interesting scene, so, together with one or two more from the crew, I made my way to the forecastle to see what would happen. The U–boatman had been unlucky enough to be collared by an over excitable 'jimmy the one.' We watched as the interrogation went on, and at one point it was clear that the prisoner was not going to give any more information. I then heard the two–ringer say to him that if he did not tell him what he wanted to know then he could put his Mae West back on, as he would be going over the side. I am pretty sure this was nothing more than a bluff. The 'jimmy,' sensing our presence, turned to us and in a quiet but firm voice ordered us to return to our quarters while he tried to get more information from the German skipper. With the two–ringer's back turned towards the German, I saw him pick up his life jacket and put it on, he then called out in broken English, 'Officer! I am ready to go into the sea.' At this point, having seen what was going on from the bridge, *Woodpecker*'s captain came down and told the prisoner to go below, where he was given accommodation in one of our officer cabooses.[39]

By now the German prisoners aboard *Woodpecker* were beginning to recover. Many of them had been wounded or injured as they escaped from their U–boat and were being checked by the medics. I can remember watching as two of them were being laid on stretchers just after they were pulled from the sea, the ship's doctor being there to organise their transfer to the sick bay. As he was seeing to these two casualties, the medic was being harassed by the 'jimmy the one' just referred to. This particular two–ringer, being something of a hot head, was telling the doctor that nobody should be sent for treatment until they gave the identity of their U–boat. This was not something that the ratings standing around wanted to see. Word of what was going on soon began to spread around the crew, and it was not long before the captain appeared and, for the second time that day, he confronted the 'jimmy the one' and ordered him to stop interfering with the doctor. After what I said earlier about a lack of compassion for the Germans who had lost their life in the action, it might seem surprising that the ordinary ratings aboard *Woodpecker* could become so concerned at the behaviour of the 'jimmy the one.' But to their way of thinking there was nothing that could be done for the dead; they had lost their life in a fair fight, but after a fair fight consideration should be given to survivors. They were uncomfortable at the sight of ordinary ratings being mistreated.

Once free to act, the doctor ordered the injured Germans to be taken to the sick bay for treatment. In the meantime, a group of uninjured survivors was escorted to the bathroom in the seamen's quarters for a hot shower, after which some spare clean clothing was found for each of them in the form of a vest, underpants, a heavy woollen polo neck sweater, a pair of grey trousers, shoes and socks. They had been badly shaken by what they had been through, but seemed happy enough to be in our hands. They were eventually given an area of the seamen's mess for their own use after it was screened off by a curtain, and with so many prisoners aboard, a decision was taken to place them under armed guard, as such I was about to discover just what the Navy sometimes meant when it issued such orders.

As I made my way to the stokers' mess after seeing the incident involving the wounded German ratings, I had to pass through one of the gangways leading to the deck on which it was situated. As I did so I came across one of the crew, a Scotsman, holding a revolver that was attached to his tunic by a lanyard. He had been detailed to take the first guard over a second group of survivors not long after they had been pulled from the sea. He called me over and asked if I had had my meal, on telling him that I had he handed the revolver to me, asking me to take over as he had not yet eaten.

The prisoners we had just taken aboard were then standing in the gangway, wrapped in blankets, ready to be taken off for interrogation. I had to stand close by, facing them, revolver in hand, hoping that none of them would make an unexpected move. After a few tense minutes I could see that the Germans were in no mood for trouble. As such I became a bit more relaxed and began fiddling with the revolver. Eventually, I opened it and saw to my surprise that the barrel held no bullets. I was mounting guard with an empty revolver. I snapped the gun closed and continued as though I had discovered absolutely nothing unusual.

At this point it should be mentioned that, some months later, in May 1944, a sentry guarding some German prisoners aboard HMS *Starling* accidentally discharged the loaded revolver he had been issued with. The result was that one of the prisoners was lightly wounded.[40]

After some time had passed, and with no sign that the prisoners were wanted by the intelligence officers, it was decided that their interrogation could wait, the reason being that the first group we picked up were still being questioned. At that we escorted them away to take a hot shower. As they stripped, we ordered them to leave their clothing on the floor and, once all were ready, they were issued with fresh clothes similar to those handed out earlier. They were then escorted to the berth that had been found for them. Once they had gone we were left to clean up the washroom, and amongst the clothes lying on the floor I spotted two vests, each with a Nazi

> symbol: an eagle and swastika. I quickly claimed them for myself and carried them down to the mess, where I washed them before taking them to the boiler room and leaving them to dry. Two hours later, when I went to get them, they had vanished. It was a pity; they would have made me a nice pair of souvenirs.

The action against *U–461*, *U–462* and *U–504* was a confused affair with regard to the aircraft involved. Some reports talk of the presence of four aircraft and these are listed below. It is possible, however, that there was a fifth aircraft involved, another RAF Halifax which was damaged early in the action and returned to base.[41] In summary it would seem that:

- The first aircraft on the scene was an RAF Liberator, 53/O. This aircraft detected the U–boat trio on the surface heading westwards into the Atlantic and called up reinforcements from the Second Support Group and three more Allied aircraft already in the vicinity.
- The second aircraft, RAF Halifax 502/S, appeared on the scene and, together with RAF Liberator 53/O, attacked *U–462*.
- The third aircraft to arrive was a USN Liberator PBY–4.
- The fourth aircraft was an RAAF Sunderland U/461.
- To add to the confusion, both Liberator PBY–4 and Sunderland U/461 made attacks on *U–461* (that is *U–461* the U–boat!).
- The RAF Liberator 53/O, after being damaged by AA fire during the action, was able to land in neutral territory (Portugal).

> The duration of a war patrol was about three hundred and fifty steaming hours, which was about fourteen days. This could be extended by oiling at sea, which we sometimes did while in the North Atlantic but never in Biscay, and after all the action just described there was still a week of the patrol to complete. We remained in Biscay during that time, and were to be provided with more excitement yet.
>
> With three U–boats in the bag Walker was beginning to push his luck, taking the group towards the port of Brest. The word was that he was trying to tempt the Germans out for a fight, if so, they obliged him in a way that could have spelt the end of us. After two quiet days towards the north of the Bay, a flotilla of three Narvik class destroyers was spotted. They were several miles from us, on the horizon, and we happened to be sailing towards them at the time

they were spotted. This, we thought, must have been the Germans' response to our patrols into the Bay. There were no U–boats in sight, but it was thought that destroyers were being used to escort submarines through the danger area of Biscay towards the Atlantic.

With the Germans in sight, we were called to action stations and ordered to put on anti–flash gear. This consisted of goggles, a white balaclava and white arm–length gloves, all designed to prevent any exposed areas of the skin from being burned during an engagement. Everyone was expecting an action at sea.

As time passed Walker kept us on a course towards the destroyers, then a tannoy announcement was made telling us that the Narvik class destroyers we were about to engage were fitted with five–point–eight–inch guns, and that their top speed was thirty–five knots. Compared to that, a Bird–class sloop carried only four–inch guns and could do only twenty knots at a push. There was no possibility of us outrunning the Germans if they decided to attack us, and there was a real possibility that just one of their destroyers could have stood off from the group, out of range from our guns, and picked off each ship in turn. Walker's response was to reduce the group's speed as much as possible and continue our course directly towards them. In the meantime, he would wait for an answer to a signal that had been sent to the Admiralty asking for reinforcements. The thought in Walker's mind was apparently that, by continuing as we were with our bows pointed directly towards them, the Germans might not be able to identify what we were. It had been said by some people in the past that our sloops could be mistaken for light cruisers; maybe it was that kind of confusion that could have led the Germans to decide that we were a more powerful force than we actually were, or that we were acting as a screen for a heavier force following behind.

No matter what the Germans may or may not have thought, we had a few nervous hours as we slowly closed the distance between ourselves and their ships. It was then announced that a signal had been received from the Admiralty saying that help, in the shape of some of the Navy's big ships, was on its way and would be with us within two hours. About ninety minutes later I was waiting to begin the watch which ran from 20:00 to 00:00, and at 19:40, just as the light was beginning to fade, my curiosity got the better of me and made me go up on deck with my friend from home, Gleeson

> who, on taking a look at the situation around the group, said that we seemed to be in a position somewhere between our arriving reinforcements on one side and the German destroyers on the other. Our help had come in the shape of two cruisers and about six or seven destroyers, and when darkness fell we took our opportunity to slip away and leave the fighting to the big boys. Not long afterwards we were ordered to stand down and remove our anti–flash gear; we could relax. At six o'clock on the following morning we tuned in to the radio for any news of the action we were sure must have followed after our departure, but if there had been a fight somebody had decided to keep tight–lipped about it.

In some places, the Report of Proceedings for this patrol suggests that the ships the Second Support Group took to be German Narvick class destroyers, were more likely to have been ships of the British 40th Escort Group. However, it seems there were several forces in the area at the time. Besides the three just mentioned there was also a covering force of British cruisers which included HMS *Scylla*, HMS *Royalist* and HMS *Charybdis*. In summary, the report states that the movements of these forces over the twenty–four hour period referred to were much confused – as were the various reports of sightings of one group by another. All that is known for sure with regard to the German destroyers is that they were certainly in the area, and that they eventually escaped the converging British forces by heading eastwards towards their bases on the French coast.[42]

> There were some false alarms during the remaining days of our patrol, but there was no more active contact with the enemy. However, we did come across some German airmen, survivors from a dogfight in which their Condor bomber was shot down.
>
> They had been in a dinghy for some time before we picked them up and added them to the bag of prisoners already aboard, but they were in good condition. Later that day we received a signal giving us the position of a U–boat sailing on the surface, and as the group closed in we were able to watch as it was being attacked by a Sunderland flying boat. This little fight was quite a vicious one, and it resulted in the loss of both the Sunderland and the U–boat.
>
> While making a bombing run the pilot seemed to make a mistake, maybe his plane had been hit by AA fire from the U–boat, but in any case he failed to pull out of his dive and crashed into the sea.

> The pilot and co–pilot were killed, but the rest of the crew, about seven all together, survived the crash and escaped from the plane before it sank. As the group got closer to the spot where it had all taken place, *Wren* was sent to pick them up as they clung to one of the wings of the Sunderland which had broken away from the fuselage and was still floating close to the place where their aircraft went down. There were also a lot of survivors from the U–boat, who were keeping themselves afloat nearby. These were picked up by *Kite*, and I have often thought about this incident through the years. Most of the men who pulled the German survivors from the sea that day were lost when *Kite* was torpedoed and sunk while escorting a Russian convoy during August of the following year. There were only nine survivors from her crew. Two of those killed were old school friends of mine.[43]
>
> We had no more contact with the enemy during the final days of this patrol, and after two weeks at sea we returned to Plymouth.

The U–boat mentioned above was *U–454*, sunk by depth charges dropped by an Australian Air Force Sunderland on 1 August 1943 at location 45.36N, 10.23W. Fourteen survivors from her crew, including her captain, were later picked up by HMS *Kite*. In the meantime, HMS *Wren* picked up the six surviving members of the crashed Sunderland's crew of twelve. The Sunderland involved was Sunderland W4020 RAAF/B of 10 Squadron, piloted by Flight Lieutenant Ken Fry. Fry did not survive.[44]

Regarding the German survivors mentioned above, it was on 31 July 1942 that *Woodpecker* was detailed to pick up six crew members of a German FW 200 Condor reported to be on a floating raft. Their aircraft had been shot down some days earlier during a dogfight with a Beaufighter from RAF 248 Squadron.

When asked about the threat posed by German aircraft over Biscay, Marsden replied that he could not remember the group ever being troubled by the Luftwaffe. In fact, according to the various patrol reports submitted by Walker up to the end of August 1943 (i.e. the end of his fourth Biscay patrol) it would appear that flights of German bombers were sometimes observed by the group. On one occasion the ships had to put up a barrage to deter what looked like an attempt by two FW 200 Condors to launch an air attack. Shortly after the FWs had been frightened off, the group was observed for a short time by a squadron of eight JU 88s. Details of enemy air activity during the patrol carried out between 3 and 16 July 1943 were as follows:

- 10 July 1943: 3 JU 88s in sight and fired upon. More a/c joined later.
- 12 July 1943: Some FW 200s approached group. A/c fired upon by 'all ships of group.'
- Later, 8 JU 88s appeared and it was learned that they had just shot down a Sunderland.
- Later still, *Wildgoose* picked up 3 German air crew from a dinghy, whose JU 88 had earlier been shot down by an RAF Whitley.[45]

It is also the case that some enemy aircraft activity was logged during the fourth Biscay patrol made by the SSG between 9–24 August 1943:

- 12 August 1943: Group of JU88s spotted; no action. HMCS *Athabaskan* and HMS *Grenville* spotted on horizon.[46]
- 13 August 1943: More enemy a/c sighted; no action.
- 19 August 1943: 3 FWs sighted; opened fire on them at extreme range – they flew off.[47]

On the face of it, it is difficult to understand why Marsden had no recollection of enemy air activity, especially so when there is a record of the group having opened fire on three occasions to deter attacks by the Luftwaffe.

The nature of the air activity witnessed by the SSG suggests that the Luftwaffe were testing the air defences of the Royal Navy's A/S forces in Biscay. By mid–July 1943 they were preparing an airborne offensive against those forces, and the activity reported by the SSG would strongly suggest that they were 'dry running' their tactics.

It is worth noting here that, during the patrol just described, there was an RAF liaison officer present aboard *Woodpecker*. Once the patrol was over he wrote an entertaining account of the various actions he witnessed at sea, which can be found in Hilary St. George Saunders': *The Royal Air Force 1939–1945, Vol. III The Fight is Won (52–53)*, published by Her Majesty's Stationery Office, 1954, and entitled, *A report by an RAF Liaison Officer aboard HMS Woodpecker in July 1943*.[48]

Operation Musketry, Fourth Biscay Patrol: 19–24 August 1943

After a short stay in port, the ships of the Second Support Group set sail for Biscay once more, but this patrol was to prove a huge anti–climax in comparison with the previous. Walker's group made no real contact with the enemy other than the odd sighting of distant German aircraft, but spent several days responding to signals from the aircraft of RAF Coastal Command, all of which turned out to be false alarms.[49] Frustrated once more, the sloops of Walker's group headed for home. It was late August 1943, and as the group sailed northwards *Woodpecker* was detached to Bristol to undergo a major refit. She would be absent from operations for about three months.

The fourth Biscay patrol ended on 24 August, and on returning to port the SSG was relieved by the 40th Escort Group, comprising the sloops *Landguard, Bideford* and *Hastings*, and the frigates *Exe, Moyola* and *Waveney*. On 25 August these ships were attacked by a number of Dornier 217s and JU 88s, 21 aircraft in total, some armed with the new 'glider bomb' the Henschel 293A. The result was that both *Landguard* and *Bideford* were hit and badly damaged; they were the first victims of the new weapon.

On 27 August, the 1st Support Group comprising the sloops *Pelican* and *Egret* and the frigates *Jed, Rother* and *Spey,* was similarly attacked, as was their covering force comprising the destroyers *Grenville* and *Athabaskan*. During these actions *Egret* was sunk with the loss of 194 of her crew of 229, and *Athabaskan* badly damaged.

It should be noted that the term 'glider bomb' used to described the Hs. 293A was a bit of a misnomer. It was actually a rocket-powered, air–launched guided missile, controlled by radio signals issued from the launch aircraft via joystick movements performed by the bomb–aimer. It weighed over a ton, including its payload of 650 lbs.

Chapter 5

Woodpecker in refit

> At the end of August 1943, *Woodpecker* was sent to Avonmouth in Bristol for a refit, and it would be another three months before we were back at sea. Apart from the regular maintenance work I was involved with, I was never told anything about the other work that was going on while the ship was in dry dock. There was a bit of an air of secrecy about things, and some of the ordinary ratings liked to gossip about the rumour that the ship was being fitted with some highly secret gear.

There may well have been some truth in the assertions made by the crew of *Woodpecker*. At the time of her refit the Germans were becoming convinced that British escort vessels were equipped with some form of radar, after having become aware that some of their U–boats had been attacked whilst on the surface in foggy conditions when visual observation would have been impossible.

Until the middle of 1943 the Allies were using long wave (1.5m) radar carried by the A/S aircraft of RAF Coastal Command, but by May of that year they were beginning to roll out a new, centimetric version, the Mk III ASV radar as earlier mentioned, which, it would seem, was also being fitted to the A/S vessels of the RN. Amongst the records at TNA, Kew, there is documentation which states that, before embarking on the patrol which ended just before *Woodpecker* went into dry dock, HMS *Wren* had been fitted with the latest ASV radar, the 215E. This would make it likely that *Woodpecker* was receiving the same upgrade as part of her refit.[1]

When *Woodpecker* put alongside the jetty in Avonmouth harbour at the commencement of her long period of inactivity, HMS *Woodcock*, her recently launched sister ship blooded during the Biscay patrol just completed, was to keep her place with the Second Support Group and take part in a number of operations whilst *Woodpecker* was in refit.

> Once the ship was in dry dock I was given some extended leave amounting to thirty–two days, so I decided to go home to Liverpool. Once a ship is in a repair yard and closed down for refit, life for

anyone staying aboard becomes uncomfortable. Everything gets cold, dampness sets in, there are no proper cooking facilities, and so on. It is far better to look for some home comforts elsewhere than to suffer the dreariness of a ship laid up; and the family home is always the best place for that.

I was soon on the train to Liverpool. Once home and settled in, I could see that life was going along much as usual. While out walking around the town centre one day, I happened to meet an old pal of mine, Jimmy Barnacle. He was serving with the RAF, and to judge by his appearance and the things he told me, he seemed to be having a very quiet war. Being a bit older than me, he had learned the trade of tailor before the war began. Now, while on leave, he would call on his old employers and pester them for a few days' work as a way of earning a bit of extra cash. There was a number of men's outfitters at the top end of Soho Street, near the city centre, where he could always find somebody willing to take him on. He was never the most reliable of people, and if ever his friends made arrangements to meet with him for a drink, they were more often than not let down when he failed to show up. Nevertheless, on that occasion I did agree to meet with him later. He kept to the arrangements and his company was more than welcome, as most of the lads we had grown up with were away on active service.

In those days a pint of beer cost five or six (old) pence, and the pubs in the city seemed to be doing a reasonable trade; in fact, they could be very lively places at times. There was plenty of work available in the war factories, the ship yards and the port; and rates of pay, if not generous, were better than they had been before the war. Obviously, there was money to be made by the bosses.

I always stayed at home during my periods of leave, so I would sometimes take my mother out to the local pub as a way of showing some appreciation for the cooking and washing she did for me. She liked to go out and enjoy a bottle or two of stout whenever the opportunity arose, saying it was heart–warming for her to see the people from the neighbourhood seeming to make the best of bad times. Rationing was in place, and sometimes, to save my mother the bother of cooking for me all the time, I would go to the YMCA at Lime Street Station where they served a decent meal that was always good value for money. The quality of the food they served was good, and three courses would cost you less than a shilling. It was because of this that the association's cafes were so popular during the war, and a lot of young servicemen regularly dined at them while on leave.

Liverpool was still showing signs of the damage she suffered during the blitz. In the area around Lord Street, Castle Street and Dale Street, where the damage had been very severe, there was not much sign that any repairs had been made since the air raids. There were a lot of stables belonging to different haulage companies in that area of the city, and I remember that many horses had been killed there during the bombing of 1941. It was a part of the city which, because it was so close to the docks, had received a lot of attention from the bombers. In fact, judging from what I saw as I wandered around the different districts of the town, it appeared that not much had been done to repair any of the buildings that had been damaged. A lot of them had simply been made safe by shoring up their walls with heavy timber buttressing, others had been demolished, or partially demolished, to stop them from being a danger to the people, leaving just flat, open spaces.

There was a lot work needed to bring the housing back up to scratch, and by late 1943 a lot of tradesmen such as builders, plumbers and electricians, had been excused war service and released from the forces to begin the work of repairing the damage done to the cities affected by the blitz. My mother's flat benefited from this system. She was moved out when the work began, and had to wait for six weeks before she could move back in. In the meantime, she stayed with one of my elder sisters.

Eventually, after seeing some of my old friends and calling on my elder sisters a few times, my thirty–two days leave was up, and at the beginning of September I made my way back to Bristol. The trains were always overcrowded during the war with so many servicemen on the move, and it was difficult to find and keep a seat during my eight–hour journey. There was never much complaining though, people had got used to it all and just got on with it. I had to stand for most of the journey, taking a seat whenever one became empty, but soon giving it up on the appearance of a more deserving case. On arrival at Temple Mead, I left the station and went straight to the dockyard to report back aboard *Woodpecker*.

A major part of the refit was the reconditioning of her twin Yarrow boilers and, together with the rest of the stokers, I was involved in this part of the overhaul. Each boiler contained about three hundred steel tubes that surrounded the furnace. Water was passed through these and heated up to make the steam needed to drive the turbines. All three hundred tubes had to be cleaned, one by one, and this was done by inserting a cylindrical wire brush on the end of a long, flexible steel spindle attached to a rotor. The tubes were about eight feet long and one inch in diameter, and every one of them had to be completely de–scaled to maintain the efficiency of the ship's engines. The men assigned to this task were divided into two teams, each team taking responsibility for one of the boilers, and as we set to work we knew we were in for a long, tiring and dirty job which took about five days to complete.

Otherwise, things were fairly relaxed during our time in Bristol. We were allowed to go to the local pubs while off duty, and this gave a long–awaited opportunity to a friend of mine, a Brummie by the name of Les. He had been hoping for such a situation all the while we had been at sea over the previous four months or so. During that time, he had appointed himself the organiser of what he promised would be a long evening's drink the next time we were in port together for any length of time. Now that we were in dock, in a town which neither of us belonged to, his chance had finally come.

He timed his arrangements to coincide with a lull in the work schedule, and on the day concerned we smartened up once work was finished and set off for the local YMCA to have a meal and get the night off to a good start. At the first pub we visited we had enjoyed just a couple of pints of beer before a fight broke out. We managed to avoid getting caught up in it, and once outside the bar we decided to go in search of a quieter pub where we could enjoy the night out. We took a stroll across a bridge to the far side of the river and asked some locals where we might be able to get a quiet drink. After some discussion we were directed to a pub that looked a bit more welcoming than the first, so in we went, and once inside we met one of our shipmates, Sammy Cornes.

All seemed well; the pub was packed and everyone inside seemed to be having a good time. After sharing a few drinks with Sammy, he decided he would go and chat to some of the girls who were standing at the bar. At that point Les and me moved off to continue with our night out, I lost sight of him for a short time before noticing that he was already at the bar ordering some drinks.

I tried in vain to get Sammy to re–join us, but he was too busy with the girls, there was no possibility that I was going to distract him. I then made my way across the floor towards my friend, and when I got close to the spot where he was standing at the bar, I saw that he had ordered eight whiskies which were by then arranged on the bar top in two groups of four. I asked who they were for and he replied, 'Four for me and four for you!'

Soon afterwards a man entered the bar accompanied by his wife. They had the family dog with them on the end of a leash and it seemed to be entirely at ease in the pub. All three of them made their way towards the bar where we were standing and, not noticing that the dog was standing behind me, I took a step back and accidentally trod on its paw, with the result that it gave out a loud yelp. This, I thought, was bound to upset its master, so I expressed my apologies before the dog's injury became the starting point for an argument. 'That's alright, Jack,' he said, 'what are you having?' This sparked a friendly conversation, during which he told us he was a merchant seaman, and as a token of his appreciation of the work being done by the Navy to protect him and his comrades at sea, he bought Les and me each another whisky before moving off to the parlour with wife and dog.

When it came to my turn to buy drinks I thought I had better match Les's generosity, so I ordered another eight whiskies; each in those days costing about two shillings. My weekly pay was thirty–five shillings, which meant that I had just spent almost half a week's pay at the bar. By this time we were both beginning to feel the effects of the scotch, but we were happy, standing there, propping up the bar and enjoying our evening out.

Just before ten–thirty the bell rang out for last orders, and as the pub had been packed and very warm we were about to feel a change of air as we left. The moment I stepped outside I felt my head begin to spin, so I reached out for the nearest support, which happened to be a lamp post. I then felt my legs give way as I slid down onto the wet pavement, the strength entirely gone from my arms. It was raining heavily by then. Groggily, I began to look around for my friend, but there was no sign of Les. I hauled myself to my feet and managed to lurch and stagger my way along the street to a shop doorway where I sat down on the step, out of the rain. I do not know how long I sat there, but sometime later a couple of matelots appeared accompanied by their girlfriends. Showing some concern for me, they asked me where I was heading. I explained that I was trying to get back to my ship, *Woodpecker*, in dock at Charlie Hill's shipyard, mentioning that I was not looking forward to spending a freezing night aboard. They decided to help and somehow managed to get me to a nearby YMCA where they booked me a room. After a few words of encouragement, they left me to recover with the aid of a good night's sleep.

When I woke up, I was completely confused by my surroundings. I had to lie back and slowly gather my thoughts. The first thing I noticed as I lay fully clothed upon the bed, was that I had lost my silk, but after sliding from the bed cover, getting onto my feet and regaining my bearings, I smartened up my appearance as best I could and made my way from the bedroom to the reception desk. I was offered some breakfast before I checked out, but I just did not feel like eating, I had not yet sobered up and there was no sign of my appetite. Heading straight for the door I left the YMCA building, and once out on the streets of Avonmouth I set off, asking for directions to Charlie Hill's dockyard as I went. About an hour later, after a taking a lot of wrong turns, I finally found my way to the gates of the shipyard. I remember, at one point in my wanderings, staggering past a queue of people at a bus stop, all of them making their way to work in the morning rush hour. I imagined I could feel their stares upon me as I swayed along the pavement, all of which only reinforced the sense of embarrassment I felt to be in such a state at seven o'clock in the morning. All the time, I could not help thinking about what had become of my friend, Les.

Eventually I arrived at the dry dock where *Woodpecker* sat, sheepishly made my way aboard and slipped quietly down to the mess where I discovered Les lying fast asleep under a table. I did not disturb him. I went over to my berth, hauled myself into my hammock and fell asleep. I had been lucky, with hardly anyone aboard the ship there was almost no activity, and I was not yet guilty of having missed a shift, which meant that I had so far escaped being placed on a charge.

When I woke up I soon became anxious about the disappearance of my silk, and the questioning it might cause if I was seen without it. My head was beginning to clear and I thought the best thing I could do was to find a replacement before its loss was noticed. A quick trip to see the Jack Dusty did the trick, but on closer inspection I could see that the rest of my uniform looked more than a little worse for wear. I had to sort it out before it came to the notice of any of the officers aboard, so I took the first opportunity I had to wash, brush and clean up all of the items I had been wearing on the previous evening, and I was soon looking more presentable than I had any right to expect. Unfortunately, the events of the previous night were not a one–off; there were to be one or two more evenings out in Bristol which did not quite go to plan. Being in dock for such long time gave the ratings of *Woodpecker* ample opportunity to socialise at the local pubs.

There was one other little adventure that might be worth telling. It happened when I got together with three of my shipmates one evening and came to the decision that we should visit a pub on the opposite bank of the Avon to that on which the dockyard stood. To get to it meant a three–mile hike to the nearest bridge and almost as much of a trudge again down the far bank. However, the thought of a six–mile stroll did not stop us from setting off, fortified as we were by the thought of a few drinks at the end of it.

After about an hour's walk, we arrived at the pub and spent a pleasant evening in each other's company. When closing time came, along with the drowsiness caused by a few pints of beer, the long walk back to the dockyard did not seem as appealing as it did when we first set out. After some discussion, it was decided that we should see if we could find a boat that we might be able to use to cross the river in, in order to return to the dockyard. One of the lads was a twelve–year man from Manchester, who remembered that there was a naval training school nearby where he had spent his first few months in the service. He was quite confident that, once we had found the place, we could search the grounds, especially where they bordered the river bank, and probably find just what we needed.

It was then October 1943, the weather was chilly and it was pitch dark, the blackout adding to gloom. We made our way to the training school with the Manchester man leading the way, and after combing part of the river bank we soon found a small skip, as we had hoped. By this time I was beginning to have second thoughts about our plans to take a shortcut. The river was not too wide at that point, but the Avon is a river of strong, fast currents. In the end I put my doubts to one side and climbed into the little boat together with my three friends, and we set course for the far bank. We had just the one oar between us, and it was the twelve–year man who knew best how to feather it, coracle style, but even with the aid of his skills we were not making anything like good progress through the water. In an effort to increase our speed the rest of us soon started to paddle with our hands.

As we approached mid–stream, one of the crew noticed a large, dark shape coming towards us, and as it got closer we began to make out that it was an oil tanker coming steadily up the river and heading straight for us. There was nothing for it, we had to turn back and paddle like hell to avoid being run down. After a frantic struggle we reached the shore we had set out from and scrambled up the embankment. Once clear of the river we decided to cut our losses; we tied up the little skip and resigned ourselves to the long trudge home.

Eventually *Woodpecker*'s refit was completed and it was time for her to take part in a test programme consisting of harbour and sea trials. The first sailing we made after we left the dockyard at Bristol took us to Cardiff, where we could test the degaussing coil which had been fitted to the hull of the ship during the works programme. These coils took the form of a copper cable attached to the outside of the hull, just below the water line. The tests took about two days to finish, after which we sailed from Cardiff to begin sea trials.

The degaussing coils just mentioned were fitted to ships to disguise them from magnetic mines, which were laid on the sea bed in shallow water. The mines' detonators were able to sense a ship's near presence by the increase it caused in the local magnetic field as it passed above, the small perturbations triggering the resultant explosion beneath the vessel.

There was a spin off in that the coils also offered protection against a type of German torpedo which was detonated by a magnetic pistol as it came close to the hull of its intended target. At one point in the war, the Germans had discovered that the depth keeping of their torpedoes was unreliable, and as a result they would often pass harmlessly beneath the hull of shallow–draft vessels when fitted with contact fuses. The introduction of magnetic fuses overcame the fault, turning what would have been near misses into effective hits, as the torpedoes would explode directly beneath their intended target.

The testing of the ship's gunnery was an important part of the trials, and it was the proving of the anti–aircraft system that provided a lot of entertainment for the crew.

An aircraft would appear at some distance from the ship towing a target that trailed about four hundred yards behind it and took the shape of a ten–foot long pennant, or sleeve, as it was called. Once the ship's ranging systems had picked up the target, AA shells were fired at it by the crews manning the four–inch guns, the obvious aim being to get the flack rounds to explode as close to the sleeve as possible. I do not know for sure what type of fuse was fitted to the shells, but I suspect they would have been timer fuses. Members of the crew who were lucky enough to be off watch while this was going on would gather on the upper decks, where they would have a good view of all the fun. These practice sessions would last for about an hour at a time and leave everyone with ringing ears for quite a while.

The ship's engines and boilers were thoroughly tested during the trials, often bringing her up to her maximum speed of about twenty knots with the boilers fully fired up. This allowed the engineers to test the safety release valves on the pressurised circuits. We would run the ship at full speed for about four hours at a time while these tests were being carried out, slowing her down to cruising speed between times. As a result of the slow–fast–slow alternations to the ship's speed, life could become pretty hectic for everyone aboard.

All of this would have been enough without the constant fire drills that were thrown in for good measure. We were being worked hard and it was understandable; after two and a half months in dock the whole crew had to be sharpened up before they went back into action. We were never given any advanced warning of a fire drill; we were simply expected to react in accordance with our training as soon as an alarm was sounded. A favourite time to put us through our paces was while we were in the act of carrying out all the essential drills that were required to bring the ship up to full action stations. It could be realistic, a bit hectic and stressful.

The fire drills would begin simply by an officer declaring an alarm and sending runners to different parts of the ship to spread the word. Besides the runners, the ship was fitted with a warning system which could give three different–sounding alarms for emergencies other than fires: one for the sighting of enemy aircraft, one for the sighting of enemy surface ships and a third for the sighting or detection of a U–boat.

On being called to action stations there were some fire safety precautions that had to be taken: all fans aboard the ship had to be shut down in order to prevent flames from spreading, all safety hatches and fire hatches had to be locked shut and all watertight compartments had to be sealed. All the drills just mentioned we practised over and over again during sea trials. Although they were usually well planned and always taken seriously, they did not always pass off in the way they were meant to.

Since the completion of her refit, a new two–ringer, an engineer officer, had been assigned to *Woodpecker*, and he was the person made responsible for overseeing the fire drills. One day, while Gleeson and me happened to be standing close to him, he ordered his runner to report a fire on the quarterdeck, the place where the ship's depth charges were stored. The runner set off at full pelt, leaving me and my friend Gleeson standing there in front of the officer trying to make up our minds as to whether or not we were expected to do something.

'Well!' he bawled, 'Did you hear what I said?'

'I heard,' I replied, still not sure what to do.

'Well! What are you going to do about it!' he snapped.

I realised we had better look sharp and think of something to do before we landed in trouble. As I began to gather my wits about me, I happened to notice that we were standing close to a fire hydrant and a coiled fire hose. This was it, I thought, now we can impress the officer, who was by then staring at us and about to explode. It was obvious, my mind told me, we had better get the hose connected to the hydrant and run it out to the area where the fire was supposed to be raging. I nodded to Gleeson to connect the rear end of the hose to the hydrant while I, with the nozzle in my hands, ran off down the port side of the deck towards the place where the fire was supposed to be. After I had sprinted a fair distance towards the quarterdeck, I began to wonder just how long the fire hose was, expecting to be pulled up sharp when it had been fully extended. On I went. 'This hose must be much longer than I thought,' I kept telling myself. Eventually, as I arrived at the quarterdeck, still going at full pelt, I glanced over my shoulder only to catch sight of Gleeson with the rear–end of the hose in his hand, matching me stride for stride along the deck. Beyond Gleeson I could see the officer looking on in horror as he stared at the piece of slapstick being played out in front of most of the crew, who were thoroughly enjoying it. At this point I was desperately thinking of the best way to get ourselves out of the situation we were in. If I turned back, I thought, it might not be the best way to do it, I could not imagine what Gleeson's reaction would be if I were to turn around and run towards him. Then I had a stroke of genius, I decided to keep running and do a full lap of the deck in order to bring Gleeson back to the position next to the fire hydrant where we started out from. He could then connect his end of the hose to it while I continued on to the place where the imaginary fire was burning on the quarterdeck.

As we dashed along the port side, around the stern, up the starboard side, across the bows and then back down the port side, all to the entertainment of the crew, I could see that the two–ringer was fuming as we approached him. He bawled at us to come to a halt when I came level with him, and as we stood there, he gave us a real tongue lashing while the crew members nearest to the scene enjoyed themselves at our expense.

There were only two courses of action open to the officer: to issue an immediate punishment to the offenders; that would be me and Gleeson, or to have the whole drill repeated time after time. Unfortunately for both of us he decided on the latter, and insisted that not only Gleeson and me were to be punished, but that the whole of the stokers' mess was to report for fire drill every day until we returned to port, and that the practice sessions would continue there until they were carried out to perfection. This did not make us very popular with our comrades.

Next day, the whole mess was duly ordered to report for drill, and there were many unhappy faces amongst them when the two–ringer appeared. He was going to be watching like a hawk as we were put through our paces again, and it was clear that he was expecting everything to go like clockwork. The level of dissatisfaction amongst the rest of the stokers was soon to be made worse by the fact that we had to wait quite some time before the drill could begin, due to a works party of seamen who were putting the finishing touches to the paintwork they had been applying to various parts of the ship.

Eventually the officer briefed us on what was expected. This time, he said, the imaginary fire was to be a fuel fire up on the forecastle (which happened to be the place where the seamen had just finished painting). Once all was ready, the exercise began when the officer bawled at Gleeson and me to get up to the forecastle and tackle the blaze. Off we went, making as much effort as we could to look fully committed. When we arrived at the site of the supposed fire we noticed that the seamen, having been over enthusiastic as usual with their paintwork, had painted just about everything on the forecastle that it was possible to paint, including the canisters that contained the fire–fighting chemicals we were about to 'spray on the fire' and their back–pack harnesses, all of which were standing ready for use against any actual fuel fire that might break out.

The paint had hardly begun to dry, and to pull on the canister harnesses would have meant that our boiler suits, newly issued as replacements for older ones, would be ruined. As we were out of the immediate sight of the officer, I suggested to Gleeson that he pick up one of the harnesses while I held the nozzle of the small hose attached to the canister mounted inside. We then began to walk about in tandem, pretending to spray foam onto the non–existent fire. It was at this moment that the two–ringer suddenly appeared, and when he saw what we were doing he flipped. He started screaming at us to put on the harnesses and fight the fire properly. It was not the time to try and explain, so we pulled on the harnesses, smearing ourselves all over with thick, battleship–grey paint. This sent the officer into a complete frenzy. The exercise was halted immediately and all members of the mess were called together to look at the state we were in. At the end of another lively rant, they were told that they would have Gleeson and me to thank for what they were about to receive over the next few days. As I looked at the faces of the stokers around me, there was not much comfort to be found in the glances returned.

By the time the next day arrived the weather had taken a turn for the worse. In the mess the stokers were not a happy bunch, never knowing when they would be called out to face whatever awaited them. As the day wore on Gleeson and me began to wonder what had happened to the promised fire drill; and when five o'clock arrived we decided it might be a good idea to go in search of the two–ringer. We called at the wardroom and asked if he was there. After a minute or two he appeared in the doorway, and it became clear that the fire drill fanatic had not yet found his sea legs. As we spoke to him, we did our best to fake some enthusiasm for a chance to make up for our performances of the previous two days, but we could sense that our man was not up for it. We were angrily dismissed and sent away with a threat as to what might be in store for us in the coming weeks. That, I can say, was the last we ever heard of extra fire drills.

Chapter 6

HMS *Woodpecker* returns to the fray

When *Woodpecker*'s sea trials came to an end, we put into Portland harbour for the inevitable five–day boiler clean. This was not a welcome job for the ship's stokers, but it would at least allow the engineers to get an idea of how they had stood up to the trials. One way of skipping work for a day, on Sundays at least, was to request permission to attend church. So, when the first Sunday in port arrived, I put an application in for attendance and was given permission to go to the catholic church in Portland. At that time Portland was home to a borstal, a kind of young offenders' institution, close to the harbour.

When Sunday arrived I left the base and arrived at Portland in time for mass, but when I entered the church I was surprised to see that there was a good number of young offenders amongst the congregation, all apparently ready to take part in the service. The church was not big, but there were quite a few people inside; scattered amongst them were the borstal boys. It made me wonder just how many of the congregation would discover the loss of a purse, wallet or other items once they arrived home. I took my place in the pews and soon found myself standing in the middle of a group of the youngsters, as they gathered around me. With the boys so close I was constantly nudged and tugged as they pestered me for money or cigarettes. I found it really annoying, and it pushed me to the brink of losing my temper which, had I done so, would have probably resulted in more trouble for me than it would for them. Once the mass was finished I took a slow stroll back to the base.

It was now early November 1943, and once the boilers had been re–conditioned we sailed to Larne in Northern Ireland for completion of the refit, some of the details of which were still being kept quiet from the ratings. It all added to our suspicions that *Woodpecker* really had been fitted with some new gear.

The previous two or three months spent in refit had provided a welcome break for the crew of *Woodpecker*, and it could be regarded as having been quite a luxury when compared with the experiences that the rest of the group were having at sea. In fact, during the time *Woodpecker* was in refit the Second Support Group carried out two more patrols in the Biscay area, during the first of which, on 17 September 1943, they went to the rescue of the crew of eleven belonging to RAF Sunderland U/461, the aircraft which sank *U–461* in the action of 30 July, as described in Chapter 4. The second was to be the group's final trip to Biscay, and after a spell of training at Tobermoray in late September, the group, still without *Woodpecker*, was assigned to escort duties in the North–West Atlantic for about two months, making use of the naval bases at Argentia and St John's in Newfoundland. During that time the ships suffered heavily in the severe autumnal storms, returning to Liverpool on 6 December for what would be a significant period of rest and recuperation for the crews, and a heavy maintenance schedule for the ships.[1]

Despite their discomfort they were to claim two more victims from Doenitz's U–boat fleet whilst on the far side of the Atlantic. These were: *U–226*, sunk on 6 November 1943 at location 44.49N, 41.13W and *U–842*, also sunk on 6 November at location 43.42N, 42.08W. There were no survivors from either boat.[2]

When *Woodpecker* left the port of Larne in November, she proceeded to Tobermory on the west coast of Scotland to continue with her working–up programme, the northern waters around the Isle of Skye being designated as a naval training area.[3] Sea trials were often conducted there, and some sea areas were used as gunnery ranges by the Navy. Everything was played out in deadly seriousness; the drills were quite intensive with the aim of improving the reactions of the ship's crew when being called upon to man the various stations as required when on active patrol. To give an edge to the proceedings, and to maintain everybody's perception of being on active duty, nobody was allowed ashore when their ship pulled into port at the end of a phase in these exercises. It was as though they were continually at sea during the whole period of the training schedule being followed.

Once these final phases of *Woodpecker's* post–refit trials were completed, the crew must have felt themselves ready to commence battle once more. It was mid–November 1943 and their comrades in the Second Support Group were still on escort duty in the North–West Atlantic. However, the Navy was not about to allow one of its recently convalesced and upgraded escorts to remain inactive in home waters for long. With *Woodpecker* temporarily detached from Walker's group a holding role was found for her, and her next active patrol was soon to commence. She had been assigned to assist in escorting a large convoy to its destination in the Mediterranean.

> After sailing from Liverpool, we joined the merchantmen in the Irish Sea and continued south without trouble. On reaching Gibraltar we pulled into harbour and lay at anchor for several hours, during which some of the crew members struck up a trading session with the local people who came alongside in their little boats, offering fruit and other things for sale.

By this time, late 1943, the Germans had been expelled from North Africa and Sicily, but with France under occupation and Italy still in the fascist camp, they continued to operate a number of air bases from which they were able to launch attacks on Allied shipping. Their submarines could also represent a threat in the Mediterranean at that time, as they were still able to operate out of the French port of Toulon and La Spezia in Italy.

> The convoy we were escorting was bound for Egypt, but *Woodpecker* did not stay with it until it reached its destination, instead we left the merchantmen after handing them over to another escort group. We then made for the port of Algiers, where we docked for about seventy–two hours in order to re–fuel while waiting for a returning convoy.

This was convoy KMF 26 (UK to Mediterranean, Fast) which left the Clyde on 15 November and arrived at Alexandria on 30 November. *Woodpecker* was with the merchantmen until they arrived off Algiers on the North African coast on or about 25 November. At that point she, together with other escorts that had been with the convoy since its departure from the UK, diverted to the port of Algiers after handing the convoy over to a relieving escort force.

KMF 26 contained many troopships carrying US and UK soldiers to Alexandria. One of these was the MTS *Rhona* which had joined the convoy at Oran and was sunk, a short time after the escort hand–over, by a Henschel Hs 293 glider bomb launched during an air attack by Heinkel He 177s and Junkers Ju 88s on 25 November. Of the 2,000 US troops aboard the *Rhona*, 1,015 were subsequently drowned, and a further 123 of those aboard were lost in the explosion and fire which followed after the missile struck. Marsden did not witness the action, as *Woodpecker* was by then en route to the port of Algiers. This was the second time his ship had avoided the glider bombs due to a timely relief. HMS *Atherstone* was amongst the relieving escorts and she took part in the rescue of survivors from the *Rhona*.

For her return trip from the Mediterranean *Woodpecker* joined the UK–bound convoy MKF 26 (Mediterranean to UK, Fast) which left Port Said on

17 November and arrived in Liverpool on 9 December. No ships were reported lost from this convoy.[4]

> Once in Algiers, a note was circulated amongst the crews of all the escorts which had accompanied *Woodpecker* into the port, warning them about the places ashore which were considered to be out of bounds. Some areas of the town were controlled by dangerous gangs whose members made a living by robbing the seamen from visiting ships. From the first impressions I got when I went ashore, I could see that life was hard. The people were certainly no better off than those at home who, it has to be remembered, were suffering the effects of the blitz and food shortages.
>
> Whenever any of us made a run ashore in the city we were always pestered by the local people, who would be tugging at our coats and making signs that they wanted to buy pieces of our uniform. It was almost impossible to get them to stop. Some sailors lost patience whenever it went on for too long, which meant that they could be a bit sharp towards the Arabs, who tended to take offence in return. Personally, I have always had a live–and-let–live approach to life and taken an interest, whenever the opportunity arose, to see how other people lived and how they made their living, rather than be antagonistic towards them, and to be fair, most of the lads I served with had a similar frame of mind. I was happy to have a look around the parts of the town which were regarded as being safe, and to buy bits and pieces which were either unusual or difficult to come by at home, especially the fruit sold in the market near the harbour.
>
> A number of MTBs had docked in port a few days before we arrived. Being open–decked boats onto which it would be easy for anybody to climb, each of them had an armed sentry. This led to an incident in which some of the local men approached one of the guards and became aggressive towards him, trying to get him to sell some of his kit. Thinking he was in danger and that his boat was going to be boarded he opened fire, hitting one of the Algerians. Whether the wounds were fatal or not, I do not know, but it was this incident that caused a lot of bad feeling towards us. There was some retaliation during the following days, with some of the locals taking it out on any unwary matelots in the town. It all resulted in at least one stabbing according to the news I picked up. Happily, *Woodpecker* soon left the port and joined the escort of a convoy

that was leaving the Mediterranean on its way back to the UK. We stayed with it for about a week, and I do not remember that we had any trouble from the U–boats before we reached home.

By the time we docked in Liverpool at the beginning of December, our old comrades from the Second Support Group had returned from Canada. It was the first time we had seen them in about four months, and after taking a look at the state of their ships it was clear that they had had a rough time and were going to be in dock for quite a few weeks.

There was to be some more home leave for me while *Woodpecker* was berthed in Gladstone dock, and I was hoping it would be spun out up to Christmas, but it did not work out that way. After about ten days in port we went shuttling around the Irish Sea, sailing between Liverpool and the Clyde before docking in Liverpool on Christmas Eve, 1943.

We were five days in port over the Christmas period during which the usual set of chores were tackled, including the inevitable cleaning of the ship's boilers. However, at this point in the war the labour force at home was being built up by an increase in the availability of men who were experienced in a wide range of skills. Amongst them were able seamen and stokers who were recovering from injuries collected during war service, or from illnesses they had caught in the course of duty. Even some of those on compassionate leave would occasionally offer themselves for work if the opportunity arose, and it was thanks mainly to this that I was able to spend the full five days of *Woodpecker*'s time in port at home with my family.

By the end of 1943, people had only the local pubs and picture houses to provide them with whatever enjoyment it was possible to have during those days. It might be surprising to say that, during all of the conversations I took part in while on leave, the war itself was hardly ever mentioned. Friends and family were not really interested in how life was at sea; they just seemed tired of it all, there was a total lack of interest in the fighting and how the war was going. If anyone showed an interest in what was happening it was the press. Most of the times we docked in Liverpool there was a welcoming party of journalists and photographers from the *Daily Mail*, the *Daily Mirror* or the *Liverpool Post & Echo*. They were mostly interested in getting a few words from the officers; the tales of the ordinary seamen did not seem to interest them at all. In fact, it was easy to get the impression they had begun to treat the ratings with contempt; not surprisingly, I suppose, as they knew they could learn nothing of interest from us. Walker seemed to have just as much dislike for the pressmen as they had for his sailors, and he always tried to avoid them.

In my experience, ratings were never forbidden to speak to the press until about this time in the war – the end of 1943 that is. To my mind this was a bit surprising when you think about the constant warnings of spies that were being put about: the everyday preaching to 'keep things under your hat,' that 'walls have ears' and all the other slogans that were used. But if you took a minute to think about it, what did an ordinary seaman really know about what was going on? How much important information did he have? The only hint of caution we were given in the early days was that we should never mention the name of the ship on which we served!

Woodpecker left Liverpool before the end of the year, still on detachment from Walker's group. We spent New Year's Day 1944 at sea somewhere between Scotland and Northern Ireland as we waited to pick up a convoy that was being assembled in Liverpool, but I do not remember there being any New Year's Eve celebrations aboard the ship; it was really not the same being at sea without the rest of the ships from the Second Support Group. We were told nothing about what we were going to be doing during this time, which was not the way things were while serving with Walker, and this rubbed off on the whole of the crew; we seemed to lose some of the team spirit created by Walker, and judging by the atmosphere aboard ship at the start of that first patrol of 1944, I don't think any of the crew would have been allowed a bit of relaxation on that New Year's Eve even if they had asked for it. We had our daily tot at half past eleven that day, as usual, but there was no splicing of the mainbrace to see in the New Year.

Apart from having to contend with some very rough seas for the first two weeks of January, life aboard *Woodpecker* seemed to have been fairly quiet. She sailed south shadowing combined convoy OS 64/KMS 38, which left Liverpool on 3/1/44. Both the Africa and Mediterranean bound portions sailed together until they reached Gibraltar, where they separated in order to head for their ultimate destinations. During the voyage south one of the escorts, HMS *Abelia*, lost her rudder when hit by a torpedo, she was the only casualty of the convoy.[5]

At the parting of the merchantmen *Woodpecker* headed for the Azores to refuel at Horta. The British were taking advantage of an old treaty with Portugal which, they claimed, allowed them the right to use the bay of Horta as an anchorage for the Royal Navy, where tankers could act as re–fuelling stations. Despite this, Portugal managed to maintain its neutrality throughout the war.[6] *Woodpecker* was at anchor for a day or so whilst at Horta before she sailed to rendezvous with convoy SL 144/ MKS 35, the SL portion of which left Freetown in Sierra Leone at the turn of the year and arrived at Gibraltar in early January 1944. She sailed from there on 6 January and arrived in Liverpool on 18 January. The MKS portion left Port Said on 21 December 1943 and arrived at Gibraltar on 1 January 1944, after which some of its ships sailed to Liverpool on 6 January together with SL 144. No ships were reported lost from this convoy. From this data, it would seem that *Woodpecker* was on the scene in the region of Gibraltar when the two convoys amalgamated.

> We were not entirely without news from the other ships of the group during the time *Woodpecker* was separated from them. Once her sea trials and working–up were completed and she had returned to her base in Liverpool, it was not long before we met up with some of our old comrades, as I have already mentioned. They returned from the North–West Atlantic in early December 1943, and during *Woodpecker*'s visits to Liverpool in December and January, we wasted no time in catching up with them and hearing about what they had been doing in Canada.
>
> One story I was told has stayed with me ever since. It was about a number of survivors from a Liberator belonging to RAF Coastal Command, who were rescued in the Bay of Biscay by Walker's group during one of the first patrols it made after *Woodpecker* had been dry–docked for refit in late August 1943.
>
> It was *Wildgoose* that went to the rescue of the aircrew after spotting their dinghy in the sea. They had been shot down some days earlier during a dogfight with German aircraft. Since then, they had been drifting in the dinghy and were in a very poor condition when they were found. I am not sure about the details of this incident; as I say, I found out about it sometime after it happened, while talking to some of the men who sailed on the patrol concerned. I believe there were seven men in the life raft, but two of them had died before they were picked up. All seven were taken aboard *Wildgoose* and it was said that, after they had been shot down, a U–boat had surfaced nearby and approached them, but the Germans did not offer

> them any help, not even a supply of fresh water. I also heard that a third airman died later while being treated aboard *Wildgoose*. It was also rumoured that Walker had been angered when he heard about the behaviour of the U–boatmen. The Biscay patrol continued for a few more days, during which the airmen were receiving medical attention aboard *Wildgoose*. I was never told what happened to the remains of the man who died after being rescued, nor of those who were beyond help when they were picked up. Whether they were buried at sea, or returned to shore, I do not know.

On 9 September 1943, *Wildgoose* rescued five members of the crew of Liberator 'P' of 224 Squadron (aka Liberator FL 959) shot down some eight days earlier during a dogfight with a number of Junkers Ju 88s. The pilot and co–pilot were killed during the action. Two of the seven survivors then died from exposure and wounds during the eight days they were in the dinghy and were buried at sea by their comrades in as decent a manner possible. Of the five surviving airmen taken aboard *Wildgoose*, Sgt. Bareham and Pilot Officer Collins died within twenty–four hours and were buried at sea.[7]

The airmen involved in this incident were later decorated for the courage they displayed during their incredible ordeal, one of whom, David Malcolm Johnstone, F/O (86904, Royal Air Force) was awarded a DSO, with R. J. Foss, F/Sgt (1313625, Royal Air Force) being awarded a CGM, and Maurice William Dilks, Sgt (1216857, Royal Air Force Volunteer Reserve) awarded a DFM. All were of No. 224 Squadron. Their citations were published in the London Gazette.[8]

F/O Johnstone's DSO citation

> This officer and airmen were members of the crew of an aircraft engaged on an anti-submarine patrol in September 1943. During the flight, the aircraft was engaged by four Junkers 88s. The captain was killed in the early stages of the combat and Flight Sergeant Foss, the second pilot, immediately took over the controls. Flying Officer Johnstone, with commendable initiative, immediately went to his assistance and rendered material help in subsequent evading tactics. The enemy pressed home their attack, however, and the aircraft was extensively damaged and caught fire, while several of the crew were wounded. Although the aircraft was fast becoming uncontrollable, Flight Sergeant Foss and Flying Officer Johnstone, by a combined effort, succeeded in bringing the aircraft down on to the sea where

> it became wrecked on impact with the water. Although under water, Flying Officer Johnstone, who was himself injured, gallantly assisted two of his wounded comrades to get clear by allowing them to step on his shoulders and head and thus to scramble through a gaping hole in the submerged portion of the aircraft. Meanwhile, Sergeant Foss assisted other members of the crew into the dinghy. For nine days, these members of aircraft crew were adrift and during this period, Flying Officer Johnstone, Flight Sergeant Foss and Sergeant Dilks displayed great courage and high morale. Throughout this ordeal, their exemplary conduct set an example of the highest order.

I really cannot leave the full heroic and harrowing account of these brave, unfortunate men of the RAF untold, and I would encourage the reader to go to Appendix 2, where I reproduce the content of documents found in the service file of J6941 F/O G.H. Wharram (RCAF), the pilot of the Liberator lost when his aircraft was shot down. Whoever placed the documents in the deceased's service file I do not know.

During the period *Woodpecker* was in dry dock at Avonmouth, the Germans began to introduce some new and technically advanced weapon systems into the Biscay and Atlantic theatres of operation. The most successful of these were the T5 acoustic torpedo and the guided (air–launched) anti–ship missile already mentioned. In the early days the term 'glider bomb' was used to describe the latter.

By late 1943, rumours were circulating that two or three of the close convoy escorts which were lost in the North–West Atlantic during the months of November and December, had fallen victims to the acoustic torpedo. This was the period during which the Second Support Group was operating in that theatre. A sure sign of the possible existence of homing torpedoes was that each of the escorts hit had suffered severe damage to their stern sections, thus confirming the suspicion that the torpedoes used in the attacks had homed in on the noise generated by the warships' propellers. All of this chimed with intelligence the Navy had gathered during previous months, and it all seemed to indicate that Admiral Doenitz had ordered his U–boat captains to alter their tactics and make the convoy escorts their highest priority targets under certain circumstances. This change, it was said, had been forced upon him due to the unsustainable losses being inflicted upon the U–boat fleet by the US and Royal Navies.

In fact, once the T5 acoustic torpedo, or '*zaunkonig*' as it was known, was introduced into service in September and October 1943, Doenitz insisted that the U–boats' objective was to remain the same: to sink enemy merchant ships using conventional torpedoes. The new weapon was to be used only to force a breach in the escort screens, should the boats fail to approach a convoy unobserved. In other words, once the U–boats came under attack from escorts, they were free to use the acoustic torpedo as an offensive weapon in their fight with the warships. They were first used in this manner on 19/20 September 1943 when U–boats attacked the escorts of convoys ON 202 and ONS 18.[9] The immediate post–combat reports sent to U–boat HQ claimed that several T5s had been used to sink twelve destroyers (certain) and score a further three probable sinkings, and that conventional torpedoes had accounted for nine merchantmen sunk. The actual figures were: three escorts sunk with another severely damaged, plus six merchantmen sunk.[10]

The introduction of the homing torpedo had presented Doenitz with the perfect means to implement his new tactics, which were aimed at regaining the upper hand in the deadly struggle being played out in the waters of the North Atlantic. As a result, Walker's sloops were later to discover just how assiduously his captains were in applying themselves to their chief's latest instructions.

As more escorts began to fall victim to the acoustic torpedo, the Royal Navy was faced with the challenge of quickly developing a set of effective countermeasures against the new weapon, which came to be known as the 'gnat.' One of the devices put into service was a piece of apparatus known as foxing gear.[11] In those days the term, 'to fox,' was commonly taken to mean 'to confuse' or 'to pretend' and true to its epithet this is, in essence, what it was meant to do to an incoming 'gnat.' The device consisted of a torpedo–shaped object, but with somewhat larger fins or stabilisers. It was towed by the escorts at a distance of about two hundred yards from the stern and emitted a noise similar to that created by the revolving screws of a sloop. The hope was that any homing torpedo fired at an escort having one of these in tow would be attracted towards it by the sound it generated, strike it, and explode harmlessly well astern of its intended target. Sometimes an escort would simultaneously maintain two of these devices in tow.

The group had been introduced to these 'noise emitters' whilst *Woodpecker* was on detachment after her refit, but Walker had discovered a serious limitation in their deployment. The towing gear, that is the cables used to tow the emitters, tended to foul on the propellers of an escort as it manoeuvred to port or starboard, or become entangled with one another. Walker always liked to refer to himself as a practical man, and having experienced some of the drawbacks of operating with the foxing gear in tow, he became wary of deploying it in anger. Instead, he preferred to use a spoiling tactic which had also been devised for use against the new German weapon. It had been noticed that if an escort were to maintain a speed of seven knots or less, its propellers did not generate a noise signal strong enough to attract the gnats. In light of this discovery, Walker was to dispense with the foxing gear as much as possible, and whenever he anticipated that the group was about to come under attack from U–boats, the drill was that his ships were to reduce speed to about seven knots. The obvious drawback with this tactic was the reduced capability of the escorts to close quickly upon a submerged U–boat.

On 21 August 1944, there would be a graphic and tragic example of what could go wrong whenever an escort deployed its foxing gear. On that day, HMS *Kite* was on escort duty with convoy JW 59, when the cables towing her two 'foxers' became entangled. Captained by a somewhat inexperienced officer at that time, he reduced her speed to about 6 knots whilst some of her crew struggled to untangle the cables. The lurking *U–344*, captained by Ulrich Pietsch, took advantage of the situation and torpedoed *Kite*, which sank with the loss of all but 9 of her crew, some of whom were Marsden's close friends from Liverpool.[12] In fact, Pietsch fired two conventional torpedoes at *Kite*, both of which struck their target amidship, all of which only served to highlight Walker's concerns about deploying foxing gear. Obviously, with *Kite* almost stationary, she would not have been emitting much noise, thus making her an unsuitable target for a T5 torpedo, but a perfect one for a conventional torpedo. Ironically, *Kite*'s captain at the time, Lieutenant Commander Campbell, was an ex–submariner. By the time *Kite* was sunk, Marsden had already experienced his own close encounter with a gnat torpedo, and his first words on the new weapons were as follows:

> With regard to the effectiveness of the new German weapons, I would soon see how good the acoustic torpedoes were, but I never saw any of the German glider bombs in action. However, I did see the kind of damage they could cause if they hit an escort, and I think it was just before *Woodpecker* went in for refit that I watched a badly damaged escort limp into Plymouth. Once she docked her crew came ashore and I met with some of them. They told me they had been hit by a glider bomb, and what they said about it did nothing to convince me that they could be stopped.

In attempting to identify the ship which Marsden was referring to, I made some tentative investigations at the National Archives in Kew, the result of which it is possible to summarise as follows (and I repeat in brief some details already mentioned):

On 25 August 1943 HMS *Landguard* and HMS *Bideford* were the first ships to be damaged by glider bombs. The attacks took place off Cape Ortegal, Spain, where the ships of the Second Support Group had been relieved by these (and other) escorts on the previous day, 24 August. On 27 August HMS *Egret* was sunk by a glider bomb off the Spanish coast near Cape Villano, she was the first ship to be sunk by the new weapon. *HMCS Athabaskan* was damaged by another glider bomb during the same action.

After checking the relevant documents available at Kew for the period immediately following the events described above, I discovered that *HMCS Athabaskan* berthed at Plymouth at the end of August 1943, after limping home from Spanish waters as a result of being hit during the glider bomb attack just mentioned. It may well have been the damaged *Athabaskan* that Marsden saw (I could find no information about the first port of call for *Landguard* or *Bideford* on their return from Biscay, though Plymouth would have been their nearest port of destination). Marsden's final Biscay patrol aboard *Woodpecker* ended on 24 August 1943, after which she was detached from Walker's group to go to Milford Haven, before going in for refit at Avonmouth. It may be the case that *Woodpecker* docked at Plymouth prior to sailing for Milford Haven, in which case both she and *Athabaskan, Landguard or Bideford,* could have been together in Plymouth before *Woodpecker* sailed for Milford Haven.[13] Alternatively, the damaged ship he saw may have been sent to the Avonmouth shipyard where *Woodpecker* underwent her refit, his memory not being correct on this occasion.

The Royal Navy's reaction to the spate of glider bomb attacks was to withdraw its A/S sloops from Biscay, pushing them some two hundred miles westward into the Atlantic, beyond the range of the Dornier 217s and JU 88s which were the launch platforms for the Hs 293.

Up until this point in the war, the beginning of 1944, Walker's record as commander of the Second Support Group was without blemish. None of the ships which comprised the group had yet been lost, and neither had a merchantman been lost from any of the convoys his ships had helped to escort during the time they were under his protection.

Since the introduction of the first of the support groups in 1943 there were, by this time, at least five in existence, and the U–boat campaign had suffered greatly from the aggressive tactics adopted by these free–ranging forces. Each of the support groups constituted a local striking force, and the tactics they adopted were distinct from the more passive or defensive tactics adhered to by a convoy's close escorts, which tended to remain in the immediate vicinity of the merchant ships they were assigned to defend, and respond only when the convoy they were escorting was attacked or threatened by U–boats. It was the task of the support groups to be continually on the offensive in order to wrest supremacy from the Germans in the Atlantic. They had a more or less free rein to hunt down the enemy and engage him at every opportunity, and by the beginning of 1944 the men of the Second Support Group must have been beginning to feel themselves invincible; they were facing a resourceful and dangerous enemy who was by no means yet defeated, but they must have been convinced that they were now beginning to dictate the terms of the battle.

Chapter 7

Walker's famous patrol. The final convoy battle of the Atlantic Campaign

The New Year was underway. It was late January 1944 and *Woodpecker* had been returned to Captain Walker's command. His battered sloops were beginning to emerge from dry dock, patched up and ready to sail once more after enduring the rigours of the storms which flailed the North Atlantic during the autumn of 1943. Once reunited, rumours began to spread amongst the crews to the effect that the group would soon be returning to escort duties in the northern waters between the UK and the USA, and that during its first patrol of 1944 it would be accompanied by two aircraft carriers, HMS *Activity* and HMS *Nairana*.[1] It was not long before the substance of these rumours was confirmed, and the group set sail from Liverpool at the end of the month to rendezvous with the escort carriers in the Irish Sea.

> *Woodpecker*, *Wren*, *Wildgoose, Kite* and *Starling*; five of the original six, were on this patrol. *Woodcock* did not sail, she was still in dock,[2] but another new ship, HMS *Magpie*, was with us, making up the number to six. One of the ships, *Magpie* or *Kite*, I cannot remember which, was in Londonderry and joined the rest of us a few days later.[3] We were in Liverpool making our final preparations for the patrol, and when the time came, all five would sail from the Mersey to the tune of Walker's anthem, 'A Hunting we will go,' playing from *Starling's* loudspeakers.
>
> *Woodpecker* was scheduled to sail from Brunswick Dock at about 02:00, which meant I was able to take the opportunity to have a few drinks that evening at some of my favourite pubs in Liverpool town centre before reporting to the dockyard and going aboard; but the night did not pass without incident.
>
> I had arranged to meet my Brummie pal, Les Summers, along with some other members of the crew, in the area of the city which

lies close to Lime Street Station. Once together we pooled our money and headed for some of the bars scattered around the city centre, determined to enjoy a last night ashore before sailing. The usual friendly atmosphere was present in the pubs we visited, one of which was O'Connor's, near Lime Street, where a local band was playing. Eventually, we arrived at another of the town centre haunts, I cannot remember which, but there were some loud American servicemen inside, all of them looking as though they had been drinking heavily for some time. We ordered a round of drinks and kept a respectful distance from them. We finished our beers without trouble, but before leaving the pub one of the lads decided to use the toilets. A few minutes later I followed him, and it was lucky for him that I did. As I entered the lavatory I noticed him standing at the urinals. Behind him stood a US Navy sailor who began to move towards him, holding a knife in a raised position. There was no doubt in my mind that he was about to plunge it into the back of my friend. I shouted a warning and the Yank turned. He then came at me, slashing at my face and chest with the knife. I managed to grab the hand he was holding the blade in and suffered some deep cuts to my fingers and palm as I did so, but I kept a grip on his wrist so he could not do any more damage with the weapon. While I was grappling with him some of my shipmates burst in and helped me deal with him. I was then led away while some rough justice was meted out to the Yank. As we were leaving the pub, the bar maid wrapped my hand in a towel in an attempt to stop the bleeding. We then quickly left before things got completely out of control.

As the night wore on it was clear that the bleeding from my hand had not been stopped by the makeshift dressing, so I insisted on going to the casualty department at Liverpool Royal Infirmary to get the wound stitched. I had been luckier than I thought. While at the hospital I discovered that my pullover had been slashed through, as had my singlet, and I was left with a small wound on my chest which, luckily, needed no attention other than a dressing. We were keen to get away from the hospital as quickly as we could in order to avoid any questions should the police arrive, so as soon as the stitches had been put in and the wound dressed, we left the casualty department and caught the last tram to Brunswick Dock from the stop outside the Adelphi public house, close to the old Arcade Fish

> Market. By then it was close to midnight. When we reported for duty after going aboard ship, things almost became worse for me. The chief stoker insisted on taking a look at the wound on my hand, and had to be persuaded not to place me on a charge for being unfit to go to sea. My friends pleaded with him and he grudgingly agreed to let it pass. Not long after, we set sail for what would be a memorable patrol.

The improvement in communications between the aircraft of RAF Coastal Command and RN escorts had progressed steadily throughout 1943, due to diligent application to the task by both parties. However, Walker was about to be working with the carrier–borne aircraft of the Fleet Air Arm and this was, perhaps, the aspect of combined forces operations which interested him most. In December 1941 he fought the convoy, HG 76, through from Gibraltar to the UK. German agents in Spain had provided U–boat HQ with intelligence relating to the convoy as it was being assembled, and this enabled them to marshal powerful U–boat forces off the Spanish and Portuguese Atlantic coast in order to intercept it when it sailed. Walker was given command of the escort forces, which included the escort carrier, *Audacity*. She was one of the Navy's smallest carriers and carried a squadron of eight Martlet fighters.

The ensuing convoy battle was fought over several days as the ships made their way north, and the end result was that just 3 of the 32 merchant men comprising the convoy were sunk, along with the carrier and one destroyer. It was only after seven days of sterling work that HMS *Audacity* was torpedoed and sunk with the loss of 73 of her crew. Before she went down, two FW 200 Condors had been shot down by her Martlets, some of which had also attacked U-boats on the surface. On the other side of the balance sheet five U–boats were sunk, causing Doenitz to regard the operation as a failure.

With regard to the sinking of the *Audacity*, it is interesting to note that pilot Eric 'Winkle' Brown, later to become famous as a FAA test pilot, was aboard her when she went down, he was one of the 225 crew members rescued.[4]

As a final word, it is known that two of the U-boats involved in the attack on HG 76, *U–434* and *U*–574, had refuelled from a clandestine depot ship in Vigo harbour, something the reader might bare in mind after reading of the Spanish trawlers mentioned earlier in the story. Both U–boats were sunk by the escorts of HG 76.

> Alarms were continually going off as we sailed through the Irish Sea, all of which made us suspect that the U–boats were on the

> prowl, but it all came to nothing. However, the false alarms were useful in the sense that, by responding to them, it helped bring everybody up to scratch. After just two or three days into the patrol, and a few days before we met the convoy we were trying to pick up, we were called to action stations when one of the sloops detected a submerged U–boat.
>
> The German skipper was probably trying to get himself in a position to attack one of the carriers, but Walker managed to get his ships in position to go after it. It was quite a short fight, the U–boat was soon sunk and we carried on with the patrol.

The U–boat destroyed by the group was *U–592*, sunk on 1 February 1944 at location 50.20N, 17.29W, which is about 300 miles SW of Ireland. The kill was credited to *Starling* and *Wildgoose*. There were no survivors.[5]

> After several hours of sailing it was announced that we were in contact with the convoy we were looking for, it was the first of four we would be guarding during the trip.[6]
>
> I do not think the merchantmen were in sight at this point, but it was clear that Walker, as usual, would be getting down to basics and making a sweep of the sea around the convoy. This was done to make sure there were no U–boats following it or lying in wait ahead of it. Once we had been with the merchantmen for a number of hours, it was decided that we should refuel from some of the oilers that were with them.

This was convoy SL 147 (Sierra Leone to L'pool) which had merged with MKS 38 (Mediterranean to UK, Slow) on 2 February 1944, the day the Second Support Group was in contact with it. Its Arnold Hague reference is SL.147/MKS.38. The escort oiler, *San Tirso*, was amongst the convoy.

During their transit of the Atlantic, convoys were permanently shadowed by close escorts. The support groups which plied the convoy routes provided additional A/S cover when the merchantmen were about to pass through an area known, or thought to be, a chosen hunting ground for the U–boats. Sometimes, rather than rendezvous with the ships, the support groups would act upon intelligence which had revealed a possible point of assembly for the wolf packs – usually derived from Enigma decryptions made by the code breakers at Bletchley. In such cases they would head for the suspected position with the primary aim of sinking the enemy submarines before they could organise themselves for an onslaught against the merchantmen. If they were not successful in engaging the enemy, the mere fact of their presence in the area would sometimes deter or disrupt the formation of a hunting pack.

> The two escort carriers in which so much faith had been placed, must have been regarded by Walker as being a liability. They were obviously important targets for the U–boats, and he must have been thinking all the time about where to position them to make them as safe as possible.

In fact, the captains of aircraft carriers were usually senior in rank to commanders of escort and support groups, which meant they had the final decision as to where to locate their vessels at sea. As an example, during their escort of convoy HG 76 in December 1941, there had been a disagreement between Walker and the captain of HMS *Audacity*, Commander D. W. MacKendrick, about where to position the carrier on the night she was sunk.[7] MacKendrick insisted on keeping his ship to starboard of the north–bound merchantmen, despite Walker's assertion that the coastal side of the convoy would probably be the favoured side for the U–boat captains to launch their attacks from.

> Having seen convoys at sea during my first trip, and on the patrols to the Med while we were detached from Walker, I was keen to take a look at the one we were then shadowing, so I took the opportunity to go up on deck. The ships were spread over a huge area, some of them almost out of sight in the haze. At a guess, I would say there were about fifty merchant vessels in view, and together with the scattered escorts it was an impressive sight.[8]

A common tactic employed by the wolf packs whilst searching out convoys in the Atlantic, was to position a string of 'look–out' boats, anything up to fifty miles apart, along a rough north–south line across the ocean. Each of these boats would patrol back and forth along the line, which would be set in such a way that it would cross the anticipated convoy routes almost at right angles. If any of them made contact with a convoy they would radio a 'first sighting signal' together with details of their own position to other U–boats in the area, and these would then converge on the location before forming up to mount a coordinated attack upon the merchantmen. One major weakness with this tactic was that the radio signals from the look–out boat could be detected by British warships and by land–based shore installations, the resulting intelligence thus providing the support groups with a clue as to where they should concentrate their offensive activities.

> The word went out, true or false, that Walker was receiving signals from the Admiralty, telling him that the Germans were organising their wolf packs for a big attack. As midnight approached we were sailing closer to the convoy, and I think it was at about this time that a U–boat was spotted lurking a mile or so behind the merchantmen. Nothing came of this sighting, but the second success of the patrol soon came about a week after we had sailed from Liverpool. It was *Wildgoose* that first detected the U–boat, and she called up reinforcements in the shape of *Starling* and *Woodpecker* to help her make an attack. This time it would be *Woodpecker* that was allowed to claim the kill, but to be fair I could never understand how the kills were assigned to a particular ship when as many three or four would take part in an attack. Here is how I remember it: After *Woodpecker* finished its first attack *Starling* still had a contact on the U–boat; it had survived. We then began to load up the racks with a second pattern. In the meantime, *Wildgoose* went in to make her attack. This was also unsuccessful. A third attack was then ordered; *Woodpecker* was going to have a second try. Walker was convinced that the U–boat had survived the first two attempts to sink her. If that was so, and she was still in one piece, there was still no sign that she was giving up the fight by coming to the surface. *Woodpecker* steamed up to the point of action and dropped her second pattern. After we pulled away it seemed as though the target had gotten away again, but there was a short delay in ordering the next attack while the area was scanned for wreckage, at the end of which *Starling* signalled that the U–boat had been sunk after her spotters had noticed a large oil slick on the surface. To make sure there was no mistake, she launched her whaler to inspect the pieces of wreckage mixed with the oil.

This was *U–762*, sunk on 8 February 1944 at location 49.02N, 16.58W, which is close to the point where *U–592* was sunk a week earlier. The kill was credited to *Woodpecker* and *Wildgoose*. There were no survivors.[9]

> About twenty–four hours after we sank the second U–boat, I was keeping the four–hour watch that began at four o'clock in the morning. Towards the end of it I had done some last–minute cleaning

> in the fan room and was very late coming off. As my final chore, I made my way out onto the deck and went towards the stern of the ship to tip the usual bucketful of waste oil and water I had collected into the sea. I looked at my watch; it was then about 10:00 and I was about to go below, but before I did I took a quick look at the scene around me and noticed that *Kite* was flying her black pennant, this was the signal that she had picked up a contact on a (third) U–boat, so I stayed where I was and watched her go into action.
>
> It was after she had dropped her pattern that we had our first experience of acoustic torpedoes, and it almost spelt the end of *Kite*. When the near miss happened I was still watching the excitement from the deck of *Woodpecker*. Suddenly, I saw a huge water spout rise from the sea. At first, everybody standing near me was stunned. They were sure that *Kite* had been hit, but then, as the water settled, we were happy to see her reappear, undamaged. She had been in line of sight, but just beyond the spot where the water spout had risen. Nobody could work out what the cause of the explosion was, but some of the crew thought it might have had something to do with the new torpedoes the Germans were using.

Terence Robertson, one of Walker's officers, claimed that just one gnat was fired at *Kite* and was detonated by the effect of exploding depth charges dropped from the sloop seconds earlier. The Germans were aware that this scenario was a distinct possibility. In their book, Morgan and Taylor state that the Allies discovered that the explosion of a single depth charge could provoke a detonation of a T5 torpedo, and that sometimes the gnat's over–sensitive trigger mechanism could be activated by the wake of a warship with the same effect.

> The hunt for the U–boat went on, but Walker was keeping our speed down to about seven knots while *Kite* and *Magpie* took it turns in to try and sink it. After many hours of a nervous hunt, Walker, in *Starling*, decided to join the fight and moved in to partner *Magpie*, taking over from *Kite* whose crew must have been happy to take a back seat after their near miss. Walker's persistence paid off, as ever, but a lot more attacks were needed before we saw some signs of success.

This was *U–734*, sunk on 9/2/44 at location 49.43N, 16.23W, again, close to the position where the first two U–boats were destroyed. The kill was credited to

Kite and *Magpie*. There were no survivors. Robertson, in *Walker RN*, claimed that *Kite* had spotted *U–734* on the surface before the attack began.[10]

> Things were really warming up. While *Kite* and *Magpie* were trying to sink U–boat number three of the patrol, *Wildgoose* had found a fourth.[11] She was too good for the German skipper, and soon claimed the fourth victim of the patrol. Everybody was on a high after this, we were all convinced that there were plenty of U–boats in action around the convoy, and they were expecting a lot more excitement.

This was *U–238*, sunk on 9 February 1944 at location 49.45N, 16.07W, the same vicinity of the first three sinkings. The kill was credited to *Starling* and *Wildgoose*. There were no survivors.

> Whenever we were on patrol, Walker liked to make sure that all of his ships had enough depth charges to make a sustained attack. Sometimes this would mean they had to be transferred from ship to ship amongst the group, depending on how they had been used up during attacks on the U–boats. After all the action we had been in, most of the sloops had used up nearly all their charges, so there was not enough left to be shared out, just at the time when it looked like we were sitting in the middle of a wolf pack. Walker had to find a way to get his hands on more depth charges before we came across any more U–boats.

Realising that this kind of situation was sometimes likely to occur, the Navy had adopted some basic measures as a means of coping with it. It was becoming clear to the high command that during the two or three weeks at sea required to mount an effective anti–submarine patrol, the sloops and corvettes could expend all of their depth charges, but the idea of their returning to the UK simply to re–arm was entirely out of the question. In every convoy, therefore, the Admiralty insisted that some of the freighters be designated to carry a quantity of depth charges from which their escorts could re–arm if need be. When asked about this specific point and the methods employed for re–stocking the escorts, Marsden stated:

> Sometimes, in rough weather, some of a ship's depth charges could be washed overboard, but there was never any danger of them exploding because they would not have been primed. All depth charges were kept in safe mode aboard ship until just a few minutes before they were used in an attack.

Despite this assertion, there is some evidence to suggest that Marsden was incorrect about depth charges having a 'safety mode' setting. In fact, German U–boat captains sometimes reported the detection of deep explosions after sinking or damaging an escort vessel, putting them down to exploding depth charges aboard their victim. Morgan and Taylor quote *Kptlt* Brauel's *U–256* attack log at the point where he described one of his successful attacks on an escort. In it, the German captain reported the sound of explosions some minutes after his torpedo had struck its target. In their analysis of Brauel's report, the writers state that the time lapse between the two events suggested these were caused by dislodged depth charges from the sinking escort detonating at 330 metres.[12]

> One of the ways we transferred depth charges from one ship to another was by lowering them, one at a time in a cradle or sling, onto the ship's motor boat. Once a full cargo had been loaded, they would be transferred to the ship in need and hoisted up onto its deck. Everything was done by hand, and with each charge weighing over four hundredweight, the whole operation involved some heavy work, especially if there was even a mild swell.[13]
>
> After the fourth U–boat had been sunk we left the convoy we were with. It was then announced that a second, slower convoy was on its way from Canada and that we would have to clear a path for it. I think it was at this point that the escort carriers left us, staying with the first convoy as it headed for the Western Approaches.

The Second Support Group had been with the first convoy, SL.147/MKS.38, between 7 and 12 February 1944. The second convoy picked up by the group was HX 277 from New York and Halifax, Nova Scotia, to the UK. It left New York on 28/1/44 and arrived in Liverpool on 13/2/44.[14]

With regard to the re-arming of the ships of the SSG with depth charges during the patrol in question, we should note that Robertson, in *Walker RN*, said that the donor ship in this instance was the escort oiler, *Thorsholm*, which is listed as having been with HX 277. However, the oiler *Chesapeake* was also listed as sailing with HX 277, and Arnold Hague classifies her as being an escort oiler carrying '58 spare DCs [depth charges].' An explosive mix![15] Arnold Hague does not list any of Walker's ships as being escorts to HX 277, which probably indicates that the SSG made contact with the convoy only to re-arm.

Before saying farewell to *Activity* and *Nairana*, it may be worth noting here that, whilst relating his story to the author, Joseph Marsden insisted that the aircrew of a Swordfish belonging to one of the aircraft carriers was lost when their machine crashed into the sea. However, the only reference to plane crashes in the logs of the carriers for the dates concerned (February 1944) are as follows:[16]

The log of HMS *Nairana* for February 1944 records:

- *5/2/44, Swordfish crashed on landing.*
- 7/2/44, Swordfish landed and crashed. Total wreck.
- 8/2/44, Wildcat crashes into barrier.

The log of HMS *Activity* for February 1944 records:

- 8/2/44, Crash of a Swordfish on deck.

There is no mention of casualties in either log, however, in a vindication of Marsden's words, three of *Nairana's* aircrew are listed in Royal Navy records as having lost their life during 'flying operations' on 5/2/44 (listed and underlined above). The victims were:

FAA, 835 Sqn, HMS *Nairana*, air operations:

- COSTELLO, Anthony F.H., Sub Lieutenant (A), RNVR, MPK (missing presumed killed).
- DALTON, John, Sub Lieutenant (A), RNVR, MPK.
- NIELD, George N., Ty/Leading Airman, FAA/FX 115137, MPK.

> Once we were with the slow convoy, we had to look for one of the merchantmen amongst the freighters which was known to be carrying a store of depth charges. Once it was found, the sloops that were running short had to sail close to her and take on fresh stocks. *Woodpecker* must have still had most of her depth charges, so did not take part in the operation.
>
> With the group re–armed we stayed with the second convoy as it passed through the danger zone without any trouble from the U–boats. We then went in search of a third convoy.

This third convoy mentioned by Marsden was HX 278 from New York and Halifax, Nova Scotia to Liverpool. It left New York on 5/2/44 and arrived in Liverpool on 20/2/44.[17] The Second Support Group rendezvoused with it on 14/2/44.[18]

> After all our recent success it took a little while for the excitement amongst the crews to settle down. There was now a sense amongst us that we would have more opportunities to add to our score. Everyone was convinced that our first victim had signalled his comrades for help once he had spotted the first convoy that we joined, which was why there were so many U–boats attempting to attack it.
>
> Once we were in touch with the third convoy, it was not long before we detected another U–boat. I think we were astern of the convoy when *Wildgoose* hoisted the black pennant, signalling she was on a contact. Once called to action stations we settled into the drill. *Wildgoose* went in to make the first depth charge attack, but this was going to be another difficult kill, not least because by this time we were all aware of the danger of a possible 'gnat' attack, and the need to keep our speed down. The chase went on for some time before *Woodpecker* was called in to try her luck. Once the charges had been rolled over the stern, we opened her up and began to pull away. We could feel the ship shudder as the depth charges began to go off. About fifteen minutes later we received a signal from *Starling* telling us that the fifth U–boat had been sunk. Once again, there were no survivors.

This was *U–424*, sunk on 11/2/44 at location 50.00N, 18.14W. The sinking was credited to *Wildgoose*. There were no survivors from this, the fifth victim of the patrol. Yet again, the U–boat was sunk within a short distance from the locations where the first four boats were sunk, all of them lying about 300 miles south–west of Mizen Head, Ireland. From the positioning of the group, it would seem that the SSG had been provided with intelligence about the location of the wolf pack's whereabouts, and had sat on top of them for about ten days as they lay in ambush for the convoys they knew would be passing through.[19]

> After all the excitement of the previous ten days or so, the expectations amongst the men were high. We were convinced that we were really on top of the U–boats and that the kills would just keeping mounting up, but it did not work out like that. We spent the next week or so shuttling to and fro in the Atlantic searching for more U–boats, but there was no sign of them. We were beginning to think they had given up the struggle because of their losses. Then we began to hear that the Admiralty was sending out warnings about the threat of more wolf packs. It was late February 1944, and

> we were about to pick up the final convoy we would be shadowing during the patrol.

This was convoy ON 224 from Liverpool to New York. It left Liverpool on 14/2/44 and arrived in New York on 2/3/44.[20] The Second Support Group was with it during 18 and 19/2/44.

On this occasion Walker's ships were to coordinate their operations with the ships of what was initially known as the B–7 Escort Group, commanded by another of the Royal Navy's renowned U–boat hunters, Commander Peter Gretton. Somewhat tired of the more restricted role of escort group commander, Gretton lobbied hard for his flotilla to be redesignated as a support group. Eventually the Admiralty agreed, and renamed his command as the Seventh Support Group. It was this force which was already on station with the merchantmen of convoy ON 224 when Walker arrived.[21] As a point of interest, when serving aboard HMS *Cossack* in 1940, Gretton was actually washed overboard during a storm, only to be thrown back aboard his ship by a following wave.[22]

> After refuelling for a second time we began to carry out our hunting sweeps around the merchantmen, and despite our thoughts that the U–boats had been driven away, we soon discovered they had not yet given up, when one was detected close to the convoy.[23] This time it was my own ship, *Woodpecker*, that was first to hoist the black pennant. We kept our ping on the target while the rest of the group came in, allowing *Starling* to take up the attack with us, but it was another long hunt, the U–boat managing to avoid being sunk on quite a few occasions. But we stuck to the task, and after so many depth charge attacks we knew that life must have been grim for the U–boatmen below. Walker also knew it and he was expecting them to crack – if he did not sink them first.
>
> I was on watch just before the hunt ended, and at about 16:00 I was relieved as daylight was fading. From the boiler room, I went straight down to the bathroom and noticed that the porthole was standing open. I was about to close it after washing at a sink, when through the open window came the sound of the guns up above as we opened fire. It was a sure sign that the U–boat had come up; the question now was: would the crew put up a fight, or would they give up the ghost and abandon ship?
>
> The sound of the gunfire soon began to increase as other ships in the group joined the attack. I then made my way up to the deck

hoping to catch sight of the action, and as I passed through a doorway and came into view of the gunners, I heard a shout from above, 'Hey, stokes! Keep your head down we're going to open fire.' I got clear as fast as I could, and after *Woodpecker* had fired a few more rounds there was a warning over the tannoy telling the crew that we were going in to ram the U–boat, which was by then fully exposed on the surface.

Expecting to feel the force of a heavy collision at any minute I went back down and ran through the ramming drill we had been taught, which was to lie down, feet towards the bows of the ship, with the soles of your shoes resting against a bulkhead. Before taking up that position it always paid to make sure you were not lying in a place where something nasty or heavy could fall on you when the collision happened. I decided the bathroom would be as good a place as any in which to avoid injury, and as I looked around for something to hold on to as the ship was lining up to make its charge, I suddenly heard Walker's voice come over a loudspeaker, warning *Woodpecker* to stand clear before he opened fire with his four–inch guns. There was a risk that, if she maintained her course, *Woodpecker* would lose her bows, if not worse; the same thing had happened to *Starling* when she went in to ram in an earlier incident, and this was probably on Walker's mind at that moment. I felt the ship peel away, circle around and come back into the attack, blazing away once more. By this time I could see the crew of the U–boat jumping into the sea. Shells were hitting their boat and throwing up splashes and spray all around as they made their escape. From what I could see, the skipper was the last man off and from what was said later, it would seem that he had done his duty by scuttling the boat rather than let it be captured. It was another example of the spirit of the Germans, and we all recognised their bravery. There were not many of our men who would have swapped places with them, and nobody was sorry for having to rescue any survivors there might be after a U–boat had been sunk. This time I think the whole crew managed to escape, and all of them were rescued by the group.

Once the action was over I found out that eighteen of the survivors had been picked up by *Woodpecker*. Being curious to have a look at them, I went to the mess where they had been gathered together. They made a sorry sight after their narrow escape and the battering they had taken while they were submerged. Later, once

> they had been interrogated, we were told that some of them had said they were aware they had been up against the Second Support Group, and that they mentioned Captain Walker by name.

The U–boat which took part in the action just described was *U–264*, sunk on 19/2/44 by gunfire from Walker's sloops at location 48.31N, 22.05W, which is about 600 miles west of Land's End. All members of the crew from this, the sixth victim of the patrol, survived and were picked up. She was the first of the new schnorkel boats to be sunk.

Commanded by *Kptlt*. Hartwig Looks, *U–264* was on her fifth patrol when she was sunk. She sank no Allied ships on that patrol. During her previous patrols she claimed a total of seven merchant ships sunk, though later analysis reduced this to three. Whilst stalking convoys between 17 and 19 February 1944 she was detected and attacked on several occasions but managed to shake off her attackers. At about noon on 19 February, she surfaced to a depth of 65 feet to raise her radio mast and transmit a signal to U-boat Control. It was then when she was detected by Walker's group. *Starling* and *Woodpecker* attacked in tandem, dropping a total of 88 depth charges between them and forcing her to the surface. Prisoners from her crew claimed that the damage sustained by their boat after each attack was slight, but that the cumulative effect was enough to convince Looks that it was time to surrender.

In ITV's landmark documentary series, *The World at War*, made during the 1970s, the Battle of the Atlantic was analysed in the episode entitled *Wolf Pack*. In it, Hartwig Looks, still cutting a dapper figure some thirty years after the war, provided an interview for the film makers, in which he described the intense sea battle fought between Convoy ONS 5, its escorts, and a large number of U–boats, which took place between 26 April and 6 May 1943 off the southern coast of Greenland. Six U–boats were sunk and seven severely damaged for the loss of thirteen allied ships. The battle was considered to be the turning point in the Atlantic struggle.[24]

> News of the sixth kill of the patrol was not long in reaching home, and it was probably as a result of this that the group, so it was said, began to receive signals from the Admiralty telling it that a welcoming party in our honour was being organised for our return to Liverpool. We would be sailing into port to the sound of bands playing, and a guard of honour led by Admiral Horton. We were going to receive a hero's welcome at Gladstone Dock!
>
> It seemed as though the Navy had decided to make a lot of propaganda from the success of our patrol; six U–boat kills on a

Above and below: Wren *being refuelled from the escort carrier HMS* Activity. Activity *was with the 2SG for the first few days of Walker's six-in-one-trip (29/1/44 to 22/2/44). Both she and a second escort carrier,* Nairana, *provided cover for the two west-bound Atlantic convoys ONS28 & ON222. However,* Activity *was also with the 2SG as part of the escort for convoys JW58 (UK to Murmansk 27/3/44 to 5/4/44) and RA58 (Murmansk to UK 7/4/44 to 14/4/44). Possibly January/February 1944 or March/April 1944.* (Gordon Canti Collection, by permission of the Maritime Museum, National Museums Liverpool)

Boarding party from HMS Wren *leaving the Spanish trawler,* Europa V, *after taking off its crew. Bay of Biscay, 25 July 1943.* (Gordon Canti Collection, by permission of the Maritime Museum, National Museums Liverpool)

Spanish crew of Europa V *about to be taken aboard* Wren. *25 July 1943.* (Gordon Canti Collection, by permission of the Maritime Museum, National Museums Liverpool)

Europa V *slipping beneath the waves after being scuttled. 25 July 1943.* (Gordon Canti Collection, by permission of the Maritime Museum, National Museums Liverpool)

Irish vessel in the Bay of Biscay. Note the republican flag painted on each side of 'EIRE.' July 1943. (Gordon Canti Collection, by permission of the Maritime Museum, National Museums Liverpool)

HMS Kite *taking U-boat survivors aboard. From the date given by Dr. Canti, we know that the action of 30 July 1943 involved ships of the Second Support Group, a number of allied aircraft and three U-boats: U-tanker U-461, U-tanker U-462 and U-504.* (Gordon Canti Collection, by permission of the Maritime Museum, National Museums Liverpool)

Incredible picture capturing the split second when a depth charge launched by HMS Wren *detonated prematurely as it was rolled over the stern.* (Gordon Canti Collection, by permission of the Maritime Museum, National Museums Liverpool)

Above: *HMS* Starling. (Gordon Canti Collection, by permission of the Maritime Museum, National Museums Liverpool)

Left: *HMS* Woodcock. Woodcock *joined the Second Support Group just before it set out on its third Biscay patrol of Operation Musketry, 23/7/43 to 6/8/43.* (Gordon Canti Collection, by permission of the Maritime Museum, National Museums Liverpool)

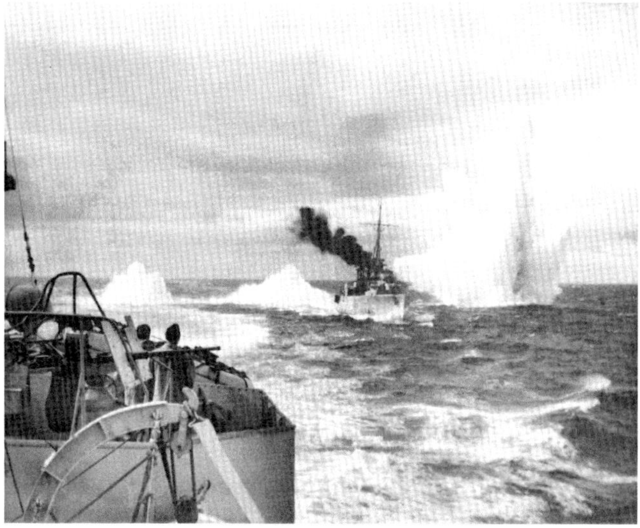

Picture taken from HMS Wren *showing HMS* Starling *carrying out an attack on U-473, sunk on 6 May 1944.* (Gordon Canti Collection, by permission of the Maritime Museum, National Museums Liverpool)

Picture taken from HMS Wren *showing HMS* Starling *carrying out an attack on U-473, sunk on 6 May 1944.* (Gordon Canti Collection, by permission of the Maritime Museum, National Museums Liverpool)

The escort carrier HMS Tracker *coming close to HMS* Wren. (Gordon Canti Collection, by permission of the Maritime Museum, National Museums Liverpool)

Above: *Dr. Gordon Canti on the bridge of HMS* Wren. (Gordon Canti Collection, by permission of the Maritime Museum, National Museums Liverpool)

Left: *The crew of HMS* Wren *relaxing during a Biscay patrol. Probably August 1944.* (Gordon Canti Collection, by permission of the Maritime Museum, National Museums Liverpool)

Survivors from U–461, *Bay of Biscay 1943. A handwritten note on reverse of this picture reads: '15 survivors off a German U–boat, picked up in the Bay of Biscay by HMS* Woodpecker, *30/7/43.'* (Private collection of Joseph Marsden)

U-boat survivors in the water, probably taken during the actions off Lorient in August 1944. (Gordon Canti Collection, by permission of the Maritime Museum, National Museums Liverpool)

U-boat survivors aboard Wren *being watched over by C.P.O. Richardson and A.B. Hamblett.* (Gordon Canti Collection, by permission of the Maritime Museum, National Museums Liverpool)

Picture taken aboard HMS Wren *showing a group of U–boat crew survivors. The German prisoners were probably from one of three U-boats: U-736, U-608 and U-385 (most likely) all sunk between 31/7/44 and 11/8/44.*

Survivors from Sunderland RAAF/B about to be picked up by the crew of HMS Wren *as they cling to a detached wing from their aircraft. Biscay 1/8/1943.* (Gordon Canti Collection, by permission of the Maritime Museum, National Museums Liverpool)

Picture taken from HMS Wren *of HMS* Starling *(U66) and HMS* Wildgoose *(U45). Possibly May or August 1944.* (Gordon Canti Collection, by permission of the Maritime Museum, National Museums Liverpool)

RAF liaison officer Jewell (on the left) aboard HMS Wren, *accompanied by one of* Wren's *gunners and Petty Officer Dawkins. July/August 1943.* (Gordon Canti Collection, by permission of the Maritime Museum, National Museums Liverpool)

Woodpecker *attended by the tug* Storm King *whose bows and two masts are just visible beyond* Woodpecker's *port side. Date 20/2/1944.* (Gordon Canti Collection, by permission of the Maritime Museum, National Museums Liverpool)

HMS Woodpecker *with the ocean-going tug,* Storm King *in attendance. The damage to* Woodpecker's *stern is clearly visible. 20 February 1944.* (Gordon Canti Collection, by permission of the Maritime Museum, National Museums Liverpool)

Woodpecker *(right) with another of Walker's sloops in attendance (left). Comparing the aft sections of the two reveals just how much of* Woodpecker's *stern is missing. Picture taken from HMS* Wren. *20 February 1944.* (Gordon Canti Collection, by permission of the Maritime Museum, National Museums Liverpool)

Above: Woodpecker *after losing her stern section. Looking closely one can see a large section of the after deck flipped up over the rear gun turret, just like the sardine tin analogy mentioned by some. 20 February 1944.* (Gordon Canti Collection, by permission of the Maritime Museum, National Museums Liverpool)

Right: *Dr. Gordon Canti posing for a picture aboard HMS* Wren *during her voyage to Russia in March/ April of 1944, as part of the escort for convoy JW58.* (Gordon Canti Collection, by permission of the Maritime Museum, National Museums Liverpool)

Picture taken in what looks like the officers' mess aboard HMS Wren, *marking the destruction of U-473. Dr. Gordon Canti is fifth from the left. 6 May 1944.* (Gordon Canti Collection, by permission of the Maritime Museum, National Museums Liverpool)

Example of the Hs. 293 'glider bomb' on display at RAF Cosford Museum. (Courtesy Shamus Reddin)

Right: *Joseph Marsden, Ceylon (now Sri Lanka) June 1945.* (Private collection of Joseph Marsden)

Below: *Flight deck crew and officers, HMS* Empress *July 1945. Joseph Marsden, standing sixth from left.* (Private collection of Joseph Marsden)

VJ Day. Flight deck of HMS Empress. *VJ Day, Trincomalee Harbour, 15 August, 1945.* (Private collection of Joseph Marsden)

HMS Empress. *Crossing the line. Return voyage from Ceylon to England, Autumn, 1945.* (Private collection of Joseph Marsden)

shafts as far as the twin screws. The whole thing looked just like a pair of giant, wilting, twisted daisies, and through the gaping hole in the ship's plating, just beyond the screws, you could see the Atlantic Ocean rolling along under a grey sky. At a guess, the engine room was flooded to a depth of about eighteen inches, and the watertight doors located about six to eight feet above floor level at the top of the access stairway were lying open.

I was with Gleeson and a few others who had gathered there, looking up at the doors, when I noticed a PO about to enter. I watched as he came in and climbed down towards the engine space. As he did so, we noticed he was holding onto a flagon of rum, and the way he was carrying it made it clear to anybody watching that it had just been taken from the ship's store. It was clear that he had not noticed us as he reached the bottom of the stairway. One of the lads, I cannot remember who, but I will always remember his speed of thought, shouted out, 'Quick! Here comes the jimmy–the–one!' This had exactly the effect we were hoping for. The PO, afraid of being caught red–handed with the rum, put the flagon down into the sea water and made off. As he did so all of us registered the spot where the prize had been dropped. One of the lads homed in on it, fished it out of the water, wrapped it in his boiler suit and off we went to the mess to splice the mainbrace. When we reached our berths it was drinks all round. Out came the cups in a flash. Nobody could believe their luck. A party atmosphere soon took over in the mess, but after sipping a cupful off I became quite sleepy and decided to make my way to my berth, where I swung up into my hammock, settled down and soon dozed off.

I must have slept for about two hours, but when I woke up it soon became clear that the drinking session I abandoned earlier had not continued without incident. One of the younger lads, let me call him Bob Weller, had drank about five cupfuls of rum and passed out. He could not be woken, so someone had thought it would be a good idea to ask for the ship's doctor to be sent down to the stokers' mess to take a look at him. When the medic arrived, he began to rouse young Bob with some light slaps across the cheeks. Apparently, it had been impossible to wake him at first but the doctor persisted, and when Bob finally came round he wanted to know who had been 'knocking him about' and became aggressive towards the medic. Things got worse from that point on, so much so that the doctor thought it best to send for a straightjacket. Young Bob was strapped into it and taken up to the sick bay. Amazingly, it all worked out in his favour, as it was at that time, or not long afterwards, that some of the crew were evacuated from *Woodpecker* and transferred to the other sloops which were still standing by.

I am sure that Bob was amongst this first group to leave the ship, still strapped into the straightjacket, and everybody in the mess, knowing what had happened, was convinced he would be facing a two–year prison sentence once he was returned to barracks. However, we were eventually to hear that he got off scot–free. The only reason we could think of for such leniency was that the Navy did not want to spoil the story of a successful patrol by putting on trial, for a serious breach of discipline aboard a crippled ship, a man who had played a full part in the success that had gone before. The feeling of everyone involved was that he had been very lucky indeed.

There were others in the mess who drank too much that day. But my friend Gleeson, who had been fairly restrained in his consumption, left the mess at one point to get some air and happened to bump into one member of the crew looking a bit worse for the wear, who was staggering along the deck towards him. Gleeson asked him where he was going, and the man said he was thinking of taking a walk to the forecastle to take in some fresh air. Luckily, my friend had the good sense to lead him to the stokers' mess where he would be out of danger. With so much of the safety rail missing from the edge of the deck it was a fair bet he would have fallen over the side had he been left to his stroll.

When both men arrived at the doorway Gleeson called on me, together with a few others from the mess, to help him get the matelot to a safe berth. Somebody pointed out that the ship's workshop was one level up from the flooded engine room, close to the emergency generator, and as such it was unlikely to become flooded unless the ship began to sink. After some discussion we decided that the workshop might well be the best place for him, and made our way towards it. As we opened the door we could see that we were not the only ones who had come up with such a plan for keeping their shipmates safe. We came across four other men in the workshop, all of them sleeping it off. To help make them comfortable, someone had opened a bale of cleaning rags and made a kind of giant bird's nest of it. The four revellers, having been laid down on the rags, were in a deep sleep. We added a fifth and left, closing the door behind us. In the workshop they would be safe from discovery, and as there was always a member of the crew keeping watch over the nearby generator, the men could be woken up if need be – or so we thought.

Not long after we left our shipmates to sleep off the effects of their drinking bout, I was detailed to take up watch in the ammunition hold. Straw was often used as a lining material for the crates in which munitions were stored, and when I entered the hold I could see that a lot of it, whether washed out of the empty crates or having been scattered around as the ammunition was removed, was now floating about in the flooded compartment and fouling the elephant's foot that was fixed to the end of the suction pipes connected to the ship's sea pumps. These pumps, six in total, were capable of pumping about one hundred tons of water per hour out of the flooded areas of the ship, so long as they were not fouled. It was now my duty to keep the straw away from the suction heads to stop them from getting blocked, and to check the pump outlets to see that they were working properly.

Half way through my watch the chief stoker came along to check on things, and while doing so he asked me where the rest of his men (my fellow stokers) were, as he had seen no sign of some of them for a quite a while. Of the twenty–four stokers belonging to *Woodpecker*'s crew, about twelve had already been evacuated from the ship, this he knew about, but of the remaining twelve, about half of them, he said, were missing. I had to plead ignorance of their whereabouts in order to protect them, but the chief could see that I was keeping something from him and warned me about the possible consequences of my attitude before he left. Later, once my watch had come to an end, I went to check on the five men we had left in the workshop. When I got there I found it empty; the men were nowhere to be seen. I was to discover later that, after they had woken up, they had somehow managed to find their way to the ship's whaler, which was being used to evacuate men from *Woodpecker* to the other ships of the group. I often wondered, thinking back, just how those five characters had managed to row the whaler (because they would have been expected to help) on anything like a straight course towards the rescue ship that took them aboard.

The matelot in whose care we had left our comrades I later found, completely drunk, lying close to the generator he had been left in charge of. By this time about half of the crew had been evacuated. The German prisoners were some of the first to go; they were transferred to *Starling*. The reason was obvious to me. With the press and cameras waiting for our return in Liverpool, these trophies of war, so to speak, were considered to be worth more than those of us left behind on *Woodpecker*. It was also clear that the first of the crew members taken to safety were mostly those of higher rank, or men with long service records; in other words, the most experienced sailors amongst the crew.

The Admiralty was keen to get the other five ships of the group under steam and heading for home as quickly as possible, so as soon as the ocean–going tug, *Storm King,* arrived, Walker decided to set off for Liverpool in *Starling* together with *Kite*, *Wren*, *Wildgoose* and *Magpie*. Once with us, the tug put a tow line on *Woodpecker* and in no time at all she was under steam towards the Western Approaches. Not long afterwards an ASDICs trawler arrived, having been instructed to watch over us as we were towed home.[25]

Once Walker's group had disappeared some of *Woodpecker*'s crew were transferred to the *Storm King*. The men now left aboard made up a skeleton crew of about twenty–five, including eight stokers, myself amongst them. All the while we were under tow, the seamen still aboard were stripping everything they could from the ship and tipping it over the side in an attempt to lighten the load on the tow line and to help keep us afloat. As the day wore on we continued to make steady progress towards Cornwall, and after several hours we were joined by a frigate.[26] At that point the ASDICs trawler was allowed to sail for home. It was to the frigate that I was later evacuated when my turn came to leave *Woodpecker*, but before being taken off the ship I was ordered to carry onto the whaler only the bare minimum of kit. I did as I was told and clambered aboard with only my little brown suitcase, into which I had crammed as many of my essentials as it would hold. We were then rowed across to the waiting frigate.

Once aboard our rescue ship, it would be less than true to say that we were received with anything like a warm and friendly welcome. She was very low on supplies, and having been diverted to pick us up her crew regarded us as being more or less personally responsible for delaying their arrival into Liverpool. I do not remember any of us being offered even so much as a cup of tea during the whole time it took to reach Liverpool; none of the frigate's crew showed the slightest interest in us. However, being a stoker aboard a strange ship I was curious to see how things looked in the engine room, and was grateful when an opportunity arose to take a look inside; unaccompanied of course. On inspection she seemed to be of a less modern design than *Woodpecker*, and I noticed she was powered by an old type of reciprocating engine.[27]

About twenty–four hours after boarding the frigate we pulled into port, and once ashore we received news that the remainder of *Woodpecker*'s crew had been evacuated by a Canadian destroyer.[28] After the last but one group of survivors had been taken off, amongst whom I was included, a heavy storm had blown up making it dangerous for *Storm King* to maintain the tow. As a result, a decision was taken to slip the line once the last of the skeleton crew had been taken off by the Canadians. Once loose, *Woodpecker* went over and lay floating, keel up, on the surface. She did not begin to sink immediately, so to prevent her from becoming a danger to shipping the Canadian skipper ordered his gunners to pump a few shells into the hull. Trapped air then escaped through the holes, and as the sea water rushed in to force out the last of the air pockets inside, she then slipped beneath the waves somewhere off the Isles of Scilly about forty miles from Falmouth.

The frigate that brought me home pulled in to Liverpool on 28 February 1944, and I was put ashore along with my fellow survivors, still dressed in the boiler suit I was wearing when I was evacuated from *Woodpecker*. I had not been offered even a change of clothing while aboard the rescue ship.

When I stepped onto the quayside of Gladstone Dock I made straight for the entrance of the air raid shelter within the dockyard. Once inside I changed into the only clean clothes I had managed to salvage before being taken off *Woodpecker*. Later, I received instructions to catch a train from Lime Street station that same night and report to barracks in Devonport on the following day. My old friend, Les Summers, had been with me aboard the friendly frigate which had just delivered us home, as such we found ourselves together in my home town, and as our train was not leaving Liverpool until midnight, it gave me the opportunity to take him home to my parents' house where we could smarten up and have something to eat.

It was my eldest sister, Mary, who had first learned of what had happened. She had been in the Grafton public house two nights earlier when she noticed some of the men from the war production factory where she worked. They were talking secretively to some of the girls from her shift. She did not realise it at the time, but her friends were being told that *Woodpecker* had been sunk. None of them told her anything about it for a little while, I suppose that was the way things were at that time; nobody wanted to be the bearer of bad news.

My mother was most puzzled as to the cause of my delay in arriving home, she had been expecting me for about a week. By then my brothers and sisters were all aware of what had happened to *Woodpecker*, but none of them had told her anything about it for fear of upsetting her. When she saw me coming through the front door of the family house, she asked why it had taken me so long to arrive. 'We caught a tin fish in the Atlantic,' I replied, 'Oh!' she said, 'I'm glad you didn't bring it home; you know I only like salmon.' All present had a good laugh and left it at that.

After having washed and smartened ourselves up, Les and me had something to eat and managed to have a few pints in the local pubs before boarding the train for Devonport.

According to the web site, *uboat.net*, *Woodpecker* was hit astern by a single T5 acoustic torpedo fired by *U–256* on 20/2/44 at position 48.49N, 22.11W. The web site, *naval–history.net*, gives the same positional data, *i.e.* some 600 miles west of Cork, but credits *U–764* with the kill. However, the greater weight of opinion comes down in support of *U–256's* captain Wilhelm Brauel's claim to have fired the fatal shot.

A translation of the segment from Brauel's war diary which covers the sinking of *Woodpecker* is reproduced by Morgan and Taylor in their publication, *U–Boat Attack Logs,* in it, Brauel states that his NAXOX radar picked up two separate contacts, each representing a ship of Walker's Second Support Group coming towards him, one to port and one to starboard of his boat. The starboard contact showed a range of 3,500 m. and is thought to have originated from HMS *Starling*, the port contact, at 2,000 m. was *Woodpecker*. Brauel then turned his boat about (after *Woodpecker* and *Starling* had passed him?) in the act of launching two torpedoes, one at each contact, this would then have then placed *Starling* on his port side, and *Woodpecker* on his starboard as the torpedoes began their flight. *Woodpecker* was hit, *Starling* escaped unscathed. As a point of interest, if Brauel did detect *Starling* and *Woodpecker* using his radar, then he must have been on the surface at the time.[29]

An Aside

If ever an example was required of just how much pressure Doenitz's U–boats were under during late 1943 and early 1944, one need look no further than *U–264*'s experiences during that period. Captained by Hartwig Looks, she was the last of the six victims of Walker's famous six–in–one trip, as we have just seen.

According to intelligence gleaned from her crew, one can see that, on 22 September 1943 she began her fourth patrol under orders to enter the Mediterranean along with *U–642*, *U–450*, *U–223*, *U–340*, *U–732*, and *U–566*.[30] The last three mentioned were sunk, either whilst attempting the passage of the straits or, in the case of *U–566*, on passage to it. The other three succeeded in entering the Mediterranean but two of them, *U–450* and *U–223*, were sunk in March 1944. *U–264* did not succeed in getting through the straits, and as a result she was ordered to sail westwards into the Atlantic and rendezvous with U–tanker *U–460* and two other type VIIs: *U–455* and *U–422*. As the four U–boats lay on the surface at their point of rendezvous, they were spotted by aircraft from the American escort carrier, USS *Card*. The ensuing result of the first engagement between *Card's* aircraft and the U–boats was that the tanker *U–460* was sunk, with the rest of the boats escaping after being strafed and depth–charged. *U–460* was unlucky in that, as she dived, one of the American Avengers dropped a FIDO – an air–launched acoustic torpedo, sometimes referred to as a 'water mine'. The FIDO then homed in on its target and sank *U–460*.[31]

The trauma for the U–boats did not end there. Later in the day, after refuelling and re–arming aboard *Card*, the American Avengers made a second sortie and discovered *U–264* and *U–422* on the surface, perhaps taking stock of the damage inflicted upon them during the morning's engagement. The result of this second encounter was the sinking of *U–422* by a second FIDO launched by the same pilot (Lt. (junior grade) R.L. Stearns of the US Navy) who sank *U–460*.

Hartwig Looks's boat, *U–264*, managed to escape after sustaining damage during the day's attacks and later docked at St Nazaire on 15 October 1943. After repairs she sailed on her next and final patrol on 2 February 1944, and was sunk by Walker's group on 19 February.[32]

Chapter 8

HMS *Woodpecker*: some reflections

With *Woodpecker's* story having come to an end, I thought it might be a good time to talk to Marsden about the day–to–day life aboard one of the Navy's little ships during the war. In the course of our conversations I would prompt him by asking questions about the kind of things that might affect a sailor's daily routine, and what follows is a compilation of his answers.

> Walker always said that his Bird–class sloops were strong enough to withstand normal sailing conditions, but that they did not stand up too well to the kind of battering they got in the heavy storms of the North Atlantic. Under those conditions, he said, the plate welding could fail and the ships begin to leak quite badly, and as an example of what he meant by this, it might help if I were to tell of my own experiences in heavy seas. The first that comes to mind happened when we were escorting a convoy towards Gibraltar in early January 1944 and sailed into a very heavy storm which could have sunk us. If I remember correctly, it was during the time that we were on detachment from Walker's Group.
>
> At about 19:30 one day, after suffering hours of strengthening gales as we headed south, the winds became much stronger, and I began to get an idea of just what our chances might be as a result. The sea was very high by then, but in spite of the worsening conditions the bosun went around the messes, blowing a whistle as he entered each, before announcing that there would be a tombola session later that night, and that it would be held at the usual venue on the forecastle. It was not long after the players had settled down to their game that it became very rough indeed.
>
> The stokers' mess was directly beneath the room where the game was going on, which meant that we could hear everything that was happening. Suddenly there was a great commotion above our heads, so much so that, along with some of the other stokers,

I left the mess and went up to see what all the fuss was about. When we arrived it was clear that the forecastle had just been swamped by a giant wave which had clearly struck the deck above with a lot of force and cracked open some of the welds, allowing the sea to pour in. Everyone in the room had been completely soaked, as had the hammocks and other gear that was stored there, and the commotion was showing no signs of ending as we entered the room.

Once things had settled down we began to make some running repairs. Later in the day, making use of some canvas and timber that had been gathered, we were able to make some stronger repairs once the worst of the storm had passed and the seas had become calmer. The coxswain was placed in charge of the working parties detailed to carry out the task, but in spite of his best efforts it was quite a while before we were anywhere near to being fully watertight. Had the storm lasted much longer, I really do not know how we would have fared. This whole incident had the effect of concentrating the mind on just how vulnerable our little ships were to the power of the sea, and after that experience I do not think I was ever again as relaxed as I used to be about the idea of sailing into stormy seas.[1]

It was during an earlier patrol while we were escorting a convoy to the Mediterranean in November 1943, again during our detachment from Walker's group, that we ran into another storm, this time I think we were out in the Atlantic. As the ship battled on through the huge seas that day, I was given a bit of a tongue lashing by one of the officers and was lucky not to have been placed on a charge, which would have been rough justice. I had been on watch in what was called the fan room, a cabin that housed a giant fan which was used to blow air towards the boiler doors to stop the flames from jumping out whenever they were opened. It was a very noisy place, and it must have been during my stint inside the cabin that an order was announced forbidding members of the crew to go onto the upper deck for the next three days due to expected heavy seas.

Oblivious to the announcement, and at that time still not too worried about the idea of being at sea in rough weather, I continued with my normal duties between 04:00 and 08:00 while on watch. Once my work was finished I went down to the mess to have a cup of tea. The men who were due on watch at midday were busy preparing lunch, which was the usual chore for the midday watch.

After a short while I decided to remove myself, feeling that my presence was making life difficult for those who were working, and returned to the fan room to check on things. The floor there had to be cleaned continually due to the build–up of leaking oil which tended to mix with the steam that condensed on bulkheads before running down the walls in little streams. To remove the slops, I would simply soak them up with a cloth and squeeze the mixture into a bucket before taking it up on deck and tipping it over the side. Floor cleaned, bucket in hand, I went off to the stern to dispose of the slops, and as I was making my way along the deck, holding on to a lifeline (a steel wire which ran the length of the deck) as I went, it seemed to me as though we were making hardly any headway. *Woodpecker* was facing into a strong gale and seemed to be standing still in the water, but she was being thrown about by the rough seas and strong winds, added to that a thick spray made things very uncomfortable for me as I staggered along the lifeline, single–handed, towards the stern. Once there I emptied out the contents of my bucket, turned around and began to make my way back along the deck. Suddenly I heard the voice of a petty officer coming from the X–gun deck above. I turned, looked up and saw him standing next to the coxswain, who was staring at me as though I was completely mad or stupid.

'Haven't you heard the orders?' he bawled. 'You're on a charge.'

I placed my bucket on the deck, cupped my hands to my mouth and asked,

'What orders?'

'There's a huge wave approaching. Pick up your bucket and get inside,' was the reply.

Once inside, thinking I was now on a charge, I went in search of the chief stoker to explain to him the reason why I had been up on deck. Just then the PO and the coxswain arrived at the covered gangway where we were standing and demanded an explanation for my behaviour. My defence was that the killick seaman, or the coxswain himself, whichever of them made the rounds to pass on the order to stay off the deck, should have made sure that all hands were told; they should, at least, have made sure that those who were on watch in places where their whistles and calls could not be heard were approached and told about the situation. Luckily, the chief stoker took my side and it was agreed, grudgingly, that the charge against me should be dropped. I suppose I should have appreciated the concern for my safety that was behind the PO's actions, but my feelings of self–pity got the better of me.

Maybe this is a good point at which to mention the sanitary arrangements aboard a Bird–class sloop. Not something that grips your imagination when thinking about the war at sea, maybe, but they were part of a sailor's daily experiences nevertheless.

The system for removing waste from the toilets aboard *Woodpecker* consisted of something like an eighteen–inch diameter pipe which had been halved along its length, with one of the halves then embedded in the steel floor of the toilet room to form a channel. There was a continuous flow of water along this channel, the stream being supplied by a pump that drew it directly from the sea. After running the length of the halved pipe the water simply poured out of the ship's side into the sea, taking with it any waste it may have picked up on its way. It was a simple and effective system of sewage disposal with the advantage that it could never become blocked.

Above the floor channel there were about five individual toilet cubicles, each fitted out with a toilet seat from which there was a clear drop to the water channel; none of them had a door; there was absolutely no privacy, but I do not remember any of the men ever being embarrassed by it. The five washbasins which stood next to the toilet cubicles shared the same drainage channel, and there was a separate trough for the urinals. The design did give us an opportunity for a bit of fun, however. Sometimes, when it was known that someone was using one of the cubicles, a fire ball made from a loose bunch of newspaper pages would be dropped into the channel and allowed to float in the direction of the occupied toilet seat.

As far as personal hygiene was concerned, the ratings were expected to buy soap for their own use at the NAAFI. It was known as pusser's soap and cost about tuppence for a large bar measuring about two inches square and nine inches in length. It came in a kind of toffee colour and contained a gritty substance which might have been soda; this we used for washing our clothes. If anybody wanted to, they could buy toilet soap for washing and showering. Fresh water was always tight while we were at sea, and everything was done to conserve supplies, such as having taps that were push–operated.

When it came to doing their laundry, the ratings usually washed their clothes in a bucket. Most men had one amongst their kit but they had to be bought ashore at your own expense; they were not an issued item. There was a steam pipe available in the ship's boiler room which served as a laundry device, it could be placed into a bucket containing cold fresh water and bring it up to boiling point if required. Like this, we could wash our kit properly before hanging it up to dry in the boiler room. The men washed themselves in a similar way, half filling a bucket with tepid fresh water from a tap in the bathroom which helped to generate a good lather from the toilet soap as we washed. The suds we then rinsed away with water taken from a special salt water tap. Finally, the salt water was rinsed from the skin using a small amount of fresh water to leave it feeling smooth and free from the stickiness caused by the sea salt. But by no means everybody shared the same level of concern for the conservation of fresh water as that usually displayed by the stokers. I sometimes watched as seamen filled up a bucket to wash no more than a handkerchief or two, and it was usually members of that same tribe who would stand under the shower for as long as the water supply was available.

As regards the question of personal cleanliness, there was never an inspection to ensure good hygiene amongst the men. Neither were the men expected to wash as part of their daily routine; it was all left to the individual. For example, some of the seamen who more or less bivouacked near the four–inch gun turrets all the time we were at sea, would not remove their lammy coats for days at a time, which was an indication of just how much attention they paid to their personal cleanliness. Not that I ever wanted to ask them how their habits allowed them to wash or shower every day.

During the later months of my service with the Second Support Group security became more of a priority than it seemed to have been in the early days. By that time we were always being reminded about the danger of letting slip any information whenever we went ashore. By that I mean that we were told never to discuss the movements of the group while it was at sea. We were also told to be always on the lookout for anything we came across during our daily duties that might look suspicious, and to report to an officer if something ever caught our attention. In complying with these instructions, I once became involved in an incident which could have led to more serious consequences for all those involved than actually turned out to be the case.

It happened while we were on a patrol in the Bay of Biscay during the summer of 1943. As I have already said, one of my duties was to ensure that everything in the fan room was safe, secure and in perfect working order, and I think I may already have explained the importance of the fan's role in maintaining the safety of the ship: its purpose was to blow air towards the boiler doors to reduce the risk of fire whenever they were opened. Each day, after finishing the morning watch, I would go down to the mess for a cup of tea, and once refreshed I would set about a list of checks and tasks designed, as I always considered them, to do no more than keep boredom at bay. The first thing on my list was a visit to the fan room for inspection and cleaning; the fan itself was mounted on a platform and secured by four large bolts which connected its base flange to the steel plates forming the platform top.

As I entered the room one day, I found one of the bolts lying on the floor with its nut and washer close by. It seemed that the bolt had come loose and fallen away. My first thought was to put it back in its place, replace the washer, screw on the nut and tighten it. But due to the vibration of the engines and the movement of the ship, the holes in flange and platform had become misaligned. It was clear that I was going to need some help to realign them, as the fan weighed something like six or seven hundredweight. When I made some checks I found that the three remaining bolts were also loose, but the thing that seemed strange to me was the fact that all the bolts had been passed upwardly through the platform and the base flange of the fan, and the nuts then screwed on from the top. I reckoned that nobody in their right mind would have made such an obvious mistake. Every fitter knows that bolts should always be passed downwards through their locating holes in order to prevent what had just happened because of the nuts coming loose. I began to wonder if I was looking at the work of a fifth columnist; not that I suspected anyone aboard *Woodpecker*; sabotage was more likely to be carried out in the shipyards and dockyards.

After reporting what I had seen to the Petty Officer I was sent to the artificers' mess to explain the situation. Three or four of them were present when I arrived to pass on my message; they listened to what I said and sent me away, promising me that they would take a look at things as soon as they had the time. I then returned and reported their response to the PO.

About three days later, after coming off the same morning watch, I repeated my usual routine and was surprised to find a second nut, bolt and washer on the floor, the first set still not having been replaced. The fan had become very loose by then, so I went once more to see the PO and informed him of the situation. This time I left him to talk to the artificers as I felt that they were not prepared to take me seriously. A few days passed with no more news about the progress of the repairs. Then, one day, I noticed a bit of a panic going on in the area of the fan room. I went to take a look and found the chief engineer artificer, together with his four assistants, all standing at the door way of the room. They had finally shaken themselves and decided to make an inspection; but by then the sea had become quite rough, and on finding the fan so loose that it was actually moving about on its mountings, they had decided it was too dangerous to try and secure it until careful preparations were made. In an effort to clear themselves of any blame for the situation, their reaction was to create a huge fuss and claim that the fault had never been reported to them. They were trying to shift the blame onto the stokers. The chief artificer saw me standing close by and began to give me a dressing down as though it had all been my fault. Luckily, the PO was standing a few feet away, and after hearing everything that was said he stepped into the row in my support.

Soon, the engineer officer was sent for and informed of the situation, and after making a brief inspection he declared that the problem could soon become worse and place the ship's safety at risk. The realisation of the size of the maintenance task now in hand began to dawn on everyone. The fan had to be secured, but before work could begin it would have to be switched off. To do that while the boiler was in operation would put the safety of the ship at risk, but to shut down the boiler and thereby reduce the ship to half speed was out of the question without permission from the Group Commander, Johnny Walker.

Everyone began to think that we might have to return to port, so there was nothing else for it; the ship's captain was told about the situation and, keen to have the situation sorted out as quickly as possible, he passed the word on to Walker via a signal to *Starling*. Eventually a plan was worked out. The whole group was to reduce speed to seven knots while *Woodpecker* ran on one boiler, this would allow the repairs to be carried out safely. Once the plan was put into action, all the necessary work was completed in less than an hour, but whether or not the basic flaw that caused the failure in the first place was ever sorted out by using split pins or nylon threaded nuts, for example, I do not know. Neither can I say that the possibility of it being sabotage was ever considered. All I can say is that, to the best of my knowledge, the fault never happened again.

Another instance comes to mind that might be worth mentioning: by the summer of 1943 a new and more powerful depth charge had been developed, and was being brought into service as quickly as possible.[2] On the return voyage to Liverpool after the final patrol we made while still armed with the old type, it was decided that we could put some of them to good use – by going on a fishing trip. The thinking behind it was that, once in port, the ship would have to unload the old weapons before taking aboard the first batch of the new pattern. Why waste such an opportunity for a bit of sport?

It was decided that we should try our luck somewhere in the Western Approaches. At the time in question we were not escorting a convoy and were only a few hours from home, so putting some of the old depth charges to recreational use was not going to interfere with the war effort. Once a large enough shoal of fish was detected, we went into action.

Some depth charges were rolled over the stern, and once the sea had settled after the explosions, *Woodpecker* closed in on a mass of senseless fish floating on the surface. At that point the ship's whaler was lowered, and with the help of a spotter was directed to the places where the stunned fish were lying about in the water. Once amongst them, the rowers went to work and gathered in a big harvest in no time. After the catch had been hoisted aboard, some of the more appetising fish were picked up by the cooks who prepared and fried them for the supper. The rest were left on the deck and members of the crew told to help themselves. In the scramble I managed to bag three conger eels after whacking each of them on the head with a length of timber and trussing them up with a length of rope. They were quite large, measuring something between five and six feet in length, and their flesh, though full of sharply pointed bones, was a well appreciated dish in those days – if not so much now.

Being aware that there was a shortage of fresh fish at home, my mind was set on making a few bob once we pulled into port, so I dragged my catch down to the fan room where it would keep fresh as it was just about the coolest place aboard the ship. I then hung them up, still trussed as they were not yet dead, and waited until they were beyond being able to sink their teeth into me, before placing all three into a large sack. Their combined weight was so great that I had later to ask one of my shipmates to help me carry them ashore. Once we had docked my business venture had to suffer something of a delay, when it was announced that all hands going ashore were to line up along the quayside before leaving the dockyard. It had been discovered that a revolver had gone missing from the ship's armoury, and a full search was to be mounted in an attempt to find it. Once the men were assembled, all bags and clothing belonging to them were searched, and when I was asked to open the sack containing my eels, the reaction as they slithered out onto the cobbled surface of the quay gave rise to a few witty comments and not a few laughs. In the end, I do not think the missing weapon was found to be in anyone's possession. I cannot be certain about it, but I think it might have been found sometime later during a search of the ship. So I was finally free to take my catch onto the streets. Once again I had to enlist some help; this time to get my eels out of the dockyard and into a side street near the Caradoc public house in the district of Seaforth.

I removed the two biggest fish from the sack and laid them on the pavement to attract customers. The eels soon caught the attention of the local people, but each time I offered them up for sale I was met with the same response; they were too big. After a while I suggested that a few families might club together, buy the fish, and share out the meat. It was an idea that was soon taken up, and I sold both eels at a price of five shillings each, which was good money when you consider that beer was selling for about four or five pence a pint, twelve old pence making one shilling in those days (*i.e.* five new pence – for the benefit of the modern reader). Business done, I dragged the remaining eel onto the tram car I boarded for the journey home, and laid it down close to the driver. He must have felt a little uncomfortable when I told him what was in the sack, as he insisted that I move it behind the stairway so that it would be less visible to the passengers. I got off the tram near Kiezer's glass works in St. Anne Street and humped my eel along for the final quarter of a mile or so to my mother's house; it must have weighed over half a hundredweight. In earlier years my mother had worked in the fish market, so she knew what to do when I presented her with the fish. She soon had it gutted and divided up into five portions, as there were five families, including my own, sharing the landing on which we lived. Each was given a share of the spoils, and well appreciated it was. I had a couple of steaks myself and thoroughly enjoyed them.

Another way of earning a few bob was to take advantage of the generous tobacco ration available in the Navy. Our individual tobacco allowance amounted to two half-pound tins per month, and for this we had to pay one shilling and eight pence. There was no point in attempting to trade it aboard ship; if anyone belonging to the crew ever exhausted their ration they could simply buy packets of Woodbines, Players or Senior Service, and the price of these items for men serving in the armed forces was much lower than that charged on Civvy Street. In the NAAFI, for example, fourpence ha'penny would buy twenty Woodbines, and sixpence was the cost of twenty Players or Senior Service. Civilians at that time were paying two shillings and sixpence for twenty Players; five times the price paid by naval ratings. We were able to take advantage of this price difference by smuggling a few packs of cigarettes ashore whenever we docked. We were then able to sell them for less than the official retail price and still turn a profit, usually something between a shilling and one shilling and sixpence per packet.

Whenever civilians came aboard ship to carry out repairs or maintenance tasks, their presence always provided a business opportunity for those members of the crew who liked to wheel and deal as though they were big players in the black market. These men could sometimes exert a bit of pressure on the canteen staff to sell them over the ration, and the extra packets purchased they would then supply to the civvies, making a small gain in the process. Most of the profits the ratings made in this manner would eventually find their way to Customs via the local bars and pubs whenever the men made a run ashore. As such, the government was hardly out of pocket from this kind of black marketeering. At least that is how we tended to see it. In selling dutied items to the civilian visitors who came aboard we ran a much lower risk of being caught 'trading in black market goods' than we would when running the gauntlet of the Customs officers manning the dock gate, should we attempt to take such items ashore ourselves. If anyone ever did fall foul of the Excise in this respect they could find themselves in serious trouble. I can recall, after the completion of one trip to sea, going ashore carrying a little white cotton bag in which I had placed half a dozen eggs and four bars of chocolate as a little present for my nieces, Teresa and Marie, as well as four hundred cigarettes. Luckily, it was raining quite heavily as I walked out of Gladstone Dock that night, and the Customs man was taking shelter a few yards from the footpath. As I was passing he called me over and asked what was in the bag. I told him about the eggs and the chocolate, expecting him to take a look, but he only asked if I had any cigarettes, to which I replied, 'No'; at that he waved me on. I was lucky on that occasion; one could expect anything up to ninety days in the lock up for such misdemeanours.

Chapter 9

To a rest camp in Scotland

After the great success of Walker's ships during the patrol that saw *Woodpecker*'s final contribution to the Battle of the Atlantic, the Navy decided that it was time to award some honours to the men of the Second Support Group. It was a well–received gesture in recognition of their dedication to the task of defeating the U–boats.

A number of medals and laurels were subsequently presented to various officers and ratings serving with the group; the medals going to individuals in cases where there was an identifiable contribution made by a particular man; the laurels, on the other hand, were simply small metal clasps, about three quarters of an inch in length, in the form of a branch of laurel leaves. These were awarded for distinguished service of a less attributable kind, and because, in the main, such triumphs as these were the result of a combined effort, it was clear that not everybody serving with the group could receive them, as it would lower the value of such decorations if it appeared that they were being handed out in bulk. It was decided, therefore, that a small number of laurels would be presented to the flotilla as a whole, and that they would afterwards be divided amongst the crew of each of the ships which had contributed to the success. As a result, a share of the awards was duly handed over to the captains of the individual ships, to be presented later to individual sailors via whichever allocation process was decided upon by the men aboard.

> In the case of *Woodpecker*, one of the laurels was presented to the ship's stokers, and it was left to the members of the mess to decide who should receive it. My pal Gleeson, being the youngest amongst us, was given the decoration. The chief artificer aboard *Woodpecker*, the man with whom I had an altercation after the incident concerning the loose fan was, I think, awarded a DSM for the part he played in making the running repairs required after our ship was torpedoed.
>
> As time moved on after the loss of our ship, many of the men from her crew were sent to Plymouth, where they would be allocated

to new ships. On reporting to barracks at Devonport, Les Summers and me were ordered to present ourselves to the medical officer for examination. Seeing that we were keen to get on with things so that we could begin our twenty–one days of survivors' leave, the doctor dealt with us quickly. Once the formalities were over, I was soon aboard a train making the return journey to Liverpool, looking forward to my three-week rest.

After just eight days at home I received a telegram calling me back to Devonport. It meant another long train journey south, and I was not very happy about having had my leave interrupted. Once back at barracks it soon became clear to me that I was being prepared to go to sea as soon as possible, and the first task for the Navy in preparing me for a return to duty was to re–kit me with the items I was unable to salvage from *Woodpecker* before she sank.

Some days later I was detailed to report to the gym, where several tables had been neatly laid out in rows, and placed upon them were separate piles of uniform items. The tables were manned by the Jack Dusties. On three separate occasions, as I passed from table to table describing the things I was short of, I was asked just how much kit I had managed to save from *Woodpecker*, and I could sense that things were soon going to take an unwelcome turn. By the end of the process a list had been made of all the items I was claiming had been lost with the ship. I was re–issued with the clothing, but a week later I was ordered to report back to the outfitters where, to my amazement and disgust, I was told that the value of the replacement items I had been issued with was twenty–four pounds and ten shillings, and that I would have to pay for them by having one pound per week deducted from my pay until the full sum had been collected. When I told them that I had been ordered to leave *Woodpecker* carrying only absolute essentials, my words fell upon deaf ears.

In fact, Alan Burn in *The Fighting Captain*, seemed to back Marsden's claims. When describing the scene at Gladstone Dock as the surviving ships of the Second Support Group sailed into port on their return from the six–in–one trip. He noted that, '… standing amongst the cheering crowd on the quayside, were some of the survivors from *Woodpecker*.' He then went on to remark that they were wearing borrowed uniforms, which tends to support Marsden's claim that he was ordered off the ship wearing the clothes he stood in.[1]

The attitude of the outfitters was that the ship's initial survival, having remained afloat for eight days before she sank, had given me plenty of time to gather up all my items of kit and take them to the rescue ship, which was ridiculous. But to give you an idea of just how much twenty–four pounds and ten shillings meant to me, I can say that, at that time I was being paid just three pounds and ten shillings per fortnight; that is, one pound and fifteen shillings per week. So I was going to be left with just fifteen shillings, that is, less than half my weekly wages, every week for the next six months. I was not a happy man and I was beginning to lose all enthusiasm for further service in the Navy.

After several weeks in Devonport, rumours began to circulate that some of the survivors from *Woodpecker* were going to be transferred to Greenock in Scotland, where they would join the crew of the latest of the Bird–class sloops, HMS *Lark*. It all turned out to be false, and in the end nobody from the barracks was sent north. Hopes of a short stay at Devonport had disappeared, and as a result our spirits began to sag once more, neither were we perked up by promises being made that we would soon be allowed to take the remaining days of our survivors' leave; we just sensed a complete lack of sincerity on the part of the Navy. However, in my case at least, they were true to their word; I was later to receive the rest of my leave entitlement, although it took some time for confirmation to come through. In the meantime chits were issued detailing some of us to report aboard the battleship, HMS *Howe*, which was berthed in Plymouth, but we would not be sailing with her. We were told that we would only be lending a hand with the boiler cleaning, the idea of which did not exactly fill our hearts with joy. I was determined to find a way to avoid the work, the more so after the way in which I had been treated over my lost kit.

Over the previous months my ears had been giving me a lot of trouble while at sea, so I thought this would be a good opportunity to report sick. While at the sick bay being examined by the doctor, he said that he found my face familiar, and I suggested to him that the cause may well have been that he had examined me just a fortnight or so earlier. This triggered his memory, 'Ah! Yes,' he said. 'You are supposed to be on your three weeks survivors' leave.' 'Yes,' I replied, 'it seems the Navy must have a desperate shortage of men if they can't allow people their full entitlement of leave.' At that point he told me that he knew some men who had been in barracks for two years, and that some of them had never been aboard a ship; at least not aboard a ship while it was at sea. I got the impression that he had more than a little sympathy for me, and the feeling was reinforced when he agreed to refer me to Stonehouse Hospital in Plymouth to be seen by a specialist.

At the hospital I had my ears cleaned and examined, and when all was done the specialist told me that I was going to be placed ashore for six months. He took my pay book and stamped it to that effect, and I reported back to the medical officer at Devonport. During the course of the interview, he informed me that I was going to be sent to a naval establishment at Aultbea in the far north of Scotland.[2] This was not something I wanted to hear; it all sounded a bit suspicious. I was beginning to think the Navy had something unpleasant in mind for me, so I asked why it was that I had to go to Scotland. His response was a bit vague, which did nothing to calm my fears. All he could say was that the base where I was to be stationed was regarded within the Navy as being a bit of a rest camp where convalescents, together with men recovering from stress and fatigue, were sent to recuperate. I was then told to take the remainder of my survivors' leave, which amounted to fourteen days, and then report to HMS *Helicon* at Aultbea.

Aultbea, on the banks of Loch Ewe, was one of the places where convoys were assembled before sailing to Russia. It was a bleak and lonely place where the sheep outnumbered the people and roamed around the naval base without fear. After my first few days at *Helicon* I soon learned to treat those animals with respect; the rams were so aggressive that the people working at the base had to arm themselves with pick axe handles whenever they were around. But the biggest problems for the servicemen stationed at Aultbea were the boredom and isolation. In an effort to stave it off, and at the same time to keep us fit, we were encouraged to play as much football as we wanted to. Matches were arranged on a regular basis and I played in goal three or four times, but soon lost my enthusiasm for it. Maybe I should have had a go in the outfield, but I had a tendency to sprain my ankles if ever I ran about on rough ground, and the pitches we played on were just unlevelled fields with hardly any markings.

The living quarters on the base were quite good; they consisted of a collection of about thirty Nissen huts, each with its own coal–

fired boiler to supply hot water and central heating. Being a stoker, I managed to bag myself a nice, steady job as the man in charge of all those boilers. Once settled into the job I struck a gentle, easy rhythm in my work, which meant that I could service all of the fires on the camp in a couple of hours or so. It was just a matter of keeping them banked up with coal and nicely damped down so that they would burn steadily without the need of attention for quite a while. The result was that I was able to lead a bit of a leisured life, and I would occupy my slack time in doing odd jobs for many of the WRNS who were stationed at the camp; there were about two hundred of them. The rest of the people stationed there consisted of a mixture of convalescing sailors, some RN seamen, RN officers and WRNS officers.

The routine at the base was similar to that aboard ship, and the watches were organised in a similar way to those we followed at sea. Officially, the Navy's middle watch runs from midnight to four o'clock in the morning, but because it was so miserable up there in the wilds of the Scottish Highlands, the servicemen agreed to make some alterations to the traditional timetable. Those who went on the watch scheduled to run from 20:00 until 24:00 would remain on duty until 01:30. This gave the reliefs an extra hour and a half of free time before taking over, after which they would have only two and a half of the bleakest hours of the day to serve, rather than four.

One of my first duties when manning the short middle watch was to attend to the boiler in each of the Nissen huts around the camp, rake out the fire and remove all of the clinker before it suffocated the flames. Once that was done, I would bank it up with fresh coke so that it would burn steadily and give plenty of hot water for the bathroom and central heating system in time for reveille.

My best efforts did not always get the appreciation I thought they deserved. When raking out the clinker from the fires it made quite a bit of noise that rattled around the internal pipe work of the huts, and this sometimes disturbed the sleep of the delicate things within. One day this led to me being confronted by an angry WRNS officer. As I set to work in the boiler room of her hut she suddenly appeared at the door, stormed in and began to bawl at me; wanting to know why I could not leave the boilers alone until people had risen from their beds, rather than disturb them at two o'clock in the morning. I explained to her that if the fires were left to burn out it would mean that everybody would be without the luxuries of a warm hut and plenty of hot water for their morning rise. She refused to listen to me, so at that point I said no more; I left the fire as it was and moved on to the next hut.

When morning arrived the inevitable happened. The Wrens in the hut where the fire had by then died down, rose to a cold dormitory and the thought of a cold wash or shower. They were not happy. As a result a complaint was made, and when I went back to the hut later that day a second WRNS officer appeared in the doorway of the boiler room, this time in the company of an RN officer. The complaint was repeated in his presence, and her performance as she made it gave all the appearance of it having been rehearsed with the help of the other WRNS officer, her of the early morning outburst, as she steered clear of explaining the reason for the fire not having been seen to. The officer decided that the complaint was serious enough to be escalated for consideration by a three–ringer, and went to fetch him. When he arrived at the scene he asked me for an explanation, and after telling him what had happened he somehow came to the conclusion that a thorough pipe–clean was required. A local plumbing firm was called out to do the job, and as things slowly settled down over the following days, life returned to normal. Nothing else was ever said about the incident, but the Wrens belonging to that hut never looked kindly upon me from that day on.

After a few weeks at the camp, I came out in a rash of painful boils on the back of my neck. The condition made life a misery, as it became difficult to sleep whenever they were in contact with my pillow. One morning, after finishing the middle watch at about four o'clock, I had my usual wash and change of clothing and was in bed by about five, trying without much success to get to sleep. I must have finally dozed off, but was soon woken up by a petty officer at about 06:00. Why he wanted me out of bed together with those who had not been on watch was a mystery to me, so I ignored him. On his second visit, he warned me that I had better be out of bed on his next return. Again, I ignored him. On his third call he ordered me to report to the door of the jimmy–the–one by nine o'clock, but I was still in no mood to comply. Eventually I rose from my bed, still groggy due to the lack of sleep, and made my way to the bathroom to wash and shave. It was not long before an armed escort arrived, placed me under arrest and marched me to the office of the two–ringer. During the interview that followed, I was accused of having sworn at the PO; something I could not deny. I was quoted at length by the aggrieved party, and I must admit it did not make for pleasant listening. At this the jimmy–the–one got excited, slammed his hand on the top of his desk and said, 'Right! commander's report for you!' So, I was going to have to face the camp commander.

Before making my appearance in front of the senior officer on the base, I visited the camp doctor and explained that the situation I was in was caused by the discomfort of the boils on my neck, as it had made me a bit irritable and short tempered. Apart from an expression of sympathy, he said he could do nothing to save me from the punishment that was coming my way. I resigned myself to it and went before the camp commander, who listened to the evidence against me and found me guilty as charged. I was given fourteen days number eleven punishment, which meant that I had to report for extra fatigues between five and seven in the evening for the next two weeks; I was on jankers, as they say in the Navy.

At that time a cinema–cum–dance hall was being built at the base, and as a way for people to get to the entrance doors without having to walk across the wet grass, a footpath made up of hard core and gravel had been laid which was flanked on each side by a line of boulders. On reporting to a chief petty officer for my first punishment duty and explaining that I was a defaulter, he ordered me to call at the stores and collect a quantity of drisco; a kind of white emulsion paint. When I returned to his office carrying the supplies I had drawn, he ordered me to paint all the boulders lining the footpath to the cinema. There was about a dozen of the stones on each side of the path, they were about three feet tall and two and a half feet in diameter, and each of them could easily have weighed a ton. Off I went and set about my fatigues. By about twenty minutes to seven I had finished painting the boulders. I did not want to hang around, killing time until the clock struck seven, so I reported back to the chief PO; it was a big mistake. I should have whittled away the final twenty minutes of my work and simply finished at the end of my two–hour stint. His response to my early appearance was that I should go back to where the boulders were, turn each one over and paint its underside. This was completely outrageous; it would have taken a squad of strong men to move boulders of that size and weight. At that point, I lost my temper and began to give my tormentor more than he expected in the way of a response. There were quite a lot of people within earshot who must have lapped it up. I became so angry that I just about managed to restrain myself from aiming a blow at him as he froze, stunned by my outburst. In the end, I told him I would rather be placed in the cells than continue with the nonsense I was expected to put up with. He stood there, rooted to the spot as I stormed off to see the master–at–arms to tell him that he might as well bang me up at that moment in time, because I was not going to go on with the number eleven. Luckily, I was in the presence of a sensible man; a big, cool–headed Cockney. He managed to calm me down and told me to return to my mess and forget all about it. Before I left his office he ordered me to report back to him in the morning, assuring me that, in the meantime, he would do his best to sort things out. The following day one of his runners came for me and told me to report to him. Once in his presence he told me that he had managed to calm the situation, and that I had been excused the rest of my number elevens. If only the world was full of men such as him!

I was to suffer the boredom of everyday life on the camp for about another three months before deciding that I could not put up with it anymore. I had to get back to active duty. So I made up my mind to speak to the base doctor and request a consultation with a specialist, as I felt my ear problem had not improved; in fact, I thought it was getting worse and would prevent me from getting the all–clear required from the medics before I could return to sea. I had been sent to Aultbea for a period of rest to allow the condition time to heal, but I now needed an answer as to how long it would be before my ears were better. In other words, I wanted to know how much longer I was to be kept in the Scottish Highlands.

While talking to the doctor he began to ask me about the details of my service before being sent to Aultbea. I gave him a short summary of my experiences, mentioning to him that I had served aboard *Woodpecker* until the time she was sunk. On hearing this he lifted my spirits by telling me he had read somewhere that Captain Walker, in an effort to retain the services of as many of his experienced crewmen as possible, was trying to find the absent members of *Woodpecker*'s crew. As he spoke to me my head began to fill with images of an escape from Scotland via a posting back to the Second Support Group. At the end of the consultation it was agreed that I should see a specialist, and an appointment was made for me in Aberdeen.

The journey from Aultbea to Aberdeen was long and tiring. After setting off one morning at about 08:00, I did not arrive at the hospital until sometime after 20:00. Once I had reported in, I was taken to a ward where I asked the nurse on duty if I could take a bath before going to bed. I was surprised when, after putting my request to the ward sister, she returned and told me it had been refused on the grounds that there were too many sick patients in the vicinity who should not be disturbed. A bit cheesed off, I went to my bed and had a good night's sleep. The next day arrived, and after being seen by the ear specialist I was told that my ears were actually on the mend. I could hardly contain my joy; it was my passport out of Aultbea. I told the doctor the reason for my happiness and explained why I wanted to return to sea. He appeared to be astonished by what I said and found it hard to understand, but agreed to pass me fit if I so wished. I returned to Aultbea hoping that I would soon be wishing everyone on the base a fond farewell. A month later, in September 1944, I was finally released, and after receiving a train pass on my final day at Aultbea, I was given instructions to report back to Devonport.

My return journey to barracks from the rest camp in Scotland was quite straightforward. The first leg was a three–hour coach journey to Achnasheen. From there I caught a train to Aberdeen, where I changed and boarded a train to Glasgow. Once at Glasgow there was a more or less direct line to Plymouth, requiring just two changes; one at Crewe, the other at Bristol.

Once back in barracks, I heard the sad news that HMS *Kite* of my old unit had been sunk while escorting a Russian convoy. This brought to mind the number of times I had tried to get a transfer to *Kite* during my service aboard *Woodpecker*. Two of my pals from home were members of her crew, one, Harry O'Brien, was with me on the day I joined up; the other was a lad named Chris McGrath. It was because they were on *Kite* that I had tried to move from *Woodpecker*; we had been friends right through our schooldays. I heard later that there were only nine survivors from her crew. My two pals were amongst those lost. None of the stokers survived.[3] Soon afterwards, I heard that HMS *Lark* had suffered the same fate as my old ship: hit astern by an acoustic torpedo.[4] She did not sink, and was later towed into port somewhere in Russia.[5] My old friend Gleeson was aboard her at the time, so it was second time around the buoy for him and, thankfully, with a similar outcome to that of the first, in that all or most of the crew survived. It was not until after the war that I saw him again, almost bumping into him in Liverpool town centre one day. He told me that, after she was torpedoed, *Lark* was towed into Murmansk where she lay berthed for about six months. During that time, he said, she was being stripped of any equipment that could be removed, all of which was then transported back to the UK aboard the ships of returning convoys. I think that brief meeting with my old friend may have been the last time I ever saw him.

At Devonport things were much quieter than they had been during the early days. We were given odd jobs to do whenever the need arose, but our greatest enemy once again was boredom. One Saturday night I found I had been detailed, together with some of the others, to prepare to go on divisions on the following day, but I was in no mood to comply. Divisions were considered by the experienced sailor to be a complete waste of time. You were expected to clean and press your kit, polish up your boots and turn out on the parade ground in perfect order. There you would be marched up and down for about half an hour before going off to Church of England service. Catholics were allowed to fall out at that point if they wanted to. None of this appealed to me in the slightest; I found it completely pointless. I just could not bring myself to go through with it, so I simply stayed in barracks when the others went off at about nine o'clock on that Sunday morning.

It did not take long for somebody to notice my absence. From that point on my name and number were regularly announced over the barracks tannoy system, along with an order for me to report to the chief stoker. I decided to ignore the calls; but they continued at regular intervals throughout the morning and afternoon until about four o'clock, with my pals advising me all the time that I should answer them. Eventually, I gave up and went off to find the chief. The reason for my absence, I told him, was that I was completely fed up with simply loafing around in the barracks doing virtually nothing for what had, by that time, been some four or five weeks. He seemed prepared to listen to what I had to say, so I pleaded with him to find a way out for me, assuring him that I was willing to consider anything he might like to offer. Luckily, he was keen to help. He explained to me that that I might yet have to wait some time for a posting to a ship, but that he would try to speed up my request in any way that he could. In the meantime he would do his best to keep me occupied. Then he mentioned that he did, indeed, have an urgent little job that required a willing hand, and that it would take me away from Devonport for a few days at least if I was prepared to do it. It was a prisoner escort duty, he said. Four men who had recently gone AWOL had been arrested by the Naval Police and were being held as prisoners in Coatdyke RNDQ, a kind of naval prison near Glasgow. He was looking for someone he thought he could trust to travel to Scotland, collect the prisoners from the detention quarters and escort them back to Devonport. I assured him that I was a man to be relied upon and agreed to take on the job. The escort was to consist of myself, another stoker from Liverpool and four seamen, one of whom was a killick.

All six of us duly reported for duty, and after picking up the warrants we travelled to Glasgow by train. We were allowed to draw our wages before we left, and in addition we were given some vouchers which we were told could be exchanged for food and drinks. The journey north was straightforward, and once in Glasgow we made our way to the prison.

When we arrived at the gaol, the usual checks had to be made before the deserters were handed over to us, ready for transportation to Devonport. We returned to the station, took our prisoners aboard the train and settled down to a comfortable journey south to Plymouth. All this time the four men had been handcuffed together in pairs. Feeling a bit sorry for them, we kept them well supplied with food, drink and cigarettes once the train had pulled out from Glasgow. Some common feelings were soon found between the prisoners and the escort as the journey wore on; one pair struck up with me and my fellow stoker, the other two, finding they had more in common with the four seamen of the escort party, made most of their conversation in that direction.

When the train arrived at Crewe, which was a busy junction on the railway, an announcement was made that we would be delayed for an hour and a half. The idea of a ninety–minute delay was better received amongst us than it was by the rest of the passengers, as it gave us the opportunity to leave the train and have a drink at one of the station bars. There was some discussion on the matter, and the killick made the suggestion that he, together with the other seamen, should leave their prisoners with me and my fellow stoker, and while we kept guard on all four deserters, they would slip off for a drink, promising to return in good time to relieve us and allow us the turn to enjoy a pint. This seemed like a good idea, so we agreed to it and the seamen got off the train. It was quite a while before we saw any sign of them again, and we began to think we had been set up, but eventually one of them returned. The prisoners were left with him while I, together with my fellow stoker, hopped off the train and went into a bar at the end of the platform. As we did so we caught sight of the killick and the two other seamen getting back on the train. We were then comfortable in the knowledge that there would be a sufficient escort with the prisoners while we were having a drink.

After a few pints of beer and a bite to eat, we became aware of a sudden commotion coming from the platform. We dashed out to see what was happening and were met with the sound of carriage doors being slammed shut, followed the sound of the stationmaster's whistle. There was a train pulling away from the station so we made a dash for it, managing to jump aboard at the last moment and immediately going in search of our party. We walked the full length of the train, and by the time we arrived at the final carriage it was clear that they were not aboard. We then asked the guard the destination and were amazed when he replied, 'London'. In our panic not to be left behind we had jumped aboard the wrong train. There was now no choice other than to ride out the journey, as the guard told us that London would be the first place where we could catch a direct connection to Plymouth. We then noticed we were without our hats; we had left them aboard the other train. Realising we would be in trouble if we were spotted without them in London, we came up with the idea of calling at the lost property office once we were off the train. There, we thought, we must surely be able to lay hands on a pair of hats. We were in luck; we eventually paid sixpence each for two hats and felt a lot better. We now had to think about how to get from London to Devonport, and we came up with the idea of reporting to a Navy office and telling the duty officer our story. After asking for directions, we soon found what we were looking for and made our way inside. The people there obliged us with a couple of train passes and sent us on our way, but not before they had warned us of what we might expect once we reported back to barracks. With their words ringing in our ears, we made our way to Paddington station and caught a train to Plymouth, ready to take whatever was coming to us. By this time my fellow stoker was beginning to worry about the plight we were in and what might happen to us as a result. In an effort to ease his fears, I suggested we should make up a story that might save us from the worst of the punishment we could get. My friend was not convinced, saying that, under questioning, even the best of stories might break down, which would make matters even worse. I agreed with him, and said that I would do all the talking when the questioning began, and just see if I could talk the both of us out of trouble. If my story was thrown out then at least he would not be in trouble for trying to cover up.

When we got to barracks we reported to the quarterdeck, which was next to the big entrance gates at the base. The Master at Arms was present, together with a two–ringer who became very interested, or puzzled, as it turned out, while he listened in to my tale of how we had come to be there, at the entrance to the base, about twenty–four hours after the prisoners we were supposed to be escorting had already reported in. After listening for a while to what I was saying he stepped across the room towards us and began to question me. In those days I had a very thick Scouse accent, and after I had rattled off my story, he looked at me and, in all seriousness asked, 'Are you a foreigner?' I said 'No,' and told him that I was from Liverpool, after which he asked me some more questions, but it was clear that he still could not grasp what I was saying. He turned to a seaman that was standing close by and asked him, 'What did he say?' 'I don't know, sir,' replied the seaman, 'I can't understand him.' At this the officer walked out of the room, but he came back a short while later to continue with the questioning. He could still make nothing of what I said, so he told me to leave and return a few hours later. When I reported back he made a final attempt to interview me, asking me all the time to speak slowly so as to give him a chance to make out what I was saying. It all became too much for him and eventually he gave up, saying that he would give me the benefit of any doubt over my responsibility for our late return, but he ordered each of us to pay seventeen shillings and four pence for the train pass we were given to make the London to Plymouth journey. I felt we had been very lucky to have escaped so lightly, and as the two of us talked about our little adventure, I soon discovered why my fellow stoker had become so worried about our situation. He told me that he had not long ago completed a ninety day stretch in a naval prison – for reporting back late from leave! It was now late summer, 1944.

Chapter 10

I join the crew of HMS *Empress*

The time dragged by at Devonport barracks, with the boredom and shore–based routine seeming to slow down the hands of the clock, but a few weeks after my return from Glasgow I was finally handed a chit assigning me to the aircraft carrier, HMS *Empress*, which was then anchored in the Clyde. It meant I had yet another train journey to Scotland to put up with, but it was a small price to pay for the chance of a better existence than that on offer at *Drake*. Before I left the base I was told that all the men originally selected to crew *Empress* had been flown to the USA some time earlier in the year, and had spent about ten weeks on the other side of the Atlantic during the commissioning of the ship. I felt disappointed at having missed the opportunity to be with them.

I arrived in Greenock eager to catch the first sight of my new ship. At the railway station I asked where I could find the jetty I had been told to report to, the name of which was written in my instructions. One of the luggage porters who lived in the area gave me some directions and I went on my way, hoping to meet someone associated with the Navy who would be able to tell me exactly where the ship was, and how I was going to get aboard.

By the summer of 1944 the Navy had converted a number of coastal trawlers to take on the role of liberty boat; a kind of water taxi used for ferrying RN crew between the shore and ships at anchor in deeper water, it was one of these which served the warships in the Clyde. Standing on the little jetty, I had to wait until it was dark before my taxi finally arrived, and as it pulled away towards the warships in the estuary, I told the skipper that I had instructions to report aboard HMS *Empress*. He acknowledged my words with nothing more than a nod of his head as he steered his boat away from the jetty. I took it that he knew his way about, so I said nothing more and simply made myself as comfortable as I could, thinking about what my new posting would be like as we chugged along. As we got further from shore it became gloomy, and soon we were in pitch darkness. The silhouette of a large ship soon appeared out of the darkness, so we pulled alongside and, thinking this was *Empress*, I climbed up the gangway to be met at the top by a sailor who spoke with a strong Scottish accent which I found almost impossible to understand. Now, for the first time, I could appreciate just what this kind of experience must have felt like for the two–ringer at Devonport when he was trying to understand my own accent.

After several attempts to catch what the Scotsman was saying, I began to make out that I had mistakenly come aboard a destroyer whose name I cannot recall. The liberty boat was still waiting at the bottom of the gangway with its pilot sensing there was a problem, so back down I went and clambered aboard once more. After some minutes searching amongst the ships at anchor, we made out the unmistakable outline of an aircraft carrier and pulled alongside. After another steep climb to the deck, I was told this time that I had just boarded HMS *Emperor*, the sister ship of HMS *Empress*! The pilot of the liberty boat, no doubt thinking that there could have been no mistake this time, had pulled away and was heading for the shore. He was hailed to return and I jumped aboard his boat for a third time. Finally, after a further search of the estuary, we came across HMS *Empress*, and at last I was able to get aboard my new ship. It was getting close to midnight.

Once the usual introductions and formalities were over with, I was assigned to the flight deck crew. This came as a surprise to me as I was a stoker, and had been expecting to be working in the boiler room. Instead, I was going to be doing the entirely new job of maintaining the carrier's catapult and arrestor gear; in effect, I would be an acting fitter.

Empress was one of the new escort carriers built in the US, they gave us quite a few of them towards the end of the war. Their reliability was not very good, and as a result they soon became known as 'Woolworth' carriers. She was a single–screw vessel intended to be converted to the role of merchantman once the war was over. It was for this reason, I believe, that all the stokers aboard her were Merchant Navy personnel.[1] They wore Royal Navy uniforms but were paid about ten pounds a month more than an RN stoker; danger money, as they liked to call it! It was difficult, if not impossible, to get those men to talk about their better rates of pay. But at least I now had the explanation as to why I could not take up my usual role of stoker. When I think about it, the whole scheme was nothing other than a disaster for the morale amongst the RN ratings serving alongside them.

The so called 'Woolworth' carriers were built in US shipyards to a basic merchant freighter design, but were fitted with a flat deck instead of the usual superstructure. They were to take on the role of escort carriers for the remainder of the war, and were smaller and lighter than the Royal Navy's fleet carriers. Some forty of them were built under a rapid construction programme. They were of a welded–plate rather than riveted–plate construction, which made them less sturdy than the genuine article, and they were also prone to mechanical failures. The intention was that they were to be converted to take up a mercantile role after the war.

During their time in America, the crew of *Empress* had been involved mostly with the commissioning of the ship and running a lot of sea and harbour trials as they learned how to maintain and handle her. There had been some testing of the catapult and arrestor gear while she was in the US, but I was told that it amounted to only a small number of deck landing and take–off trials. This meant that there was a lot of work to be done to bring the ship and its flight deck crew up to scratch, and over the coming weeks we took part in a lot of joint exercises with the Fleet Air Arm as a part of a general working up.

From Greenock we made several trips into the Irish Sea, usually to the area around the Isle of Man where we worked through the training schedule, staying at sea for about two weeks at a time. During that time there were no aircraft stationed aboard the carrier, those that we trained with were based ashore and would fly out over the Irish Sea to work with *Empress*. About twenty of these aircraft, which included Swordfish, Avengers and Seafires, were assigned to work with us.[2] The pilots, like the ship's crew, were worked hard as they went through a heavy training programme. The FAA demanded a lot from them, and before they were considered to be qualified for carrier–based flying, they had to make four perfect daylight landings on the flight deck. Once that milestone had been passed, they were expected to make four perfect landings at night.

We soon learned that when an aircraft is coming in to land on the deck of an aircraft carrier, the people best placed to judge whether or not it is going to touch down safely are those belonging to the flight deck crew. These men can watch the aircraft's approach relative to their own position on the flight deck and estimate the chances of a successful landing. However, it was not just the Fleet Air Arm pilots who were learning their trade during those early exercises, many of the men on the flight deck were also novices at the job of being able to tell correctly whether or not to signal a pilot to abort his landing, it was something gained only from experience. All of this meant that a lot of nerve–wracking work was done aboard *Empress* in an effort to improve the team work between the pilots and flight deck crew.

As I say, the FAA pilots were very reliant on the flight deck crew to bring them down safely, and as the batmen guided the pilots coming in to land, they would signal them to 'go around again' by firing flares into the sky if they judged their approach to be wrong. The amount of time they had to make their decisions was sometimes very small. To me, seeing all of this for the first time, a pilot's life under these circumstances was a very risky game. To give an example of the dangers they faced, I can remember one attempted night landing being aborted at the last moment, only for the pilot to lose control and crash into the sea. He managed to climb out of the cockpit before his machine sank, but he then had to wait quite a while to be rescued by the Isle of Man lifeboat. Apparently unshaken by his experience he returned to flying duties on the following day.[3]

For me, life aboard the carrier was different in many ways from that aboard a sloop; not least because I was not now in the role of stoker; but I have always enjoyed the challenges of moving into a new job, and having been given the chance to work with the Fleet Air Arm I was finding it to be varied and interesting. I suppose the main reason for my happiness was my escape from the dreariness of an existence at HMS *Drake*. To my mind there was no comparison between barracks life and life aboard ship. I should also add that one of the main reasons for joining the Navy, rather than the Army, was that I knew that I could be sure of having three cooked meals a day. The idea of living on tinned rations never did appeal to me, and I was not keen on the idea of sleeping and living rough during the kind of campaigning the land war would demand. During the many years which have passed since the end of the war, I have often thought about this, and I can now say that, the more I think about my decision to go to sea, the more I consider it to have been the best thing I could have done.

In the Navy there was never any shortage of food, the quality, quantity and variety of which, in my opinion at least, left nothing to be desired. The only regular item on the menu that made me a little queasy was rabbit, which was served every Saturday aboard *Empress*; but as there was no alternative, I was faced with the choice of eating it or going hungry, and on every occasion my hunger got the better of my queasiness. Breakfast usually consisted of one rasher of streaky bacon or a couple of boiled eggs, some cereal or porridge and a cup of tea. Lunch was more varied and the portions larger. Tea tended to be a light meal. Such a routine was a new and appreciated luxury for many a young sailor at that time, especially when compared with the unpredictability of the home life shared by many working–class families.

Just before Christmas, on 16 December 1944, HMS *Empress* sailed from Scotland to begin her journey to the Far East, where the war against Germany's ally, Japan, was nearing a critical stage.[4] She was to be part of a large carrier force being assembled at Colombo and Trincomalee in what was then Ceylon. Her full operational complement, including pilots, aircraft fitters and flight deck crew, would be some eight hundred men.[5]

Shortly after leaving the Clyde we ran into some very stormy weather as we sailed through the Irish Sea. Several members of the crew became very sea sick during that part of the voyage; something I did not expect to see. When we arrived off Plymouth about three days later, we lay at anchor for a few days until the weather improved. Once the storm had passed the ship entered Plymouth harbour and went into dry dock for some ten days, the reason for which I never found out. However, a few days after coming out of dock we were sailing to meet the ships we were going to join for the first part of the journey to the Far East.[6]

On New Year's Day 1945, *Empress* left Devonport and headed north into the Irish Sea. After berthing at Belfast for about twenty–four hours, she then left port to pick up a convoy that was bound for the Mediterranean.[7] Once with the merchantmen she sailed south again accompanying them on their way, however she was not acting as an escort carrier whilst with the convoy. None of the aircraft held aboard her were operational, they were without aircrew and simply stored in the hangars below deck. In essence, *Empress* was acting as an aircraft ferry during her voyage to India, and was under the protection of the convoy escorts rather than providing them with air cover.

Before continuing, the reader should be aware that the carrier–borne Far East campaign of 1945 was apparently conducted under a regime which sought to inform all members of the task forces involved exactly what it was that they were attempting to achieve during each mission they took part in. It would seem that this enlightened approach, adopted by the Royal Navy in particular, was a vast improvement when compared with the more *de haut en bas* attitude which prevailed during the early years of the war, when ratings were expected to simply get on with their duties in ignorance of the strategic and tactical contexts of their mission. Bearing this in mind, the reader should allow for the certain level of awareness which Marsden was able to display when talking of the wider picture relating to the naval operations in which he was involved.

At Gibraltar, we stopped to take on fuel and other stores while the rest of the convoy continued on its way.[8] *Empress* followed on alone, sailing through the straits of Gibraltar and eventually arriving at Malta, where we anchored offshore for a good few hours. After the short halt we were on the move again, sailing past the port of Alexandria on the way to Suez, where we entered the canal and headed south towards the Red Sea. Once through we sailed for Aden, where we arrived in late January 1945.[9] It was another short stop, during which we simply got on with the work of taking onboard some fresh food and water. While at the quayside some war supplies were put ashore for the Army garrison there, and once that was done we continued on our way. By this time the invasions of France and Italy seemed to be going well. It was easy to notice that we had been without an escort for the whole of the voyage from Gibraltar, and that we had sailed the length of the Mediterranean without any sign of the enemy. The only thing I could make of it that was that, by then, the Navy must have been very confident about the situation in the Mediterranean.

A lone carrier plodding her way to Suez would have been an easy target for the U–boats.

Our next stop was at Bombay where we docked for several hours but I did not manage to get ashore, something I was keen to do simply to see how people lived in that part of the world. I was, after all, a working–class lad with little chance of ever seeing this part of the world again once the war was over. I was so ignorant of it all that I had not even given much thought as to what to expect once we arrived at Ceylon. For the moment I was enjoying the sights and experiences of the East, and even at this point in our journey we, the ordinary ratings, were still unsure about what we would be doing in Ceylon.

By this time the heat was beginning to have an effect on the crew; everybody aboard was suffering. During the cooler part of the day, if we were not on duty, we would keep ourselves fit by exercising and jogging around the carrier deck.

The work of the flight deck crew throughout the voyage consisted mainly of maintaining the ship's arrestor wire and catapult gear, as well as the inspection and testing of other pieces of equipment. No aircraft were flying from *Empress* at the time, but we had to maintain the ship at an operational level. The FAA squadrons we were going to pick up were already based in Trincomalee.[10]

The ship's catapult, or accelerator as they sometimes called it, was a hydraulic device for launching aircraft from the carrier, and as well as routine maintenance, we were also expected to run regular tests on the system. The tests we carried out were obviously not the same thing as real aircraft launches. All we could do was to tense the catapult up to half pressure and release it, after which it would be drawn in, tensed up and fired again and again, before being inspected. The hydraulic pressure required to launch an aircraft was 3,000 psi, which meant that our test firings were carried out at only 1,500 psi, which meant we would be leaving a lot to faith when it came to the real thing. After leaving Bombay we sailed for about two days towards Cochin. We were still without escorts and did not see any before arriving at our final destination.[11]

At this time in the war there was a lot of interest in football amongst the Indian population, and almost every ship docking at Cochin would be asked to put up a team against one raised by the local people. Not long after *Empress* had berthed we were challenged by the people of the port to a match, and we were more than happy to take it up. A team was picked to take on a side of bare–footed players from Cochin, quite a novelty to us and one we were keen to see, especially as the pitch was very stony and completely bare of grass. On the day of the match some stands were created by parking as many vehicles as possible around the touchlines, and there was quite a lot of push and shove on vehicle bonnets, trailers and roofs as everyone tried to get a good view of the game that was about to kick–off. I reckon that there were between ten or fifteen thousand Indians looking on.

As well as being without any kind of boots, the Indians had no kit. The Navy did what it could and came up with a set of shirts and shorts for them. I wish I could tell you the final score, but I could not, with any certainty, say which of the two teams came out on top, let alone remember the result. Our stay in Cochin was short but enjoyable; about two and a half days or so, and it was there that the Hellcats we had ferried from the UK were taken from the ship's hangars and hoisted ashore.[12] We also unloaded some supplies for the army before sailing.

Our next port of call was Colombo in Ceylon, and we were docked there for quite some time, it was one of the bases used by the East Indies Fleet.[13] We were now finally about to team up with the FAA squadrons we would be working with, the first of them being an Avenger squadron that was based at an airfield in Colombo.[14] Once the ship was ready the aircraft flew out to join us, giving the flight deck crew the first chance since leaving the UK to test the arrestor gear as they landed on deck.

With the aircraft aboard we sailed for Trincomalee. It was now early February 1945, and whenever we left harbour we were now never without a destroyer escort.[15] However, during the patrols we made towards the Andaman Sea we would always be accompanied by supporting cruisers and other warships, including minesweepers.

The photo–reconnaissance missions, which were a regular part of the flying operations launched from *Empress*, were usually carried out by small flights of four aircraft.[16] I suppose the reason they kept in small groups was that they could give each other support while on patrol, these flights usually lasted for about two hours. If longer patrols were sent out we would fit each aircraft with an auxiliary fuel tank slung beneath the fuselage. These had a capacity of two hundred and fifty gallons and were filled with high octane aviation fuel, which meant that the aircraft were never allowed to land on the carrier with the tank still attached; they had to be jettisoned into the sea before making their landing approach. It must be said that the most frustrating thing about our sea patrols were the mechanical failures that affected the carriers; they were very unreliable. As a result, there was always a heavy maintenance programme to be tackled whenever we returned to port. This meant that, after two weeks at sea, the ship would sometimes spend several weeks in dock while efforts were made to get her sea worthy in time for the next patrol. As a point of interest, I can say that, when fully operational, *Empress* could manage, at best, about eighteen knots into a head wind while she was launching her aircraft.

Operation Stacey 22 February – 6 March 1945

The first active operation I experienced while with *Empress* began in late February1945.[17] One of the aims of the mission was to gather photo reconnaissance information which would help us to find out where the Japanese bases were in Sumatra.[18] The aircraft used on these missions were Hellcats, four of them were based aboard *Empress* during the patrol.

After being at sea for about four days, one of the Avenger squadrons aboard HMS *Ameer*, another carrier on the patrol, was giving air cover to the task force. One time, as her aircraft circled the ships, they were mistakenly identified as enemy fighters and fired at by some of them.[19] Luckily, the mistake was corrected before any of them were hit. It all resulted in an investigation to find the cause of the mistake, and I think the committee came to the decision that the pilots were to blame. It was claimed that, at one point, they had flown towards the task force with the sun directly behind them, making it difficult to identify what they were, which was why the ships' gunners opened fire. But it ought to be said that the whole task force was in a high state of alert at that time. Reports had been received warning that there were Japanese aircraft operating in the area and that we should be prepared for *kamikaze* attacks, something that the crew of *Empress* had not yet seen. No doubt all of this contributed to the nervous tension amongst the ships' crews; or, to put it another way, everyone was just a bit trigger happy, they treated every approaching aircraft as a *kamikaze* until told otherwise. In the end, the Japanese air force did not make an appearance that day.

It was during this patrol that *Empress* launched her aircraft in anger for the first time. According to what was said, the photo reconnaissance missions seemed to have been a success, and as we got closer to the islands of Malaysia the Hellcats were launched to give air cover for the ships. After the return of one of these flights we were told that our fighters had taken on Japanese aircraft and shot some of them down.[20] These actions took place far out of sight from the ship, so I can only state what I heard from the reports that were circulated amongst the crew after the fighters had returned.

It was not long before mechanical problems began to affect the ship's catapult system. Investigations were made by the engineers while we were at sea to find the cause of them, but the only information I got was that the accelerator could not be fully repaired until we were in port. In the meantime, the number of launches we made from the carrier was reduced to a minimum. Once the fleet had completed its mission people began to hail it as a success. Personally, I had no way of knowing what was actually achieved; but I knew we had not lost a ship, and that *Empress* had not lost any of her aircraft, and for me that was good enough.

Operation Stacey was a purely photographic reconnaissance mission of Penang and the Kra Isthmus between latitudes 7°N and 10°N, and of Northern Sumatra.

We returned to our base in Ceylon, and by early March *Empress* was in Tricomalee harbour undergoing the usual inspection and maintenance works needed to keep her seaworthy. A special plan designed to fix the problems we were having with the ship's catapult system was worked out, and after two days in port we sailed to Colombo where the repair facilities were better. Once in dock, we set to work on the plan and found out that the fault had been caused by the fact that each time the catapult was fired, the cable by which it pulled an aircraft along the flight deck had to run through a guide in the form of a metal sheave. On inspection the guide was found to have fractured in operation, causing excessive wear to the outer wires of the cable.

For some strange reason the ship did not carry any spare sheaves at that time, and there were no replacements available from the stores at the dockyard. There were only three solutions to the problem: wait for the arrival of a new part from the US, repair the broken one, or try to manufacture a replacement at the nearest engineering works; of these it was decided that the latter was the best solution. The whole situation was typical of the kind of maintenance problems we had to put up with in relation to our 'Woolworth' carriers. The aircraft launch–slings were also a cause of trouble. These were made up of a length of cable with a metal hoop at each end. The hoops were placed on special hooks which were part of the undercarriage of the aircraft; the centre of the sling was then connected to another hook attached to the end of the accelerator cable. When the catapult was fired it would literally drag the aircraft along the deck using the sling that connected the two, and as it left the ship the sling would simply fall away into the sea. Before a sling was selected for use it was our responsibility to inspect it for any flaws. If two or more of the plaited wires it was made of were broken, which was a common problem, it could not be used; it went over the side.

Since first arriving at Colombo at the end of January 1945, *Empress's* mechanical problems meant that she had been able to carry out just one war patrol. It was now late March; about three weeks since the catapult failure occurred, and we were still waiting for a replacement sheave. Eventually the new part arrived, and we set to work to make the accelerator system operational.[21] Once the sheave was in place it was decided that we should carry out some test launchings in open water, which meant the carrier would have to leave Colombo harbour.

Rather than use a serviceable aircraft to carry out the tests, which would mean risking the loss of both it and its pilot if things went wrong, the engineer officer in charge came up with the idea of using a Barracuda airframe instead; that is, a raw aircraft body from which the engine, guns and other equipment had been removed.[22] Once it was hoisted aboard the flight deck the crew began to make the Barracuda shell up to a weight equal to that of a fully fitted out aircraft, which was about six tons. To do so we had to fill the cockpit with bags of cement that had gone hard and some bags of sand. Once it was ready, the airframe was attached to the catapult and everything was prepared for a launch. That done, the catapult's hydraulic pressure had to be brought up to operational launch level, and while that was going on a lot of people, most of them senior officers who had come aboard to observe, were gathered nearby waiting to see if the accelerator could be passed as being serviceable. There was a short delay as the oil pressure was ramped up, but finally the order to launch was given and ... BANG!

When the catapult was triggered, it tore the undercarriage clean away from the fuselage of the Barracuda. As the wheels shot through the air the rest of the aircraft belly flopped onto the deck.[23] There were some stony faces amongst the top brass as orders were barked out to check the effect that the failed launch had had on the catapult system; all of which looked still to be in good working order. We had to think quickly about finding something else to use in the next test. The Barracuda airframe was then cleared from the accelerator track and pushed over the side, before the ship's piano was brought up for the following attempt. This was launched with complete success, the whole thing flying a good distance through the air before crashing into the sea giving everyone who witnessed it a good laugh. I suppose it was a good way of defusing a lot of pent–up tension amongst the observers.

We now felt that we were ready to get our Avengers airborne, and all went to plan with the first three launches. The aircraft, once up, circled the carrier before returning to land on deck, giving us the opportunity to test the arrestor gear. I do not recall there being any further problems during the trial, and when it ended *Empress* sailed for Trincomalee.

Once in harbour it was decided that further work on the accelerator was still required, and it was another three weeks or so before the engineer officers decided that all was well. The resulting trials were conducted using Avenger airframes to begin with, and once we felt sure that our problems were now behind us, we completed the trials with some of our operational Avengers, successfully launching and landing several aircraft. It was late March 1945.

Operation Bishop 27 April – 9 May 1945

By the end of April 1945 *Empress* was ready to sail, which meant we could set out on our second patrol with the East Indies Fleet.[24] The photo reconnaissance aircraft were aboard, along with some fighters, but the Avengers were not with us; they were all Hellcats. This time the second carrier was HMS *Shah*, and we were heading for Car Nicobar in the Andaman Sea to carry out air strikes. While the Hellcats were at work the heavy cruisers, together with a number of destroyers, went in towards Nicobar to bombard some of the shore targets, *Empress* and *Shah* stayed miles out at sea. Floating mines were a big danger, and we had to a keep a watch for any that might come near. Whenever one was spotted the ship would steer clear, and if the currents caused any of them to drift towards her, the marksmen would try to set them off with rifle fire.[25]

After about two days the task force sailed away from the islands before returning to make a second attack some days later, and when we re–joined the cruiser force we were told that a Dutch cruiser which was with it had been hit by artillery fire from the shore.[26] Two Dutch ratings were killed and were afterwards buried at sea. About four or five days later we returned to action, and the aircraft aboard *Empress* were sent to carry out more missions over Car Nicobar. As the Hellcats returned from one of these, we were to suffer the loss of one of our pilots when he crashed into the sea while trying to land. The plane sank out of sight, taking the pilot with it before a rescue could be mounted.[27] I never found out the true cause of the crash, but it was said that this plane was one of many hit by AA fire while over the islands.

Once the action was broken off the task force headed for home, but not without a few scares. We were called to action stations on at least two occasions when air attacks were expected, but they never materialised. It was now early May 1945, and before we arrived back in Trincomalee we received news that Germany had surrendered. The end of the war was now drawing close, and from that point on everyone was hoping to stay safe until the Japanese decided to throw the towel in.

Operation Bishop was designed as a move to make use of some of the battleships in the Far East. These were to proceed to Car Nicobar and Port Blair to provide cover for the amphibious landings at Rangoon in Burma. The main task of the fleet was to provide a sustained off-shore bombardment of Japanese airfields. The carriers *Empress* and *Shah* were to provide air cover for the battleships and cruisers, and to launch strafing attacks upon shipping resources in and around Port Blair.

Once at Trincomalee it was said that the ship's catapult had again been noisy during operation, and after making an inspection the engineer officer in charge decided that a complete change of the oil in the catapult's hydraulics system was required. Two days later we set sail for Colombo where we were to carry out the repair plan designed to fix the problem. It took a few days to complete the work before we could come out of dry dock and put to sea to carry out trials, but it was to turn out to be a very short trip. We were only a few hours out of Colombo, on our return to Trincomalee, when we suffered an engine failure due to a fault in the ship's fuel supply system.[28] As a result we were forced to return to port under tow, where we were to remain for about two months until all our problems were cured. It was mid–May 1945 and we did not put to sea again until mid–July. In the meantime we continued with harbour trials, trying to sort out the catapult system.

Apart from dealing with the accelerator problems, the next two months passed without incident. Meanwhile, the carrier force in the East Indies continued to be built up, and in early June it was decided to make the escort carrier, HMS *Begum*, operational. For some months she had been used only as an aircraft ferry, making a number of return trips between the UK and the Far East. As a result, her accelerator and arrestor gear were unserviceable through lack of use. Once this equipment was re–conditioned she would become a reserve carrier. She was another one of the converted merchantmen built in the US.

It fell to us, the acting fitters aboard *Empress*, to sort out *Begum*'s problems, and it was to be a long, hard, filthy job. The reason we had to do it was that there were no fitters amongst *Begum*'s crew who were properly trained for the work now required.[29] All twenty–five of the accelerator/arrestor gear fitters from *Empress* were transferred to *Begum*.

After three fifteen–hour shifts we finally had her gear in working order. The ship was then almost ready to take part in operations, but before she could be allowed to sail with the task forces, we had to make sure that the work just finished had been effective.[30] She was assigned a squadron of aircraft to carry out trials and we, the fitters from *Empress*, had to remain aboard as she left the harbour to begin exercises in open waters. Some hours after leaving port a flight of Avengers came into sight and took up a position about a mile from the ship before being signalled to land. The first aircraft that came in made a perfect landing, but as the second made its approach things began to go wrong. The usual drill, and the first rule of self–preservation for the flight deck crew as an aircraft made its approach, was always to keep an eye upon it. If the angle, speed or height of its approach were not judged to be correct, a warning flare was fired as a signal to the pilot to accelerate and climb away from the ship. As he brought his aircraft in, the second pilot was signalled to abort and duly accelerated away. He then came in for his second attempt, but he did not succeed in touching down. He failed to catch any of the arrestor wires as his aircraft passed the whole length of the ship, just a few feet above the deck, before clipping one of the barriers at the end of the flight deck and tipping, nose down, into a gun turret just beneath it. Unfortunately, two of *Begum*'s seamen were standing in the turret at the time. They were using it as an observation point to watch the practice landings. It was said that after so many months of being with *Begum* and seeing her used only as an aircraft ferry, they had decided to take a close look at how life would have been if she had been fully operational.

As the nose of the Avenger dipped into the spot where they were standing they were caught by its propeller blades and killed.[31] The plane then somersaulted into the sea and began to sink with the pilot still inside the cockpit. All hands rushed to the edge of the flight deck and began shouting, encouraging him to free himself from his harness and escape, but as his machine slipped out of sight beneath the waves the commotion on the deck began to die down. Everybody thought the pilot was lost. I had just turned my back, certain that he had gone to his death, when a loud cheer went up as he bobbed to the surface. He was a Canadian, and as he waited to be rescued from the sea he was given some entertainment by the crew of our destroyer escort.[32] As its crew tried to launch one of their two whalers, which by then contained the ship's doctor and four rowers, something went wrong. Maybe one of the pulleys had locked or snagged as the boat was being lowered, but the result was that the whaler flipped over, tipping the doctor and crew into the sea where they bobbed about in their Mae West. A second whaler then had to be launched to go to the aid of the rescue team. Once they had all been pulled from the water the boat moved across to the pilot and picked him up. All returned safely to the destroyer. The Canadian was completely uninjured and apparently unshaken by his experience, but I do not know if by that time he had been made aware of the fate of the two seamen. He wasted no time in getting airborne again

Begum's carpenters were detailed to build two coffins for the victims of the accident. Once the bodies had been placed inside, they were transferred to the destroyer. I was included in the party that carried out the ship–to–ship transfer using one of the whalers belonging to the escort, and by the time the caskets were hauled up and laid on deck, the victims' blood had begun to ooze from their seams and congeal on the hot metal surface.

In contrast to the story just told, life in the Far East was not always without its fun. For example, I can remember one piece of slapstick comedy that happened aboard *Empress*, and it took place in front of just about the whole of the ship's company. It happened during the ship's boxing tournament which took place in April 1945. As an extra bout the ship's padre had insisted on fighting one of the more wayward members of the crew. The man concerned was at that time serving a sentence in the ship's lock–up after having been found guilty of an assault on another member of the crew. He was a known bruiser. The organising committee attempted to talk the padre out his mission, but he would hear none of it. In order to give him a chance, the committee decided to clamp a ball and chain to his opponent's ankle just before he got into the ring.

When the opening bell sounded, someone in the crowd hurled a huge cabbage at the prisoner which struck him full on the chest, rebounded from his body and landed on the canvass. Unflustered, he picked it up and moved as fast as he could across the ring, dragging his ball and chain behind him as he approached the padre. When he got within arm's reach he smashed the churchman over the head with the giant cabbage before he could swing a punch, knocking him out cold. I need not describe the reaction of the spectators.

It was now late June or early July 1945, and the ship's crew was being encouraged to bathe in Trincomalee harbour whenever she was in port. There was a special pipe, 'hands to bathe,' which was the signal for all of those who wanted to take part to report on deck. A ladder was rigged up to take them from the deck down to the water, but some of the ratings had no fear of jumping from the flight deck into the sea; a drop of about forty feet. A shark net was sometimes put out, if not, a small motor boat was launched to patrol the swimming area and make sure that nobody got into difficulties or strayed too far from the ship. I do not think, by the way, that the risk of shark attack was all that great.

Despite the precautions the swimming always carried a risk of accident. I remember being in the water one day when I noticed that one of the bathers was wearing a life jacket. As I got close to him his Mae West suddenly began to deflate, and in his panic he grabbed hold of me, pulling me under the surface. After swallowing a lot of sea water in the struggle I managed to free myself from his grip. Luckily, a pal from home, 'Ginger' Breen, was watching from an alcove on the ship's side just beneath the flight deck. Realising the danger I was in he dived from the platform and came to my aid, keeping me afloat until I got my breath back, before helping me out of the water. Another sailor went to the aid of the man I had been struggling with and pulled him to safety. I was unhappy about what had happened, and I could not understand why a non–swimmer had been allowed to join the bathing party. It was also the case that the Navy was not supposed to take non–swimmers into its ranks, and I knew that the swimming ability of every recruit was tested during basic training. Nobody was allowed to continue with the course until they proved they could swim at least two lengths of the pool and could keep themselves afloat by treading water for at least three minutes. We had regular swimming exercises at a local college while at Great Malvern, and even after qualifying, a man could be called upon to do a standard swimming test. These were performed while wearing a canvas suit, which became heavier with the water it soaked up as you swam the required distance. It was no easy test, and most were struggling to stay afloat by the time they had completed it. All that said, I did not report the incident.

Another strange incident occurred while I was aboard *Empress*, and it was something that left me angry for quite a while. It involved an attempt to have me transferred to the Army, and it all began at about noon one day while the ship was in port. At the time I was standing on the flight deck, talking with some of the ratings from my works team, when an officer's runner came up to us and asked for me by name. When I answered his call he told me that I had to report to the ship's office, but he could tell me nothing about the matter as I walked some of the way back with him, wondering what it could all be about. When I entered the room the Master–at–Arms was sitting at his desk. He began the conversation by telling me that, at that point in the war, the Army was in need of a helping hand, and as it was obvious to him that I was showing no interest in the Navy, he wondered if I might like to consider a transfer. My reaction was to refuse his suggestion point blank. I made it clear to him that I had joined the Navy for the duration of hostilities and that I meant to see out the war as a sailor. There was not a chance that I would agree to anything that would land me in a khaki uniform. He looked a bit stunned by my response, but before he could speak I asked him to justify his claim that I had shown no commitment to the Navy. His reply was that I had never bothered to seek confirmation as Stoker, First Class, and that this was proof enough for him that my heart was not in it. I then turned the tables on him by telling him that I had made a request for confirmation to Stoker No.1 while I was on *Woodpecker*. The next step, I explained, was that I should have been called to attend an interview before a panel of experts who would have questioned me about the technical parts of my job, and if all questions were answered to their satisfaction the promotion would have been granted. I was telling him something he already knew, but at least he could see that I had made myself familiar with the process of seeking confirmation in my rank. It is worth noting here that, after twelve months serving as a stoker, a man was automatically given the rank of Acting First Class Stoker, and that came with an extra shilling a day in pay. The confirmation that the Master–at–Arms was talking about was just a confirmation of the rank of Stoker, First Class; but there was no further rise in pay when that happened. In my case, the interview part of the promotion board had been postponed due to the sinking of *Woodpecker*.

Luckily, while I was in barracks waiting for a posting to another ship after *Woodpecker* had been lost, I decided to put in a second request for promotion, half suspecting that my first submission had gone astray. I heard nothing more about it before receiving my draft chit for HMS *Empress*. All of this I explained to the

Master–at–Arms, and on hearing my story his attitude changed completely. He dismissed me, and within two days I stood before him again. This time he told me that I could forget all about a move to the Army and that he had arranged my promotion board with the engineering officer for a few days later. I then went before the three–ringer who chaired the meeting, and after answering about half a dozen questions that were put to me about the technicalities of my job, I was confirmed in the rank of Stoker, First Class. The officer's parting advice was that I should look after myself as it would not now be long before the war was over. He wished me luck and sent me on my way. I was more than just a little relieved at having avoided Army service.

During one of our visits to Colombo I took the opportunity to go ashore with some of my shipmates. As we wandered around the town we visited some of the small shops where alcohol was served, enjoying a few drinks here and there as we made a tour around the port area. While in one of the bars, I noticed an Indian or Ceylonese who was carrying a small, varnished wooden box, it was about nine inches square and five deep, and there was a red cross painted on its lid.

There were some regular sailors amongst the crew of *Empress*; 'twenty–two–year men,' as they were known, and I used to enjoy talking with them, listening to some of the tales they had to tell. Two of them had served on the China station and knew a lot about the stories of the way of life in the Middle and Far East, and it might have been from the things they said that I became more open minded about the foreign cultures I was seeing for the first time.

The man with the box was going around the customers in the bar asking if anyone was suffering from corns, for which he claimed he had a fool–proof cure. One of the men of the old China station, a typical Geordie, was among the group I was with so I asked him if there was any truth in what the man was saying. Geordie was a no–nonsense type who I had some respect for after watching him dive from *Empress's* flight deck into Colombo harbour, about forty feet below, whenever there was a 'hands to bathe' call. He thought nothing of it. I remember one time, after sharing a conversation with him on the flight deck, he turned to me and said, 'I'm just going for a swim, I'll catch up with you later,' and at that he went straight over the side, making one of his dives into the harbour with hardly a splash as he broke the surface.

To return to the situation in the bar: Geordie insisted that these corn curers, as they were known, were as good as their word, so I asked the medicine man to take a look at my toe. In the past I had seen sailors trim the heads from their corns using a razor blade in an effort to get some relief from the pain they caused. It was not something I ever thought of doing myself because I always had a nagging feeling that the cut could become infected and lead to blood poisoning. Before we began the procedure, I asked the native if he was claiming the cure would be a permanent one. He assured me this was the case. Half convinced, I agreed to let him treat me. We stepped outside the bar onto the pavement, and as I sat down I handed him his fee of two rupees, about three shillings, before he started his work. He took a scalpel from his box which he used to scrape away the hard skin from the surface of the corn and reveal its head. Next, he made a small cut across the top from which a trickle of blood appeared. Finally, he took out a length of tapered rubber tubing about as long as a man's finger and placed the wide end over the head of the corn, he then put the narrow end between his lips and began to suck the air from the tube. After a few moments he pinched the tube closed between his finger and thumb and held it in place for about a minute before removing it from my toe, only to reveal the head of the corn still in place. At that point I was about to ask for my money back and send him away, but my friend told me that it sometimes needed a few attempts before the corn came out. On the second attempt, after he had removed the tube from the corn he flicked it with his finger nail and out it popped onto a piece of paper he was holding, it was a small red, carrot–shaped core about three eighths of an inch in length. Finally he put a piece of cotton wool over the hole in my toe and that was the last time I was ever troubled by the corn. In fact, I have never had any new corns since that day. All the time he was treating me he had been showing me a collection of letters he had received while he was working in London. I was keen to know why his time in England had come to an end, but he never gave me an understandable answer.

I must now return to the subject of the sailor's daily ration of rum in order to give an idea of how much it was valued by some, and how others could come to regret a bit of over indulgence.

About six months after I joined HMS *Empress,* I lost my taste for the sweet, daily tipple; the 'tot,' and the reason for it stemmed from the day of my twenty-second birthday (9 June 1945) which I celebrated aboard the carrier. I had decided that I was going to enjoy a celebration drink that day, but I did not expect it to reach the level of excess that it did.

During the process of serving out the rum to the crew, and for half an hour or so after everybody had been served, the men would sit around sipping their drink and chatting before making their way to the galley to get their lunch. This routine usually began at about eleven thirty in the morning. As I entered the room I could see that about half the men of my mess, some twenty–five in all, were lined up waiting for their daily tot; the rest might not yet have reached their twentieth birthday, which meant they did not qualify for the ration, or that they were on watch at that particular time. The Liverpool contingent amongst the crew amounted to about sixty men, and the 'Scousers' are a clannish people, never slow to find an excuse for a party. As a result most, if not all of them, on hearing that it was my birthday were offering me 'sippers' or 'gulpers' from their tot. The rum was always mixed in even measure with water (sometimes more) and a tot would be about enough to fill an egg cup. By tradition it was only the chiefs and petty officers who were allowed neaters – an undiluted tot – and the pilot of *Empress*'s motor boat, present at the time, held one of those ranks. This always struck me as being a bit strange; I would have thought that the man in charge of the ship's motor boat ought to be kept as sober as possible, but to add to the merriment the motor boat pilot gave me his full measure of neaters that day.

The drinking session went on for about two hours, and the thing about navy rum was that, with its high content of Demareira sugar, the more you drank the longer and stronger was your craving for more. At the end of the two–hour session I was completely drunk, and soon fell asleep. When I woke up I found that I had been tied to a bunk by my shipmates for the sake of my own safety. I managed to free myself after a while and began rummaging around in my locker, for what reason I cannot remember, but my head by that time was still nowhere near clear. Someone close by asked me what I was doing and by my reply, which I cannot remember, it was clear to him that I thought it was by then only about four thirty in the evening. I was wrong by about six hours; it was ten thirty. I went to the bathroom, had a cold wash, and did the best I could to clear my head before reporting for my next watch. I was very lucky that I did not end up on a charge or worse that day. One of the men from my mess told me that I had fallen down a stairway consisting of twenty–five steps, which probably explained why I felt so rotten – apart from the hangover, that is.

After the experience just described I could not face the thought of taking a full daily tot ever again. I continued to line up with the rest to receive my ration, but I would give it away; something which was strictly against the rules. Sadly, it soon became the cause of arguments amongst my friends as to whose turn it was to have my tot. I was not happy about that and decided that it should not go on, so I began to think of better ways to palm it off.

Things such as sugar, tea and milk were hard to come by in any quantity during the war. As such they had become items of luxury. That being the case, I decided to see if it was possible to trade my daily tot for some of those articles, so I made my way to the galley one day and quietly put my offer to one of the cooks. As a tester, I offered him that day's tot and asked him if he could supply me with a brew of tea in return. This he did without hesitation, keen to hear what kind of bargain I wanted to strike in order to continue the trade. When I explained to him what I had in mind the change in his manner was incredible. I had happened to hit upon a rum rat. His eyes lit up as he asked me to confirm what it was that I was asking for as a trade for my daily tot. I listed some the items that took my fancy, and he said he would fix me up with a bit of what I wanted. Pushing my luck, I told to him that I did not have a tea pot to mash my tea in. 'Don't worry,' he said, 'come back in an hour.'

When I returned the trade was ready. He had collected half a dozen tins of Libby's milk, a seven–pound jam tin that he had made into a kind of bucket by fitting it with a small handle, and inside there was a pound of tea and two pounds of sugar. All of this for the price of just one tot of rum per day for the next few days! As I made off with my booty my first problem was to find a place to hide it. If my little hoard was discovered I would probably find myself in some serious trouble. My friend, Ginger Breen, and two more of my mess mates, could hardly believe it when I showed them what I had brought to share between us. We found a quiet little room beneath the flight deck; this was to be our tea room, boiling water being supplied on demand by the friendly rum rat in the galley. I kept him

> happy with a continual supply of 'halfers' and his gratitude was boundless, always making a point of asking me if I was alright for supplies and passing them over whenever we ran short.

It was at about this time, the end of June 1945, that, with Germany's surrender, the realisation amongst the Allied servicemen that the war was coming to an end was firmly established, and it seems to have engendered a bit of a de-mob spirit amongst them. Whilst reading through *Empress*'s log for July 1945, I came across the following entry recorded for the 2nd of the month:

> John MacX X X, Jnr Engineer, T****: Admonished and logged for the following offence: Was, on 29th June 1945, guilty of an act to the prejudice of good order and discipline on using the ship's broadcasting system without authority at about 23:45.[33]

One can only imagine what it was Mr. MacX X X was broadcasting over the ship's tannoy, but it would seem that a bit of the hang-loose spirit was percolating through the junior officer ranks. In an effort to track down any other references to Mr. MacX X X, undoubtedly a Scotsman judging by his full name, I found the following recorded in *Empress*'s log entry for 3 September 1945:

> John MacX X X, Jnr Engineer, T****: Admonished and logged in accordance with instructions contained in KRAI (Kings Regulations and Admiralty Instructions) 509 for the following offence: Was guilty of an act to the prejudice of good order and naval discipline in contravening captain's standing order no. 6 by exceeding the amount of his wine bill for the month of August 1945.[34]

As I read this snippet I could not help imagining Mr. MacX X X, letting his hair down once again, probably at the news of Japan's surrender. Who could blame him?

Chapter 11

An encounter with the Kamikazes

Operation Livery 19–26 July 1945

Late July1945. *Empress* was ready to go to sea again after weeks in Trincomalee harbour. From there we sailed towards the island of Car Nicobar and the Andaman Sea once again.[1] The war against the Japanese was now nearly over, and the idea seemed to be that of keeping up the pressure on them as we prepared to invade Japan itself. This time we had a squadron of Hellcats aboard.[2] We were with a task force belonging to the East Indies Fleet, and it looked as if we were going to strike a heavy blow.[3] The carrier *Ameer*, the battleship *Nelson* and the cruiser *Sussex* all sailed with us.

After a few days at sea *Empress*'s reliability problems struck again. This time the fault was in the tripping gear, a cam–operated lubricating pump on the propeller shaft. As the gear began to fail it gave less oil to the shaft, causing it to get hot. This meant that the heat would be transferred to the main bearings that held it in place. To run like this for any amount of time would have been a big risk; if the bearings seized up then the ship would lose all power. So we were ordered to reduce speed to minimise the danger and to prepare to return to Colombo. While the preparations were being made we kept up with the task force as best we could, but we were slowly falling behind.

The crew was determined not to throw in the towel and return to base if we could help it, and after a full assessment of the problem was made the ship's engineers were able to work out how it might be fixed. They eventually made some running repairs that allowed the carrier to continue in the trail of the task force without losing touch, and on the following day we were close enough to take part in the operation.

Early that day, five Japanese aircraft appeared above the ships and began to position themselves for an attack on the *Sussex*.[4]

Two of them broke away from the group in what looked like a suicide attack. But while they were still at good distance from her, *Sussex's* anti–aircraft guns opened up, bringing one of them down. The second avoided the flak and began to dive towards the cruiser, but it was hit by more fire as other ships joined in the barrage. As it closed in on the cruiser the plane kept on being hit, but the pilot managed to steer it into the side of the warship. As it struck home there was a quite a big explosion, but it had hardly any effect, the ship's armour plating was obviously strong enough to withstand the blast. When a third Japanese plane began to dive towards the *Ameer*, the guns of all ships were able to give it their full attention and it soon burst into flames. All we could do was look on as it approached the carrier, but before the pilot could close the distance between himself and his target he smashed into the sea.

During five days in action we lost two of the minesweepers that were with us. These were trying to clear a path through the minefields which lay in the approaches to the islands we were attacking. One of them hit a mine in its path,[5] but the other one was hit by a *kamikaze* on the last day of the action.[6] There were a number of casualties from each ship, and some of those caused by the suicide attack were brought aboard *Empress* for emergency treatment before being transferred to the *Nelson*.

Throughout the operation our Hellcats were carrying out strikes on targets far over the horizon, out of sight from the carriers. The intensity of the air battles meant that there was a lot of activity aboard the carrier as the fighter–bombers returned to be re–armed and refuelled before being launched again. But it was good to see just how much work we could get out of the catapult system that had been giving us so much trouble. However, the engine prop shaft problems continued to cause trouble throughout the mission, and I was not the only man aboard who thought about the consequences if we lost all power and became a sitting duck for the *kamikazes*. Happily, it was not to be that way. We managed to stay with the force, straggling along behind as the ships made their way back to Ceylon. We docked in Trincomalee at the end of July, 1945.

Operation Livery was designed to clear the approaches to Phuket by minesweeping, thus allowing ships to come close in and carry out off–shore bombardments. The aircraft carriers were present to provide air cover and to launch air strikes against appropriate targets such as small ships, railway locomotives and grounded aircraft.

The fault in the tripping gear which had given us so much trouble during the patrol was soon corrected while we were in dock, and the ship was ready for her next patrol within a week, something that came as a surprise to us.

Operation Carson 10–15 August 1945, aborted 11 August on news of the surrender of Japan

At the start of August 1945, rumours that Japan was about to surrender ran thick and fast around the fleet as we set out towards Malaya and Sumatra.[7] After just a few days at sea we received orders to return to port, the reason being that the Japanese had agreed to surrender.

The victory over Japan was announced on the day we docked at Trincomalee. That night I witnessed the celebrations that took place to mark VJ Day, when the sky around the harbour was lit up by a huge fireworks display.[8] The effect on the men was easy to see, everybody's spirits were lifted as they began to think they would soon be on their way home. No more war!

The joy amongst the servicemen gradually faded over the next few days, as the air became thick with rumours that our return home might not come as quickly as many had expected, and morale soon began to sink. Most of the men, myself included, had signed up for service during hostilities only (HO) and we were unhappy about the idea of extending our service into peacetime.

It was some time before we began to hear the reason for the sudden surrender of the Japanese. Word then began to spread that they had sued for peace after two of their cities had been destroyed by powerful bombs. It was not the first time we had heard stories of new and powerful weapons being developed. Nothing had ever come from them in the past, so there was a lot of wariness about it amongst the servicemen. No matter what we were told, it was not until the official news of the surrender was broken that we finally began to relax. We had been fully expecting to see action in support of an invasion of Japan at some time during the coming months, and for the war to drag on into 1946. The fact that Japan had raised the white flag came as a great relief to all of us and we did not think too much about how she had been brought to her knees, we were just thankful that it was all over.

The end of the war did not stop everything dead in its tracks. The fleet continued to sail on so–called missions, which were really nothing more than training exercises made up to keep everyone busy, but nobody was being fooled; Japan was beaten, and well beaten in the Far East and everybody knew it. In the meantime, the men were becoming restless, they wanted to know how much longer it would be before they would be sailing home. We had done our bit, and every one of the mock missions carried out brought with them the usual dangers of being at sea, especially for the pilots and naval ratings aboard the carriers.

During the next few weeks, the grounds for the rumours about delaying our de–mobilisation were confirmed when officers began to break the news to us that we might not all be going home as soon as we had hoped. It was explained that, with so many of its ships scattered throughout the world, the different squadrons would have to wait for the arrival of replacement crews before the serving men could return home. As this kind of talk began to circulate the mood of the men became ugly and mutinous. Riots broke out at the big naval barracks in Colombo, where buildings were set on fire and the whole complex smashed up by the troops and naval ratings stationed there.

There was a fairly swift reaction. The authorities began to put out promises that the men would, after all, be de–mobbed at the earliest opportunity, and these announcements played a large part in calming the situation over the next few days. True to their word the powers that be began the process of sending troops to their various homelands sooner rather than later. Within a few weeks, *Empress* was given the task of ferrying home about two hundred New Zealanders, together with a group of four hundred Australians.

Whilst we were on our way to Australia we 'crossed the line,' and whenever that happened it was a tradition in the Navy that the crew should have a bit of fun, mostly at the expense of those who were making the crossing for the first time. When the day of the carnival arrived a timber frame was erected on the flight deck, it was then lined with canvas sheeting so that the whole thing formed a large, temporary swimming pool about five feet deep and fifteen feet square.

A ducking stool was set up at one end, the rear legs being attached to the frame of the pool by a pair of hinges. All of the crew were expected to dress up in any old outfits they could make up, and it was common to black–up faces and bodies to give the proceedings an even more tropical flavour.

All of the first–timers were told to take their place on the ducking stool. A welcoming party of about five matelots was ready in the pool, and when the man on the chair was tipped into the water he was given a good ducking before being tossed out onto a rope mat. While this was going on the next first–timer was prepared for his dip. At the same time, sailors dressed as policemen would search the ship looking for likely criminals. These were arrested and placed on trial. Inevitably, all criminals were found guilty by the jury and were given to the only punishment being handed down on the day – a good ducking. After a few of the Aussies and Kiwis had suffered this fate they formed up in a large gang and came to the decision that the members of the jury deserved a ducking for their verdicts, so into the pool they all went. With thoughts of home in everybody's mind the whole day passed off in the best of humour. No drink was allowed, it was good, clean, simple fun.

Our first stop was Melbourne, and on arrival at the port all the Australians were disembarked. We were berthed there for a very short time, less than a full day I would say, before putting to sea again and setting course for Wellington, New Zealand. It was there where all the Kiwis were put ashore, and I can remember that, during our five–day stop, we celebrated Guy Fawkes night on 5 November 1945. It would seem that the pull of the southern seas had had an effect upon some of *Empress's* crew, as a good number of them went missing ashore, never to return. On leaving New Zealand we set sail for home, returning along the same route we had taken on our outward journey to the Far East almost a year earlier, re-crossing the Indian Ocean, the Red Sea, Suez and the Mediterranean. I can remember nothing in the way of incident from that journey. There was only one thought in everyone's mind. We would be home for Christmas!

Chapter 12

A trip to Germany

It was mid–December 1945, and after the long journey from Wellington *Empress* pulled in at Greenock on the Clyde. Once ashore I was given the usual train pass and detailed to return to Devonport.

Things at home seemed to have become grimmer since I left for the Far East twelve months earlier. Maybe it was just me having spent a year in hot, bright weather but, as far as I could tell things showed little sign of improvement from the way they were in December 1944. Now that the war was over there was not much work available, and there was also a real shortage of materials such as timber and metals which, I thought, would set back any recovery people were hoping for. Many men were still with the armed forces, which was just as well, because if they had all been de–mobbed as soon as the war had ended they would have flooded the labour market.

Towards the end of 1945, efforts were being made to release men from the forces in some kind of organised way. At Devonport each man was given a demob number when he arrived at the base, this was meant to indicate their position on the waiting list for the release system that was in operation. The number I was given was forty–five, and I supposed this to mean that I would be amongst the forty–fifth batch of men to be de–mobbed from *Drake*. There was no official explanation of what the number meant in terms of an actual release date, but we were told that would depend on the rate at which reliefs became available. I do not know how many young men were deciding to join the armed forces at that time, but I think I can safely say that all the replacements arriving at Devonport during the first few months following the end of the war were young lads who were being conscripted under the National Service Act.

At the barracks, life did not consist of lazy days waiting for the arrival of our replacements. I myself had been at the base for about three weeks when I was ordered to act as a relief for a stoker who was serving aboard a ship stationed at Kiel in northern Germany. I cannot say that I was happy about it at first, and I had a suspicion that the new posting might become the cause of a delay in my own release. But, as usual, I was unhappy with the dreariness of barracks life, and after a second thought I began to look forward to another, hopefully short, adventure.

Once issued with my pass I caught a train to Hull, and when I arrived there I reported to a small naval establishment where I billeted overnight. After a comfortable night's rest I rose at four o'clock in the morning, and once I was ready for the journey I was taken to the local docks in a military jeep driven by two Royal Marines, my kit bag and hammock stowed behind the rear seats of the vehicle. I was then put aboard a civvy ship for the crossing of the North Sea, and assigned a comfortable little cabin all to myself which I thought was a luxury. Once my belongings had been stored below with the rest of the cargo the ship set sail for Cuxhaven.

I had been given instructions that, on my arrival in Germany, I was to catch a train to my final rail destination which was the city of Hamburg, and from there make my way to Kiel, some seventy miles away, by other means. The instructions went on to say that I need not bother waiting for my kit to be unloaded after I had disembarked, as it had been arranged that it would be collected from the ship by the port authorities at Cuxhaven and transferred onto the train I would be taking to Hamburg. The address to which I was to report had been written on the tally attached to my luggage, but whether it was the fault of the port authorities, or the German Railways, it failed to appear. I was to see nothing of it for about two months.

After another good night's sleep I had my breakfast aboard the ship once it had berthed at Cuxhaven, and after going ashore I made my way to the main station where I caught a train for Hamburg. All appeared to be going smoothly. However, when the train pulled in at my destination, I left the carriage and made my way along the station platform to the goods wagon, expecting to find that my kit had been unloaded, but there was no sign of it. I explained what I was looking for as best I could to the German railwaymen who were on the spot, but it was impossible to make myself understood, so I tried to ask them to delay the departure of the train until a search for my kit could be made, but it was non–starter. As the train pulled away I decided to make my way to the address I had been given, there was nothing else for it.

During the train journey into Hamburg I had plenty of opportunity to see the amount of damage caused by the bombing. The distance between Cuxhaven and Hamburg was about fifty miles, and it looked to me as though anything and everything that could have been considered to be a target had had the attention of the bombers; it was awful. All of what I had seen on that short journey should have been enough to prepare me for what I would find in Hamburg, but after stepping out from the main exit of the station into the centre of the city, I could hardly take in the sight that met my eyes. There was barely a building still standing. Huge areas of the city had been reduced, literally, to rubble. I could see that the railway station had been badly damaged but that some repair work had been done and more was going on. But apart from that it did not seem that any rebuilding on a big enough scale had really started. My mind began to wonder back to the dark days of 1941 when Liverpool was bombed; but this was worse, much worse.

As I walked away from the station into the streets, I was quite surprised to notice that the Germans seemed completely used to the presence of British servicemen amongst them. I neither felt, nor saw, any sign of hostility from the German people towards the forces for the destruction of their city. This was some ten months after the war with Germany had ended, but there was still a curfew in place, which meant that all Germans had to be off the streets by ten o'clock at night, and this made me think that the forces were still a bit jittery. Speaking for myself, I can only say that, unarmed and alone, walking freely about the city, I felt completely safe.

After a brief look around what was really just a city of ruins, I decided that it was time to make a serious effort to find someone in uniform who might be able to help me with the final leg of my journey, as I had still to get from Hamburg to Kiel. I spoke to a British soldier who I met on the streets, and he told me there was a road link in place between the two towns which was mainly used by British Army transports. The best way to make my journey to Kiel, he said, was to hitch a lift. I was not comfortable with the idea but with no alternative I decided to take his advice, and once I was convinced that I had found the road I was looking for, I waved down a wagon that looked as though it might be heading in the right direction. As the truck drew up the driver said he was on his way to Kiel and told me to hop in the back, as I did so I found there were already several men aboard. About half of them were British soldiers in full uniform, the majority of them unarmed, the rest were Germans, also in army uniform. At first, I was a bit unsure about the situation, half expecting to see signs of friction between the soldiers of two armies who had been at each other's throat, but as the lorry trundled along the road I became more relaxed as I could see that both groups were quite happy in each other's company.

It was about an hour's ride to Kiel. The road had been repaired, but all along the route, on either side, I could see only dereliction in places where there used to be life. It was difficult to grasp the scale of it. It reminded me again of the damage caused by bombs and fires that I had seen in Liverpool, but this was a hundred times worse; there was no comparison between the two. The people on the streets appeared to be completely demoralised; as well as the destruction of their homes there were food shortages to put up with, all made worse by the freezing cold weather of the early spring. The people of Hamburg must have been as convinced as I was that reconstruction on the scale needed to rebuild their city was beyond anyone.

We were soon in the outskirts of Kiel, so keeping a eye open for any sign that we were getting close to the harbour area as we entered the city, I managed to hop from the back of the lorry as it slowed down in what looked like a promising place. Without my kit bag and hammock, and carrying only the little brown suitcase that was with me when I was taken off *Woodpecker*, I set out to see if I could find anyone connected with the Navy. It was not long before I came upon a hut standing at the entrance to one of the docks. It was being used by British sailors, so I stopped there and explained I was due to report aboard the destroyer, HMS *Zealous*. A phone call was made, and as a result of what was said I was told to wait until a motor launch arrived to ferry me to the ship. It was now early April, 1946, the weather was very cold and I was grateful to be sitting in the warmth of the sentry hut. When the launch arrived, I was surprised to see that it was manned by two German servicemen. They explained to me that *Zealous* was tied up at a buoy in the canal, so I climbed aboard and, more relaxed in the company of the German sailors than I might have been earlier, I was ferried out to the ship.

Once aboard *Zealous* I reported to the guard on the quarterdeck, presented my papers to him and was told to go to the stokers' mess below. As I passed down through the decks I soon began to feel the benefit of the electric heaters that were pushing out some well appreciated warmth, the early springtime weather had quite a nip to it. When I got to the mess I explained why I had been sent, and that I had been separated from my kit when I was put ashore at Cuxhaven. They seemed concerned about my situation and ready to help, and in short time a small group of them went off to find the Jack Dusty and ask him to provide me with some replacement kit. They soon returned carrying a hammock and a blanket, and I was able to rest assured that, at the very least, I would have enough bedding to guarantee me a comfortable night's sleep. I was then sent to the chief stoker to report the loss of my personal kit. On hearing my story he reported it to the engineer officer, and so on it went up the command structure. The Navy's system of administration was better than I gave it credit for because, despite my lack of faith, my kit managed to follow my movements from that point on until it eventually caught up with me in Devonport sometime later.

Once I felt settled in, I asked my new shipmates what things were like ashore. Kiel, they were all agreed, was a miserable place, not somewhere to find the kind of atmosphere present in a dockside pub in England. In turn they asked me a bit more about how I had come to lose my kit, and as I told them my story one of them pointed out that my trousers were on fire! I had been standing too close to one of the electric heaters, and they had caught alight. Everyone saw the funny side of it, and after dousing the flames I was left with a large hole in one trouser leg.

Before I got a name for being troublesome, or accident prone; a bit of a Jonah, I thought it best to patch up my trousers instead of asking for a replacement pair of bell–bottoms. Using the black collar from the back of my tunic as spare material, I made a rough and ready job of the repairs. Once done, and quite happy with my appearance, I went ashore aboard the ship's motor boat, keen to see if things in Kiel were really as bad as my new shipmates said they were.

Once in town I found my way to the local YMCA, and was about to enter when I realised that I did not have any German currency with me. Just then two matelots came out of the building. They seemed quite approachable, so I asked if they would mind exchanging some cash with me, asking them if they knew what the rate of exchange was. They looked at me in amazement and told me to keep my money, then simply handed me a big bundle of German banknotes, telling me they were more or less worthless. With a large wad of cash in my tunic pocket I made my way inside and had a cup of tea and something to eat. The atmosphere inside was quite relaxed, I remember clearly a German band playing the tune of Jealousy; it was a popular song at the time. On my way into the building I had noticed a group of German children playing in the street, close to the door of the YMCA, and as I watched them for a while, I saw that they would try to cadge bits of food from people as they made their way out of the cafe. Bearing this in mind as I paid for my meal I bought a few cakes and handed them out as I was leaving. The young boys were quick to show their gratitude for my little effort and, taking the opportunity to look at them more closely, they did not seem to me to be too badly off. It was clear, however, that food was by no means plentiful. One thing that struck me was the way they approached me and took the cakes I was handing out. There was no rush or snatching at the little I had, they were very well mannered towards me as they waited for their share.

As I made my way from the YMCA I asked some passers–by if there were any bars in the area where I might get a drink, and was directed to one which was one of the few buildings in the area still standing almost undamaged. There were not many people inside; just a smattering of British servicemen and some local German civilians. Both groups seemed at ease with each other, though I noticed there was no attempt to mix; maybe that was simply due to the language barrier. From all I had seen so far, I was gaining the clear impression that most of the German people were just glad that the war was now over, and that they simply wanted to get on with their lives as best they could. It was just the kind of feeling people had at home.

After a few drinks I made my way back to the dock and caught the shuttle service to the ship. I was back aboard by eleven o'clock, and after stringing my new hammock, using sixteen clews at each end, I slung it and climbed in for my first night's sleep aboard *Zealous*.

Next day, I was taken to the boiler room and introduced to the man I was about to relieve, and I was surprised, once more, to find that we had a German sailor working with the stokers. He was one of about four ex–servicemen, still in uniform, who had been employed aboard the ship since she docked. The Germans, I could see, were more than happy to be working with us, the skipper had assigned one to each of the messes, and as payment for washing dishes and carrying out other such chores they were allowed to help themselves to something to eat once we had finished our meal. These little extras were in addition to the pay they got for doing the regular jobs they had been hired for.

After I had been aboard *Zealous* for about four days we received orders to sail for Portland. I had had enough time by then to take in some of the details concerning my new surroundings and shipmates, and what I saw was not very impressive. I noticed that we had some young recruits aboard amongst whom, I regret to say, the level of personal hygiene left a lot to be desired. After washing at a sink they would leave a filthy tide mark of scum around the bowl, and as I looked around I could see that other areas of the bathroom had been left in a less than clean state. Some of the boys had open sores on their face and, on the whole, they did not present a healthy sight at all. Inevitably, it was not long before my own face became dotted with sores. There was no doctor aboard *Zealous*; many ships' doctors had by then been transferred to shore jobs with the Navy, or had been de–mobbed, so I made an appointment to see a medical officer once we were in Portland.

We arrived at our destination about two or three days after sailing from Kiel, and after having my medical examination I was surprised to be told that I was going to be sent to Portland Naval Hospital. My complaint had been diagnosed as impetigo. Once again, I could feel the frustration, not to say the anger, rising within me at the Navy's lack of attention to the health of the young men in its ranks. The use of a basic routine to encourage personal cleanliness, coupled with proper inspection routines for the living quarters and toilets, would have prevented the all too frequent outbreaks of medical conditions often associated with poverty. When I arrived at the hospital I was admitted for two weeks under treatment.

One of the doctors who examined me said that he would administer a treatment which, if I understood him correctly, seemed nothing other than weird. He said that he was going to bleed me from the thigh and then inject some of the blood into my ear. The thought of this gave me a sleepless night, but soon afterwards my complaint began to clear up, and I can only think the shock I got when I heard about the treatment that was being considered was the cause of my quick recovery. My skin complaint having disappeared, I was soon told that I could return to my ship, and after being discharged from the hospital I reported back aboard *Zealous* where I was immediately given fourteen days sick leave. I collected my train pass and set off for home.

It was now May or June of 1946. There was not much work available, food rationing was still in place and there were severe shortages of many items such as cheese, eggs and fruit. Tropical fruits, such as oranges and bananas, were almost completely missing from the shops. It all reminded me of the time when I brought home some tangerines. While I was aboard *Woodpecker* we had called at Algiers after escorting a convoy into the Mediterranean shortly before Christmas 1943, once in port I went ashore and bought some pieces of fruit from a local shop near the quayside. After weighing them out, the shopkeeper placed them into little individual straw bags that gave them a kind of tropical appearance. I stored them away when we sailed, and when I got home I shared some of them out amongst the toddlers who lived close to my mother's flat. I became quite sentimental when some of them, never having seen such things during their short life, could not tell me what they were.

There was still no organised football underway in England, so a trip to Goodison Park or Anfield was out of the question, the official league had not been re–started by then. Some of my old pals from the neighbourhood were already home, having been de–mobbed, others were still with the forces waiting for their release. I passed away my two weeks leave having the occasional pint of beer with old friends and, despite the general shortage of all kinds of things, the breweries never seemed to run dry. On thinking about it, I found it surprising that most of my friends and family had survived the war, but I had, indeed, lost a young cousin and a young nephew, which was loss enough for anyone, I suppose. Of my friends, apart from the two lads who were lost when the *Kite* was sunk, the only other death I was aware of was that of the son of one of the neighbours on the landing, Mrs Mulcahy. Joe was just seventeen when he was killed while serving aboard one of the Navy's heavy destroyers.[1]

Once my two weeks leave were up, I returned to Portland and reported back aboard *Zealous*. She was one of what were called the Navy's Battle class destroyers. Fast, heavily armed ships, with deck–mounted torpedo tubes. She had at least three sister ships, the names of which escape me, and together with two of these she had been selected to take part in a sea race from Portland, eastwards through the Channel, then north along the Kent coast before entering the Thames, then finally up the river to the finishing line at the dockyard of Woolwich Arsenal. It was probably something dreamt up by the Navy to keep down the level of boredom amongst the crews of its ships.

On arrival at our destination we were told that *Zealous* had finished second in the three–horse race, and we were later told that we had kept up an average speed of thirty–four and a half knots for the twelve hours of the competition, about twice the speed we could have gotten out of *Woodpecker*. We were happy to learn that our journey had not been completely meaningless; apart from the technical information gathered during the course of the race, each of the three ships had carried some cargo for delivery to the Arsenal, and on arrival at Woolwich we unloaded a large quantity of munitions which were returned to store. While berthed in London, the ships' crews were allowed two days ashore to take in the sights of the capital. To my eyes it appeared that the city had benefitted from a lot of tidying up since the blitz. It certainly presented a better sight than Liverpool did; something which made my stop–over quite enjoyable.

Once our two–day break was over and all hands were back aboard, we sailed for Falmouth, where *Zealous* lay tied up for five days. There was nothing much to do during those post–war months, and it began to look as though the Navy was running out of ideas for keeping us busy. This suspicion was soon strengthened when news began to circulate that we would shortly be setting off on a 'showing the flag' trip. All was confirmed when we received our orders to sail for Manchester, which to me was not the first place that would spring to mind for such a mission. On leaving Falmouth, we sailed through the Western Approaches before turning northwards into the Irish Sea, and after a couple of days we arrived at our destination after sailing up the Manchester Ship Canal. Judging by the high number of visitors that came aboard, it seemed that our presence had aroused a lot of interest in the Salford and Manchester area.

The proximity of home, it is just thirty miles from Manchester to Liverpool, allowed me to make a few return journeys between the quayside and my mother's house. In fact, two of my younger sisters, Mags and Tina, came to visit the ship one day, bringing with them the two young daughters, Marie and Teresa, belonging to my eldest sister, Mary. Some years later, one of them reminded me of the time when, as a child, I had carried her aboard what she seemed to think had been a submarine. When I explained to her that *Zealous* was a surface ship she replied, 'Yes; but when we got aboard you took me down a few flights of stairs.' It is funny how the logic of a child's mind can sometimes work.

Chapter 13

De–mobbed

After the ship had spent five days in Manchester, my relief finally came through in July 1946. There was not much ceremony about the way in which the news was given to me, the coxswain aboard *Zealous* simply approached me one day and told me to collect my kit together, as I was about to leave. I skipped off to my berth, packed my kit bag, folded my hammock, and began my journey to Devonport after a home visit to Liverpool. The baker who made the daily deliveries of bread to the ship while she was berthed in Manchester gave me a lift to the local railway station, from where I made the first leg of my journey by taking a train to Liverpool. On arriving at Central Station, I stowed my belongings at the left luggage department and walked the short distance to the family home where I slept the night. On the following day I left for Devonport on the midnight train.

Back at barracks the same old routine was still in place. I was told which mess to join and to wait for any news concerning my release, which might come during the daily nine o'clock announcement. By a stroke of luck I even managed to get back one of my old jobs: that of looking after the fuel stocks at the barrack's cinema where there was a regular delivery of coke. The lorry would arrive, tip its load of about two tons outside the building and leave me to shovel it down through a hatch into the cellar below. It might seem strange that I can describe the return to that kind of work as a stroke of luck, but believe me, any job that relieved the boredom of barracks life was more than welcome.

Finally, after about eight weeks in Devonport, my chit arrived and I was told to report to the gymnasium on the following day, bringing all the items of my kit with me. This was it! The news I had been waiting for. After rising and having a good breakfast, myself, along with all rest for de–mob that day, arrived at the gym in groups of about twenty at a time, carrying kit bags and hammocks as instructed. Once we had answered to our names in a roll call, we were loaded onto a lorry and driven to St. Budeaux, near Saltash, where we were to be officially de–mobbed. It was early September 1946.

It had been decided that all de–mobbed men would be allowed to keep whatever items of uniform they stood in when they reported to St. Budeaux. This might sound like an act of generosity on the part of the Navy, especially so when you remember what had happened to me after *Woodpecker* was sunk. But at the start of our service we had all been issued with two suits; two sets of navy uniform that is. Since then, many of the men had bought a third set, bit by bit, during the time they were in the forces. I also took up the habit of putting away half a crown per week, which I liked to spend at the tailors whenever I had the need, or took the fancy, of replacing some of my standard items. It was a common thing to do which stemmed, I think, from the fact that the tailors measured their customers before making up the ordered garments. Like that, you stood a good chance of having a set of clothing that came close to a proper fit; the standard items were usually ill–fitting. Be that as it may, we were expected to hand in two complete sets of uniform on de-mob, and it was the self–purchased items that we tended to keep. This might explain the apparent generosity of the Navy in allowing us to keep the uniform we were wearing when we arrived at St. Budeaux, but in effect we were being allowed to keep a uniform we had bought for ourselves.

Once our items of kit had been checked in and our kit bags and hammocks collected, we were each left with our small brown suitcase and a small, cotton cord–pull carrier bag. Everyone was then allowed to choose a set of de–mob clothing. There was a pile of shoes on the floor of the hall where we were gathered, and after rooting around in the jumble most were able to pick a pair that took their fancy and were of a decent fit. Trilbies and suits were available in abundance, all quite obviously having been bought in bulk by the ministry. Judging by the appalling quality on view I would say that some of the suppliers must have made a big profit from it all. The clothing was so cheap and ill made that some of the men refused to accept what was on offer and were given a voucher to be used at a tailor's shop on civvy street. I decided to choose a grey striped suit, a pair of socks, a pair of shoes, a shirt and tie.

Once changed into our new clothes we were given details of the de–mob payment we would receive. Mine came to eighty–three pounds, which was forwarded to me about three weeks later. It was quite a sum of money in the eyes of many, though if you thought about it, it might soon begin to appear less generous when weighed against our war service. A fortnight or so later my final wages came through, and three years after that I received five pounds in prize money. Naval captains, I was told, had received about three thousand pounds as their share. So much for a burden shared.

In the de–mob hall I met up with some of the Liverpool lads I had joined up with on 5 November, 1941. It was the first time we had seen each other since that day. Strange it might be to mention, but with so much catching up to do, I cannot remember any of them wanting to talk about their war experiences. I do not know if this was something deliberate, or just the natural tendency to look to the future after what we had been through. In fact, one of the lads in the group was an elder brother of my pal, 'Ossie' O'Brien, who was killed when *Kite* was sunk. Once the formalities were completed we caught a train to Bristol where we had to wait for a change to take us on to Liverpool, and as there was quite some time to kill we decided to go to the YMCA near Temple Mead station and have a meal together before continuing with our journey. About twelve hours after leaving Devonport we arrived at Liverpool Lime Street.

The employment prospects in Liverpool were hopeless, and I was a full month looking for work without success. In the end I had to report to the unemployment benefit office in Renshaw Street, and after assessing my claim they decided to award me the sum of fourteen shillings a week, a pittance from which I had to hand over a fair share to my mother as help towards my keep. I was lucky if by the end of the week I had saved enough to enjoy a couple of pints.

In an attempt to stave off the boredom of a life without purpose I would, of an evening, visit one of the half dozen or so local cinemas. They provided a welcome break for many, and I suppose it was all in the cause of a bit of make–believe; people just wanted to pretend that they were sharing in the world they saw on the screen and to forget about the demoralising effect of their daily lives. During daylight hours I travelled the length and breadth of the city looking for work. One of the few opportunities available was that of manual labour on the many demolition sites around the city, but I was determined to accept such employment only as a last resort. Like many others I felt that I had given a lot for the sake of the country during the previous six years or so, and all I asked in return was the opportunity to learn a trade. I wanted to pick up a skill that would allow me to earn a decent living.

It is my long–held belief that the government should have been much more willing to lend a hand immediately after the war. Thousands could have benefitted from a well–run training scheme and they, together with their families, would have had the advantage of a father in work bringing home a wage, and the country, maybe, would have made a quicker recovery from the war than was actually the case. Prospects being so bleak in Liverpool, I decided to leave town in my search for work. My father was good enough to give me a pound which was to pay for my travel to the Black Country to see if there were any opportunities to be had there. I set off, full of hope, and although there did seem to be a lot of activity in Coventry and Birmingham, I was not lucky enough to get the early break I was looking for. I then struck out for London and continued my search for work in Canning Town.

After a short time I got a job at the Ford car factory, working in the engine assembly plant. It was my responsibility to fasten clamps to the moulds into which molten metal was poured to cast engine blocks. The working conditions were dire and dangerous, and it was difficult to keep up with the pace demanded by the speed of the production line. I returned to my digs every night totally exhausted and aching from head to toe as a result of the non–stop work at the plant. After a week in the job I decided that kind of work was not for me, and I made up my mind to leave.

During those early post war months power cuts were a common thing due, I suppose, to a higher demand for power from what was still a recovering power supply situation. In order to improve the country and get industry on its feet again, the government had begun a big power station construction plan, and I was soon able to find a job at one of the sites.

I began by working as a hod carrier and general labourer with the bricklayers before being moved on to help the joiners in making up shuttering panels; these, once erected to form moulds, would hold the poured concrete which formed the floors and footings of the buildings going up on the site. As the weeks passed by, I was encouraged to persevere with this work by a string of promises that I would soon be moved onto the tools. There was now a chance, I thought, that my long–awaited hope to become a carpenter was finally within my grasp.

In anticipation of a decent period of employment at the site, I moved into the temporary accommodation blocks close by; they were made up of a collection of Nissen huts with canteen facilities included, and were set up by a local landlord. Conditions there were not at all that bad when you made allowances for the effects of the war; and the level of cleanliness at the little complex, always a concern to me, I found to be quite acceptable. With eight or ten men sharing a dormitory, the accommodation could not be said to have been overcrowded by the standards of the time.

As the summer wore on the working deadlines on site became so demanding that a night shift was introduced; so, together with about six of the men I was working with, I volunteered to switch shifts. We worked seven nights a week in order to earn as much as we could while the job lasted, although the rates of pay could not be said to have been in any way generous. The construction site was dominated by a huge crane, and as work continued the need soon arose to extend the reach of its jib. This was done by adding a new central section in the arm, the work taking about five or six days to complete. Once the crane was ready for use again, I was expecting the fitters to run some trials to make sure that all was well, but nothing much was done. One night, shortly after the job was completed, the crane was brought back into use. We had a need to use it almost immediately to lift a load of scaffolding poles and move them across the site to a place where they were required.

As the load was lifted away and swung along the jib I noticed that the crane became unstable. I am not sure if it was because the new section of the jib had been badly fitted, or because it was now just too long, or, on the other hand, because the load being lifted was too heavy, but whatever the reason was, the whole structure began to sway. Soon I could hear the sound of bolts being sheared under the strain, and it was clear that the crane was beginning to fail. Standing close by and realising what was about to happen, I decided the best thing to do was to stay as cool as possible and try to judge which way it was going to topple if it fell.

I tried to get the rest of the men not to run off in any direction as the crane began to collapse, yelling at them to keep an eye on it as it fell so that they could avoid being hit by the shower of metal that was beginning to rain down, but I could not stop the scatter. I was lucky. From where I stood, I could make out the structure of the crane against the sky, and as it came down I could see that I was going to be safe, so I stayed where I was. Sadly, some of the others were not so lucky. Two were killed and several injured as the tower and jib hit the ground.

I continued working at the site after the accident, but I was never offered the chance of picking up a skill, something I still really wanted. Other promises and offers were made to me, but with winter approaching I knew it would soon be time for the building trades to scale back their work until the good weather returned. Eventually, with word coming from home that things were beginning to pick up, I returned to Liverpool, where I remain to this day.

A lot has happened in my hometown during the past sixty years or so. I have witnessed a lot of the changes that have taken place during that time, and it would be nice to give my impressions and opinions of it all. But that, as they say, is another story and not one for these pages.

Appendix 1

RAF liaison officer's report on his time spent on patrol with the Second Support Group[1]

Jack Bernard Jewell of the RAAF was almost certainly the author of the the report containing the following description of the action which took place on 30 July in the Bay of Biscay. Acting as a liaison officer, he was assigned to HMS *Woodpecker* during the Second Support Group's Biscay patrol which ran from 23 July to 6 August 1943.

Jewell appears in one of Dr. Gordon Canti's photgraphs, in which he is seen in conversation with two of HMS *Wren*'s crew.[2]

> …… It was at this point that the Admiralty were at last able to make available a surface hunting group to co-operate with Bromet's aircraft. It was composed of the sloops *Starling*, *Wren*, *Woodpecker*, *Kite*, and *Wild Goose* under the command of Captain F. J. Walker, 'that great U-boat hunter', as Slessor calls him. For the next six weeks this force and the aircraft of Coastal Command wrought havoc among the U-boats. What happened on 30 July, when No. 502 Squadron and No. 461 Squadron RAAF and Walker's sloops between them sank every one of a group of three U-boats in transit is vividly described by the Royal Air Force Liaison Officer [Jack Bernard Jewell, RAAF] on board HMS *Woodpecker*.

About 8.30 [he records] the fun really started:

> What a terrific day! A Sunderland and a Catalina were around and they signalled that no less than three U-boats were on the surface about ten miles ahead. The Senior Naval Officer in *Kite* made the signal 'General Chase'. Off we went at full speed, line abreast – a grand sight – smooth blue sea and blue sky – all ratings and officers at action stations. Soon we saw the aircraft circling low and diving to

> drop depth charges. Two of the U-boats were visible by this time and the Sunderland dropped a couple of depth charges plumb on either side of the conning tower of one of them. That broke the U-boat's back and he disappeared pretty quickly, leaving some survivors and a raft in the water. Simultaneously, all our ships had opened fire with 4-inch on the second U-boat. He, too, left survivors who had to wait until U-boat No. 3 had been located and dealt with. Not unnaturally, No. 3 dived in some haste and we were now set the task of finding him beneath the surface. It was like great cats stalking an oversized mouse. *Kite* found him first and dropped a pattern of depth charges. Then *Woodpecker* set about him and dropped depth charges. *Kite* got a 'fix' and with his direction we proceeded to lay a 'plaster', which is rather what the name denotes. *Wildgoose* repeated the dose, but while she was doing so the first patches of oil were observed and soon it was coming up in great quantities – the sea stank of it. Wood and other wreckage came up too. This was about 3.30 p.m. We recovered various things. *Wren* found some German clothing. The evidence was decisive and the ships (which had been shielding one another during the action) reformed and made off to pick up survivors. We picked up seventeen, including the captain and 1st officer. The other ships picked up a further fifty or so altogether. Ours were in or clinging to a rubber float, shaped like a big rubber ring. Some were injured. One had a bullet in his stomach and a broken ankle. They were mostly shaking with cold and/or reaction from their experience. Several of them were truculent. Some had never been in a U-boat before – possibly never to sea before.

The sloops were able to collect more than a hundred prisoners from the U-boat victims of our air and sea forces. It was on this day that one of these strange coincidences, when fact far surpasses fiction, occurred – Sunderland 'U for Uncle' of No. 461 Squadron RAAF met and destroyed *U-461*.

A week passed and then the naval force returned, receiving as they reached Plymouth Hoe a signal of congratulation from the Commander-in-Chief, who took the salute as the leading ship passed by playing 'A-hunting we will go' on her loud hailer. Such successes were gratifying and fully bore out the dictum that 'the best U-boat killing machine is a really well trained and experienced team of air and surface craft'.

The joint pack hunted together until August when once more the enemy changed his tactics. The loss of four U-boats in the first two days of that month in the Bay of Biscay was evidently felt by him to be too severe. He abandoned, therefore, the attempt to traverse those waters on the surface and chose instead the safer method of hugging the north coast of Spain and moving as far as possible submerged. Walker's sloops and Bromet's aircraft at once followed the U-boats to the new area. Now, however, the British air and sea forces were far from their bases and close to those of the enemy. They were in fact almost within his grasp, for he, too, had not been idle and had a new weapon. On 25 August, the naval vessels watching the Spanish exit from the Bay were attacked by glider-bombs. One sloop was damaged. Two days later the enemy sank HMS. *Egret* with heavy loss of life and severely damaged HM destroyer *Athabaskan*. In the application of common prudence, the surface vessels had to be withdrawn some two hundred miles to the westward out of easy range of German aircraft. Co-operation with Coastal Command suffered in consequence. Nevertheless, the patrols of the Navy's vessels were continued until mid-September when information was received indicating that the U-boats were reappearing once more in the North Atlantic. This was a danger signal which could not be ignored, and the ships were therefore withdrawn from the Bay and sent farther north. Not until nearly a year later did they reappear in the Bay at a time when the rapid advance of Eisenhower's forces south-westward from Normandy compelled German submarines to evacuate the Biscay ports.

Appendix 2

Content of documents found in the service file of J6941 F/O G.H. Wharram (RCAF)[1]

Below is a transcript of a letter from W/C A. Cloustom, Commanding Officer, No.224 Squadron, to the Air Ministry (Casualties Branch) dated 25 September 1943, referring to the loss of Liberator FL959, 3rd September 1943:

> Liberator FL959 (F/O G.H. Wharram) took off from Gibraltar at 1030 hours on 2 September 1943, to carry out anti-submarine sweep in the Bay of Biscay. At 1615 hours, whilst in position 44.00 N, 11.00 W, Liberator was attacked by four Ju.88s. After combat, Liberator was forced to ditch. The captain (F/O Wharram) was killed in action.
>
> The full report of events by F/O D.M. Johnstone [I include below]:
>
> The crew was as follows:
> Pilot – J6941 F/O G.H. Wharham [sic for Wharram]
> Pilot – 1313625 Flight Sergeant Foss, R.J.
> Navigator – 138822 P/O W.R. Collins
> Flight Engineer – 569893 Sergeant Bareham, D.H.
> WOP/AG – 1216857 Sergeant Dilks, M.W.
> WOP/AG – 11123y4 [sic for 1112371] Sergeant Maloney, R.A,
> WOP/AG – 136708 P/O J.R. Wilcox
> WOP/AG – J8754 F/O J.C. Miller
> Passenger – F/O Johnstone
>
> Sergeant Maloney was killed in the ditching process.

The remaining members of the crew (Flight Sergeant Foss, F/O Collins, Sergeant Bareham, F/O Miller, Sergeant Dilks, F/O Wilcox and F/O Johnston) were in a dinghy for some days.

F/O Miller and F/O [sic] Wilcox died on 7th September and 8th September 1943, respectively, and were both buried at sea,

The remaining members of the crew were rescued at 0945 hours on 9 September 1943 by HMS *Wildgoose*, but P/O Collins and Sergeant Bareham died on board ship.

The following personnel survived the ordeal and are now in hospital:
Flight Sergeant R.J. Ross [sic for Foss]
Sergeant M.W. Dilks
F/O Johnstone

I was on the return journey to United Kingdom from North Africa where I had been engaged on Investigational flights of enemy S,E. [Special Equipment or radar]. Jamming in different areas and had stopped at Gibraltar to collect kit, etc. I had intended to continue my journey on the night of 1 September by Courier plane, but hearing that some 224 Squadron Liberators also returning next morning I saw F/O Warram, the captain of the plane and obtained permission to return with his crew on the morning of 2nd September.

My principal reason for doing this was that I should have an excellent opportunity to gain experience in the operation of the Mark 5 ASV on the aircraft.

The trip was uneventful until about 100 miles north of Finisterre, the weather along the Portuguese coast was cloudy with visibility frequently poor, but on entering the Bay it cleared up 2/10 thin strato-cumulus at about 5,000 feet. At about 16.10 hours BST an Irish ship was sighted on the starboard bow and about 16.15 hours an SE contact 12 miles to port was obtained and the aircraft turned to investigate. Owing to the rate of which the contact range decreased I told the Captain that it might come from an aircraft. Course was resumed and shortly after at about 16.20 hours the Gunners reported the approach of four aircraft identified as Ju.88s. One of these overtook us rapidly and I saw it pass ahead of us on the port side and when about 400 yards ahead turned sharply and made a frontal attack at the same time as the Pilot was turning and climbing to port.

At the same time as the Ju.88 opened fire I saw the tracer from Mid-Upper turret pass over its wings and nose. However, the burst from the Junkers scored direct hits, there was an explosion in the cockpit, and the Captain cried out that he was 'done for' and died in a few seconds. The Second Pilot told me to remove the Captain's body, and started to climb towards the clouds. I had the greatest difficulty in moving the Captain's body, partly because of rigor which set in very rapidly and the difficulty of moving him without interfering with the controls, partly because I was in a somewhat weak condition with the Enteritis which I had contracted at Gibraltar. However I managed to shift him eventually and at the request of the second pilot, sat in the first pilot's seat to take over in case he was knocked out. When requested to do so, I gave additional control on the rudder or elevator to assist in the evasive action and kept a lookout on both sides to give warning of the direction of attacks when the intercom had broken down.

The first phase of the attack lasted about 20 minutes and after the first frontal attack, consisted mainly of rear and beam attacks. Every available use was made by the second pilot of the very poor cloud cover, in particular two further attempts at frontal attacks were frustrated in this manner. The Mid-Upper turret became unserviceable quite early in the attack and the rear turret was put out of action shortly after the rear gunner had reported seeing one of the Ju.88s in trouble after getting a burst from the side guns and the rear turret. It was seen to be climbing at a stalling angle, emitting smoke. The attacks then ceased for a few minutes but were resumed again by three only of the enemy aircraft. They knew obviously of our helplessness for they flew around taking various shots at us from no deflection rear attacks closing in from 400 to 50 yards firing continuously to full deflection beam attacks. No.2 engine was already out of action and had been feathered. No.3 engine went after emitting a 30 foot flame; there was a flame in the after part of the fuselage.

The aileron control had gone and every surviving member of the crew was wounded, some seriously, so at 1700 hours the second pilot decided to ditch while there was still some control left. The enemy broke off the attacks when they saw we were ditching; the approach was made skilfully especially considering the condition of the aircraft and the fact that the second pilot was wounded in the hands and legs. The aircraft appeared to stall in tail first, our first impact being followed by a more violent one which knocked me out although I had braced carefully. I felt water rushing over me and saw a patch of light above me and swam about 15 feet upwards before I surfaced in time to see the tail of the Liberator going under; it had broken in two after the impact, and saw the dinghy with three of the crew in it and several others swimming about. When we all got in there were seven of us and a body floating with head submerged which we took to be that of the rear gunner who had been seriously wounded in the back.

The condition of those in the dingy (*sic*) was as follows:

Myself – shrapnel wounds, hands and ankles
Collins – deep wound left leg
Miller – side and back crushed. Bullet wounds, buttock and feet.
Wilcox – front of right leg blown away by cannon shell.
Dilkes – bullet wound left leg
Foss – bullet wound in hand; shrapnel in knees.

In the dingy (*sic*) there were just paddles, pump, signalling flag and repair outfit and for supplies altogether we had two tins of water and five tins of emergency rations. There was no means of dressing the wounds except by covering them with handkerchiefs,

About one hour after ditching we sighted what we thought was a ship and attracted its attention by waving and flashing a mirror, as it turned towards us we saw it was a U-Boat in Arctic camouflage, a dirty yellow colour. The decks were crowded with men; as they passed they shouted to us what I took to be in German, 'Allies or not Allies' and when some of us replied British they carried on without slackening. I noticed a four-barrelled A.A. gun aft of the conning tower. They altered course south after leaving us. That night we had a difficult time as Miller was in great pain and we were all very cramped and felt it almost impossible to sleep.

3 September – Drifting north most of the day. We tried to repair single seated dinghy which we had in tow, so that we could put Miller into it but it persisted in getting waterlogged. We each had a few Horlicks tablets and a small piece of chocolate. In the evening a Sunderland was seen heading North about three miles to the East of us, but we failed to attract its attention. During the night the sea became rough and breakers swamped the dinghy at frequent intervals.

4 September – Drifting North East most of the time. Attempted to catch fish using a boat pin and string with chewing gum as bait, with no success. Sea choppy, necessitating frequent baling out. Weather continuing cloudy but fine. Sighted aircraft in evening about six to eight miles to South, too far off to attract attention.

5 September – Drifting East. Weather fine. The seriously wounded men are developing gangrene. In the afternoon a Sunderland and Liberator was seen but did not notice us. Shared first tin of water, about three to four tablespoons each. Situation at night increasingly difficult due to coldness and cramped position.

6 September – Drifting East then South. In the evening a Sunderland heading North East passed about one mile to the South and apparently saw us just after passing, turned and circled us. They dropped a Sea Marker, then a Mae West filled with cans of water, first aid and emergency rations, but unfortunately no distress signals. Another Sunderland took over later in the evening, dropping more flame floats. After dark a Catalina patrolling overhead picked us up with search light, flying down the line of markers. Later another Catalina took over but failed to find us with its searchlight, probably because it did not swing the light as the first Catalina had. The search was abandoned about midnight.

7 September – Drifting South, a Sunderland passed about three miles to the East, heading South during the morning, but failed to see the dinghy. Miller had become delirious and we gave him two injections from the first aid ampoules. Two tins of water were left as we had drunk about one tin each overnight from the supply dropped by the Sunderland. Wilcox also showed signs of collapse and delirium. Both he and Miller, and Collins had been drinking sea water. Miller died just after dark and was put overboard, and during the night Wilcox got rather out of hand, trying to bite and interfere with those near him. We gave him injections and he decided to go over the side. We made no attempt to stop him as he was getting out of hand.

8 September – Sighted by a Sunderland, and afterwards by other aircraft, including a Halifax and Catalina which appeared overhead and dropped more supplies. We tried to signal them to land, but apparently they could not obtain permission. Bareham was in a very weak condition, and delirious, and Collins also showed signs of weakening. Some of the supplies dropped upwind, or to one side of the dinghy. In the afternoon the cloud dispersed and no aircraft were seen. Fortunately distress signals had been dropped so that when during the night a Catalina was heard, we let off some signals and the aircraft dropped flares around us which were seen by the Sloops which had been looking for us for several days.

9 September – Two Sunderlands appeared early and homed the ships onto the dinghy. We were taken aboard and put in hot blankets and given coffee to drink. In spite of every attention, Bareham died the following night and Collins on the following day.

The three survivors – myself, Flight Sergeant Foss and Sergeant Dilks – were landed at Liverpool 12 days later, having received the very best of care and attention from the ship's company.

I do not feel it necessary to say much about those who failed to survive, although Wilcox impressed me considerably by his resolute conduct until his collapse, and Collins continuously exerted himself in the interests of the others. I though Flight Sergeant Foss's handling of the aircraft during the action was most skilful and resourceful, the ditching, carried out without flaps or aileron control, and in a wounded condition, was an outstanding achievement. Sergeant Dilks showed throughout a stolid indifference to danger and continued to operate the wireless even when seriously wounded. During the long spell in the dinghy he continued stolid and uncomplaining, and took his full share in baling, pumping and other activites,

D.M. Johnstone,
Flying Officer.

Obituary for Gordon Canti

After the war Gordon Canti worked as a pathologist at St Bartholomew's Hospital in London and latterly at Charing Cross Hospital. He specialised in diagnosis of lung cancer and wrote chapters for several influential textbooks on clinical cytology and oncological pathology.

Gordon retired in 1987 at the age of 70, and in 1988 he published a book called "A Colour Atlas of Sputum Cytology". He was a keen gardener and moved to a thatched farmhouse in Corfe, Somerset, where he established a beautiful garden. Christine, to whom he had been married for 66 years, sadly predeceased him in 2014. In June 2017 he celebrated his 100th birthday surrounded by his four children and their spouses, six grandchildren, and nine great grandchildren. In January 2018 he died peacefully at home.

Bibliography

Published Sources

Burn, Alan, *The Fighting Captain* (London: Leo Cooper, 1993).
Dimbleby, J, The Battle of the Atlantic (United Kingdom: Penguin Books, 2015).
Hessler, Gunter, *The U–Boat War in the Atlantic*, Facsimile edition by Lt Cdr A. Withers, (London: HMSO, 1989).
Macintyre, Donald, *U–Boat Killer*, (London: Seeley Service, 1976).
Macintyre, Donald, *The Battle of the Atlantic*, (London: B.T. Batsford, 1961).
Morgan, Daniel and Taylor, Bruce, *U–boat Attack Logs,* (Barnsley: Seaforth, 2011).
Robertson, Terence Robertson, *Walker RN*, (London: Evans Brothers, 1956).
Saunders, St George, *The Royal Air Force 1939–1945, Vol. III The Fight is Won (52–53),* (London: HMSO, 1954).
Wemyss, D.E.G., *Relentless Pursuit*, (London/Aschroft: Wrens Park/Cerberus, 2003).

Unpublished Sources

Archival References

Report of Proceedings, Second Support Group, 3 July – 16 July, 1943., ADM 1/12673, The National Archives
HMS *Starling*, Report of Proceedings, Second Support Group, 17 June – 30 June, 1943. ADM 217/186, The National Archives
HMS *Starling*, Report of Proceedings, Second Support Group, 9 Aug. – 24 Aug. 1943. ADM 217/187, The National Archives
HMS *Wildgoose*, Report of Proceedings, Second Support Group, 3 July – 16 July, 1943., ADM 217/202, The National Archives
HMS *Kite*, Report of Proceedings, Second Support Group, 23 July – 6 August, 1943., ADM 217/214, The National Archives
HMCS *Athabaskan*: bomb damage. ADM 267/8, The National Archives
HMCS *Athabaskan*: damaged by enemy action. ADM 358/3028, The National Archives

Log of HMS *Activity*, ADM 53/118759/60, The National Archives
Log of HMS *Begum*, ADM 53/120953, The National Archives
Log of HMS *Empress*, ADM 53/119374, The National Archives
Log of HMS *Empress*, ADM 53/119375, The National Archives
Log of HMS *Empress*, ADM 53/121327, The National Archives
Log of HMS *Empress*, ADM 53/121327/28, The National Archives
Log of HMS *Empress*, ADM 53/121328, The National Archives
Log of HMS *Empress*, ADM 53/121329, The National Archives
Log of HMS *Empress*, ADM 53/121330, The National Archives
Log of HMS *Empress*, ADM 53/121331, The National Archives
Log of HMS *Empress*, ADM 53/121333, The National Archives
Log of HMS *Nairana*, ADM 53/120112/13, The National Archives
The Admiralty's Pink List, ADM/32, The National Archives

Online Sources

Naval–history.net: https://www.naval–history.net/WW2CampaignsUboats4.htm, Data source for German U–Boats at war during 1943.

Uboat.net: https://uboat.net/, Comprehensive data source for German U–Boats.

U–boat Archive: http://www.uboatarchive.net/BritishInterrogationReports.htm, Naval Intelligence Division (NID), Interrogation Reports from captured U–boat crew.

Arnold Haig Convoy database: http://www.convoyweb.org.uk/hague/

The London Gazette 29 October 1943, https://www.thegazette.co.uk/London/issue/36226/supplement/4765/data.pdf: Citations for David Malcolm Johnstone, F/O (86904, Royal Air Force) No.224 Squadron, DSO. Sergeant Maurice William Dilks (1216857, Royal Air Force Volunteer Reserve) No. 224 Squadron, DFM.

Royal Air Force Commands, 26 November 2013, http://www.rafcommands.com/awards/a–gripping–story–behind–an–adventurous–citation/, Mr Hugh A. Halliday, *A gripping story behind an adventurous citation*.

Casualty Lists of the Royal Navy and Dominion Navies, World War 2, https://www.naval-history.net. Researched & compiled by Don Kindell, all rights reserved.

Now defunct web site relating to HMS *Kite*, http://www.hmskite.com/kiteintro.html.

The story of the survivors from the SS *St Mary*, by D.S. Davies, Captain of the SS *St. Mary*, www.39–45war.com/st%20margaret.html.

Royal Australian Air Force (RAAF). Fighting the U–Boats, http://www.3squadron.org.au/subpages/raaf.htm.

http://www.merseyfire.gov.uk/Historical/blitzCronology2.htm (accessed 4 September 2018).

http://www.merseyfire.gov.uk/Historical/blitzCronology2.htm (accessed 4 September 2018).

naval–history.net: https://www.naval–history.net/xGM–Chrono–10DD–37J–HMS_Jaguar.htm, (accessed 9 September 2018).

naval–history.net: http://www.naval–history.net/xGM–Chrono–10DE–Fernie.htm (accessed 9 September 2018).

Warsailors.com: https://www.warsailors.com/convoys/on164.html (accessed 23 March 2019).

https://en.wikipedia.org/wiki/List_of_Allied_convoy_codes_during_World_War_II

Royal Air Force Commands, www.rafcommands.com/archive/01665.php (accessed 23 March 2019)

Mersyside Fire and Rescue Service, http://www.merseyfire.gov.uk/Historical blitzCronology2.htm.

Warsailors.com, https://www.warsailors.com/convoys/on164.html.

Wikipedia, list of convoy codes used by the Allies during World War II, https://en.wikipedia.org/wiki List_of_Allied_convoy_codes_during_World_War_II.

Royal Air Force Commands, www.rafcommands.com/archive/01665.php.

Endnotes

Preface

1. A war correspondent, Sonderführer-Leutnant Lothar-Günther Buchheim, accompanied *U–96* on her seventh patrol. Thirty years later he wrote about his experiences on board in a book entitled *Das Boot*. Lehmann-Willenbrock served as the model for the commander portrayed in that book. uboat.net: https://uboat.net/men/willenbrock.htm, accessed on 30 December 1922.
2. *U-202*'s Fourth Patrol: *Unsuccessful Attempt to enter Mediterranean*: *U-202* left Brest towards the middle of December, 1941, and made an abortive attempt to break through the Straits of Gibraltar. At 0100 on 17 or 18 December, when about to enter the Straits, she was attacked by an aircraft which dropped four bombs. These caused little structural damage but the engines were made unserviceable. For 36 hours *U-202* lay on the bottom in 50 fathoms of water before re-surfacing to head back to Brest. She arrived at her base on the last week of December. (*N.I.D. Note.* This report may refer to an aircraft attack (U/812 Squadron) at 2141 on 19th December, 1941, two and a half miles off Cape Spartel.
   CB 04051 (72) U202 Interrogation of Survivors, at: *https://www.uboatarchive.net/U-202A/U-202INT.htm*, accessed on 30 December 2022.
3. uboat.net: https://uboat.net/men/commanders/737.html, accessed on 30 December 2022.

Chapter 1: The Liverpool blitz

1. Brunswick Dock was damaged during the first air raid on Liverpool, which took place on 17/18 August, 1940.
   Web site of the Merseyside Fire & Rescue Service dedicated to the history of the Liverpool blitz:
   http://www.merseyfire.gov.uk/Historical/blitzCronology2.htm (accessed 4 September 2018).
2. The author searched the editions of the *Liverpool Echo* held on microfilm at the British Library for July, August & September 1940, and did not find any

reference to the display of wrecked German aircraft in Liverpool. It leaves open the possibility that such an event may have taken place later in the war.

3. The public air–raid shelter which Marsden refers to was situated in Blackstock Gardens. It took a direct hit on the night of 21 December,1940. Christina Mary Marsden, aged 15, is listed among the fatalities caused by the explosion.
4. On 3 May 1941, the steamer SS *Malakand* was berthed in Huskisson Dock, Liverpool, taking on a cargo of munitions. That night Liverpool was subjected to a heavy air raid, in the course of which the ship's cargo caught alight and exploded, destroying a number of buildings located on the quay side. There is some debate as to the actual cause of the explosion. Some accounts say that a barrage balloon that had caught fire during the raid drifted onto the ship and set light to its cargo. Other accounts claim the ship was hit by a bomb. It was this ship that Marsden was helping to load as the German bombers attacked.
   http://www.merseyfire.gov.uk/Historical/blitzCronology2.htm (accessed 4 September 2018).
5. The official record of the Liverpool blitz records the hit close to Thurlow House, the tenement block where Marsden lived. Maps showing the location of the explosion place it at Rose Hill, the street closest to Thurlow House. Although Marsden claims it was a land (parachute) mine that caused the damage, the official record, which distinguishes between the type of ordnance at each bomb site, doesn't classify the Rose Hill device as a parachute mine, incendiary or oil bomb, which indicates that the local police and fire services considered it to have been an HE device (i.e. bomb).

Chapter 2: Answering the call; life in barracks

1. Gloucester held its Warship Week between 22/29 November, 1941. HMS *Jaguar*, a J Class Destroyer, was adopted by the town. The ship was lost on 26 March 1942 whilst carrying out anti–submarine operations in the Mediterranean off the coast of Egypt. Torpedoed by *U–652*, 193 of the ship's company were lost. There were 53 survivors.
   naval–history.net: https://www.naval–history.net/xGM–Chrono–10DD–37J–HMS_Jaguar.htm, (accessed 9 September 2018).
2. HMS *Fernie* was a Hunt class destroyer. During March 1943, she was engaged in convoy escort duties in the North Sea and the English Channel. In August 1942 she was nominated Reserve HQ ship for the Dieppe raid. Marsden's assertion that she was involved in escort duties with the Russian convoys at the time he was assigned to her is incorrect. She survived the war.

naval–history.net: http://www.naval–history.net/xGM–Chrono–10DE–Fernie.htm (accessed 9 September 2018).
3. Local name for Cornish pasties.
4. Marsden always referred to the ships of the Second Support Group as 'Bird–class' sloops. In fact they were of the Modified Black Swan–class.

Chapter 3: My first days aboard HMS *Woodpecker*

1. Warsailors.com: https://www.warsailors.com/convoys/on164.html (accessed 23 March 2019).
2. Arnold Haig Convoy database: http://www.convoyweb.org.uk/sc/index.html?sc.php?convoy=120!~scmain (accessed 23 March 2019).
3. Arnold Haig Convoy database: http://www.convoyweb.org.uk/kmf/index.html?kmf.php?convoy=11!~kmfmain (accessed 23 March 2019).
4. Arnold Haig Convoy database: http://www.convoyweb.org.uk/mkf/index.html?mkf.php?convoy=11!~mkfmain (accessed 23 March 2019).
5. Note: the convoy codes mentioned have the following meanings:
   ON: Outward bound for North America (Liverpool to Halifax, Nova Scotia). Used for convoys sailing between July 1941 to July 1945.
   SC: North Atlantic route; slow convoys (Sydney, Nova Scotia to Liverpool) reverse of ON
   KMF: UK to the Mediterranean and occasionally onward; fast convoys; reverse MKF. Used for convoys sailing between October 1942 to May 1945.
   MKF: North Africa via Gibraltar to Liverpool or the Firth of Clyde; Mediterranean to the UK Fast; reverse of KMF. Used for convoys sailing between. November 1942 to June 1945.
   WS: UK to Gibraltar, Freetown, Sierra Leone, the Cape of Good Hope and the Middle East or India, or for dispersal (non-troopships). Used for convoys sailing between July 1940 to August 1943.
   For a comprehensive list of all convoy series identifiers see: https://en.wikipedia.org/wiki/List_of_Allied_convoy_codes_during_World_War_II, which references, Arnold Hague: *The Allied Convoy System 1939–1945* (2000) ISBN 1-55125-033-0 (Canada). ISBN 1-86176-147-3 (UK).

Chapter 4: My first taste of action

1. Gunter Hessler, *The U–Boat War in the Atlantic* (Facsimile edition by Lt Cdr A. Withers, HMSO) Ch. VIII, p.44 & Vol. II, Appendix, p.121.
   naval–history.net: https://www.naval–history.net/WW2CampaignsUboats4.htm, see entry for 1 June 1943 (accessed 9 September 2018).
   uboat.net: https://uboat.net/boats/u202.htm (accessed 9 September 2018).

2. Donald Macintyre, *U–Boat Killer*, pp.17–20, 59–61.
3. Report of Proceedings, Second Support Group, 17–30 June 1943. ADM 217/186, The National Archives, Kew, (h/forth, TNA).
4. U–boat Archive: Interrogation of Survivors *U–202*, CB 04051 (72), Naval Intelligence Division (NID).
   U–boat Archive: http://www.uboatarchive.net/U-202A/U-202INT.htm, (accessed 27 March 2019 via http://www.uboatarchive.net/BritishInterrogation Reports.htm).
   Note: The document provides a comprehensive list of casualties from *U–202* (via the assistance of Mr. Tony Cooper).
5. Note on convoy code:
   HX: Inward bound to Liverpool from Halifax, Nova Scotia and New York City; North Atlantic route; fast convoys. ON: Reverse (outward bound from UK on the same route). Used for convoys sailing between September 1939 to June 1945.
6. Arnold Haig Convoy database: http://www.convoyweb.org.uk/hx/index.html?hx.php?convoy=241!~hxmain (accessed 23 March 2019).
7. Arnold Haig Convoy database: http://www.convoyweb.org.uk/hx/index.html?hx.php?convoy=241!~hxmain (accessed 23 March 2019).
8. Casualty Lists of the Royal Navy and Dominion Navies, World War 2, http://www.naval-history.net/xDKCas1944-02FEB.htm.
9. Alan Burn, *The Fighting Captain* (London: Leo Cooper, 1993), p.132.
10. Admiralty document: *Extension of Dangerous Areas in the English Channel and the Bay of Biscay* (Memorandum by the First Lord of the Admiralty issued on 27 October 1940). National Archives, Catalogue Reference: cab/66/13/8. This document defines the first extension of sea area covered by the 'sink–at–sight' policy. It seems that this area was later extended, as Walker's report on one incident relating to commercial shipping quotes: 'The boats were operating in the prohibited area laid down in P.C.W.O.100 (1)(d).'
11. Report of Proceedings, Second Support Group, 17–30 June 1943. ADM 217/186, TNA
12. Macintyre, *U–Boat Killer*, pp.99–106.
13. Gunter Hessler *The U–Boat War in the Atlantic* (Facsimile edition by Lt Cdr A. Withers, HMSO) (London: HMSO, 1989) Ch. VII, p.12.
    Report of Proceedings, Second Support Group, 17–30 June 1943. ADM 217/186, TNA.
    uboat.net: https://uboat.net/boats/u119.htm (accessed 9/9/2018).
14. Report of Proceedings, Second Support Group, 17–30 June 1943. ADM 217/186, TNA.
15. Ibid.

16. Report of Proceedings, Second Support Group, 17–30 June 1943. ADM 217/186, TNA.
    Donald Macintyre, *The Battle of the Atlantic*, pp.176–178.
17. Hessler, *The U–Boat War in the Atlantic*, Ch. VII, p.12.
    Report of Proceedings, Second Support Group, 17–30 June 1943. ADM 217/186, TNA.
    uboat.net: https://uboat.net/boats/u449.htm (accessed 9 September 2018).
18. During its blockade of the Bay of Biscay the Royal Navy provided the A/S sloops and frigates with support from cruiser forces, which could come to their aid if they were threatened by heavier German surface forces. The cruiser which had the airman under observation in this case was HMS *Bermuda*.
    Report of Proceedings, Second Support Group, 23 July – 6 August 1943. ADM 217/214, TNA.
19. Report of Proceedings, Second Support Group, 3-16 July 1943. ADM 217/202, TNA.
    Royal Air Force Commands, www.rafcommands.com/archive/01665.php (accessed 23 March 2019) contains a statement claiming that Davidson 1195435 was shot down on 12 July 1943 and was rescued up by a ship of the Royal Navy.
    Errol W. Martyn, in his book, *For Your Tomorrow*, Vol. 2, also states that Davidson was rescued by a Royal Navy ship.
20. Button–tossers – a naval slang term for signallers. It is a corruption of the original, 'bunting tossers', the name given to the men who hoisted the signalling flags aboard the Royal Navy ships; 'bunting' being the official name for the kind of worsted cloth from which the flags were made.
21. This was Captain Walker.
22. Report of Proceedings, Second Support Group, 3–16 July 1943, ADM 1/12673, TNA.
    U–boat Archive: Interrogation of Survivors *U–607*, CB 04051 (74), Naval Intelligence Division (NID), http://www.uboatarchive.net/U–607INT.htm, (accessed 7 September 2018 via http://www.uboatarchive.net/BritishInterrogationReports.htm).
    Note: The document provides a comprehensive list of casualties from *U–607* (via the assistance of Mr. Tony Cooper and Mr. Roger Griffiths).
23. Alan Burn, *The Fighting Captain*, pp. 93–94.
    Report of Proceedings, Second Support Group, 3 July – 16 July, 1943. ADM 217/202, TNA.
24. Note: *Starling* was not with the group on this occasion. She had sustained serious damage to her bow section during the previous patrol when she sank a U–boat by ramming. To add insult to injury, as she went in for the kill on

that occasion, another of Walker's ships fired a pom–pom shell at the enemy craft, which passed through *Starling*'s bows at more or less the same instant she struck the U–boat. Captain Walker and his officers were aboard HMS *Wildgoose* during their second Biscay patrol.

25. Gunter Hessler, *The U–Boat War in the Atlantic* (Facsimile edition by Lt Cdr A. Withers, HMSO) Ch. VI, p.85, Ch. VII, p.11 & Ch VIII, p.34.
26. The Spanish trawlers were: *Buena Esperanza, Campanal, Don Antonio, El Viro, Europa V, H de Valterra, Montenegro*. Note: *H de Valterra* was spared to convey the Spanish trawler men to the mainland.
Report of Proceedings, Second Support Group, 23 July – 6th August 1943. ADM 217/214, TNA.
27. Hessler, *The U–Boat War in the Atlantic*, Ch. III, p.93.
Macintyre: *The Battle of the Atlantic*, p.89.
28. The boat boarded by *Wren* was: *Europa V*: (*Europa V* sunk at 20:02 in position 44 deg. 40 min. N, 10 deg. 51 min. W).
Report of Proceedings, Second Support Group, 23 July – 6 August 1943. ADM 217/214, TNA.
29. The boats boarded by *Woodpecker* were: *Buena Esperanza* and *Don Antonio*.
Report of Proceedings, Second Support Group, 23 July – 6 August 1943. ADM 217/214, TNA.
30. The trawlers were registered at the Spanish port of Vigo.
Report of Proceedings, Second Support Group, 23 July – 6 August 1943. ADM 217/214, TNA.
31. The boats were operating in the prohibited area as laid down in P.C.W.O.100 (1)(d) as referred to in the document,
Report of Proceedings, Second Support Group, 23 July – 6 August 1943, (ADM 217/214 TNA).
Document reference: Catalogue Reference: cab/66/13/8, TNA.
32. See article by the Cuffley Industrial Heritage Society on the Sunderland Flying Boat, http://www.cuffleyindustrialheritage.com/page56.html (accessed 7 September 2018).
Gunter Hessler, *The U–Boat War in the Atlantic* (Facsimile edition by Lt Cdr A. Withers, HMSO) Ch. V, p.42. Ch. VII, p.22 (provides details of the RAF airman's cock & bull story to the Germans).
33. Walker, in his report to the Admiralty, claimed that one of the RAF aircraft involved in the action signalled 'Congratulations' to his group.
Report of Proceedings, Second Support Group, 23 July – 6 August 1943. ADM 217/214, TNA.
34. Report of Proceedings, Second Support Group, 23 July – 6 August 1943. ADM 217/214, TNA.

Gunter Hessler, *The U–Boat War in the Atlantic* (Facsimile edition by Lt Cdr A. Withers, HMSO) Ch. VII, p.13.
Interrogation of Survivors *U–462*, CB 04051 (82), Naval Intelligence Division (NID) http://www.uboatarchive.net/U–462INT.htm (accessed 7/9/2018 via http://www.uboatarchive.net/BritishInterrogationReports.htm).
Note: The document provides a comprehensive list of casualties from *U–462* (via the assistance of Mr. Tony Cooper).

35. Report of Proceedings, Second Support Group, 23 July – 6 August 1943. ADM 217/214, TNA.
Gunter Hessler, *The U–Boat War in the Atlantic* (Facsimile edition by Lt Cdr A. Withers, HMSO) Ch. VII, p.13.
Interrogation of Survivors *U–461*, CB 04051 (81), Naval Intelligence Division (NID), http://www.uboatarchive.net/U–461INT.htm (accessed 7/9/2018 via http://www.uboatarchive.net/BritishInterrogationReports.htm)
Note: the document provides details of casualties and survivors from *U–461* (via the assistance of Mr. Tony Cooper).
36. The full story of this affair may be found at https://en.wikipedia.org/wiki/USS_Hobson (accessed 31 July 2024).
See also: Report CB 04051 (81), Naval Intelligence Division (NID), http://www.uboatarchive.net/U–461INT.htm (accessed 7 September 2018 via http://www.uboatarchive.net/BritishInterrogationReports.htm) with the assistance of Mr. Tony Martin.
37. The third boat was *U–504*, sunk by depth charges on 30 July 1943, at location 45.33N, 10.56W by *Wildgoose* and *Woodpecker*. There were no survivors from her crew of 53. Report of Proceedings, Second Support Group, 23 July – 6 August, 1943. ADM 217/214, TNA.
38. Marsden may have been mistaking a junior German officer amongst the survivors aboard *Woodpecker* for the commander of *U–461* or *U–462*, but according to Alan Burn, the commanders of both U–boats were picked up by HMS *Kite*. See RAF liaison officer's story in Appendix 1.
Burn, *The Fighting Captain*. p.99.
39. This was Lt. Cdr. R.E.S. Hugonin, who was in command of HMS *Woodpecker* from 16 November 1942 to 6 October 1943.
uboat.net: https://uboat.net/allies/warships/ship/3920.html (accessed 7 September 2018).
40. Terence Robertson, *Walker RN* (London: Evans Brothers, 1956) pp.196–196.
41. Report of Proceedings, Second Support Group, 23 July – 6 August 1943. ADM 217/214, TNA.
Terence Robertson, *Walker RN*, pp. 126–129.

42. Report of Proceedings, Second Support Group, 23 July – 6 August 1943. ADM 217/214, TNA.
43. These were Harold O'Brien and Christopher McGrath. Marsden had made a number of requests to join the crew of HMS *Kite* in order to be with his pals. He was lucky that they were all refused. None of the stokers aboard *Kite* survived the sinking.
44. Gunter Hessler, *The U–Boat War in the Atlantic* (Facsimile edition. by Lt Cdr A. Withers, HMSO) Ch VII, p.13.
    U–boat Archive: Interrogation of Survivors *U–454*, CB 04051 (83), Naval Intelligence Division (NID), http://www.uboatarchive.net/U–454INT.htm, (accessed7/9/2018viahttp://www.uboatarchive.net/BritishInterrogationReports.htm).
    Note: the document provides details of casualties and survivors from *U–454* (via the assistance of Mr. Tony Cooper).
45. Report of Proceedings, Second Support Group, 3–16 July, 1943. ADM 217/202, TNA.
46. It should be noted that, before the completion of the patrol they had just commenced, *Athabaskan* and *Grenville* were attacked by German aircraft carrying the new Hs 293 anti–ship guided missile. *Athabaskan* was seriously damaged.
47. HMS *Starling*, Report of Proceedings, 9–24 August, 1943. ADM 217/187. TNA
48. See Appendix 1.
49. Report of Proceedings, Second Support Group, 9–14th August, 1943. ADM 217/187, TNA.
    In Walker's report of proceedings, he refers to this patrol as being 'uneventful.' He makes mention of the fact that the group made sightings of enemy aircraft shadowing his ships but they did not make any attacks.

Chapter 5: Woodpecker in refit

1. By the time she was sunk, *Woodpecker* had been fitted with Radar Type 272 for surface warning and Type 285 for fire-control of the main armament, which comprised three twin 4-inch mountings. Another radar version, Type 286P was also fitted and gave limited warning of the approach of aircraft and ships.
   Report of Proceedings, Second Support Group, 23 July – 6 August, 1943. ADM 217/214, TNA.
   Gunter Hessler, *The U–Boat War in the Atlantic* (Facsimile edition by Lt Cdr A. Withers, HMSO) Ch. VI, pp.86–90 & p.106.

Chapter 6: HMS *Woodpecker* returns to the fray

1. Robertson, *Walker RN*, pp.132–157.

2. Robertson, *Walker RN*, pp.149–152. Note, Robertson mistakenly refers to *U–226* as '*U–220*'.
   Hessler, *The U–Boat War in the Atlantic*, Vol. III, Appendix III, p.110 & p.115.
   uboat.net: https://uboat.net/boats/u226.htm (accessed 9 September 2018) & https://uboat.net/boats/u842.htm (accessed 11/2/2023),
3. Walker did not place too much faith in the theorists and tacticians based at Tobermoray. He preferred to put his trust in the skills of U–boat hunting acquired by personal experience, and although he allowed his ships their allotted time at the training base, he tended to retain faith in his own anti–submarine tactics developed, honed and refined at sea.
   Burn, *Fighting Captain*. p.15 & p.67.
4. Arnold Haig Convoy database: http://www.convoyweb.org.uk/kmf/index.html?kmf.php?convoy=26!~kmfmain. (KMF 26) (accessed 20/1/2020).
   Arnold Haig Convoy database: http://www.convoyweb.org.uk/mkf/index.html?mkf.php?convoy=26!~mkfmain. (MKF 26) (accessed 20/1/2020).
5. naval–history.net: https://www.naval–history.net/xGM–Chrono–18SL–HMS_Woodpecker.htm (accessed 9 September 2018).
   Arnold Haig Convoy database: http://www.convoyweb.org.uk/os/index.html?os.php?convoy=64!~osmain (accessed 20 January 2020).
   Warsailors.com database: http://www.warsailors.com/convoys/mks35.html (accessed 12/2/23).
   The Admiralty's Pink List, ADM/32, TNA.
6. Donald Macintyre says that he took his ship, HMS *Walker*, into Punta Delgarda, on the Azores island of San Miguel, for re–fuelling in February 1942.
   Macintyre, *U–Boat Killer*, p.65.
7. Burn, *Fighting Captain*, p.106.
8. *London Gazette*, 29 October 1943, https://www.thegazette.co.uk/London/issue/36226/supplement/4765/data.pdf (accessed 8 September 2018).
9. One definite victim of the new 'gnat' torpedoes was the escort HMS *Lagan*. Severely damaged on 20 September 1943, she limped into Liverpool on 24 September and was later written off. 29 of her crew were killed in the attack.
   https://uboat.net/allies/warships/ship/99.html (accessed 12 February 2023).
10. Hessler, *The U–Boat War in the Atlantic*, Ch. VIII, pp.25–26.
11. This was simply a noise generator designed to lure T5 acoustic torpedoes away from the sound generated by the screws of an escort's propellers.
12. uboat.net: https://uboat.net/allies/merchants/ship/3327.html (accessed 25 March 2019). Kite was torpedoed and sunk by *U–344* at 73° 01'N, 3° 57'E. On the following day *U–344* was herself sunk by a Swordfish operating from the aircraft carrier HMS *Vindex*.

13. HMCS *Athabaskan*: damaged by enemy action, ADM 358/3028, TNA.
    HMCS *Athabaskan*: bomb damage, ADM 267/8, TNA.

Chapter 7: Walker's famous patrol. The final convoy battle of the Atlantic Campaign

1. The Second Support Group joined the escort carriers *Activity* and *Nairana* in the Irish Sea on 29 January 1944 before heading into the North Atlantic. The carriers did not stay with Walker's ships for the full duration of their patrol, both were back in Greenock by mid–February having turned for home on 9 February 1944.
   Log of HMS *Nairana*, ADM 53/120112/13, TNA.
   Log of HMS *Activity*, ADM 53/118759/60, TNA.
2. HMS *Woodcock* went into dock for repairs in late December 1943. The work was completed by 21 January 1944. She then joined the Seventh Escort Group.
   Robertson, *Walker RN*, p.155.
3. HMS *Kite* was not in Liverpool with the other ships of the group. She sailed from her port of berth some hours later and rendezvoused with them somewhere off the Irish coast.
   Burn, *The Fighting Captain*. pp.124–125.
   Log of HMS *Nairana*, ADM 53/120112, TNA.
4. Hessler, *The U–Boat War in the Atlantic*, Ch. III, pp.90–91.
5. Gunter Hessler, *The U–Boat War in the Atlantic* (Facsimile edition by Lt Cdr A. Withers, HMSO) Ch. VIII, p.44.
   uboat.net: https://uboat.net/boats/u592.htm (accessed 9 September 2018).
6. Arnold Haig Convoy database: http://www.convoyweb.org.uk/sl2/index.html?sl.php?convoy=147MK!~slmain. (accessed 24 March 2019).
7. Macintyre, *The Battle of the Atlantic*, pp.129–130.
8. SL.147/MKS.38 comprised 82 merchantmen and 19 escorts. In fact, in his book, *The Battle of the Atlantic*, Jonathan Dimbleby mentions a convoy which covered an area of some five square miles.
9. Hessler, *The U–Boat War in the Atlantic*, Ch. VIII, p.44.
   uboat.net: https://uboat.net/boats/u762.htm (accessed 9 September 2018).
10. Robertson, *Walker RN*, pp.172–173.
    Daniel Morgan and Bruce Taylor, *U–boat Attack Logs*, p.xxvii and p.xxxi.
    uboat.net: https://uboat.net/boats/u734.htm (accessed 9 September 2018).
11. Hessler, *The U–Boat War in the Atlantic*, Ch. VIII, p.44.
    uboat.net: https://uboat.net/boats/u238.htm (accessed 9 September 2018).
12. Daniel Morgan and Bruce Taylor, *U–boat Attack Logs*. pp.379–382.
13. Robertson, in *Walker RN,* describes a different method of transferring depth charges between ships at sea, that of hauling them across on a line from one

ship to the other. This was the method used during the course of the patrol being described.
Robertson, *Walker RN*, pp.174–175.

14. Robertson, *Walker RN*, p.174.
Arnold Haig Convoy database: http://www.convoyweb.org.uk/hx/index.html?hx.php?convoy=277!~hxmain (accessed 26 March 2019).
15. Robertson, *Walker RN*, p.174.
Arnold Haig Convoy database: http://www.convoyweb.org.uk/hx/index.html?hx.php?convoy=277!~hxmain (accessed 25 March 2019).
16. naval–history.net: http://www.naval–history.net/xDKCas1944–02FEB.htm (accessed 8/9/2018).
Log of HMS *Nairana*, ADM 53/120113, TNA.
Log of HMS *Activity*, ADM 53/118759/, TNA..
17. Robertson, *Walker RN*, p.175.
Arnold Haig Convoy database: http://www.convoyweb.org.uk/hx/index.html?hx.php?convoy=278!~hxmain (accessed 25 March 2019).
18. Warsailors.com database: http://www.warsailors.com/convoys/hx278.html (accessed 12 February 2023).
19. Hessler, *The U–Boat War in the Atlantic*, Ch. VIII, p.44.
uboat.net: https://uboat.net/boats/u424.htm (accessed 9 September 2018).
20. Robertson, *Walker RN*, p.177.
Arnold Haig Convoy database: http://www.convoyweb.org.uk/on/index.html?onz.php?convoy=224!~onzmain (accessed 24 March 2019).
21. Terence Robertson correctly states that the second escort force on the scene was the Seventh Support Group. There was (and still is) a degree of confusion when talking about escort groups and support groups; and people tend to interchange the words 'support' and 'escort', when talking about these formations, especially the Seventh Support Group – as explained in the chapter.
Robertson, *Walker RN*, p.177.
22. Dimbleby, J. *The Battle of the Atlantic*, p.121.
23. The escort oiler with the convoy was the *Vanja*. Arnold Haig Convoy database: http://www.convoyweb.org.uk/on/index.html for ON.224. The U boat detected was *U-264*.
24. Gunter Hessler, *The U–Boat War in the Atlantic* (Facsimile edition by Lt Cdr A. Withers, HMSO) Ch. VI, pp.104–105.
U–boat Archive: U–boat Archive: Interrogation of Survivors *U–264*, CB 04051 (99), Naval Intelligence Division (NID), http://www.uboatarchive.net/U-224INT.htm (accessed 9 September 2018 via http://www.uboatarchive.net/BritishInterrogationReports.htm).

Note: this document provides details of casualties and survivors from *U–264* (via the assistance of Roger Griffiths).

25. ASDIC trawlers were (ex) commercial trawlers which had been fitted with armaments, usually three–inch or four–inch guns. They were used as armed escorts for fishing fleets as well as other duties.
26. This could only have been HMS *Azalea*, a Flower class corvette launched in 1941.
27. HMS *Azelea* was a Flower class corvette. Most of the ships of her type were fitted with a reciprocating, four–cylinder, triple–expansion engine.
28. The Canadian ship was *HMCS Chilliwack,* a corvette.
29. uboat.net: https://uboat.net/boats/u256.htm (accessed 9 September 2018). naval–history.net: https://www.naval–history.net/xGM–Chrono–18SL–HMS_Woodpecker.htm (accessed 9 September 2018).
    Daniel Morgan and Bruce Taylor, '*U–boat Attack Logs*' pp.380–382.
30. CB 04051 (99) *U–406*, *U–386*, *U–264* Interrogation of Survivors https://www.uboatarchive.net/U-406A/U-406-386-264INT.htm (accessed 13 February 2023).
31. U–boat Archive: http://www.uboatarchive.net/U-264A/U-264.htm. (accessed 30 March 2019).
32. Hessler, *The U–Boat War in the Atlantic*, Ch. VIII, pp.32–33.

Chapter 8: HMS *Woodpecker*: some reflections

1. In fact, Walker was scathing about the design and build quality of the sloops he commanded. In his Report of Proceedings submitted at the end of the Biscay patrol which ran from 9–14 August 1943, he included a statement describing the inherent weaknesses of the modified Black Swan class of sloops.
   Report of Proceedings, Second Support Group, 9–14 August 1943. ADM 217/187, TNA.
2. In 1943, Torpex, an explosive 50% more powerful than TNT, was introduced along with a more streamlined depth charge casing. The combination of the two improvements resulted in a faster sink–rate of the weapon and a much heavier 'punch' on detonation.
   uboat.net: https://www.uboat.net/allies/technical/depth_charges.htm (accessed 24 March 2019).

Chapter 9: To a rest camp in Scotland

1. Burn, *The Fighting Captain*. p.141.
2. This was the shore establishment, HMS *Helicon*, located at Aultbea on Loch Ewe.
3. HMS *Kite* was sunk on 21 August 1944 by *U–344* at location 73.01N, 03.57E, *en–route* to Murmansk. Of the 226 officers and men aboard only 9 survived.

uboat.net: https://uboat.net/allies/merchants/ship/3327.html (accessed 24 March 2019).

4. HMS *Lark* was severely damaged on 17 February 1945 (later written off), in position 69.30N, 34.33E, *en–route* to Murmansk. All but three of her crew survived. naval–history.net: https://www.naval–history.net/xGM–Chrono–18SL–HMS_Lark.htm (accessed 26 March 2019).
5. *Lark* was towed into Murmansk in the Kola Inlet and later declared a total loss by the Navy. naval–history.net: https://www.naval–history.net/xGM–Chrono–18SL–HMS_Lark.htm (accessed 26 March 2019).

Chapter 10: I join the crew of HMS *Empress*

1. Merchant Navy personnel were allowed to serve aboard RN ships whilst wearing RN uniforms and retaining Merchant Navy pay rates, after agreeing to sign a T–124X form.
2. *Empress* was used for pilot training by 768 Squadron, based at Ayr (Avengers, Hellcats, Fireflies, Seaflies, Sea Hurricanes, Swordfish), 766 Squadron, based at Inskip (Swordfish) and 1772 Squadron, based at Burscough (Fireflies). The aircraft mentioned in the log entries of *Empress* for November 1944, when most of the training was done, are mainly Swordfish and Fireflies. Log of HMS *Empress*, ADM 53/119374, TNA.
3. *Empress*'s log for November 1944 contains the entry: 'One Swordfish made forced landing in sea. Royal Manx Lifeboat (RML) attended. [The] crew of three [later] reported safe and well.' Log of HMS *Empress*, ADM 53/119374, TNA.
4. *Empress* set sail from Greenock for Devonport on 16 December 1944. Log of HMS *Empress*, ADM 53/119375, TNA.
5. Some sources give the full complement as 890 officers and men.
6. *Empress*'s log for 1 January 1945 states that she sailed from Devonport to Belfast [before rendezvousing with convoy KMF 38 on 5/1/45]. Log of HMS *Empress*, ADM 53/121327, TNA.
7. This was convoy KMF 38 which left the Clyde on 5 January 1945 and arrived at Gibraltar on 10 January. Arnold Haig Convoy database: http://www.convoyweb.org.uk/kmf/index.html?kmf.php?convoy=38!~kmfmain (accessed 24/3/2019).
8. *Empress*'s log for January 1945 states that she refuelled at Gibraltar. Log of HMS *Empress*, ADM 53/121327, TNA.
9. *Empress* arrived at Aden on 23 January 1945. Log of HMS *Empress*, ADM 53/121327, TNA.

10. *Empress* made the trip to the Far East ferrying a number of F8F Hellcats. The aircraft were stored below in the hangars for the whole journey and were disembarked at Cochin on 29 January 1945.
Log of HMS *Empress*, ADM 53/121327, TNA.
11. Marsden was incorrect when he stated that the *Empress* was without escort for the *whole* of the journey to the Far East. When she made her departure from Belfast on 6 January 1945 she joined convoy KMF 38, en route to the Mediterranean, which was under escort. The ship's log entry for 10 January 1945 states that HMS *Malcolm* and HMS *Wolverine* joined the escort [at Gibraltar]. At that point, *Empress* halted for refuelling whilst the convoy continued towards its destination. Once refuelled she made the rest of the journey to the Far East unescorted.
Log of HMS *Empress*, ADM 53/121327, TNA.
12. *Empress* docked in Cochin on 29 January 1945 and sailed for Colombo on the following day.
Log of HMS *Empress*, ADM 53/121327, TNA.
13. *Empress* docked in Colombo on 31 January 1945 and sailed for Trincomalee 2 February.
Log of HMS *Empress*, ADM 53/121327/28, TNA.
14. *Empress* embarked 845 Avenger Squadron, 804 Hellcat Squadron and elements of 888 Hellcat Squadron, Photo Reconnaissance (PR), whilst at Colombo.
Log of HMS *Empress*, ADM 53/121328, TNA.
15. *Empress* was in Colombo for four days before sailing to Trincomalee. Her log for February 1945 details the ships she sailed with from Trincomalee whilst on exercise and operations.
Log of HMS *Empress*, ADM 53/121328, TNA.
16. This was 888 Squadron PR Hellcats.
Log of HMS *Empress*, ADM 53/121328, TNA.
17. This was Operation Stacey (22 February – 6 March 1945). The first task for the operation was to carry out photo reconnaissance of the Kra Isthmus and Penang. Missions were also flown to photograph Sumatra, Niass, Simalung and the Banyak Islands.
Admiralty War Diaries for the Eastern Fleet, February 1945, http://naval-history.net/xDKWD-EF1945.htm (accessed 24 March 2019).
18. On 1 March 1945 *Empress*'s Hellcats of 804 Squadron were amongst the first group of British escort carrier–borne aircraft to engage and destroy Japanese aircraft, three of which (two Oscars and a Dinah) were shot down without loss.
Admiralty War Diaries for the Eastern Fleet, February and March 1945, http://naval-history.net/xDKWD-EF1945.htm (accessed 24 March 2019).

19. In *Empress*'s log for 25 February 1945, it states that nine aircraft were 'detected' and [later] identified as 'friendly'. It does not mention any AA fire from the ships.
    Log of HMS *Empress*, ADM 53/121328, TNA.
20. The only enemy aircraft destroyed by the fleet's carrier–borne aircraft during Operation Stacey were the two Oscars and one Dinah referred to in f/n 18 above.
21. There is an entry in *Empress*'s log for 2 April 1945 which states '*catapult sheave landed*'.
    Log of HMS *Empress*, ADM 53/121330, TNA.
22. A Barracuda airframe was used for the test launch, its weight being made up with bags of sand.
    Log of HMS *Empress*, ADM 53/121329, TNA.
23. The test failure is noted in the ship's log.
    Log of HMS *Empress*, ADM 53/121328, TNA.
24. This was Operation Bishop (27 April – 9 May 1945) which was a covering operation for the invasion of Rangoon. *Empress* sailed from Tricomalee on 27 April 1945 with 20 Hellcats of 804 Squadron aboard which were to carry out strikes against the two airfields located on Car Nicobar island: Admiralty War Diaries for the Eastern Fleet, April and May 1945, http://naval-history.net/xDKWD-EF1945.htm (accessed 24 March 2019).
25. There are references to the avoidance procedures taken when floating mines were spotted in *Empress*'s log for May and July 1945, but there is no reference to sharpshooters being employed to detonate the mines: Log of HMS *Empress,* ADM 53/121331/33, TNA.
26. Later investigations of this incident aboard the Dutch cruiser HNLMS *Trompe* were to reveal that the casualties were caused when a 5.9–inch shell fired from one of *Trompe*'s guns detonated prematurely as it left the muzzle. There is an entry in *Empress*'s log for 2 May 1945 mentioning the burial at sea of the Dutch casualties: Log of HMS *Empress*, ADM 53/121331, TNA.
27. The Hellcat pilot lost on his return from carrying out airstrikes against Port Blair on 6 May 1945, was S/Lt (A) Scott RNVR, Hellcat JX 803. His aircraft had been damaged by AA fire: Log of HMS *Empress*, ADM 53/121331, TNA.
28. *Empress* suffered 'catastrophic engine failure' on 14 May 1945 and was towed into Trincomalee by the cruiser HMS *Black Prince*: Web site, http://www.royalnavyresearcharchive.org.uk/ESCORT/EMPRESS.htm#.XiSw5iOnzIU, (accessed 19 January 2020).
29. HMS *Begum* spent most of its early life as an aircraft ferry. It was not until June/July 1945 that it was decided to prepare her to act as an operational carrier. She embarked her first operational aircraft during that period:

832 Avenger Squadron: Web site, http://www.royalnavyresearcharchive.org.uk/ESCORT/BEGUM.htm#.XiSzjiOnzIU (accessed 19/1/2020).

30. In fact, *Begum* never took part in any operational patrols whilst with the East Indies Fleet. Instead, she was used as an offshore deck–landing and take–off trainer in the coastal waters of Ceylon, during July 1945. She was later nominated to take an operational role in Operation Zipper (August 1945) but was grounded shortly after leaving Trincomalee harbour and withdrawn from the mission: Admiralty War Diaries for the Eastern Fleet, July 1945, http://naval-history.net/xDKWD-EF1945.htm (accessed 24 March 2019).
31. *Begum's* log for 9 July 1945 states that 'one a/c crashed port side; overside. One rating, C/JK 392768, P Cain, killed. Pilot S/Lt Lowell picked up by HMS *Nubian.*' No other casualties are mentioned. Sadly, the log of HMS *Nubian* is not in the public domain, so it is impossible to refer to it for a description of the pilot rescue: Log of HMS *Begum,* ADM 53/120953, TNA.
32. The pilot was S/Lt. Lowell.
33. Log of HMS *Empress,* ADM 53/121333, 2 July 1945, TNA
34. Log of HMS *Empress,* ADM 53/121335, 3 September 1945, TNA

Chapter 11: An encounter with the Kamikazes

1. This was Operation Livery (19–27 July 1945). During the operation targets on the Kraa Isthumus were attacked and military targets at Huatsei were bombed by aircraft from the fleet.
   Admiralty War Diaries for the Eastern Fleet, July 1945, http://naval-history.net/xDKWD-EF1945.htm (accessed 24 March 2019).
2. Four Hellcats of Squadron 896 were embarked aboard *Empress* on 15 July 1945. Log of HMS *Empress,* ADM 53/121333, TNA.
3. *Empress* was part of Force 63, Group 1, engaged in Operation Livery (19–25 July 1945)
   Admiralty War Diaries for the Eastern Fleet, July 1945, http://naval-history.net/xDKWD-EF1945.htm (accessed 24 March 2019).
4. This action, which took place on 26 July 1945, is mentioned briefly in *Empress's* log. The Admiralty War Diary statement is that three *Kamikazes* were shot down; two by *Sussex*, one by *Ameer*.
   Log of HMS *Empress,* ADM 53/121333, TNA.
   Admiralty War Diaries for the Eastern Fleet, July 1945, http://naval-history.net/xDKWD-EF1945.htm (accessed 24 March 2019).
5. This was the minesweeper HMS *Squirrel*. Seven ratings were lost with their ship: Admiralty War Diaries for the Eastern Fleet, July 1945, http://naval-history.net/xDKWD-EF1945.htm (accessed 24 March 2019).

6. This was the minesweeper HMS *Vestal*. She was the last ship of the Royal Navy lost to enemy action in the Second World War. Casualties from *Vestal* were brought aboard *Empress* before being transferred to HMS *Nelson*. Fifteen ratings were lost with their ship.
   Log of HMS *Empress,* ADM 53/121333, TNA.
   Admiralty War Diaries for the Eastern Fleet, July 1945, http://naval-history.net/xDKWD-EF1945.htm (accessed 24 March 2019).
7. This was Operation Carson when *Empress* was part of Force 61, which sailed on 10 August 1945 to attack shipping and airfields around Penang and Medan.
   Log of HMS *Empress,* ADM 53/121334, TNA
   Admiralty War Diaries for the Eastern Fleet, August 1945 http://naval-history.net/xDKWD-EF1945.htm (accessed 19 January 2020).
8. VJ Day is marked somewhat laconically in *Empress*'s log as follows: 'Dressed ship with masthead ensign. VJ Day': Log of HMS *Empress*, ADM 53/121333, TNA.

Chapter 12: A trip to Germany

1. Joseph Mulcahy was killed when his ship HMS *Aldenham* hit a mine shortly after she had landed a group of partisans in Croatia on 14 December 1944. *Aldenham* was the last of the Royal Navy destroyers to be sunk during the Second World War. Only 67 from her crew of 189 survived.
   naval–history.net: http://www.naval–history.net/xGM–Chrono–10DE–Aldenham.htm (accessed 9 September 2018).

Appendix 1: RAF liaison officer's report on his time spent on patrol with the Second Support Group

1. Hilary St. George Saunders: *The Royal Air Force 1939–1945, Vol. III The Fight is Won (52–53)*, Her Majesty's Stationery Office, 1954.
   A report by an RAF Liaison Officer aboard *HMS Woodpecker* in July 1943.
2. Australian War Memorial: https://www.awm.gov.au/advanced-search?query=AT%20SEA%2C%20BAY%20OF%20BISCAY.%201943-08-06.%202058&collection=true&facet_type=Photograph.

Appendix 2: Content of documents found in the service file of J6941 F/O G.H. Wharram (RCAF)

1. *http://www.rafcommands.com/awards/a-gripping-story-behind-an-adventurous-citation/* (accessed 16/8/2023) With thanks to Hugh A. Halliday for his article, '*A gripping story behind an adventurous citation,*' published Royal Air Force Commands, 26 November 2013.

Index

Convoys.

Places.